The Modernity Bluff

The Modernity Bluff

Crime, Consumption, and Citizenship in Côte d'Ivoire

SASHA NEWELL

The University of Chicago Press
Chicago and London

Sasha Newell is assistant professor of anthropology at North Carolina State University.

The University of Chicago Press, Chicago 60637
The University of Chicago Press, Ltd., London
© 2012 by The University of Chicago
All rights reserved. Published 2012.
Printed in the United States of America

21 20 19 18 17 16 15 14 13 12   1 2 3 4 5

ISBN-13: 978-0-226-57519-3 (cloth)
ISBN-13: 978-0-226-57520-9 (paper)
ISBN-10: 0-226-57519-5 (cloth)
ISBN-10: 0-226-57520-9 (paper)

Library of Congress Cataloging-in-Publication Data

Newell, Sasha, author.
    The modernity bluff : crime, consumption, and citizenship in Côte d'Ivoire / Sasha Newell.
        p. cm.
    Includes bibliographical references and index.
    ISBN-13: 978-0-226-57519-3 (cloth : alkaline paper)
    ISBN-10: 0-226-57519-5 (cloth : alkaline paper)
    ISBN-13: 978-0-226-57520-9 (pbk. : alkaline paper)
    ISBN-10: 0-226-57520-9 (pbk. : alkaline paper)   1. Urban youth—Côte d'Ivoire—Social conditions—21st century.   2. Urban youth—Côte d'Ivoire—Economic conditions—21st century.   3. Social status—Côte d'Ivoire.
I. Title.
    HQ799.8.C8N48 2012
    305.2350973'091732—dc23

                                                              2011041970

CONTENTS

ACKNOWLEDGMENTS

Over the years this book's parts have been unearthed and exposed to the brilliance of many, many people, whose insights have reshaped it in countless ways. I can only hope it reflects a portion of their perspectives and suggestions. This work began as an undergraduate thesis at Reed College under the direction of Gail Kelly, in the form of an investigation into the historical and cultural context of la Sape. Robert Moore introduced me to metonymy and metaphor during that year, and it changed the theoretical direction of my work completely. Some of the key ideas from that project found their way into my dissertation at Cornell University, which benefited immensely from my committee: Jane Fajans, Vilma Santiago-Irizarry, and Sandra Greene. Sandra Greene's close reading and attention to historical depth and fact-checking accuracy kept my ethnographic lens sharp. Vilma Santiago-Irizarry and Fred Gleach were essential guides to the navigation of adventurous anthropological waters, both intellectual and academic. Jane Fajans and Terry Turner launched me not only on my first career as a fledgling anthropologist but also on my second one as a faculty gardener, and I thank them for their unabated support and hospitality over the years. The guidance of A. Thomas Kirsch provided a firm and crucial foundation to my thinking, and the classes I took with James Siegel have proved increasingly important to my understanding of anthropology as my own theoretical evolution has progressed.

The fieldwork for this book was generously funded by grants from the Mario Einaudi Center for International Studies at Cornell University and the Wenner Gren Foundation. I wrote the first draft of my manuscript while under an Andrew W. Mellon Foundation Postdoctoral Fellowship at the University of Illinois in Champaign-Urbana. The Department of Anthropology at the university was a welcoming and wonderful temporary home, and I would particularly like to thank Matti Bunzl for his generous mentoring and advice over the years. While in Illinois I had the great fortune of participating in the African Studies Workshop at the University of Chicago and gaining from the discussions at that magnificent refuge for scholarship and debate. I am especially indebted to Jean and John Comaroff, Ralph Austen, Robert Blunt, and Jennifer Cole for their comments. I also thank my fellow Ivoirianists Mike McGovern, Karen Morris, and Joseph Hellweg for their insights. I was later sheltered by the inestimable Department of Anthropology at the University of Virginia, and I would particularly like to thank Susan McKinnon and Ira Bashkow, whose warmth and friendship were matched by their generous help and critical guidance. The welcoming department at the College of the Holy Cross, especially those within our lively writing group, also provided encouragement, assistance, and insight over the last few years. Other people who have read and made a significant impact upon this work over the years include Anna Pandey, Christophe Robert, Erik Harms, Jacob Rigi, Cymene Howe, Hong An Tran, Andy Graan, Laura Bellows, Ellen Moodie, Jean Allman, Rupert Stasch, Jeff Dixon, Ara Francis, Renée Beard, Ann Marie Leshkowich, Nina Sylvanus, and Paul Manning. My editor, T. David Brent, has shown patience and encouragement through this, process and I thank him for his confidence in my work. Most importantly, my research would not have been possible without the many Ivoirians who hosted me and taught me how to navigate the streets of Abidjan. Jean-Pierre Dibangoup and his children Christian, Nancy, and Caroline shared their home with me and probably saved my life during the violent elections of 2000. Madame Kone was a wonderful neighbor, inviting me to delicious meals. Many friends contributed their knowledge, offered their protection, shared their food, and showed me the sweet life of Abidjan, including Ernest, Jean-Luc, Papis, Aurelien, Alexandre, Hervé, Claude, Djedje, Paul-Aimé Ecare, Nicole, Adou, Baldé, Ousmane, Ange, Kouame, Souba, Brico, Arthur, and Dedy. The greatest thanks go to Noël-Aimé Kouassi and Nini, who treated me as their own family, who accompanied me to places I could never have gone otherwise, and who responded to my endless questions with great honesty. The off-the-grid lifestyle my parents gave me, combined with regular overseas travel and a steady stream of foreign exchange students, undoubtedly provided the basis for my anthropological leanings, while my brothers' gaming skills have taught me as much about bluff and virtual social worlds as any anthropological theorist. While in Champaign-Urbana I was lucky enough to encounter my greatest source of both high-flying inspiration and critical on-the-ground perspective, Diana Arbaiza, with whom I share not only my life in this world, but the imagined, discursive worlds we have constructed together. She is my greatest friend, my true collaborator, my sharpest critic, and my love.

Pieces of this research have been previously published, and I appreciate the permission given to reuse this work in its new form. An earlier version of chapter 1 was published using the same title in 2009 in the *Journal of Linguistic Anthropology* 19 (2): 157–84. Chapter 5 is a revised and expanded version of a piece called "Migratory Modernity and the Cosmology of Consumption in Côte d'Ivoire," from an edited volume called *Migration and Economy: Global and Local Dynamics*, published in 2005 by Alta Mira Press. Extracts from chapter 2 were originally found in "Estranged Belongings: The Moral Economy of Theft in Abidjan, Côte d'Ivoire," in *Anthropological Theory* 6 (2): 179–203, in 2006.

INTRODUCTION

What's society built on? What's society built on? What's society built on?
It's built on bluff . . .
It's built on words. (Stereolab 1996)

The act of imitation is a matter of national pride in Côte d'Ivoire. A local tailor of *griffes colés* (counterfeit brand labels) named Dalbé told me
proudly that Ivoirians were the very best imitators of Europeans. "When
Ivoirians imitate, they don't do it at 50%, they imitate at 100%." There
is no shame then, in being derivative. It is precisely in the ability to imitate with precision that many urban Ivoirians locate their sense of prestige.
Ivoirians used the word *bluff* to describe both the act of artifice through
which young men and women project the appearance of success and the
people who performed it: *les bluffeurs*. A combination of dress, attitude,
physical comportment, and spendthrift practices, the bluff is not only a
performance of success beyond the financial means of the actor in question, but also a demonstration of the cultural knowledge and taste of the
urbanized citizen. It is a demonstration of the superior person one would
embody all the time if one had the money for it, a display of potential.
While the performance would seem to be an act of deception, an illusion
meant to fool the audience into believing in the success of the performers,
it paradoxically would seem to skewer such impressions by drawing attention to its own performativity—it is explicitly a bluff.

Within my first few weeks in Abidjan, the capital city of Côte d'Ivoire,
I found myself seated on a rickety wooden folding chair in a *maquis* (outdoor bar) in the middle of the street, as loudspeakers blared local pop music and the clientele danced and sang along enthusiastically. Several still-
operational streetlamps illuminated this spot of brightness in the darkened

dirt streets. I sat with my friend Leguen[1] and his accomplice, Billy (both in their thirties), who were celebrating a successful forgery scam by "wasting the table," spending their earnings extravagantly on beer and food and flashing their roll of cash. Almost every available inch of the table was covered with beer bottles, and young men at surrounding tables aggressively encouraged each other to buy more. The women were dressed in African wax print material cut in body-hugging European fashion, while the men wore U.S. and European name brand clothing: Nike, Adidas, Façonnable, Fubu, Docksiders, Hilfiger.[2] Several of the larger men wore tank tops revealing massive musculature. Almost everyone had a cell phone displayed prominently. The audience cheered as the DJ put on the latest Ivoirian hit, and a young man jumped out of his chair and began a frenetic dance. The crowd opened a space and encouraged him as he gestured rhythmically, displaying in a mock fighting style the number of bottles on his table, then accentuating through his movements each expensive piece of clothing on his body. A group of men entered with an exaggerated swagger, frowning and avoiding eye contact. One signaled the waitress and in a loud voice demanded a case of beer and a bottle of whiskey. Watching through the corner of his eye, the young man dancing returned to his overladen table and ordered five Guinnesses. Another called over a friend from a neighboring table and began to talk in low tones, passing over a cell phone that was immediately pocketed by the recipient. When the waitress attempted to clear empty bottles, he stopped her angrily and insisted that all remain. The DJ announced the presence of freshly returned migrants from France, who were paying for their champagne with "real French francs," and the crowd cheered, all eyes turning to their table to witness the ensuing acts of luxury.

This portrait of Abidjan's lively nightlife in the fall of 2000 describes a central mystery that continues to confound accounts of postcolonial Africa.[3] The rolls of money being flashed and spent, the prominently labeled clothes, the expensive drinks, and the cell phones were all part of an elaborate performance of success and modern citizenship that was disconnected from the economic reality of the performers. While to all appearances this crowd was living the good life, many of those present that night, including my friend Leguen, would struggle to find enough money to feed themselves the next day. Many might see this behavior as defying the logic of economic rationality and even consider these actions to be tragically misguided imitations caused by the consumer culture brainwashing of globalization. Others would decry these acts as a loss of culture and a betrayal of their traditions. Indeed, scholars have recorded these kinds of reactions throughout the colonial history of Africa, from Europeans and Africans alike (Magubane 1971; Martin 1994; Ferguson 2006).

This book sets out to demonstrate how such public activities made sense from within an urban Ivoirian cosmology of social practice, building from that local perspective to rethink connections between mimesis (the magic of the copy) and the postcolonial relationship to modernity. I demonstrate the ways in which these appropriations of the material of otherness were in fact key to the urban production of an "Ivoirian" national identity, one which grew to have enough power to produce new forms of xenophobia directed around national boundaries. Ultimately, this new urban sense of national identity has played a part in the divisive violence that has claimed so many victims in the last ten years.

The scene described above was not merely one of self-destructive wasting of resources in competitive potlatch, for there was a wonder and irresistibility about these acts of abandon; they radiated an allure that was contagious and difficult for all surrounding it to resist. More importantly, the audience and performer alike were well aware of the "real" economy underlying such performances, but the performance was socially important and effective anyway. Understanding why consumption worked like this, and what kinds of effects display had on social life, is the key puzzle around which this book revolves. Ultimately, I use this Ivoirian example to explore the role of the fake in social life more generally, examining its troubled history in the relationship between Africa and Europe as well as the role of the counterfeit in the construction of modernity itself.

The *bluffeurs* par excellence were unemployed Ivoirian men between fifteen and thirty-five who earned their income through the informal economy, men who were often characterized as *nouchi*, a slang term for a hoodlum or bandit. Although this would seem to indicate a group on the fringes of society, Côte d'Ivoire's economy had reached such desperate dimensions that the "shadow" economy could be considered the dominant or, as Janet MacGaffey (1991) puts it, the "real" economy, as in so many other contemporary African societies (Mbembe 2001; Simone 2004; Apter 2005; De Boeck and Plissart 2006; Ferguson 2006). Because success within this informal economy depended upon strong social networks through which goods, information, and security flowed, the streets of Abidjan could be described as a moral economy in the sense that the maintenance of social relationships often outweighed the importance of profits, that economic transactions served to accumulate people more than things (Newell 2006).

Money and luxury goods were thus a medium for the investment in social relations. Much as in Geschiere's (1997) discussion of how Cameroonians interpret modern capitalist relations in terms of witchcraft, in Abidjan's zero-sum economy too much individual accumulation produced negative reactions such as the alienations of social relationships, theft, witchcraft accusations, or magical attack. Any dramatic increase in wealth was clear evidence to people's friends and family members that they were not fulfilling their social obligations to share income. In such a world, the accumulation of real capital was dangerous and often invited violent aggression, and so economic success required careful social negotiation. These problems affected even the truly rich, living in neighborhoods like Cocody and Riviera, though these had greater means with which to build loyalty through patronage.

However, for Abidjanais *nouchi* youth in the *quartiers populaires* (low-income districts), the display of transitory wealth and the knowledge of what it meant to live as though money were no matter could actually enlarge one's reputation and build stronger social support. As in De Boeck's Kinshasa, any surplus beyond the "bare minimum" was "immediately dispersed, injected into a broader social network" (De Boeck and Plissart 2006:242). Spending above one's means in a public setting was also to purchase for one's friends, thus overcoming the crippling effects of social obligations within a moral economy. To bluff was to build a network, to deceive was to distribute wealth, allowing for personal gains in reputation without risking the social ties necessary for survival and success. During my fieldwork, bluffing involved a dance called the *logobi*, through which brand logos were displayed. This phenomenon later metamorphosed into the internationally followed musical genre of *coupé-décalé* (scam and scram, cut and move) popularized by Douk Saga and his Jet Set entourage (Kohlhagen 2006, McGovern 2011).[4] This scene included the act of *travailler* (to work), in which the audience threw money at the dancer in appreciation of his *travail*. Dancing was also referred to as "wasting," and a good dancer would be encouraged by calls of "gaspiller, on te din" (waste, we are watching you). In this way the bluff collapses and inverts oppositions of production and consumption—to waste is to work.

In calling their performance of success a bluff, urban Ivoirian youth signaled at once that their actions were mimicry and that such mimicry could in fact produce success. Similarly, in a game of poker, by pretending one's cards are better than they are, one can make value out of nothing, as if by magic. Bluffing is essential to winning the game in the long term, so deceit is expected, valued, and productive. In a section of society in which the ability to scam was both an art and a means of survival, the bluff was a form of exchange and a meter of social hierarchy: *nouchi* took not only prestige but real profit from their target in a successful deceptive transaction. "Faking it," despite appearances (or rather precisely because of them), could have real effects, and that was something to be celebrated. Thus, Abidjan's residents saw the difference between the "look" people were able to project and their material position in life as a positive transcendence of their surroundings rather than an artificial put-on. This was in part an appreciation of the quality of the specific actor's performance, but in a deeper and more important sense, this was an appreciation of the nature of performance itself, the ability of metaphor to produce reality rather than merely comment upon it, for illusion sometimes participates in the construction of reality.

Indeed, for anthropologists the role of projected imagery and the social imaginary in the construction of reality should be familiar territory. If, as in "voodoo death," a person who has been magically murdered through the pointing of a bone or lime spatula can really die, then certainly it should not be surprising that the mask of success can make social success (Fortune 1932; L. Warner 1937; Lévi-Strauss 1963; Siegel 2006). The presence of "our" symbols as the metaphors in question should not interfere with our ability to appreciate the ways other cultures can put them to use.

In this book, I challenge the cultural presuppositions underlying our understanding of the fake in order to recast anthropological theories of the relationship between mimesis, modernity and postcolonial identity. The bluff, by acknowledging itself as deceptive illusion and yet demanding that everyone act as though it were real, challenges precisely the boundaries between the real and imaginary explored in contemporary Africanist literature.[5] Apter (2005), in a particularly relevant example, has traced connections between postcolonial African state spectacle, Nigerian 419 scams, and the magic of money, demonstrating how the postpetroleum Nigerian economy has been built upon duplicitous illusions and counterfeits in an effort to make money out of magic. As the Comaroffs have put it, "postcolonies are quite literally associated with a counterfeit modernity, a modernity of counterfeit" (2006:13). Is there a particular connection, then, between postcolonial identity and the mimesis of modernity? And what do we (or more to the point, those in the postcolonies) mean by modernity? What are the consequences of mimesis for understanding contemporary global relations, new nationalisms, new subjectivities?

Ivoirian Nationalism and Urban Popular Culture

The idea that imitation is a matter of Ivoirian national pride brings up another kind of question that runs through this book: Who is Ivoirian? A fraught question in any country, this has become the dominant problem of Ivoirian politics, as since the death of the first president, Félix Houphouët-Boigny, in 1993 politicians such as Henri Bédié, Robert Guéï, and Laurent Gbagbo have increasingly drawn on new concepts of nationalism and anti-immigrant sentiment in order to consolidate their followings. In such a context, "Ivoirian" has become an increasingly politicized word, a word whose contested signification has brought about killing, suffering, and instability. However, as tempting as it may be to blame the "politics of the belly" (Bayart 1993) for the political devastation of this formerly successful country, I believe this nationalist diatribe fell upon an audience all too ready to believe in a cultural separation that had not been so clear only a decade before. Thus, this book seeks to trace the origins of the dichotomization of Ivoirian society within a nascent urban popular culture that I suggest reshaped the significance of cultural identities across the nation.

While political tensions had been growing since the rise of multipartyism in the early 1990s, they became truly destructive in September 19, 2002, when a rebel army from the north called the Force Nouvelles attempted a coup d'état, demanding proper representation for northern residents in the national government. While their efforts were stopped midway—producing a boundary between northern and southern zones that until quite recently was policed by U.N. peacekeeping forces and the French military—neither side was able to overcome the other and a long-term standoff ensued, interspersed with many acts of violence and terror (International Crisis Group 2003, 2004, 2007). Liberian mercenaries from the waning neighboring war were incorporated on both sides, further increasing violence. Every year from 2005 onward President Gbagbo promised elections that never materialized. The country was symbolically reunited in 2007 when Guillaume Soro, the former leader of the rebel army, was made prime minister, but many suspected him of selling himself for personal power, and both elections and rebel disarmament continued to be delayed.

When the elections finally did take place on November 29, 2010, both Gbagbo and Ouattara claimed victory, and Ivoirians themselves seemed unable to determine which was the real and which the fake. After a delay in the count, the electoral commission announced that Alassane Ouattara had won by 54% to 46%. However, the head of the Constitutional Council, a friend and ally of Gbagbo's, tore up the election results and declared the election a "masquerade." He argued that the results of nine districts of Côte d'Ivoire—all strongholds of support for Ouattara—were fraudulent. After eliminating these false results, Gbagbo would win the election by 51.45% to 48.55%. Thus, Gbagbo, who had managed to stay in power five years beyond the end of his mandate (a post many Ivoirians said he never legitimately won in the first place), declared himself president for another five years. Gbagbo accused his opponents of "faking it," of pretending to be Ivoirians when they were not, and of rigging the votes when they could not get enough legitimate Ivoirians to vote for his opponent. In so doing, he used national anxieties over authenticity to draw attention away from his own performance of legitimacy. While the U.N. recognized Ouattara as the winner, Gbagbo resisted, asking his followers to reject foreign intervention that was trying to oust his legitimate leadership because he would not collaborate with the French. The result was a stalemate, as Ouattara hid out in a dilapidated luxury hotel with no institutional power while Gbagbo was cut off from much of his funding and international recognition. All attempts at mediation and diplomacy failed. On April 11, 2011, French troops arrested Gbagbo and placed him in Ouattara's custody. While from an international perspective this may have been long overdue, within Côte d'Ivoire the collaboration of the French in the final takeover may cast doubts on Ouattara's legitimacy in the future, at least in the eyes of Gbagbo's many supporters. Rather than transcending oppositions, as intended and hoped for, this "masquerade" of an election ended up merely reiterating the divisions that had riven the country apart to begin with.

This book examines the relationship between urban popular culture and the increasing symbolic exclusion of northern Ivoirians and the children of immigrants from citizenship within political discourse. Despite a steadfast reputation for political stability, when the civil crisis began in 2002, Côte d'Ivoire suddenly tumbled into the ranks of African nations stereotypically characterized in the media by their irrational violence structured by timeless ethnic oppositions. This is a representation I wish to contest here, suggesting instead that the instability of contemporary Ivoirian politics is closely linked to the cultural processes underlying the bluff and its relationship to the imagination of modernity. This is an issue I will treat in much further detail in chapters 1 and 6.

My fieldwork during 2000 and 2001 took place precisely in the time period leading up the attempted coup d'état of 2002, which sparked the Ivoirian crisis. As the electoral process became muddled by military manipulations and accusations were leveled concerning the citizenship of the most important candidates for president, new forms of popular culture were flourishing and transforming the very idea of Ivoirian culture. Drawing from my research in the streets of Abidjan during the elections of 2000, at a time when the divisive categories of "north" and "south" were first developing political salience, I believe that a key feature of the Ivoirian crisis can be found outside the usual political economic sphere in the nebulous, capricious territory of popular culture. Indeed, I suggest that from within the bustling streets of Abidjan's *quartiers populaires* a new imagination of Ivoirian national identity was in the making, a process launched in a cultural efflorescence linked to urban social life that first really came into its own in the 1990s.

It is not that the idea of national identity was new. The nation's founding president, Houphouët-Boigny, had made the construction of shared national identity a state priority and put in place numerous policies to achieve it. He built an integrated national education system, he insisted on French as the national language (thereby avoiding the problem of whose local language was dominant), and he installed incentives for internal migration, encouraging Ivoirians to move to the southwest cocoa-growing region of the country and theoretically weaken ethnic boundaries while launching economic productivity.

Houphouët also initiated an open-border immigration policy, giving legal residence to practically anyone who requested it and even attempting to give immigrants the right to vote. Ivoirians continue to speak proudly of this welcoming period in their past. Theoretically, this provided the country with an endless supply of cheap labor, while Ivoirians could take the more prestigious administrative positions, run businesses and plantations, serve in education, and so on, which probably allowed the country to achieve its economic stature in the sixties and seventies. As a result of these policies, over a third of Côte d'Ivoire's population today are immigrants and a far higher, unknown percentage the children of immigrants.[6] The great majority of immigrants come from Burkina Faso and are of Dioula ethnicity; according to the 2000 census (which counted only legal immigrants and not their naturalized children) their numbers had reached 2,238,548, making up 14.6% of the total Ivoirian population (INS 2000). As early as 1961, the Burkinabe accounted for 90% of plantation labor (Rouch 1961). They were followed by people from other neighboring West African countries such as Mali, Ghana, Guinea, and Nigeria. Houphouët thus discouraged a discourse of autochtony as a part of national identity (Cutolo 2010:529). Not incidentally, his reign lasted until his death in 1993, such that his personal vision of Côte d'Ivoire is deeply ingrained in the social latticework.

But Houphouëtist policies were not only top down, their content was for the most part empty of indigenous cultural content (Chappell 1989). Since all *local* culture was ethnically marked, it was difficult to draw on any symbols of Ivoirian identity without being accused of tribal factionalism. I suggest that it was the emergent urban popular culture, developed on terrain that both colonists and the Ivoirian state had enforced as ethnically neutral or "extraterritorial" (Dembélé 2002:139), that allowed for the development of a sense of national identity among citizens themselves as the twentieth century came to a close. However, this popular culture forged in southern cities valorized urban identity and symbols of modernity, rejecting anything that smacked of "tradition" or the *paysan* (peasant) and producing a confusion between the *citadin* (urban resident) and the *citoyen* (citizen).

Thus, the political problems of 2000 were spurred on by a new form of urban culture forged by lower-class urban youth in search of an alternative model for identity. Their motivations did not concern nationalism at all, but rather a class struggle against elitist hierarchical evaluations based on differential access to symbols of French "civilization." They attempted to supersede this system by emphasizing their lower-class identity while legitimizing it through the appropriation of U.S. fashion and to some extent linguistic style and music. Many of their borrowings were linked to African-American hip-hop culture, to which they were drawn by its associations with lower-class urban scenarios close to their own experience, as well as by certain parallel forms of consumption not so far removed from the bluff: think of the symbolism of cars, expensive liquor, clothing, and hypertrophied heterosexuality in U.S. hip-hop videos (Mukherjee 2006). Because these representations were from a cultural source considered even more powerful than the French, such appropriations challenged the superiority of elite consumption practices. At the same time, because this new value system celebrated the incorporation of influences from a wide variety of local ethnic groups, these cultural products formed the basis for an understanding of Ivoirianess that could not have existed before.

Henri Bédié, the successor to Houphouët-Boigny, sculpted the discourse of *Ivoirité* to prevent his competitor Alassane Outtara from winning the presidency by claiming Outtara was not a true Ivoirian. However, the success of Bédié's political machinations was inseparable from popular visions of overlap between autochthony and modernity—each category paradoxically contained within the other. Cutolo (2010) demonstrates how a group of academics and intellectuals consolidated elite ideology around the concept of *Ivoirité* as a curious hybrid: part adumbrated autochthony based on the groups present at the colonial genesis of the nation in 1893, part vision of national modernity structured around Baoulé ethnicity as the model for cultural citizenship. While Cutolo presents this new self-affirming elite discourse as a causal factor in the disruption of the nation-state, my fieldwork uncovered this same overlap between autochthony and modernity being forged simultaneously in the popular, grassroots construction of identity. I argue that this new understanding of Ivoirian nationality was a product of the dynamic intermixture and urban sociality of a city that had grown from fifty-eight thousand to over well over two million between 1948 and 1990.

While this reimagining of "Ivoirian" was centered in Abidjan and implicitly excluded residents from rural northern regions, the diffusion of popular culture through media and migration makes this study relevant to understanding Ivoirians in general. While urban culture should not be considered nationally representative, it is possible to speak of an Ivoirian popular culture with national significance, just as it is possible to discuss the urban culture surrounding hip-hop in the United States as affecting U.S. culture generally. A city like Abidjan is a porous place, a place made up as much by its movement in and out as by anyone who lives there. The ideas and tastes of the city are produced by this circulation into and back outward throughout the rural interior, pushed like the pumping of a heart by the economic and cultural motivations for migration. Every one of my closest contacts left the city for a visit to a village at some point during my fieldwork, and I frequently encountered new arrivals or visitors to the city linked to my network. In addition to the conventional media like radio and newspapers that spread cultural products with near instantaneity, the city is itself a kind of medium, broadcasting through the circular migrations of its residents. Urban cultural productions such as fashion, slang, and genres of music and dance do not belong solely to the city that spawned them; these things are Ivoirian, their significance made national in scope by the media, even if their epicenter remains Abidjan. As Piot (1999) has demonstrated so beautifully, the village is "remotely global," interconnected in intricate and intimate ways with wider cultural worlds.

At the same time, the concept of "Ivoirian" spread throughout the nation by this urban popular culture was not inclusive of the nation, but carried implicit hegemonic evaluations of style, value, and urban acculturation that made some Ivoirians appear to be less authentic citizens than others. From within this urban subculture, evaluations were the reverse of what one might imagine; authentic autochthony was more likely to be indicated by what Ferguson refers to as "cosmopolitan" style—with references to externality—than by "localist" imagery (1999:97).[7] Indeed, it useful to here to draw on Ferguson's use of style as a way to talk about cultural pluralism and disrupt the fallacy of cultural holism; he argues that style should not be seen as transparently connected to social identity or group, but rather as a personally cultivated performance. In Côte d'Ivoire this stylistic conflict effected not only urban identities, I would argue, but extended to wherever the influence of urban popular culture had reached. Thus, we are not talking about north versus south or even urban versus rural, but about a conflict of taste that shaped Ivoirian society as a whole. However, while I agree with Ferguson that style is individually motivated, I cannot follow him in severing it from social identity (1999:96–98), for social actors often do read style as the self-evident expression of group identity. This was precisely the problem faced by those who refused to perform urban style in the city: they were assumed to be foreigners and excluded from the category "Ivoirian." Thus, while I will employ the word "Ivoirian" throughout this text to refer to cultural productions I consider to have national significance, it should always be understood that such cultural products or styles are not consumed monolithically, but from conflicting evaluatory schemas.

Yere and *Gaou*: Authenticity and the Cosmology of Modernity

Given the importance of modernity in these new forms of popular culture, it is no coincidence that the bluff was an expression of the modern, urban identity of the actors. It was proof that they had transcended the villagers, who they believed had no comprehension of good taste and fine living. Thus, a *bluffeur* was someone who had truly arrived in the city, no longer a migrant laborer but a *citadin*, an urban resident (Newell 2005). The bluff was modeled upon images of North Atlantic[8] modernity (what they called *Beng*) conveyed in the global media's representation of hip-hop culture. The objects of desire for most Abidjanais between the summer of 2000 and that of 2001 were baggy pants, jeans, basketball jerseys, tracksuits, and thick gold chains. They used street names like Biggie, Tupac, and Tyson, along with others drawn from characters from action films, such as Rambo and Scarface. Furthermore, they insisted on the authenticity of the North Atlantic products they consumed—they had to be "real" name brand products, such as Dockers, Adidas, Nike, Fubu, Façonnable, Kappa, Docksider, and Timberland—and they were terrified by the prospect of being caught with a fake product. To wear a fake was to reveal one's inability to discern the "true" product from its imitation. Thus, we see a strange combination of the necessity for the objects to be "authentic" even as the performance itself was recognized as *faire le show* (to make a show), or as bluffing.

Indeed, the ability to discern the fake from the real in everyday life was not only a crucial survival skill in an economy built upon conning people, but also the principal proof of one's modernity. The distinction between urban and rural was usually cast through the polyvalent opposition between *yere* and *gaou*, a polysemous opposition whose ramifications run throughout the book. I was told the Nouchi word *yere* originates in the Dioula for "seeing," that it describes someone "qui voit claire," but other interpretations of the word's etymology include "self," "authentic," and "true." *Dozos* (traditional hunters typically of northern ethnic origin who are feared for their powerful bulletproof magic) utilize the term *dozo yere-yere* to differentiate authentic *dozos* from impostors.

However, according to Drissa Kone, a *dozo* who worked closely with Joseph Hellweg (2011) in his research, the word also signifies clarity or openness. Examples he provided included the phrase *nya yere*, which means "open eyes," or the verb phrase *ka da yere*, "to open the/a door." He also cited a television show in which an actor shouted "Je vais te yere!" as in, "I'll make you see," or "I'll 'open' your eyes to the truth about who's right/ in charge!" Drissa concluded, "Quand tu es yere, tu vois clair." The French phrase *il voit claire* was often used in connection with the *féticheur*'s ability to see into the mystical goings-on of the otherworld, where witches, spirits, and *jinnis* are at work, and it seems that word *yere* refers to more than ordinary clarity of sight. Thus, there would appear to be a semiotic connection between authenticity and the ability to see beyond the surfaces of things to the inverse, behind-the-mask realm where potency exists.

Participants in the criminal economy, however, apply this concept to the art of the scam. *Yere* describes someone who cannot be scammed, while to *yere* someone is to steal from them. By contrast, a *gaou* is a fool, someone incapable of discerning his surroundings, and therefore someone easily duped. Since savvy urban citizens were likely to gain part of their income from the second economy, recent arrivals to the city and immigrants were the likeliest targets of their cons. *Gaou* qualities were thus readily associated not only with rural origins but with the large population of African immigrants in Abidjan, categories which overlapped dangerously in *nouchi* perspective.

At the same time, urban youth applied this opposition to taste and connoisseurship concerning consumption. A *gaou* did not know how to dress, or how to differentiate between a counterfeit and the real thing. Likewise, commodities and clothing of Euro-American origin were *yere* in relation to Ivoirian-made products (and U.S. clothing was more *yere* than French clothing), while Ivoirian products were often superior to those made in other African countries. Geographic locations, both migratory destinations and origins of valued consumer goods, were arranged hierarchically according to this logic. *Yere* would thus seem to connect "true" or "authentic" qualities with symbolic openness to external forces, but with different valences according to differing competing discourses. From the perspective of the traditional hunting society of the *dozos*, a true *dozo* was one with the ability to connect with the otherworld of the spirits, to see clearly where normal people cannot see, whereas for the urban Ivoirian youth, an authentic Ivoirian was someone capable of distinguishing and absorbing value in the world of modernity.[9] Thus, the competitive performance of *faire le show*, or bluffing—the central act of identity production for young Abidjanais men—was not simply a display of money and foreign goods, but also a display of the cultural mastery of the symbols of modern identity, differentiating them from "untrue" Ivoirians incapable of making such distinctions.

Not only was citizenship linked to one's access and proximity to sources of authentic modernity, but the urban Ivoirian vision of power relations on a global scale between nations was also inscribed in this cosmology of relative modernity (Malkki 1993). The outlines of this "mapping" of cultural power seems to parallel general North Atlantic perspectives on cultural value (oppositions such as First and Third World or developed, developing, and underdeveloped come to mind), but the underlying principles organizing classification are quite different. In a manner quite similar to Wyatt MacGaffey's (1968, 1972) research on Kongolese perceptions of "the West," the ordering of nations corresponds to cosmological ideas about relationships between the visible world and the otherworld of the spirits, in which real-world success comes from connections of mediation with the world of externality.[10] I describe this vision as a nested hierarchy of cultural evolution, in which Abidjanais are to rural Ivoirians and African immigrants as Europeans are to Ivoirian migrants, and the U.S. to France.

The fear of inauthenticity and the nervous detection of fakery in the social environment extended during increasing moments of political instability in 2000 and 2001 to the suspicion that one's neighbors might only be posing as Ivoirians. As politicians struggled for predominance, the question of their citizenship was quick to surface, and such concerns rapidly spread to the voting populace. The possibility of fraud in a country where bribery is quite normal immediately made questionable even the documents meant to insure authentic citizenship. As one newspaper headline read in 2001,

ALL THE FOREIGNERS WILL HAVE IVOIRIAN I.D.: CÔTE D'IVOIRE IS IN DANGER ("Tous les Étrangers Auront des Pièces d'Identité Ivoiriennes" 2001)[11]

The chief mechanism behind this attempt to identify and remove the "fake" Ivoirians was *les rafles* (raids), in which military police would round up large groups of people and demand to see identification papers. If none could be produced, one had to bribe the policeman or be carted off to jail. Increasingly, as political tensions over national identity mounted, people who either looked Muslim or had a Muslim-sounding name had their papers torn up or burned on the spot, under the pretense that they were fakes. The emergence of such activities in conjunction with a new political discourse of *Ivoirité* came as a shock to people within and outside Côte d'Ivoire who continued to believe in a history supposedly free of ethnic and religious strife—though as McGovern (2011) reminds us, this representation ignores the instability of the precolonial period. In this sense the urban reimagining of modernity in Côte d'Ivoire became imbricated with both a paradoxical glorification of fakery as a mark of Ivoirian pride and a growing paranoia over people's ability to fake Ivoirian identity itself. I now turn to a consideration of the relationship between this cosmology of mimetic modernity and the urban setting that produced it.

Sapeurs and *Bluffeurs*: Discourses on African Mimesis

In asking the question of why exactly Abidjanais youth were investing so much of their limited economic resources in the consumption of U.S. and European clothing and public "waste" of money, we are immediately drawn into complex questions of mimesis and identity and their relationship to a fraught colonial history of hierarchy, racism, and the ideology of social evolution in Africa. The problem of mimesis is one that has plagued anthropology from very early on, for any attempt to understand the enactment of "Western" cultural practices by the Other is tied up in identity politics themselves. As Bhabha (1994) has argued, because the European colonial empire played a double game by encouraging "natives" to abandon their cultural practices and recognize the superiority of European ones, but at the same time barricading access to European identity, the interpretation of mimesis reproduces colonial discourse. Both representations of native authenticity underlying mimetic enactments and those that describe successful "acculturation" reinforce ideologies of modernity and the hierarchies they continue to legitimate.

To celebrate mimesis as a transcendence of the boundary between the

"West and the Rest" runs dangerously close to the idea that true success lies within so-called modern lifestyle, and that the Other should leave behind their former, less accomplished cultural past and take part in the culture of the global modern. This aligns much too well with the colonial project of the civilizing mission to be comfortable to the anthropologist. To say on the other hand that such acts are a performance of modernity, that there is an underlying difference beneath the superficial sameness of the act, is to suggest that postcolonial performers are not "really" modern, thus denying them access to the very identity they seem to be seeking.

Unfortunately, we find ourselves on very sensitive and unstable ground in any attempt to investigate this set of issues, for "the fake" is a loaded term, and imitation is generally disparaged in North Atlantic cultures as an unworthy, dubious, and even dangerous entity. There seems to be a fear of clothing's potential to confuse social categories; such acts are seen as dangerous artifice. As Goffman put it,

> Society is organized on the principle that . . . an individual who implicitly or explicitly signifies that he has certain social characteristics ought in fact to be what he claims he is. In consequence, when an individual projects a definition of the situation and thereby makes an implicit or explicit claim to be a person of a particular kind, he automatically exerts a moral demand upon the others, obliging them to value and treat him in the manner that persons of his kind have a right to expect. He also implicitly forgoes all claims to be things he does not appear to be and hence forgoes the treatment that would be appropriate for such individuals. The others find, then, that the individual has informed them as to what is and as to what they *ought* to see as the "is." (Goffman 1959:13)

Thus, actors and audience alike are morally obligated to pretend that appearances correspond to social "reality." When someone dressing "above their station" is unmasked in the U.S. context, not only is their authenticity and personal valor questioned, they sometimes face negative social repercussions. Furthermore, in connecting modernity with mimesis in the postcolony, we invite Bhabha's critique that the very concept of mimicry is inherent in the colonial politics of keeping the Other "almost the same, but not quite" modern (1994:86). The overall effect, as Ferguson (2006) puts it, is squeamishness. Part of this embarrassment seems to be produced by the misperception of irrationality, the idea that the causal role between consumption and success is reversed here. The product of Protestant ideology, U.S. culture considers proper consumption the just reward of hard work, and to spend in proportion to income—our addiction to credit cards and crushing national debt notwithstanding. The line between modern and primitive is often presented precisely as that between the producers of originals and those that merely imitate (Taussig 1993). As Gable writes, this is especially the case for Africans, for whom the line between the modern and its mimics is typically racialized, representing would be boundary crossers as "aping" whites, such that "Africans are modernity's monkeys" (2002:578).

But postcolonial imitators are also often represented in some way as betraying their own culture by adopting these trappings of North Atlantic culture. As Ferguson (2006) describes, anthropologists, who often want to "speak to power" from the position of the disenfranchised, seem embarrassed in the face of such obvious respect for the ex-colonials or neocolonials (or the anthropologist themselves). Like anxious parents, we hope for "our" colonial subjects to be fighting back with all the "weapons of the weak" they can muster, and thus, the dominant anthropological position on mimesis describes it as a form of resistance.

Ferguson uses Jonathan Friedman's (1994) work on Congolese *sapeurs* as a primary example of how wrong such a tack can go. For him, Friedman's analysis of African men obsessed with wearing expensive designer label suits goes too far when it suggests that the mimesis of modernity is really a kind of "tradition," in which motivations are primarily directed by magico-religious belief (Ferguson 2006). Such an explanation risks denying the agency and political relevance of a movement whose actors are clearly not interested in being traditional, and who, above all, seek membership in the global community of the West, which the concept of modernity walls off from the "Rest." But while Ferguson's argument clarifies many unspoken assumptions of the study of mimesis and brings our attention to the political claims people might be making in acts of mimesis, it downplays the significance of culture in the use of symbolic action. Gable considers that Ferguson "ventriloquizes" African voices as critics of anthropology without properly situating them ethnographically:

When he asserts that the Africans he quotes are claiming "global citizenship," are they appealing to a kind of universal morality—one that is associated with a Western discourse and culture—precisely because they share "an education" (and therefore a culture), even though they differ as to nationality, ethnicity, and so forth? Or are the discursive tactics they deploy also typically African—not mimicry at all, but creative borrowings of Western formats and media to say quintessentially African things about the responsibility putative kin have toward one another in an emerging global community? (Gable 2002:575)

Ferguson's article glosses over the different reactions Africans with "Western" educations and those without might have to something like Jean Rouch's film *Les Maitres Fous* (1954). Clearly not all "Africans" will have the same reactions to these kinds of representations, and varying degrees of exposure to pervasive North Atlantic stereotypes of African behavior will probably have an effect upon this.

The literature on La Sape, a Congolese movement of young men wearing designer suits, is a particularly relevant case with which to demonstrate the course I try to sail between Friedman's "consumption as tradition" and Ferguson's mimesis as a purely political outcry for membership.[12] I appreciate and make use of both these perspectives, but I seek an intermediate space between them. La Sape contains dynamics strikingly similar to the Ivoirian bluff while retaining its own characteristics and dynamics, and the comparison is one I would like to draw out more extensively elsewhere. Indeed, my first field research involved Congolese immigrants in Paris, before I received funding for my project in Côte d'Ivoire. But my purpose in describing the movement here will be to illustrate the multilayered complexity of consumption, laying the groundwork for the ways in which this book will approach Ivoirian stylistic performances.

La Sape reached its peak in the late 1980s but continues to exert and influence to this day. Sometimes referred to as an acronym (S.A.P.E., or Société des Ambianceurs et des Personnes Élégantes), La Sape began with Congolese youth who made the journey to Paris for the purpose of buying authentic suits from the highest fashion labels, which they brought back in order to seal their reputation back home (Gandoulou 1984, 1989). In Brazzaville they became celebrities of elegance, followed by crowds of appreciators and underlings who carried their things for them. Hierarchies were highly elaborated, with ranked clubs within which actors vied for leadership, and clothing duels were a regular occurrence at important cultural events. Being seen was so important to the *sapeurs* that they attended all kinds of social functions, including weddings, baptisms, and funerals, where their own activities sometimes overshadowed the purpose of the event. Much as in the Ivoirian case, I believe these consumption practices were linked to a cosmology of modernity in which Europe was seen as a locus of power that could be drawn upon through consumption and migration. The authenticity of the clothing was crucial at the beginning, and the role of Paris as the "center of the world" became a key part of Congolese efforts at building reputation and wealth (Gondola 1999). However, my field research on *sapeurs* in Paris in 2000 indicated that as the movement spread beyond its origins to other African countries, *sapeurs* increasingly emphasized the "art of dress" and claimed a kind of cultural expertise and connoisseurship that could not be simply bought. Modernity was expressed through progressively nuanced performances of taste, and the *sapeurs* sought to differentiate themselves from other African mimeticians through the maintenance of a specifically Congolese national relationship to fashion.

Friedman (1994), emphasizing the "you are what you eat" approach to consumption, has described the *sapeurs'* relationship to North Atlantic consumer goods as akin to the cannibalism practiced in traditional Congolese warfare, in which actors incorporate the power of their enemies through literal acts of consumption. The clothes are not simply surfaces covering the person, but carry metaphysical efficacy—what Friedman refers to as "lifeforce"—from Europe. He also demonstrates how the hierarchically ranked clubs seem to reproduce the kinship and political system of the Kingdom of the Kongo, in which ranked clans competed with one another for proximity to the king (W. MacGaffey 1986).

While my own fieldwork on *sapeurs* indicates that Friedman is largely right about the symbolic underpinnings of La Sape, the problem with his portrayal is that it can easily lead the reader to exoticize and primitivize these actors, the very same who are sacrificing everything to achieve an identity associated with modernity. This is precisely what Ferguson finds fault with, for he reads Friedman's portrayal as yet another boundary-drawing act, in effect casting these would-be "moderns" back into primitive and unchanging traditional Africa. This problem is exacerbated by Friedman's dichotomous approach to cultural comparison, arguing that Congolese consumption is socially determined while Europeans express and construct individual lifestyles, thus confirming an opposition between "modern" and "not."

While Friedman's culturalist interpretation ends up reifying cultural boundaries in problematic ways, I think Ferguson focuses too exclusively on the political economic motivations of mimesis. After all, as Gable (2002:576) pithily remarks in his critique, shouldn't we expect the appropriation of symbols to take place in terms *appropriate* to the actor's culture?[13] How can we assume that the modernity to which all these imitators seek entrance is the same one, simply because they use the same signifiers to reference it? This is precisely the problem the debate boils down to: is modernity an objective reality explained as the material differentiation of the world into haves and have-nots through the rise of a global capitalist world system, or is modernity a culturally specific explanation of global inequalities, one therefore subject to multiple incarnations and interpretations and whose existence is fundamentally indemonstrable because it is culturally relative?

Indeed, I was told by a Congolese man who had adopted the street name of Kennedy: "La Sape is a religion. We do not believe in one overarching God, but in a sense we are all gods, gods of La Sape" (personal communication, 1998). Such a perspective on the value of clothing clearly indicates a more complex motivation for mimesis than claiming membership in the community of moderns, even if this is also a key desire for Kennedy. Further evidence of the importance of local cultural frameworks in such acts of mimesis can be found in Bazenguisa-Ganga's early arguments that urban youth from the Kongo ethnic group were using clothing to criticize the cultural legitimacy of the Mbochi ethnic group that had taken power from Patrice Lissouba (of Kongo ethnicity) through a military coup (Bazanquisa 1992).[14] Since the Kongolese had been local intermediaries with European culture since initiating contact with the Portuguese in 1491, the superior mastery of the symbols of European identity was a crafty and potent way of undermining the political legitimacy of the elite in the 1980s when La Sape was formed.

I think that both Congolese and the Ivoirians I focus on in this book were trying to gain access to the benefits of modernity, as Ferguson argues, but that their understanding of modernity and of the role of mimesis in relating to it were culturally inflected, if often in contradictory and polyvalent ways. This is not to say that their interpretation of modernity was wrong, for I believe the conception of modernity reified as reality by North Atlantic cultures is a form of discourse through which the real is culturally constructed. Sapeurs and bluffeurs are architects of this discursive construction as well, remaking the modern in their performances. In this book, I explore the close links between cultural constructions of modernity and the ideologies surrounding mimesis, in order to understand both African postcolonial efforts at attaining "modernity" through consumption as well as the relationship between fears of mimesis and the cultural construction of so-called modern identity in North Atlantic cultures.

Mimesis and Masking: Real Fakes and
the Elusive Illusion of Modernity

Theories of consumption have long been dominated by the idea of surface imitation, of counterfeit identities, of passing, and have continually failed to take account of other cultural possibilities for evaluation in the act of consumption. Perhaps the model of fakery or the counterfeit is misleading, if only because it is so value laden in our own society. If the bluff is explicitly a bluff and yet remains a positive and constructive act, we are no longer in the realm of the poser but rather of the performer.

I suggest here that our reactions to mimesis have been insensitive to the culturally specific nature of the image. Indeed, Mbembe is instructive here in his description of the "autochthonous status of the image" in Cameroon. He says that the obverse and reverse of the world, its visible face and the hidden forces of the other side, "were governed by relations of similarity, relations far from making the one a mere copy or model of the other. . . . The invisible was in the visible, and vice versa, not as a matter of artifice, but as one and the same and as external reality simultaneously—as the image of the thing and the imagined thing, at the same time" (2001:152). In this sense, Mbembe suggests that the figurative capacity, the power to project an image, an illusion, can be considered in this context the power to bring to life the thing for which the image was a metaphor, to conjoin the world of the living and that of the shades or spirits. He continues: "It is to that extent that the world of images belonged to the world of charms. For the power to represent reality implied that one was having recourse to that sort of magic and double sight, imagination, even fabrication that consisted in clothing the signs with appearances of the thing of which they were precisely the metaphor" (2001:153). Representing was to re-present, to bring forth. The figurative principle Mbembe refers to here is the logic underlying many African masking practices, in which the mask is understood both as a performance and at the same time as a reality: simultaneous multiplicities. The mask is the literal presence of the spirit entity it represents, even when the audience is almost necessarily aware that it is witnessing a performance by human actors. Some "masks" in Cameroon don't even involve covering the face; the identity is indicated merely through makeup, clothing, and ritual role, and yet the audience recognizes the presence of something other than the person who normally inhabits the human body—it is no longer a person, but possessed by the character of the mask and unrecognizable as anything else during the course of the ritual (Argenti 2007). Thus, the secrecy often surrounding the donning of masking costumes, or the common claim that no woman can know that masks are performed by men, cannot be taken at face value, but rather as public secrets, secrets known by all but never spoken of (Bellman 1984; Picton 1990; Taussig 1999). The mask is thus a paradox: at once a figure to be taken literally, and whose powers and identity are believed to be real and to influence the course of society, and at the same time a costume worn by human actors, a performance recognized by its audience as theater. We must then consider the possibility that like the ritual mask that both is and is not the ancestor it represents, the bluff has the capacity to conjoin the real and imaginary, illusion and authenticity.

Let me be clear that this is not an explicit cultural link in Côte d'Ivoire. The young men and women who appreciated the bluff were quite scornful of masks, referring to them as "old things." Perhaps this was because the hundreds of masks piled on the floors of market stalls in the city were not authentic spiritual items, but as Steiner (1992a) has documented, made for North Atlantic consumption—and so bereft of their metaphorically indicated flip side. Occult objects tended to be kept hidden; whenever they were revealed I noticed a certain respect and even fear of their power. It was hard to tell whether these things were hidden because of shame of believing in "tradition" or because their owners wanted to avoid accusations of sorcery. As Vogel (1997) makes clear in her treatment of the Baoulé (a central Ivoirian ethnic group) relationship to art objects, the value of masks and other sculptures was in the spiritual content of the object rather than their aesthetics, and these objects were mostly kept concealed and if ever revealed only in semilit, inebriated environments. Ironically, the visibility of these figurative objects, despite their purpose as images, was not socially encouraged. "Baoulé objects, on the other hand, are important in invisible ways" (Vogel 1997:76). It is their ability to contain spirits and deities and mediate with the otherworld that gives these objects force, a force indicated visually but not visually produced.[15]

It is the act of representation itself that seems to have power, as in Harry West's wonderful anecdote of the antiwitchcraft theater troupe in Mozambique that mimicked acts of sorcery on stage in order to demonstrate how evil they were. An audience member told West during the performance that their representation was so accurate that it could only have been performed by people who were capable sorcerers:

> "You see the way they eat human flesh?!" He asked me, genuinely scandalized.
>
> "But surely they are just *acting out* what they *imagine* sorcerers do?" I responded.

"Exactly. . . . Who can imagine such a thing without doing it!?" he asked
me, clinching his case. (West 2008:54)

When West confronted the leader of the troupe with this accusation, asking
rhetorically for confirmation that they were not indeed sorcerers, the actor's
shocking but apparently sincere response was "I don't know" (2008:54). In
the right social contexts, at least, representation is performative in Austin's
(1962) sense—it makes present, it discursively produces its object. This is
in fact the logic of magical efficacy, performative signifiers that produce
their signifieds (Tambiah 1979). Language is the magic through which we
shape and transform our world.

The mask at once conceals and reveals the invisible that lies behind it.
The visible image is not therefore a copy, "but the visible and constructed
form of something that always had to conceal itself" (Mbembe 2001:153).
Given the central importance of masking in a wide variety of Ivoirian ethnicities (Green 1987; Adams 1988; Steiner 1992b; Förster 1993; Vogel 1997),
I suggest that the figurative logic of the mask is at work in contemporary
public performances, a kind of visual grammar informing the work of
image-making illusions. This is not to say that Ivoirians are mired in a traditional culture blocking them from access to modernity, but rather that
Ivoirian modes of producing and communicating connections to power
are culturally informed, whether that power be one of contact with dangerous beings living just outside everyday perception or with dangerous
people living across the ocean.

And just as Abidjanais may bluff modernity in this doubled figurative
sense, modernity itself, the "original" that so carefully polices the constant
counterfeiting practices of those nipping at its heels, is in fact built upon
the production of copies. Steiner (1992a) describes a wonderful scene in a
market in the heart of Abidjan, in which a tourist attempts to buy a mask
in trade for his Seiko watch. The tourist anxiously examines the mask for
authentic signs of its age and use, while the hawker searches for someone
to verify that the watch is not a counterfeit Seiko. Modernity's constant
search for authenticity is predicated upon the social inability to differentiate the real from its imitation in a world where mass reproduction is the
mode of production. How indeed can we separate the legitimate large-scale
copying of one's own commodities from counterfeiting, when most brand
name items subcontract their production to countries with cheap labor,
the same places (often the same factories) where counterfeit goods are being manufactured? Indeed, it is copying, not originality, that lies concealed
beneath the masquerade of modernity, even as this deceptive surface of

reproduced "authenticity" produces a real boundary with real economic effects: a performative speech act on a global scale.

Abidjan: The Urban Setting

Abidjan is one of those places where one is least likely to find social order, a hodgepodge of immigrants and ethnicities thrown together in a fragmentary grid constructed by colonists who have mostly departed, over which a disintegrating state struggles to hold onto the illusion of control, and over whom the influence of the elite must be characterized as ambivalent at best. A city of approximately four million now, it was built on what was practically *terra rasa*, a village of fourteen hundred in 1912. In 1934, when it was declared the capital, it had grown to eighteen thousand, and from there to fifty-eight thousand in 1948, and since that time it has grown exponentially and increasingly free from urban planning (Diabate and Kodjo 1991:119–20). Like its larger colleagues, such as Lagos and Kinshasa, Abidjan's growth rate has far outpaced its infrastructural development, and many sections remain without plumbing and electricity.

At the center lie the two original quarters of the city built by the French, Plateau and Treichville. Plateau was the French residential and administrative center of Côte d'Ivoire but gradually evolved into the Manhattanesque financial district, complete with flashing neon billboards and grand esplanades. Only up close does the observer spot the decay of this sector. Many of the twenty- to thirty-story skyscrapers are falling apart, with broken elevators and windows propped open due to lack of air-conditioning. There are almost no residents in this quarter, which empties at night.

Figure 1. Treichville from my apartment. In the distance you can see the skyscrapers of the Plateau district. Just to the left of the lamppost is one of the most powerful "ghettos" or criminal hangouts.

Across the lagoon lies the original African quarter, Treichville, constructed by the French in a grid pattern with the explicit intention of preventing the Africanizing of the city. As Réné Charbonneau, a French colonist, wrote in 1954,

> This indigenous metropole is worthy of serving as an example. . . . Under the Dioula influence, that is from the Islamized northerners, this quarter could have become a quasi-mysterious city, full of detours and walled-in houses, like traditional medinas. *Et bien, non.* Open space, turned outward toward its arteries, it has demonstrated that its inhabitants knew how to evolve in an intelligent and healthy manner. It is even possible that one day this new agglomeration will take a step in advance and that Abidjan-Treichville will become Treichville-Abidjan. The menace has nevertheless been avoided. (Diabate and Kodjo 1991:96)

He was perhaps right about Treichville's destiny as the origin of Abidjan's culture, but the direction it took was probably not quite the *mission civilisatrice* the colonist had in mind. The gaps within the grid were quickly localized into *cours communes* (collective courtyards) in which I was told that the public life of the village was reproduced, though certainly in a more cosmopolitan, ethnically integrated manner. Such public courtyards contained

Figure 2. A typical Treichville street. In the center children cluster around an outdoor video game center. The television is protected from theft by a cage, and the player pays the proprietor for their time. Open drainage runs down the side of the street.

a single fount of water for as many as ten apartments, a single shared toilet, and a single stall with a drain where people could take turns bathing. All cooking took place outdoors in the public space of the courtyard. It was from such a space that the *bluffeur* would emerge and lend the muddy, garbage strewn streets an aura of glamour.

Methodology

Despite groundbreaking works of scholarship by the likes of Simone (2004) and De Boeck and Plissart (2006), who all seek to describe the fluid forms of urban organization through which survival is made possible, the processes and structures through which African cities work remains mysterious and puzzling to North Atlantic eyes. Following in the Hobbesian tradition, many of us have long assumed that the social contract requires the intervention of the state. In order to come to terms with African urban social life, we must pay attention to the micropolitics of sociality in a society where the state, rather than providing the infrastructural framework within which society unfolds, is encompassed within the informal economics and the face-to-face interactions of social networks. Through what kinds of social practices do people survive and organize themselves when the state services and institutions prove unreliable?

In one of the earliest and nearly forgotten urban ethnographic explorations, A. L. Epstein wrote: "Despite the apparent confusion of the urban scene, it is equally patent that the Africans who live in Ndola do not compose a mere aggregation of individuals nor a disorganized rabble" (1992:51). Epstein points out that it is through the production and maintenance of social networks—networks that typically extend all the way from the rural hinterlands to the metropolitan centers—that urban residents produce infrastructural elements and institutional supports through which the navigation of the city becomes possible. These invisible forms of organization are so powerful that newly arrived migrants from the villages regularly find their friends and family upon arrival, despite unstable residence patterns and largely unmapped zones of informal housing.

I spent the first month living with a family in the elite quarter of Riviera III while exploring various *quartiers populaires* in order to choose which would be most effective for my research. In November (after the dangerous electoral period) I moved to an apartment in Treichville. I had made my first contact, Dedy, in Treichville several weeks before, and so I had already begun forging a personal network around his part of the quarter by the time I moved in. Treichville itself is subdivided into many tiny neighborhoods, each centered on a local *maquis* or coffee kiosk, in which locals congregate at all hours to discuss the politics and gossip of the day. I thus traced out connections from Dedy's friends and family to their friends and family following the snowball sample approach, gradually developing a widespread social network of my own. I used this same approach to expand my network outward from a group of young men who socialized on a corner near my apartment on the opposite side of Treichville. It was indicative of the interwoven nature of Abidjan's social fabric that these networks of separate origins eventually interconnected and overlapped in multiple locations.

In order to make my intervention in the social life of these contacts as unobtrusive as possible, I conducted most of my research informally, following my friends on their various errands and activities, and participating in social events, spending many hours sitting on the corner and talking, going to a *maquis*, or eating with them at the street vendor stalls where most young men found their meals. Although I took an active part in these conversations, I also let conversations take their natural course and follow the topics that were of greatest interest to the other participants. I actively attended a wide variety of social events, including many church services, funerals, weddings, palm-wine gatherings on Sunday mornings, birthday parties, baptisms, political rallies, dance rehearsals for music videos, and district meetings with the mayor. Some had their own ideas about what my research should be about, and I followed their leads and suggestions whenever possible. Although my focus was on *nouchi* youth, I conversed with a wide variety of people from differing age groups, ethnicities, classes, education levels, and national origins. To supplement this primary form of research, I also conducted a series of formal hour-long interviews.

Dedy was in his early thirties and had spent his whole life in Treichville (though he had traveled around Côte d'Ivoire quite a bit). He was an ideal informant because he prided himself on knowing everyone and yet kept a certain independence from all social groups. Dedy had once been involved in serious crime, but after he attempted a trip to Germany and was repatriated before leaving the German airport, he dropped out of his former circles, ashamed that he had not succeeded. However, he still maintained many of his contacts and employed them whenever he was able to gain some profit or social influence from them. His street name was Chef du Village, and he considered himself a sort of public defender. He stopped for every street dispute, heard both sides of the controversy, and aggressively argued for whichever side seemed to have the better case. His sense of justice was so acute that he had at least once taken the side of strangers against his own siblings when he thought the latter were in the wrong. He used his imposing physical presence to weight his side of the argument, and in fistfights he thought nothing of stepping into the blows in order to defend the loser. This was an important source of income for him, as people would usually give him something for his efforts. Dedy was always in search of a *manzement* (literally, something to eat, a slang word for any source of income) and performed a whole range of activities from impersonating police officers to get bribe money from thieves, to acting as a marriage counselor for his neighbor, to assisting white people, to occasionally stealing when the opportunity presented itself. Mostly he paced the streets, often late into the night ("That's when you catch the hoodlums at work," he told me), always in search of people he knew and any bits of information that might lead to money. In this manner, he usually succeeded in paying his rent. His live-in girlfriend, Mimi, took care of electricity bills through her job as a maid, from which she got leave only two days each month. Dedy was Gouro and Mimi was Baoulé, from a family several blocks away. Dedy's father and a couple of siblings lived only three blocks away in the opposite direction. After living with Mimi for seven years, Dedy discovered that a considerable portion of her family's dislike for him stemmed from his not having followed proper Baoulé custom and asked the family formal permission to live with their daughter by offering a considerable gift. Such, Dedy bemoaned, were the difficulties of urban life. Dedy also managed to maintain several girlfriends, sometimes even bringing them to his house while Mimi was at work. Although everyone who shared his *cour commune* therefore knew of his affairs, Dedy assured me that they would never dare tell Mimi, because they were too frightened of him.

I met my other principal social group in the neighborhood surrounding my apartment. The area was called France-Amérique and was divided from the rest of Treichville by one of the city's major arteries. It was reputed to be the wealthy part of Treichville, mostly because at one time it had been the home of a number of French colonists, whose villas had now been subdivided into tiny, run-down apartments like my own. A group of young guys aged eighteen to twenty-two spent copious amounts of time on a corner a block away from my apartment. Christophe, Solo, Mory, and Henri were cousins linked to the Baoulé family that owned the *cour commune* just next door. They all shared the same room off the courtyard; their only furniture was a queen-size bunk bed in which six of them slept. Almost ten years older than the rest, Henri was getting his degree as a pharmacist and spared no effort to demonstrate his intellectual superiority. Luc was the nephew of an unrelated woman who rented in the *cour commune*, but he had become best friends with the others of his age group, and he usually slept in their room. He had moved to town in order to go to school but was having trouble getting the funds together to continue his post-secondary-school education as a mechanic. Finally, Olivier, otherwise known as Doctor H, was an old friend of Solo's from an elite family. When his father had died his stepmother's family had cut him off, and he had fled to Abidjan. He slept on the floor in the same room as the other young men in the family. With the exception of Henri, none of the group was in school any longer, and few of them had a steady source of income for any length of time, but they found earnings from a variety of informal sources. Compared with many groups their age that actively engaged in mugging people, picking pockets, and other scams, this group was only marginally connected to the criminal world. Nevertheless, they were quite knowledgeable about its inner workings, as several of them had formerly been deeper in the criminal system. Through this group, I met many of the other youth in the neighborhood, including those who were much more "in the movement," as they put it. I also regularly attended the Sunday *bangidrome* (palm-wine gathering) in their courtyard, where I encountered many of the older family members and neighbors from the surrounding area.

As is quite evident in the above paragraphs, this study focuses primarily on male networks. This limitation reflects both the gendered valence of public display in the streets of Abidjan and a series of methodological problems I encountered in my research when I tried to cross gender lines. Women were an integral part of the bluff, both as actors in their own right and as accessories to male display practices, and I represent their perspective on the social issues of this book whenever possible. Women engaged in the bluff in significant ways, but their ability to call attention to themselves in the space of the *maquis* was severely curtailed by norms of propriety. In public, women were at once necessary to male performance and a threat to its success, because they had the power to undo the bluff by demanding food and liquor beyond the means of the *bluffeur*, exposing the underlying poverty beneath the performance of wealth. The bluff was thus a performance not only of wealth but also of masculinity, a masculinity that I suggest was strongly effected by an urban Ivoirian interpretation of European gender norms in which women are meant to be consumers and men providers.

Those willing to take on the reputation of the *godrap* (trouble girl) could con men out of their meager fortunes by exploiting the public sphere to demand money and goods. Those who played along, however, could build their reputation both through their own mastery of style and through the success of their successive boyfriends. Indeed, I show that men and women

depended upon each other's divergent forms of social network and economic activity for economic survival and prestige-building activities. My
problem in investigating this terrain came from the difficulties of separating myself from this sexual economy, in which I was seen, by virtue of my
race, as a source of potential profit. Thus, the women I was most interested
in talking to, the *godraps*, were the ones who were most set on transforming our relationship into a sexual one, even implying to others that this
relationship existed despite my continued resistance. For this reason, the
bulk of my conversations with women came through either older women
or women who were in a relationship with one of my friends.

Insofar as possible I negotiated my research through natural channels
of social relationships in an effort to receive the most honest information
possible from my informants. While they were always aware of the awk-
ward fact that I was studying them, we did become engaged in the kinds
of reciprocal exchanges through which relationships were maintained. My
knowledge of society in Abidjan is therefore limited to a relatively small
segment of the population, almost all of the members of which were in
one sense or another indirectly interconnected, even though my network
ultimately spanned categories of age, ethnicity, and religion and had representatives scattered across the city. However, these limitations provided the
possibility of in-depth contextualization of the processes through which
social relationships, identity, and reputation were produced in such a complex and seemingly chaotic social arena.

Outline of the Argument

The first chapter discusses the emergence of the street language called
Nouchi (Newell 2009b), an urban slang originally produced by criminal
networks that became widely fashionable in Ivoirian urban popular cul-
ture, taking on the role of a pan-ethnic national language. Arguing that
French and Nouchi represent alternative modes of enregistering modernity,
I use this as a model for understanding the emergence of a new grassroots
form of nationalism which challenges the state-imposed understanding of
Ivoirian identity structured by its apparent proximity to French culture.

The second chapter theorizes underground economies in terms of social
networks and moral economy. Because many Abidjanais living in *quartiers
populaires* scorned legitimate work as fit only for immigrants from other
parts of West Africa, the focus of economic production in Treichville was
informal exchange and theft. This informal economic sector was structured by social networks inscribed with fictive kinship ties and hierarchical

patron-client relationships. I found that, surprisingly, the direct economic benefits of many of the transactions I recorded were so limited that I could only conclude that their actual benefits lay in the real of social capital. The construction and maintenance of social networks was the principal tool for urban survival, and hierarchical positions within these networks produced quite real economic benefits, as well as protection from accusations of theft or acts of theft against oneself. This chapter lays the socioeconomic foundation for the motivations and efficacy of the bluff, explaining where actors attained their resources and why it was worth spending them on making *le show*.

The bar was the space of the bluff: the performative production of social hierarchy through the mimesis of financial abundance. In the third chapter, I examine how men displayed large sums of cash, expensive clothing, and the ability to buy vast quantities of alcohol in an effort to seduce women and impress their peers. By spending everything they had for the pleasure of the group, urban youth attempted to diffuse the envy they garnered through their success. In this way, both internal differentiation of the network and the group's sense of itself as a collectivity were produced in the same act of ritual display. I compare these as performances of masculinity continually threatened by women's ability to unmask the bluff, even though women typically remain complicit in order to take advantage of their men's reputation and resources while they last. Men and women depended on each other for access to differently gendered social networks, explicitly exploiting each other for access to economic resources.

The fourth chapter introduces key concepts of metonymic consumption and the role of brands in authenticating performative modernity. Urban youth considered the ability to bluff an index of modernity, evaluating everything from individuals to consumer goods to ethnicities and nations in terms of the opposition *yere* and *gaou*, forming a cosmological map of hierarchical global relations, interconnected by flows of goods and people embodying different degrees of *yere* modernity. Abidjanais transformed themselves through a semiotic "magic" by which they absorbed and embodied value. The image of success became success itself; appearance and reality became inseparable. Metonymic incorporation of the "authentic" anchored the illusory performance, providing external legitimacy to the play of surfaces. I compare this cosmological structure with that of masking performances and occult understandings of *derrière l'eau* (the realm "behind the water") as the space of death.

International Ivoirian migrants went to the source of value, which they referred to as *Beng* (the Occident, the land of the whites), and were transformed into sources of value in their own right. In *nouchi* terms, they had become *bengistes*, people from the "land of the whites," and in this way contact with them carried prestige in its own right. In the fifth chapter, I explore Ivoirian representations of Europe and the U.S. and the migration process, analyzing them as a local theory of geographic space in relation to power. I highlight the overlapping relationship between consumption and migration; cosmologically, both are symbolic processes in which people absorb modernity through contact with otherness, embodied within physical objects or geographic space. Approaching migration as something both culturally motivated and productive of culture, this chapter approaches movement not as something that takes place between cultures, but rather as something from which cultures are produced (Hahn and Klute 2007).

In the final chapter, I interpret the Ivoirian political crisis in terms of my analysis of Ivoirian popular culture. I argue that much about the war can be understood by examining stylistic oppositions between *bluffeurs* and those they despise as *gaous* and what these reveal about divergent representations of modernity in relation to *Ivoirité*. Because my fieldwork was situated in the period leading up to the civil war, I was uniquely situated to see how people were imagining these oppositions and which cultural categories were salient and which were not. While the international media have treated this war as another example of primal ethnic opposition and religious war, I argue that ethnicity and religion remain fluid categories in urban environments, dynamic categories of urban sociality rather than age-old cultural rivalries. As representations of a pan-ethnic Ivoirian popular culture have multiplied in the media and on the street, an increasing sense of national identity has emerged from the street in opposition to former state-distributed representations Ivoirian identity. Paradoxically, these popular efforts to define Ivoirianess have led to an increasingly alienated portion of the populace, as those who rejected the values of *nouchi* culture have been excluded from emergent interpretations of national identity. Politicians have transformed the language of social division from a discourse of relative modernity and migration to one of innate ethnic difference and invasion—and yet groups on either side have continued to distinguish themselves on both sides in terms of a stylistic opposition between inwardly directed localist visions of civilization and externally motivated cosmopolitan ones. By examining the link between popular culture and imagined communities (Anderson 1991), I challenge the assumption that national identity is primarily shaped by hegemonic state discourse.

I conclude by considering the concept of modernity in relation to mimesis more generally, especially the relationships between mirroring surfaces, masking, and counterfeits and the kinds of socioeconomic transformations modernity is supposed to entail. By arguing that mimesis can be both "fake" *and* effective (and therefore in some sense "real"), I provide new possibilities for understanding the contradictions of postcolonial identity. Briefly tracing the relationship between fear of mimesis and the ideologies of modernity that arose together in Europe from the sixteenth century onward, I demonstrate the inseparable linkage between a concern with inauthenticity and the defense of privilege that the concept of modernity has always been. Bringing together turn-of-the-century theorists like Simmel (1950, 1957) with postmodern thinkers like Baudrillard (1998), I think through the ramifications of a social system in which dialectical processes of imitation and differentiation lead to the progressive mass counterfeiting of signifiers of authenticity, causing the recurrent fear that meaning itself is being eroded. But it is not meaning itself whose boundaries are mimetically undermined, but the sacral status of social hierarchy, which can only reproduce its set-apartness by consuming ever-new signs of its own differentiation. Thus, modernity itself is a bluff, one that has helped to produce some of the greatest socioeconomic inequities the world has yet experienced.

ONE

Enregistering Modernity, Bluffing Criminality: How Nouchi Speech Reinvented the Nation

The time seems to have come to speak of the French World, just as once we spoke of the Roman World, . . . [forming] a republic under the domination of a single language. [It is] a spectacle worthy of this language, that this uniform and peaceful empire of letters which extends over the diversity of peoples, and which, more durable and strong than an empire of arms, accumulates equally the fruits of peace and the ravages of war! (Rivarol 1808:1)

We *nouchi* just keep deforming. There is French in it, mixed up Dioula,[1] Baoulé, you name it. No matter what, deformations of French. (Christophe)

On the June 16, 2009, the Ivoirian state recognized the cultural significance of Nouchi for the first time by initiating a conference of "scientific study" with the revelatory title "The Nouchi in Côte d'Ivoire: Momentary Linguistic Expression of the Dissatisfaction of Youth, or the Potential Alternative of an Ivoirian Identity in Construction?" ("'Nouchi' au Scanner des Spécialistes de la Langue, Le" 2009).[2] The minister of culture and *francophonie* called it "a historic day," officially valorizing a language which until quite recently was scorned by many as the crass and corrupted speech of criminal youth. The Ivoirian register of Nouchi, a slang widely associated with urban youth, criminality, and impoverished education, has throughout its brief history been a dynamic symbolic rallying point in the refashioning of Ivoirian national identity. The politics of postcolonial identity are carried out here through the enregisterment of modernity in language (Agha 2007): one's way of speaking can become an embodied form legitimizing hierarchy by signifying the modern. The ability of language to index such affiliation reveals processual struggles over the semiotic associations of speech which shape local understandings of indigeneity, civilization, and citizenship. Abidjanais say street gangs originally created Nouchi as a code language to shut out the P.J., or Police Judiciaire, the undercover cops who infiltrate *les ghettos* (criminal hangouts). But today not only is Nouchi spoken with pride and imitated widely by youth of all classes and from all over the country as well as the Ivoirian media aimed at them, but also more and more often it is the language spoken at home and thus the first language of many Ivoirians. It has traveled with the Ivoirian diaspora in Europe and through the medium of the Ivoirian pop sensation of *coupé-décalé* is now being imitated and spoken throughout Francophone Africa. Much like the youth language *bahasa gaul* studied by Smith-Hefner (2007) in Indonesia, this informal youth speech has migrated from a language considered to be the speech of "marginals" and "delinquents" to a central form of popular discourse bridging diverse social groups. As Simon Akindes says in an interview with Siddhartha Mitter (Mitter 2007) on afropop.org, "Nouchi spread from the bottom up, which is very interesting. A lot of people didn't like it, especially the Ivorian elite that was connected to the outside world. . . . But of course it's just like slang in many countries, it is not the language that is going to be used for official business, it is not the language of instruction, but for its purpose of expression [of] people's concerns, people's problems, it is very, very important." Nouchi is thus a case of language moving against the current of social hierarchy, traveling from the "corrupted" French of Ivoirian society's most marginal members to a form of discourse associated with Ivoirian national pride, a journey filled with contradiction, ambivalence, and conflicting evaluations.

I suggest here that the excitement generated by Nouchi stems from the enregisterment of modern urban identity in a language indigenous to Côte d'Ivoire. The Ivoirian state has encouraged a worldview of modernity centered on French language and culture, and the evaluation of speakers in terms of the purity of their French has been an important instrument of class reproduction. Nouchi provides an alternative to this state-imposed modernity of externality, locating modernity within urban Ivoirian speech. As a hybrid of French and multiple Ivoirian ethnic languages, Nouchi unites the pragmatic speech indexes of autochthony and modernity, formerly diametrically opposed within the state project of francocentric modernity. The case of Nouchi reminds us to look beyond state attempts to control language evaluation (Irvine and Gal 2000), beyond the symbolic class resistance of slang (Roth-Gordon 2009), to examine how the indexical connections between linguistic registers and identity can reshape political orders and hierarchies even when their origins stem from the streets rather than the state. At the same time, it provides the material to examine how colonial and postcolonial ideologies of modernity are incorporated into language practice and imposed on the representation of the language of others, invoking forces external to the nation-state in the construction of local hierarchies. The symbolic role of language in the production of modernity (Bauman and Briggs 2008) can be appropriated and used to hierarchize by the very subalterns initially subordinated by it.

Unfortunately, in precisely this way the grassroots productions of national identity associated with Nouchi have served to divide the country rather than unite it, excluding those who are deemed "uncivilized," "rural," or "northern" from rights to citizenship and encouraging a conception of *Ivoirité* that problematizes the historical role of immigration. Nouchi became a symbol organizing a conception of modern, urban Ivoirian culture that excluded both foreign migrants and rural Ivoirians who didn't "get it," and as with so many burgeoning nationalities, this new sense of shared *Ivoirité* fractured the nation itself.

The Abidjanais with whom I spoke to liked to emphasize the novelty of Nouchi, consistently citing its emergence in the early 1990s, a time of great cultural upheaval in Côte d'Ivoire. It was in 1990 that Côte d'Ivoire had its first multiparty elections, and the period leading up to this moment was filled with demonstrations, riots, and violent conflicts at the university between a politicized student population and the military. The year 1990 also marked the first free press, and with it the efflorescence of hundreds of (mostly ephemeral) independent newspapers. *Zouglou*, the first Ivoirian popular music, based on traditional rhythms and simple electronic instrumentation combined with a creative focus on satirical, often politicized lyrics. Produced by some of the same rebellious university students, it combined critical political discourse with the "corrupted" French of the streets. This music came with a new urban Ivoirian style involving handkerchiefs tied around the head and the knees of ripped jeans, as well as a variety of new dance forms through which Abidjanais youth *misent en valeur* (place value on) their clothes and bodies. Nouchi was thus at once an integrative force bridging social gaps between ethnicities as well as class and, more significant, a *sign of the process* of urban cultural integration. Arriving in this charged cultural moment, Nouchi became an important contested sign in a popular struggle to redefine what it means to be Ivoirian, a struggle that, as we shall examine in further detail in the final chapter, has unfortunately metastasized into a civil crisis, delegitimizing the state, transforming the postcolonial relationship with France, and throwing the very definition of citizenship into question.

Nouchi, I argue, is a crucial symbol for understanding these identity politics, because it has played an important role in creating a grassroots sense of national identity among the lower-class youth. In the 1990s Nouchi changed the existing opposition between modernity (French) and indigeneity by providing an alternative model of modern language that was unquestionably Ivoirian and simultaneously a performance of urban cosmopolitanism, a connection to the modernity of otherness. Such a shared sense of national identity would not have existed without the unifying productions of urban popular culture that crossed over preexisting ethnic divisions and produced a shared sense of identity. It was this urban understanding of Ivoirian identity, reflected in Nouchi, as connected to modernity and excluding those that did not ascribe to the performance of modern identity, that gave the word *Ivoirité* such political efficacy to mobilize the division into north and south.

In thinking through the politics of Nouchi, I want to keep in mind Inoue's (2006) representation of language as "vicarious," separating the discourse about a language form from the speakers associated with it. Just as the phenomenon of "women's language" in Japan was in large part a product of male intellectuals talking about women speaking, eventually leading to real women who speak in this manner as a symbol of Japanese national identity, Nouchi is "cited" or "voiced" by many people other than those who are supposedly its original speakers, and such citations carry evaluative weight that changes the character of the language itself. At the same time, it is precisely these citations and reproductions and imitations of Nouchi that have made it something more than an obscure argot unintelligible beyond the limited networks of Abidjan's criminal scene and turned it into something that stands for Ivoirian identity both within and outside the country. Nouchi exists in that all Ivoirians believe it exists; but it has no objective, identifiable existence, in the sense that there is no agreement on precisely what Nouchi is, but rather a continual struggle over the right to define it. Indexicality, Inoue writes, "constitutes reality not by naming and pointing to a preexisting object but by inverting the order of the indexed and indexing"; it is the pointing that produces the object (2002:21). Through a variety of such processes of indexicality, including acts of self-identification and expression, scornful "acts of alterity" (Hastings and Manning 2004), and mimetic appropriations of alterity, Nouchi was symbolically produced, and its existence provided the imaginative space for the construction of *Ivoirité*.

Les Nouchis: Speaking of "Gangsters"

Nouchi speech is enregistered by reference to a stereotypic speaker, a new urban figure, the *nouchi*.[3] The form of speech and this stereotype of urban identity are dialectically intertwined, each producing the other. When I asked what a *nouchi* was, Ivoirians almost always responded: "un bandit" (gangster, crook). Thus, the identity of Nouchi began with the alterity of accusation. Indeed the complexity of Nouchi as a register and the conflicting interpretations of its role in Ivoirian life were the result of strategies surrounding this axis between alterity and identity. Some Ivoirians scornfully rejected the alterity of the criminal lifestyle and the corrupted speech associated with it, some lived this lifestyle proudly as their identity, while others attempted to bluff their involvement by appropriating alterity. As is so typical of the judgments cast on speakers of slang, calling someone a *nouchi* was often a way to point out his or her dubious moral standards and class origins. Thus, Papis (who I knew to be a thief) told me that "*nouchi* means *voleur, bakroman, vagabond* [thief, homeless person, vagrant]. It is not something to be proud of. You don't say, 'I am a *nouchi*'; you accuse other people of being *nouchi*." His friend Abdou (a recent arrival from the north) explained that "*nouchi* are youths who come from the north and have no parents and everything they have ever had in life they found in the streets."[4] The label could also be used in a more inclusive yet patronizing tone: "Yeah, I know them, they're just little do-nothing *nouchis*." This was the sort of statement one often heard from a *vieuxpère* (an authority figure in the criminal network), who could make his living without engaging directly in criminal activity, and thus looked on it and his peons that did this work with a sort of condescending fondness. Finally, Papis's assertions to the contrary, one also encounters the proud statement of identity: "Je suis un *nouchi!*" Used in this positive context, to be *nouchi* is to have urban know-how, to be able to live by one's wits alone, and above all, to be tough. If once it had a literal connotation of "gangster," for many it is now a more metaphorical identity. To be *nouchi* is to live by gangster ideals, to be self-sufficient, confident, unstoppable—the urban warrior. The word *nouchi* itself means "nose hair" and is said by some to refer to the moustaches of cowboys in U.S. westerns—icons of the masculine renegade hero, much like the Hindubill of Kinshasa, who named and styled themselves after the filmic Wild West (De Boeck and Plissart 2006).

Being *nouchi* was a continual performance, down to the very presentation of the body. "You can't just say something Nouchi and be *nouchi*," Dedy coached me; "you must act the act." *Nouchi* youth were also very particular about their dress, wearing preferably only name brand labels imported from the U.S. which they flaunted in the dance of the *logobi*, the act par excellence through which youth demonstrated their urban, civilized status. Pierre, a young man training to be a judge who had grown up among the Treichville *nouchi* youth, explained, "You can tell who is *nouchi* by the way they are dressed, but especially by their mouth, by the way they stand and move. Even if a *nouchi* wears a tie, you can still tell he is *nouchi*." There were particular poses, hand gestures, eye and mouth expressions. One of the most prevalent greetings—"En forme? . . . Oui, en forme" (In good shape? . . . Yes, in good shape)—was accompanied by making a fist and pumping the arm up toward the chest as though about to flex the muscle. The *nouchi* struts, arms swinging, unhurried, uncaring, but always alert. One night while walking with Dedy I noticed what seemed to be a limp and asked him if he had hurt himself. He replied that this was the walk of a *loubard* (see below), and that he walked this way at night because anyone who saw him would know that he was too *nouchi* for them. Dedy continued his lesson:

> If someone comes up to you and asks for something timidly you can respond politely, but if they approach you like a *nouchi*, "rendre a Cesar ce qui appartient a Cesar." A true *nouchi* couldn't give a shit if you are older or even stronger. He will still act rudely, threaten to beat you up (but if he thinks it will really come down to an unequal fight, he flees). Even if they are talking to the president, *nouchi* will not change their attitude. If they meet a woman they don't know, even an older woman, they will call her "little sister." "Ehh, petit soeur, je viens te trouver ce soir, on sort ensemble, ya pas drap . . ." [Heyyy, sister, I'll come by tonight, we'll go out, no problem . . .] When she says no, they don't give up. "Non, ya foé, on sort, je viens a dix-huit heures" [No, no worries, we'll go out, I'll come at six]. They always show confidence, it is the art of the bluff.

As we saw in the introduction, the bluff was a key mode of expression for Abidjan youth. This required a symbolic mastery of a culture from which they were excluded, a proof of potential membership. Acts of deception were crucial to successful cons through which *nouchi* survived, and the display of success was a key way of building the social networks that formed the principal means of support and accumulation. But the bluff of material success through which figures in the criminal network asserted their status was combined with another kind of bluff, signaled by Dedy in the last line of his statement above. Being *nouchi* was itself already a bluff, as social actors felt compelled to project the part of the street tough, full of artful confidence and cunning. The bluff of being tougher and more streetwise than the next kid was just as crucial to navigating the social space of Abidjan's streets as the ability to project wealth.

Indeed, Pierre highlighted the performative bluff of *nouchi* identity, suggesting that if I were being harassed, I should never show fear, never back down, but rather adopt the tone of voice and manner of the harasser, and he would soon leave me alone. In fact, I was told on several occasions I was too *mogol*, a word referring to "men like women: lazy, soft, not showing enough force." I was told I should walk in a more macho manner and speak Nouchi as much as possible. Survival in such circumstances depended on the ability to bluff *nouchi* comportment. In this sense, not everyone is as *nouchi* as they might pretend, and in the semiotics of Ivoirian urban youth culture since the 1990s, many people *want* to index their relationship to the *nouchi* criminal networks. The question is not one of differentiating between authentic Nouchi speakers and their imitators, because the concept of the bluff challenges the very basis of authenticity. Even the most hardened *nouchi* openly discusses the performance of *nouchi* qualities, because the bluff is a straightforward acknowledgment of skillful deceit. Thus, for the majority of its speakers, Nouchi is really an appropriation of alterity, the staging of a "bluff." *Nouchi* identity is ambivalently grounded in a stereotype of lawless urban hooligans, who serve as a model to be actively imitated by a wide variety of Abidjan's youth in the art of the bluff. While some people maintain more active connections to the life of the streets than others, everyone is a *bluffeur*, because bluffing is itself integral part of being *nouchi*.

Loubard, Boss, and *Bakroman*: Further Stereotypes

Nouchis are defined not only by reference to stereotypical positive models, but also in contradistinction to stereotypical others, such as the *loubards*, a divergent form of youth culture related to but not identical to the *nouchi*. While *loubard* is a French word meaning "youth living in a poor suburb, belonging to a gang whose comportment is asocial" (according to the 1997 *Robert Micro Poche*), urban Ivoirians have attributed a more specific identity to the term. A *loubard* is a *nouchi* whose way of life is based on physical force rather than cleverness and cunning (for an illustration of the typical *loubard* see fig. 3 below). "*Loubards* are people who live by force alone. They are not *nouchi*, though they speak it. They do not work; when they want something, they simply take it. They are not afraid of anything, not even death," Dedy told me. Like the *nouchi*, the *loubards* have a particular walk, a lumbering, almost drunken strut, with swinging shoulders and arms out as though their muscles were so big that they couldn't drop their arms to their bodies. They look like cowboys in a western movie continually about to draw their pistols. A *loubard* exudes strength. The sheer mass of the *loubard's* body seemed to cause a certain nervousness on proximity, and even Dedy was trepidatious around them. Although *nouchi* and *loubards* interacted continually, often as part of the same groups and networks, they distinguished themselves from one another. A *nouchi* was not a *loubard* because the former didn't need strength to get along, but relied on their wits and toughness to survive. In 2001, while the *loubards* danced the *zeguei*, a dance made up of fixed poses and subtle muscle flexing, the *nouchi* danced the *logobi*, a fast-paced dance based on street fighting and the display of the brand name labels. The *loubard* was not necessarily looked down upon by the *nouchi*. The difference was a stylistic choice within the criminal scene rather than qualitative distinction, and the two engaged with each other with restrained respect, even if it was sometimes accompanied by discomfort.

Nouchi identity was further conceptually opposed to the *boss* and the *bakroman*. Abidjanais youth tended to call anyone wealthier than themselves *bosses*, but the category was epitomized by the political elite living in the villa-ridden district of Cocody. According to stereotype, *les bosses* drove air-conditioned Mercedes, wore French designer clothing, went shopping in the giant, florescent-lit supermarkets, and spoke *gros-gros français* (fat-fat French). The *nouchi* dreamed rather than perceived the *boss* way of life, as it revolved almost exclusively in realms inaccessible to them. A *boss* always worked in an office behind a desk, the only source of income that deserved unambiguous respect in the *nouchi* worldview: "Ivoirians count on an office job" goes the refrain of one famous pop song by the Garagistes. *Nouchi* regarded this elite world with intense ambivalence, struggling between admiring emulation and disdainful resistance. For *les bosses* were at once the prime targets of their criminal efforts and the desired object such activities are meant to achieve; despite their scorn of the *choco* (greasy) French and refined mannerisms of the elite, the *nouchi* I met often dreamed of leading a "proper" and successful life someday. But stylistically speaking, *nouchi* rejected the *évolués* ("the evolved," a holdover from French colonial terminology for educated Africans), preferring expensive sportswear and U.S. hip-hop style to French dandyism, signifying urban know-how's triumph over class hegemony.

On the other side, *nouchi* opposed themselves to the *bakroman*, their term for homeless people (literally, "sleeping man"). In Dedy's words,

The *bakroman* is like the *nouchi*, only worse. Even the *nouchi* is afraid of the *bakroman*. The *bakroman* is a *nouchi* who has no home; they sleep in the cinema. They are very dangerous because they don't care about anything. You can call the police and they don't give a shit. If the police take them to prison they say "thank you" because their life is already worse than prison. In prison at least they have food and shelter. They would just as soon kill you as not. They cannot speak French, nor can they speak the language of the father and mother. They have no ethnic group anymore, they no longer know what it is. They can only speak Nouchi. They have no papers, no I.D.

However, the closer I looked, the stranger and less defined the distinction between *nouchi* and *bakroman* appeared. I had also heard *nouchi* defined as "someone who doesn't have a home" and when I asked the speaker how *nouchi* was different from a *bakroman*, he said with some confusion "a bakroman is someone who sleeps on tables in the street." Dedy himself spoke only Nouchi, he never learned his ethnic language beyond a couple of greetings, yet he would never be considered a *bakroman*. In fact, I only encountered a couple of individuals who could be unambiguously pointed out as a *bakroman*; the identity was more a figment of daily conversation than of daily life. The salient aspect is defined negatively: they had no family, no ethnicity, and no language besides Nouchi, leaving them with "no I.D.," no identity. *Bakromen* are thus collective representations of the danger of becoming too *nouchi*, of losing oneself in the ethnic phantasmagoria of the city, of being trapped within the slang they created to escape the restrictions of normative society.

For the "original" Nouchi speakers—those Goffman would describe as "natural figures" (1974:524)—speaking Nouchi was a means of self-location within a particular street subculture that was quick to exclude outsiders while staking hierarchical claims according to one's abilities to inhabit *nouchi* lifestyle through speech. *Nouchi* are "urban warriors" who struggle for survival through their acute knowledge of the city and its social networks and their ability to endure hardships and pain in the pursuit of the dream of a "proper" life, taking the *manzements* they need from those too ignorant or too sheltered to see through their deceptions. While it is quite tempting to read this as a negative portrait of low-class "hoodlums," in the failing economy of the late 1990s and first years of the twenty-first century, the illicit economy was a normal mode for many male Abidjan residents. Thus, proximity to a hierarchical positioning within the criminal networks structuring that economy was an important means of access to both prestige and material accumulation.

Yere and *Gaou*: *Nouchi* Hierarchy and Modernity

Nouchi gangs had once been highly structured, according to their own oral history, but by 2000 they were made up of fluid social networks of patron-client ties. These relationships were constructed as metaphorical father-son relationships in the opposing terms *vieuxpère* and *fiston* (I will discuss these further in the next chapter).[5] The cultural legitimation of these hierarchical relationships was found in the organizing opposition of *yere* and *gaou*, as discussed in the introduction. The concept of *gaou* collapsed representations of "low value," "undeveloped," and "immigrant." *Yere* then implied a superior degree of urban modernity, coordinating a hierarchical evaluation of space (in which the United States was more *yere* than France, which surpassed Côte d'Ivoire, which in turn stood above Burkina Faso) with the flow of people and things across these boundaries (Newell 2005). Côte d'Ivoire was a stepping-stone to modernity in this cosmology and thus internally differentiated between those for whom it represented a step up already and those who were preparing to take a step further.

Within the language ideology of the *nouchi*, the language par excellence of the *gaou* was Dioula—ironically so, since it is widely recognized that Dioula makes up the largest portion of Nouchi's lexical content, making Abdou's earlier association between *nouchi* and northerners all the more poignant. The Dioula language and ethnicity were themselves the product of urbanization (Launay 1982); Dioula, a Mande derivative, was a language of trade associated with an ethnic group that extended across Côte d'Ivoire's borders with Burkina Faso and Mali and made up the largest portion of immigrants.[6] Despite the recent and urban derivation of both this language variation and the ethnic group associated with it, and despite its continued importance as a vehicular language in the market, many *nouchi* stereotyped Dioula as northern, Muslim, and uncivilized: in other words, as *gaou*. Thus, while the Dioula language remained an important part of the urban fabric and a crucial contributor to Nouchi itself, there was a strong symbolic opposition between Nouchi and Dioula, an opposition that was both a product and a producer of the cultural divisions in Ivoirian society leading to the political crisis. Just as speaking Nouchi was to mark oneself (accurately or not) as a street hoodlum, to speak Dioula was an index of northern, Muslim identity and made one a likely target for *nouchi* aggression or cons. In other words, within this evaluative distinction between two contemporary pan-ethnic languages lie the roots of the xenophobia that has nearly shattered Côte d'Ivoire in recent years.

Speaking Nouchi well was *yere*, and therefore to speak Nouchi was to be urbanized and modern. In Nouchi, Abidjan is called Yere City. Within this formula was the reversal of the hegemonic ideology of linguistic performance in terms of the French model. Here we find gangsters in the streets of the *quartiers populaires* who evaluated speech according to modernity, but a modernity defined in opposition to that associated with speaking perfect French. Because Nouchi was originally produced by speakers seeking to limit their audience to those in the know, it was in some sense a moving target, continually shifting to retain its impenetrability to casual observers and varying to degrees of mutual unintelligibility from one part of town to another. As Ferguson (1999) has suggested, some of the signification that happens in urban locales is intentional noise—it communicates its incommunicability in order to distance the speaker from the static codes of "traditional" identities. Thus, when I introduced words I had learned in Marcory to my resident experts in Treichville they protested that some *faux type* (poser) had been instructing me, or that I had learned the language of the *panomans* (pickpockets), not "true" Nouchi. Seen from within a criminal network, any Nouchi unrecognizable to them was illegitimate, while at the same time, Nouchi too recognizable outside their network was equally worthless, for it had lost its exclusivity. This drove Nouchi speakers to innovate perpetually to maintain their distinction. Yet, it was this vicarious production in local media and among those outside the *nouchi* networks that objectified and commodified Nouchi as an icon of Ivoirian modernity. Even in its mediated form, speakers of Nouchi were aware of its inherent ephemerality and continually sought to learn the latest and most recherché words. The novelty and excitement of proving that one was *yere* and in the know was part of how Nouchi projected its sense of urban modernity.

Within this formula we can see the germination of Nouchi's spread from a limited niche language scorned by society at large and designed to be incomprehensible to a nationwide phenomenon in which the registers of social value were drastically transformed and in many cases inverted. In order to understand how Nouchi became a sign of Ivoirian national identity, I will now provide a historical exploration of language ideology in Côte d'Ivoire from colonialism to the present. I will then return to the Ivoirian reception, mediation, and appropriation of Nouchi.

Ivoirian Language Policy and the French Model of National Identity

Côte d'Ivoire came into being as an independent nation in 1960 but has retained close and largely unquestioned ties to France through most of its postcolonial history. It was once renowned for its political stability and economic success based on its near monopoly of the cocoa market, but both of these have slipped away since the death of president Houphouët-Boigny in 1993. One of the central issues for this fledgling nation was how to produce an overarching sense of national identity in a country made up of well over sixty ethnolinguistic groups, whose discourse of a nascent state was explicitly anti-"tribalist," discouraging overidentification with one's ethnic group. This project was inherently as well as discursively modernist; Houphouët-Boigny wanted to usher the country and its population into the "modern age" through the appropriation of the French civilizing mission, to use French culture to unite the nation. In one of his characteristically eloquent speeches, Houphouët argued that the word "revolution" had "one R too many" for Côte d'Ivoire: *evolution* was the guiding ideology of his program (David 2000:64). Ivoirians grew to think of themselves as one of the most modern African nations; indeed, modernity became a distinguishing feature of national identity as the "Ivoirian Miracle" of economic success was sustained by waves of cheap immigrant labor from "less developed" countries. But this project of the national mimesis of modernity formed the basis for the differentiation of social hierarchy based on proximity to the standard of French culture. The standard of Frenchness and especially French language was held up as a measure through which to exclude those who had not achieved one's own level of acculturation (Touré 1981). As such, national identity for the average Ivoirian was more a relationship of alterity than identity, a negotiation with the culture and language of the former colonizer. To be Ivoirian was to be modern, but it was also to become the Other (i.e., French).

At the same time, within a nation of great ethnic diversity brought together only under French rule in the nineteenth century, and only ideologically united under Houphouët in 1960, Ivoirian identity was something state imposed—insisted upon by political leaders. Indeed, at independence, the only thing that seemed unambiguously shared by this multitude of ethnic groups was their experience of French culture. Thus, it is worth briefly examining the French colonial ideology of the relationship between language and civilization, especially since it was explicitly adopted by the Ivoirian state.

During the colonial period, the French implemented what Rivarol referred to (see the epigraph to this chapter) as "the empire of letters" (1808) in an attempt to transform the culture of their colonies through the power of language—a project they were ironically still in the process of completing at home in France (Bourdieu 1991). Ideologically, justification for French education in the colonies was sought in terms of its functional benefits as a unifying discourse: "French was taught, they [the colonists] argued, because there were simply too many African dialects to master" (Conklin 1997:84). Hence the importance for Côte d'Ivoire of Delafosse's (1904) studies, which emphasized linguistic polyphony and so immediately justified suppressing the "useless" multitude of indigenous languages in favor of French (Adegbija 2000:86).

More importantly for understanding the enregisterment of modernity in Ivoirian language ideology, the supposed civilizing capability of the French language was a central factor underlying French language policy, particularly once William Ponty took the role of governor general of the West African colonies in 1907 (Conklin 1997). One of his principal interests was education, especially concerning French language. Ponty argued that

> even if we admit that the child who returns to his family after an elementary school education rapidly loses the French language, he will not be able to erase the memory of the uplifting notions which, through the intermediary of this language, we will have caused to penetrate. The words may disappear, but the ideas will remain, and the ideas, which are our own and whose use endows us with our moral, social and economic superiority, will little by little transform these barbarians of yesterday into disciples and auxiliaries. (Conklin 1997:84)

Within the worldview of the *mission civilisatrice* (the ideology that colonialism would justify itself through the civilization and eventual assimilation of its subjects) not only was speech thought to be "transparently emblematic of social, political, intellectual, or moral character" (Woolard 1998:19), but the relationship was also causally inverted, as French colonists tried to improve the moral fiber of their subjects like so many Pygmalions by teaching them French. Charles de Gaulle himself spoke of France's mission to "make available to the world a language perfectly adapted to the universal nature of thought" (C. Miller 1990). The *mission civilisatrice* relied on the principles of magic, hoping that the law of contiguity would transform its subjects' minds by teaching their tongues. Modernity was so enregistered within French colonial language that it was believed to be transferable through speech itself.

Analyzing Francophone African literature, Christopher Miller argues that the assimilationist policies of French colonialism shaped the entire literature of former French colonies in a manner distinct from that of the British indirect rule, binding the literature of Francophone postcolonies to the French language (1990:183). This relationship was explicitly valorized by one of Africa's most significant literary and political leaders, Léopold S. Senghor, who wrote of *francophonie* as a world movement: "It is a spiritual community, a noosphere around the earth.[7] In short, more than language, *francophonie* is French civilization; more precisely, the spirit of civilization is French culture" (1977:80). Like De Gaulle and Rivarol, Senghor espoused the inherent propensity of the French language for clarity, abstraction, and rationality, as well as believing it to embody a shared spirit of French culture. Thus, the enregisterment of modernity in the French language was transferred into postcolonial language ideology.

The Ivoirian state, particularly concerned with the project of unifying an ethnically diverse population, proclaimed in the first article of the constitution: "La langue officielle est le français" (The official language is French) (Turcotte 1980:424). The disdain with which elite Ivoirians looked on indigenous languages is exemplified by an Ivoirian applied linguist named Atin: "Without written form, which wasn't the least of their problems, without a palpable cultural tradition in literature or thought, devoid of any scientific or technological terminology, the indigenous languages were frankly dysfunctional" (Turcotte 1980:425).

Citing dangers of "tribalism" should ethnic groups maintain their linguistic differentiation, the state prescribed French as the method of national integration. For some, these lessons seemed to produce the desired effect. Maury, an avid self-proclaimed master of Nouchi, nevertheless told me, "The way we are divided into eighty-one ethnic groups, how are we going to communicate if not in French? No, colonization was good for Côte d'Ivoire. What would we have done to integrate ourselves otherwise? It's not even possible." Education was conducted almost entirely in French, regardless of the subject being taught. No political speech was given in any Ivoirian language (Adopo et al. 1986:83). Radio and television included a very limited and carefully bounded representation of indigenous languages but were heavily dominated by French.

Spitulnik argues that the supposed neutrality of colonial language actually represents the naturalization of its dominance. Thus, she writes of English in Zambia: "English as 'neutral' thus masks class dimensions and the hegemony of those who command its usage" (1998:175). Lafage's analysis of the role of French in Ivoirian society parallels this argument, stating that "in fact, it can be said that the differing degrees of acquisition of the official language correspond to a hierarchical system in Ivoirian society" (1978:57). At the heart of the process of national integration is an internal differentiation, a gradient scale around "the norm." Thus, the imposition of French as a national language during independence served to keep those who had profited most from colonial contact, the *evolués*, in positions of power and economic gain. The official language legitimated this emerging elite cadre's social superiority and supposed advance along the path of social evolution through their linguistic performance.

The explicit association between speaking French and degree of civilization had strong effects on the Ivoirian evaluation of speech. Kouamé, an unemployed man in his late forties, compared the former president, Bédié, to a villager for his linguistic ineptitude and poor sense of style: "No matter how dressed up he was, I could always tell he was a *gaou*. From the first time I saw him I said, 'No, he can't even speak French, he doesn't know how to dress.' When he traveled the world he stood there in awe, dumbfounded. It was so obvious he had spent his life in the village." Ivoirians revered French as a language that expressed more noble sentiments, a more "cultured" mentality, a more refined persona—characteristics which Ivoirian elites considered to be a mark of nationality vis-à-vis other West Africans. French was considered "beautiful," while the language of their villages was "ugly," and when people spoke French "well" in poor *quartiers* like Treichville, they were looked on with admiration, sometimes even applauded (though too much of this could be criticized as *choco*, or the "greasy" French of someone putting on airs). Therefore, while Francophone linguistic performance was an index of Ivoirian social hierarchy, it also carried more profound associations of one's personal development on the ideological path of "cultural evolution," a path which Ivoirians saw extending beyond Côte d'Ivoire to the universal.

Urban Cultural Integration and the Ivoirianization of French

Despite tendencies toward the preservation of French purity implied by such language ideology, urban centers, especially Abidjan, were from the very beginning arenas for the transformation and localization of French. From a population of only 58,000 in 1948 (Diabate and Kodjo 1991:120), Abidjan has grown to over four million today,[8] and faced with such exponential growth and intense diversity, it has faced many of the same linguistic issues cited by Epstein (1992) in his studies of urban language in the Copperbelt in the 1950s. As a focal point for the migration of Côte d'Ivoire's diverse ethnic groups as well as immigration from all over West Africa, Abidjan was a place in which French was necessary as a lingua franca with which to engage in everyday interactions on the street. In the process, generations of youth growing up in the city spoke French as their first language; simultaneously, as French was learned by word of mouth rather than in school, it became increasingly Ivoirianized. As Michel (a middle-class phone technician in his thirties) explained, "Now there is a difference between villages and cities. In the village everyone learns French in schools, but it is really only the young who are still learning who are able to speak. The rest converse in tribal language. It is really the opposite situation in town, where everyone speaks French and people only speak their tribal language at yearly gatherings of their region. In my family we speak French practically all the time." In this way, the urban environment became closely associated with the French language. But more importantly, it became a space where the French language became Ivoirian, as it was transformed from the pragmatic realm of communicating across cultural lines to the first language of those growing up in this space.

The resulting transformations of French produced what is most typically referred to in the linguistic literature as *Français Populaire Ivoirien*, or FPI (Lafage 1978; Kokora 1983; Adopo et al. 1986; Gnamba and N'Guessan 1990; Chumbow, Sammy, and Bobda 2000; Kouadio 2005). In a Web interview, Akindes described its development in the following terms:

> In the first place it was "Moussa's French." In the Ivory Coast there were a lot of immigrants from Burkina Faso; it actually started long ago when Burkina Faso was Upper Volta; they came to Ivory Coast to work by themselves, and also there were waves of workers that were recruited by the French to come and work in the Ivory Coast before independence. And so the French that was used to address them, to talk to these people, and to uneducated people in general, was a kind of broken French. But that French developed gradually by itself, especially in places like Yopougon and Abobo in Abidjan, and in every metropolitan area. The language developed, and it developed by itself. (Mitter 2007)

Indeed, the propensity of Ivoirians to transform French to their own purposes was both documented and valorized by one of its most famous authors, Ahmadou Kourouma, in his groundbreaking novel *Les Soleils d'Independances*, in 1968. Until this time, as Christopher Miller (1990) documents, Francophone African literature remained entirely in classical French despite the increasing localization of the French language in speech in the postcolonies, demonstrating the incredible power of French language ideology. Kourouma's book, though entirely in French, makes use of the rich practices of translating local Ivoirian idiomatic expressions into French, written in a manner that tried to capture the way Ivoirians thought in French. The book was a direct challenge to the norms of Francophone African literature as well as Ivoirian state language policies (a state parodied in the book as the rulers of the fictitious Côte d'Ébène).[9]

The matter of the Ivoirianization of French was one of grave concern for the Ivoirian state as well as a variety of French and Ivoirian linguists, many of whom feared the irreparable corruption of the French language. As Inoue (2006) has demonstrated in Japan, modernization projects often produce particular reified identities who are seen as in opposition to the ideals of national identity, and linguistic studies themselves become a part of this process of reification. Kokora, for example, argued that French should be confined to a specific governmental role and kept "pure," while quotidian activities should be carried out in indigenous languages: "If this minimal linguistic organization is not undertaken very soon Ivoirian French will rapidly go off course and become degraded" (1983:147). Even Lafage, typically quite sensitive to hierarchies of language, wrote in one of her earlier studies that "great efforts must be deployed if we wish to avoid the expansion of FPI and the creolization of French" (1978:66).[10] Until the first decade of the twenty-first century, scholars almost universally saw Nouchi or *Français Populaire Ivoirien* as a danger to be avoided, an impure and imperfect language resulting from undereducated people mistakenly trying to appropriate the symbolic power of French. In this sense the language that most people spoke in the cities of Côte d'Ivoire was considered a dangerous corrupting force upon the nation by the country's ruling elite. As we saw at the beginning, it was only in the summer of 2009 that the state recognized Nouchi as potentially connected to Ivoirian identity and worthy of attention.

Because the degree to which speakers could approximate "proper" French determined their ability to attain modern status, many elites referred to FPI scornfully as *Petit Moussa* (little Moussa, a name associated with migrants from the north) and likened it to the speech of peasants. *Fraternité Matin* published a humor column recording the French of the streets called *Petit Moussa*, depicting the speech errors and idiomatic expressions lower classes were prone to make (it also included translations of some of these expression, just like the Nouchi columns to follow). Its heading included a cartoon caricature of a peasant, an image of the friendly but "ignorant" recent arrival from the village (in Nouchi terms, a *gaou*).[11] This column's vicarious representation of "popular" Ivoirian French reproduced the hierarchical stratification of French speakers. Yet important cultural processes were at work in Ivoirian cities, embodied in the linguistic practices of *Français Populaire Ivoirien*. French provided a middle ground outside ethnic constraints, through which a new Ivoirian popular culture was developing something that could be shared throughout the country as a source of Ivoirian identity but that went unseen because of the ideologies of modernity and class stratification.

The Emergence of Nouchi and the Self-Recognition of Ivoirian Popular Culture

Rather than contenting themselves with an "impure" or "corrupted" French which could only serve as the emblem of their social deficiency, in the 1990s urban criminal youth actively transformed their "popular" French into the sign of a new urban identity. They rejected the purity of the French language as well as the position of France as the symbolic center of Ivoirian cultural hierarchization. Criminal networks began to transform and play with the rules of FPI, making up some words, actively borrowing others, and purposefully making the language unintelligible. To cite Akindes again,

> So as time went and as the stigma of that language being associated with immigrants started fading away, what happened was that the youth appropriated it. So it became the language of the *maquis*, the *allocodromes*: the *maquis* is the African restaurant, usually open restaurant where people gather and talk, but it was also a place of cultural activity. . . . And there is a culture that developed around those places and around the language. So in many different places people started using that type of French. (Mitter 2007)

Thus, we see the formation of a new urban popular culture around shared experiences of eating, drinking, and speaking—an emergent, vehicular form of culture that allowed Abidjanais lower-class youth to invert the hierarchical schema of indexical ideology, placing themselves at the center of modern Ivoirian culture. For these were not simply spaces for the merry consumption of victuals and the exchange of pleasantries around a table: these were contested spaces of display, in which actors vied for their reputation of success through the bluff. And through such performances that blurred the lines between the real and the fake and proved their ability to live as gloriously as the crème of Ivoirian society, Ivoirian urban youth staked their claim to their piece of the modernity pie.

Nouchi is not simply "an aristocratic intention," as Bourdieu (1991) says of slang, or an antilanguage that forges itself always in opposition to the standard (Halliday 1976), for like the Ivoirian standard (Parisian

French), Nouchi derives its authority from the externality of modernity. Rejecting French elitism, *nouchi* youth sought out the streetwise authority of U.S. popular culture, and in doing so they undermined the hegemony of the French language in Côte d'Ivoire. Reflecting the changing norms of enregisterment, Ivoirian studies of Nouchi since 2000 now argue that FPI (or Nouchi, depending on the terminology they choose to adopt and its ideological ramifications) is an Ivoirian language and should potentially be considered its own standard (Boutin 2003; Kouadio 2005). Sonaiya writes that "over time, these peculiar usages became accepted through processes of vernacularization, with the Ivoirian community insisting on them as evidence of its appropriation of the French language" (2007:440).

Standard French and Nouchi both serve as indexical icons of the modernity of their speakers, but in opposed ways.[12] While the Standard French of the elites iconically indexes a concept of cultural superiority based on refinement and control, Nouchi's generativity and performance—its purposeful introduction of neologisms—are also icons of modernity, the urban modernity of the streets, just as Spitulnik (1999) brilliantly suggests for Town Bemba. Furthermore, its French syntactic structure combined with large lexical incorporations from English mark its modern and Western qualities. Nouchi contains expressions like *je vais me wash* (I am going to bathe) or *il est wanté* (he is "wanted"), *bizness* (illicit economy), *boxing* (forgery), *dribbler* (to avoid or escape), or "Le Black" (the black market of Adjame). Another form of created word was more a cultural borrowing, a tributary naming of things after the idols of U.S. television and movies, or even after more local stars. *Ken*, an opportunity to make money or an object to sell, comes from the name of David Carradine's character in the old television show *Kung Fu*. The Nouchi word for magic is *Mcgaiveur*! The street names *nouchi* used to refer to one another in public and under the rubric of which they attained fame often referenced U.S. pop culture. Among those I encountered were Tupac, Biggi, Rambo, le Rock, and Scarface. These references, drawn from English language and U.S. pop culture, further indexed the opposition *nouchi* made between U.S. and French modernity, and their efforts to supersede the passé stylings of the elite.

Nouchi also contains a highly egalitarian ideology of production (though ultimately, the dissemination of words was tightly controlled by networks). As Gros Guerrier, a muscle-bound *loubard* introduced to me as "the father of Nouchi," told me, "the language of Nouchi was created like that, little by little, around a table in a *maquis*, we talk, we discuss, and words come to our heads. If you are Baoulé, maybe it is Baoulé words that come, and you put those words into French phrases." Nouchi indexes

Ivoirianess because of this street ideology of creative production combined with the incorporation of ethnic languages from Côte d'Ivoire, making it a perfect vehicle for the association of "the people" (in both the semiotic and the political sense). Not only are there people walking around with the title "father of Nouchi" and many others who can claim to have invented a word, but also, because Nouchi incorporates much of its lexical content from indigenous languages such as Dioula, Baoulé, and Bete, its speakers declare themselves definitively Ivoirian, autochthones. Indeed, Ivoirian linguists and state officials were dismayed by the prevalence of FPI (and later of Nouchi) precisely because these influences were seen to distance Ivoirian culture from the modernity the state was so proud of producing.

Thus, from its fluid efforts to resist standardization to its indexical references to modernity in content, Nouchi proclaims its urban origins. At the same time, through its explicit localization of French and incorporation of indigenous language, it is clearly an Ivoirian modernity that is expressed. In this way, Nouchi has become a source of national pride for some Ivoirians, especially as it has been incorporated into cultural products exported internationally. I now turn to the dramatic spread of Nouchi from the *bluffeurs* of Abidjan's criminal scene to a wider national audience through its appropriation by large-scale media and adoption by university students.

Vicarious Banditry: The Mediation of Nouchi

In the years leading up to my fieldwork in 2000, Nouchi exploded into the popular consciousness of Ivoirian society, invading pop songs, television broadcasts, and newspaper comic strips. University students and elite teenagers who were brought up speaking French adopted it as their hipster lingo. One university student enthusiastically exclaimed to me in a hallway outside his classroom, "Yes, I speak Nouchi all the time, because I find it's chic, it's like cool, you know. Or as we say in Nouchi, it's *enjaillent* [thrilling]. Lots of students speak Nouchi more naturally than French." Such elite uses of Nouchi cannot be written off as dominant hypocorrection (Bourdieu 1991), for it is an explicit imitation of the language of the street, a reversal of the hegemony of French normative speech. Speaking Nouchi became a kind of vicarious banditry, in which urban youth sought to participate in the value system of *nouchi* criminal hierarchies, claiming *yere* status by speaking what they heard or read as Nouchi language. Nor was this limited to the urban context, for I was told that even in the north children were learning Nouchi and insulted when it was implied that Nouchi speech belonged solely to Abidjan. Indeed, there is evidence of a cultural merging between students and *nouchi* youth, as students became increasingly violent and styled themselves not only linguistically, but sartorially and economically from the street networks.[13] Indeed, the Jeunes Patriotes militias (Young Patriots, an informal network of armed groups supporting Gbagbo) that sprang up after 2002 were indistinguishable from the *nouchi* criminal youth in terms of both appearances and behavior. As Michael McGovern commented, "Perhaps poor and working class criminal elements considered the student thugs to be 'soft,' but they were fighting one another with machetes, killing students from competing student unions, and using theft, beatings, rape and murder as means of extorting and punishing fellow students" (personal communication).

The media also promoted Nouchi and encouraged learning new words. *Gbich!*, a weekly humor magazine, included a "Petit Dico Ivoirien" (Little Ivoirian dictionary) regularly, signed by "les loubards Ilpolo." In this way, the authors explicitly highlighted the illicit underworld connotations of the words and their origins, while simultaneously providing access to "authentic" Nouchi words, in a sense commodifying *nouchi* identity. Many newspaper cartoons even had a *lexique* or at least a series of definitions along the bottom, though not all Nouchi terms were translated. Although this urban language was prevalent enough to appear in cartoons, not all readers understood it. Different cartoons chose to translate different terms in a seemingly arbitrary manner; there seemed to be no established idea of which words the average reader might know.[14] But it was commonly assumed that everyone wanted to know, and part of the pleasure of reading these papers was to test one's knowledge of Nouchi and learn new words.

Music was and continues to be one of the most powerful disseminators of Nouchi. When a DJ played a new Ivoirian rap song by two singers reputed for their Nouchi skill (Power and Turbo of the group Rien à Signaller), he told his audience with great excitement that this song was an opportunity to enrich its Nouchi vocabulary. In the heady days of the early 1990s, Ivoirian students came up with a new pop music combining traditional Ivoirian rhythms with synthesizers and humorous political lyrics. *Zouglou*'s lyrics, like newspaper cartoons, were almost always in an approachable Nouchi that employed and familiarized key elements of the lexicon. Ivoirians learned the words to many of these songs by heart, sang them in the street, and quoted lines from them frequently in conversation as aphorisms. Thus, these songs had the potential to strongly affect popular discourse, and sometimes even carry new words into popular language (as in the case of Power and Turbo). *Zouglou* has since been replaced by *coupé-décalé*, a new form of Ivoirian music first produced by Ivoirian illegal migrants in Paris and now exported not only to Côte d'Ivoire but to much of Francophone Africa , dispersing Nouchi slang and becoming a new source of Ivoirian pride.

Another fascinating example of Nouchi in popular media is the Nouchi. com Web site, a dictionary of Ivoirian slang. Unlike most dictionaries, which dispense knowledge of standard language in a typically top-down fashion, Nouchi.com allows all visitors to the Web site to add their own words or alternative definitions (this having begun already in 1999, before "wiki" was a household word). This would seem to reflect the egalitarian ideology of Nouchi production, even if in practice Nouchi innovation is controlled by hierarchical social networks. The very concept of a Web site for Nouchi is somewhat bizarre, as the great majority of *nouchi* I encountered at the time had never set foot in an Internet café, this despite the ready availability such cafés for more computer-adventurous West African immigrants.[15] The site is respected enough to be linked to Abidjan. net, which is certainly Côte d'Ivoire's most important Web site for news, discussion, and cultural information.[16] It seems likely that the readers and contributors to the site are mostly elite Ivoirians who enjoy Nouchi as a form of entertainment.

Not only was the populace eager to gain access to new Nouchi words, but advertisers were equally keen to capitalize on the popularity of Nouchi. The Coca-Cola Corporation chose to advertise itself with the phrase "Abidjan *enjaille* Coca-Cola" plastered across billboards with images of Ivoirians driving convertibles. Unfortunately, whoever wrote this ad was not quite fluent in Nouchi. While undoubtedly trying to convey the idea that Abidjan enjoys Coca-Cola in its own exciting local dialect, they neglected that unless used reflexively, as in "Abidjan *s'enjaille* avec Coca-Cola," *enjaille* means "to titillate" rather than "to enjoy" (*enjailler* is a combination of "enjoy" and *jaillir* [spurt, ejaculate]); thus, the billboards actually suggested that Abidjan sexually stimulates Coca-Cola. In any case, Coca-Cola thought of Nouchi not as a corrupting criminal slang, but rather as something with enough widespread popularity and cachet that it would add glamour to its brand identity.

Purity and the Perils of Degeneration: Anxious Interpretations of Nouchi

However, the fact that Nouchi was a desirable model imitated by many Ivoirians, that its speakers had successfully enregistered an alternative evaluation of the modernity of their speech, did not mean that all Ivoirians were willing to abandon their attachment to the French standard. As Nouchi spread from the secret argot of Abidjan's notorious gangsters to the language of youth in general, Nouchi's associations with lawlessness and flagrant criminality caused a panic among the Ivoirian elite. In the spring of 2001, when a couple of French expats teaching at the Lycée Français of Cocody presented a project on Nouchi with their students at the Centre Culturel Français, I watched the audience accuse them of being irresponsible and counterproductive. The teachers were told that their role as educators was to discourage children from using this slang language, not expose them to it. One audience member asked, "What will happen if children are unable to distinguish between Nouchi and French? What if they leave school still unconsciously slipping Nouchi into their speech?"

In a similar vein, my landlord, a son of Baoulé nobility who had spent fifteen years in France and was considered very rich by our neighbors, exclaimed:

> The fact that we [Ivoirians] had no common language originally explains why we have such a bizarre national French now. We have adapted it to our own purposes and localized it because it is our national language. But this is why I think university students today are held back in literature and law, because their French is not good enough. If they just went to France for a while to improve their French it would go much faster. I dated a very intelligent university student getting a degree in pharmaceuticals. But she often asked me to explain myself because she did not understand French at my level. Likewise, when Ivoirians speak among themselves, I often cannot understand what they are talking about without asking them.

Notice that, like De Gaulle, my landlord associated French with logical thought itself. Older Ivoirians at this time worried about their ability to communicate with other Ivoirians as Nouchi took on greater ideological strength, replacing the concept of FPI. Concern over the corruption of the French language could be heard from secondary school students, from mothers who had never gone to school, from teenagers on the street. Jerome, of northern origins and probably not yet twenty, worked as an attendant at an Internet café. Although he enjoyed speaking Nouchi, his feelings about it were ambivalent:

> Don't you think it is a bad thing? I think that it is damaging for kids who are trying to learn French. These days even teachers will use Nouchi when they are forgetting themselves; in midexplanation it just slips out. I guess it can be

a good thing, though, depending on how it is used. When I was a little kid in Abobo, the guys who spoke Nouchi were real hoodlums, guys who scared me. People who spoke Nouchi were the ones you didn't want to be around; they were a bad influence. But today Nouchi seems to be something for everyone, so maybe it is changing.

The *nouchi* themselves, despite their pride in breaking the rules of French, making up words, and defying comprehension to the uninitiated, expressed anxiety over their ability to speak French "properly." A cartoon (see fig. 3) perfectly expresses the ambivalence held by *nouchi* over their linguistic capabilities. Gnamankoudji Zekinan is a *loubard* who lives to fight. Here he puts up a job announcement requesting someone to fight him "morning, noon, and night," but his French is so bad that a crowd gathers to make fun of it. He is insulted and asks in Nouchi what *gaou* has dared to insult his French. This gangster, who is supposed to epitomize the authority-defying anti-French values of the *nouchi*, is worried about the quality of his written French and how it reflects on his image. The ideal then, is to be capable of speaking French faultlessly yet *choose* to speak Nouchi. Indeed, as the politics of citizenship took on force, a lack of capability in French was often taken as a sign that the speaker might be an immigrant, an untrue Ivoirian. I often witnessed people badgering the *marchands ambulants* (walking salesmen) and food vendors about their inability to communicate properly, accusing them of being *gaou* foreigners, insisting that they were villagers and knew nothing.

The Nouchi terminology to describe the phonetic differences in speech between classes is an opposition between "dry" and "greasy." Ivoirians (and other Francophone Africans) are said to *parler sec* (speak dryly), meaning that they pronounce their syllables clearly and slowly, with too much effort. In contrast, "real" French and the elite are said to speak *choco*. My friends spoke of how often the language in French films was too *choco* and no one could understand the actors because the syllables slid into one another. *Sec* was also used to describe someone's lack of skill with a language, as when a *nouchi* falteringly attempted to speak English with me. As he walked away, someone in my group muttered scornfully, "Anglais sec-là" (Dry English, there). But speaking French too well inappropriately met with the most disapproval and could bring about direct confrontation, as when my friends accused a youth named Mathieu of trying to speak *choco* around me because I was a *graté* (whitey).

Most important here is the way in which the evaluation of language flips back on itself according to context, at one moment accepting the dominant

Figure 3. This *loubard*, a muscle-bound type of *nouchi* who lives to brawl, has written an advertisement looking for someone to fight. However, when the crowd laughs at his mistakes in French, he becomes angry and threatens to beat up whoever dared to make fun of him. One man admits his guilt when the crowd scapegoats him, but the *loubard* says he will fight the rest of the crowd, since they were dishonest.
(*Gbich*! 84, no. 12 [May 18–24, 2001].)

ideology valuing "pure" French, a minute later reveling in a speaker's prowess in Nouchi. Abidjanais speakers echoed these contextual value shifts by transforming their speech patterns, just as Mathieu did in my presence. But both in speech and in their evaluations of speech, Abidjanais displayed a great deal of ambivalence between French and Nouchi as divergent models of "good" speech, each making claims to being the truer expression of modern urban identity.

Nouchi and Nationality Identity

The pervasiveness of Nouchi in contemporary Ivoirian speech is no longer in doubt. Kouadio writes that "Nouchi has reinforced its position in youth culture to such a point that it has become the first language, or at least the most spoken language of youth between ten and thirty years old" (2005:1). Nevertheless, contradictions surrounding Nouchi as a basis for identity are summed up in this snippet of conversation recorded during my fieldwork in 2000.

HENRI: People here grow up hearing so much Nouchi, they can never even arrive at mastering French. Only those who get to *Troisième* even get close. We just can't help mixing Nouchi in.

OLIVIER: Don't other countries have Nouchi too?

HENRI: All countries have some kind of Nouchi, but not as strong as ours. Ours is a real language. It is part of what makes Ivoirians different from other Africans.

Here we see at once the anxiety over the corrupting influence of Nouchi upon French expression combined with a pride in Nouchi as a "real language" that distinguishes Ivoirians from other Africans. In the twenty-first century, Nouchi has become a national export, initially traveling through the African diaspora with *zouglou* breakthrough hits like "Premier Gaou" by Magic System and later truly taking off with the sensation of *coupé-décalé*, which samples Congolese *soukous* and overlays lyrics in Nouchi. Born in Parisian nightclubs catering to the African diaspora, *coupé-décalé* has become one of the dominant music genres of the African continent, carrying Nouchi with it in its path. Both music and language are forms of Ivoirian national production rather than connected with a specific ethnicity. Nevertheless, Nouchi's criminal origins continue to be advertised (Kohlhagen 2006), as *coupé-décalé* signifies something akin to "scam and scram" in Nouchi. By enregistering both modernity and autochthony, Nouchi provides a space within popular culture from which to escape the dilemma of postcolonial Franco-centrism without favoring any particular ethnicity—a source of national identity that is packageable, exportable, and outside state control.

The significance of products like *zouglou, coupé-décalé*, and Nouchi for imagining Ivoirian national identity is not easy to convey to a U.S. audience. The transformation from a nation employing French culture as a bridge to national unity in the 1960s to one exporting local popular culture to a global audience is profound. At an ethnographic level, my argument here follows a historical process of shifting indexicality, in which Ivoirian French was transformed from the language of the uneducated poor to the language of criminals to a language signifying a shared, if contested, Ivoirian popular culture. Ironically, this final incarnation is the enregisterment of a form of speech that was originally intended to be unintelligible to the average Ivoirian. Ivoirian youth appropriated Nouchi speech as an alternative evaluatory scheme whose potency stemmed from the rejection of the postcolonial position of dependence on French culture, asserting their creative rights over the means of communication and indexing the urban modernity of the imagined *yere* streetwise warrior who survives through wits, performative style, and the duplicity of illusion. As a consequence, the negative representations of FPI and Nouchi presented by the state and elites only fed the glamour and expressive potency of Nouchi in the eyes of youth cut off from any productive avenue in the failed postcolonial economy (Diouf 2003; Argenti 2007).

Nouchi defies typical narratives of hegemonic language ideology and the nation, where the state works through language standardization to produce national identity and "improve" its population while any deviance from the standard is treated as morally suspect (Anderson 1991; Bourdieu 1991; Silverstein 1996). Speakers of slang in such accounts are woebegone heroes resisting hegemony and rule-bound standards to insist on their own distinct identity and style, only to find their "distinction" to be the mark of inferiority (Bourdieu 1991). Jennifer Roth-Gordon's (2009) insightful investigation into connections between slang and citizenship suggests that processes of enregisterment have produced new categories of citizenship, tracing the productive possibilities of indexicality outside state control. But in the end, these distinctions become fodder for the middle class and state to "attribute the position of marginality" to speakers of *favela* slang. Nouchi is a counterexample to this kind of narrative, a case in which slang is cited and reproduced by upper-class youth in order to appropriate its alternative modernity in contradistinction to the "traditional" modernity of Frenchness. As the marked category of slang has expanded to become the unmarked first language of a large percentage of the population, especially in urban environments, so-called slang has become the norm. But this is a norm increasingly distant from the "street warrior" model from which it derives, as its appropriation by upper classes defies its intention of unintelligibility.

Both French and Nouchi enregisterments of modernity play upon an imagination of Côte d'Ivoire as a stepping-stone between Africa and the West, a gateway to modernity. Urban Ivoirians portray African immigrants to Côte d'Ivoire as gleaning modernity just as Ivoirians in turn absorb modernity in their own travels to Europe. But while the postcolonial state encouraged a hierarchical but encompassing citizenship based on the mimesis of French culture as evolution, the reimagination of *Ivoirité* produced by *nouchi* street hierarchy has progressively excluded populations they consider *gaou*—often placing them in the constructed category of Dioula. It is worth pointing out that because Nouchi contains so much Dioula, thus relying upon the very language it ideologically excludes, it has the potential to serve as a cultural bridge through which to integrate a more holistic sense of Ivoirian identity. Certainly many people with "Dioula" names speak Nouchi, some of them as a first language. Whether or not Côte d'Ivoire is now a political space in which this is possible remains to be seen.

Faced with the phenomenon of Nouchi, we are wont to label it and list its characteristics. But rather than treating Nouchi as an objective "thing" to be studied for its exciting linguistic features, we can think of it as a series of value judgments and citations that produce a "language" in the sphere of public discourse. That is, Nouchi exists as a "language" because of the debates surrounding its use and its speakers in the Ivoirian public sphere. As such (and not in its original form as an encoded argot), it became an organizing symbol for Ivoirian society in the negotiation of an emerging national identity, and so enregistered precisely the cultural distinctions that brought about the Ivoirian crisis in 2002. Nouchi's vitality and dynamism are continually renewed by the collective struggle over whom it is associated with, for it is this struggle that gives Nouchi its semiotic relevance and indexical punch.

Until Houphouët's death in 1993, the Ivoirian state made a concerted effort to assert a foreign language as the official standard, a standard which proved more capable of representing social hierarchy than producing a shared sense of belonging. Instead, it was the popular culture of the city, simply out of the need for daily communication and social interaction, that produced an Ivoirian semiotic space in opposition to the French and free from association with any particular ethnic group. But this space was itself hotly contested, simultaneously scorned and appropriated, and it came to enregister a regional opposition between an urban south and an estranged north. Nouchi's ability to integrate linguistic material from a wide variety of languages is an important factor in urban cultural integration, and it is also a *symbol* of that integration. At the same time, Nouchi speakers explicitly evaluate themselves in relation to the images of U.S. gangs they imitate. Nouchi draws on U.S. street sources of cultural legitimacy in order to construct an alternative social hierarchy harnessed to a popular reimagining of Ivoirian identity. The bluff of modernity in which they are engaged, an appropriation of alterity that is at the same time a performance of self, becomes the stereotypic model from which *Ivoirité* could be produced as a public object. It is through these conceptualizations of the external, these varying imaginings of modernity according to differentiated social positions within Côte d'Ivoire, that an Ivoirian (as opposed to ethnic) selfhood is forged. But here again, it is the mimetic performance of the bluff, through which Ivoirians model their speech, clothing, and musical taste upon the media's stereotypic figure of the *nouchi* criminal, that creates the possibility of a "real" Ivoirian identity. It is the shared performance of alterity that allows the public object of identity to emerge. In this case, this newly constructed Ivoirian national identity has tragically produced a radical alterity within the country itself, leading to precisely the kinds of ethnic conflict it was supposed to prevent. As I shall explore further in chapter 6, the production of an "Ivoirian" identity by urban street youth simultaneously produced its imagined alter ego, the counterfeit Ivoirian—the uncivilized Other falsely attempting to proclaim the right to citizenship.

TWO

Bizness and "Blood Brothers": The Moral Economy of Crime

Because of their historical predicaments, postcolonies tend *not* to be organized under a single, vertically integrated sovereignty sustained by a highly centralized state. Rather, they consist in a horizontally woven tapestry of partial sovereignties: sovereignties over terrains and their inhabitants, over aggregates of people conjoined in faith or culture, over transactional spheres, over networks of relations, regimes of property, domains of practice, and quite often, over various combinations of these things; sovereignties longer or shorter lived, protected to a greater or lesser degree by the capacity to exercise compulsion, always incomplete. (Comaroff and Comaroff 2006:35)

The Infamy of Treichville

Less than a year before my arrival, Treichville had been the center of the Abidjan mafia, the home of Jon Pololo, a legendary—and in many people's eyes, heroic—bandit who had dominated the underground economy of Abidjan for many years. He can be read as the founding culture hero of the *nouchi*, an origin myth of sorts working as a charter for *nouchi* identity as well as stereotypic alterity. This personage not only figured highly within rumor networks (many people have personal stories involving him), but was also a media icon in his own right. He was considered by many to be the first *nouchi*, the originator of both the style and the language itself. As Dedy told it,

He was a Bete who lived in Treichville. He was killed in the coup d'état because everyone was afraid of him. He was too powerful, many people followed him as their leader, and he was known to beat and kill soldiers. When he wanted a woman, he would just take her and throw her over his shoulder, like this. One time he did the same to me. He took me to an alley and demanded money. I pleaded with him not to kill me, and he showed me the knife he was going to do it with, but in the end he let me go.

Pololo was a celebrity, so famous that even elites know him by name to this day, and one of Côte d'Ivoire's most popular musicians, Ismaël Isaac, wrote a song about his death. He even made television appearances, as Jean-Luc tells in the following description:

> When he was twenty-two he visited Europe. But there he killed a white man. It was outside a nightclub, and they harassed him until . . . he pulled out a pistol and killed the guy. So they sent him back here. That's why despite all his money he was never able to leave the country. But here he made music and he went on television. He looked so sharp. That day, all the gangsters watched television. He said he was the king, and that all that he commanded took place.

According to popular belief, when the military finally caught him they tried to shoot him but, as Jean-Luc continued, "it didn't work, it didn't hurt him at all. So they were forced to hook him up to two trucks and pull him apart." This is then the model on which *nouchi* identity is based. He made his living through crime, yet he was eloquent, always confident, and flamboyant. He always got what he wanted and he backed down to no one. And he was so tough that not even bullets could kill him.

Treichville's collective memory of this time is one of terror and impotence, for in those days, people told me, gangs would rob you in broad daylight, on the most crowded streets, and no one dared protest at all. The elite family with whom I lived during my first month in Côte d'Ivoire could rarely be convinced to enter Treichville at all, and the women in the family never did. They all listened to my stories of life there incredulously. But especially among the *nouchi* who compared themselves to warriors fighting for survival on the streets, Treichville's criminal reputation was also a mark of pride, for this was the toughest quarter, and it was here that they had made their way in the world. Zokis, a resident of Koumassi, related the following:

> Socially, Treichville has a higher proportion of hoodlums [than Koumassi]. This is because Treichville really used to be the capital of the *nouchi*, the center of the mafia. So today Treichville is populated by the descendants of yesterday's *nouchi*. If you have a child in Treichville, people will always say he is

a hoodlum, even if he makes it as far as the United States. The networks are very strong there since everyone is the child of former mafia. All the youth here are *Gros Bras* [Big Arms, a synonym for *loubard*] All they do is lift weights. Me I'm not *loubard*. I used to be really in shape and do the vagabond thing, but now I have work at the port and I don't have time to work out. But I still have all my old vagabond friends, who come and wake me up in the morning [i.e., the friends who brought me to meet him that morning].

Although the former mafia-style structure had now largely dissolved, most young men's income was still directly or indirectly connected to crime, and the ability to *yere* someone was a valued skill in this community. Victims were *gaous* despised for their ignorance of how to protect themselves in the city. While my *nouchi* friends were quick to offer protection from more hostile bandits that might seek to rob me, they were equally quick to make fun of me when I was foolish enough to entrust an acquaintance with money to order us food. When I realized the man wasn't going to return, I accosted his *vieuxpère* (superior in the hierarchy) for not keeping his *petit* (underling) in line, he said, "What do you expect, you were *gaou* enough to give money to a *nouchi*?" Thus, Treichville residents expressed conflicting and often ambivalent opinions about its criminal tendencies, proud of their fortitude, wit, and sheer survival, relieved that they no longer lived under such constant threat of crime, but ashamed that they were no longer the center of illicit exchange.

This same dilemma could be found at the individual level when it came to sources of income. Abidjanais men were often reluctant to admit what they did for a living. Occasionally, this was because they didn't trust me, or that they worried that I might disrespect them for any criminal behavior, but just as often, they were loath to admit to their Ivoirian friends that they supplemented their informal trade with a low-level part-time job. For *nouchi* men, most of the available work was considered so demeaning that it had to be avoided or hidden from one's community. It may seem surprising that illicit dealings would be considered more honorable, but Jon Pololo offered a model of criminality as social justice. In a television interview of Pololo, he justified criminal behavior in a phrase echoing Hobsbawm's ([1969] 1981) concept of social banditry. As Jean-Luc related it to me, "They asked if he had stopped his life of crime and he said yes. So why didn't he stop other people from doing that? He lets that happen because there are rich people who lack respect, who give nothing to the poor. One must redistribute a little. People who are proper, who know how to share, we leave them alone." As we shall see in this chapter and the next, this

Robin Hood ideology of redistribution was crucial to the maintenance and hierarchization of social networks. *Nouchi* youth were aware of the injustice of their position in the social hierarchy and felt that they were already owed something by the political elite from which they stole.[1]

The Economic Underpinnings of the Bluff: Illicit yet Moral Economies

One of the first questions people ask when they hear about Ivoirian youth with no jobs wielding wads of cash and dressing in brand name clothes is "But where do they get the money to do this"? I cannot claim to have satisfactory data for a reliable response, since both legitimate and illegitimate labor were shrouded in secrecy. Indeed, the problem was exacerbated by the liability of publicly known income, since one was obligated to share it with a wide network of people should they demand it, and so most of my friends were not very forthcoming about their day-to-day saving and spending. Furthermore, MacGaffey and Bazenguissa-Ganga advocate against the inherently judgmental use of the term "illegal" economy, for the boundary between legal and illegal "is a political one, established by the dominant to maintain their power and control" (2000:5). But how do we even begin to determine who establishes "legality" when the only agents of the state encountered on a daily basis are active participants in the "illegal" sphere? And when the most feared local authorities are not police officers but renowned gangsters, by what criteria is the legitimacy of a transaction established? For this reason, I do not believe the distinctions among legal, informal, and illicit economies are tenable for my analysis. As the Comaroffs put it, "Politics and crime, legitimate and illegitimate agency, endlessly redefine each other. The line between them is a frontier in the struggle to assert sovereignty or to disrupt it, to expand or contract the limits of the il/licit, to sanction or outlaw violence" (2006:11). In Abidjan, a wide spectrum of behavior exists: not everyone is a criminal by any means, not everyone is shut out of formal employment, but many people make significant portions of their income in ways that will not register in the statistics recorded for formal economic analysis. Most income is hidden not only from the analyst, but also from one's closest friends and family, so there is little hope of an objective accounting. Nevertheless, I witnessed enough to glean the essentials of how survival worked in this system, to lay bare the paradox of secrecy and deception joined at the hip with fame and bonds of mutual trust that lies at the heart of Abidjan's economic life.

In this chapter I explore the social and economic underpinnings of the bluff. I demonstrate how crime and community can be mutually constitutive in a city where the second economy is really the primary one, where sociality necessarily transgresses boundaries of ethnicity and kinship on a daily basis, and where social order is often an ad hoc construction adapted to the moment by the people present. As recent Africanist scholarship by Simone (2004) and De Boeck and Plissart (2006) has shown, the incredible rate of expansion of African cities in recent decades has not been accompanied by the same rate of infrastructural growth. For a variety of reasons including internal corruption and external manipulations of structural adjustment policies, the state has been unable to provide for or to maintain order among urban populations. And yet "Africans do make cities that, in many respects, work" (Simone 2006:358). The architect Rem Koolhaus has heralded this new form of bottom-up centerless urbanization in Africa as "an announcement of the future," predicting the demise of the twentieth-century city as we know it (Packer 2006). In order to come to terms with African urban social life, we must pay attention to the micropolitics of sociality in a society where the state, rather than providing the infrastructural framework within which society unfolds, is encompassed within the informal economics and the face-to-face interaction of social networks. Hart's (1988) study of urban informal economy in Africa suggests that much of it takes places in the interstices between kinship and contract, between behavior regulated by tradition and that regulated by the state, outside the control of either. It is instead trust-based relations of voluntary friendship upon which such economies rely, exchanges and obligations neither between strangers nor between close kin. I argue here that the criminal transactional sphere, despite its reputation of deviance and questionable values, was ultimately organized according to a form of moral economy.

By "moral economy," I denote a system in which people often exchange for the purpose of maintaining and accumulating social relations, rather than merely for the purpose of maximizing their profits (Thompson 1971; Scott 1979). Of course, in some more abstract sense, people profit from their social relationships, but the point is that the social relationships take priority, or rather, that the maintenance and accumulation of these relationships is its own kind of profit. Ralph Austen writes that "the central trope of the various efforts to define moral economy has been an opposition between, on the one hand, the maximizing individual and ever-expanding market of classical economy and, on the other, a community governed by norms of collective survival and believing in a zero-sum universe—that is, a world where all profit is gained at someone else's loss" (1993:92). In describing a system of moral economy, I am not implying that there is no such thing as individualistic profit maximization, or that moral economy is about valuing community to the exclusion of individual motivation, but rather that consideration of community and one's place within it interlocks dialectically with considerations of self-promotion which are as likely to conflict with as to complement so-called moral strategies.

Social connections are a liability, a collection of obligations that weighs down personal accumulation, but they are also the buoy keeping most people afloat. As Simone writes, "The pressures for maintaining function cohesion within the framework of extended family systems and the practices of resource distribution that go with it are enormous. There is a preoccupation on the part of many residents in African cities with the extent to which they are tied to the fates of others who they witness 'sinking' all around them. At the same time, they hope that the ties around them are sufficiently strong to rescue them if need be" (2004:4). Thus, the key aspect of moral economy I want to emphasize here is the idea of a zero-sum world, where all profit is understood to be someone else's loss. In such a world, there is a continual tension between centripetal forces of hierarchical accumulation and leveling mechanisms of redistribution, for the moral obligation to share one's earnings with one's friends and family must be honored. Financial accumulation can only be achieved by controlling the flow of information, the *radio trottoir*, or "sidewalk radio," which in turn requires a position at the nexus of broad social networks (Ellis 1989; De Boeck and Plissart 2006). Thus, it is through the investment in social connectivity that people paradoxically overcome the anchoring obligations of their social networks. Before delving further into the dynamics of network and urban economy however, I must turn to the question of how "work" is understood by Ivoirian urban youth, for it is this evaluatory schema that directs many youth toward the fluid social architecture of the second economy.

The Illegitimacy of Labor

Sitting in a *maquis*, I struck up conversation with a youth slouched over his beer, who kept sighing to no one in particular, "Life is hard." I asked him what he meant:

> First, there is something blocking you in everything you try. There is no work anywhere. My father died a year ago and I have lost contact with my mother. With no parental advice I have no direction, no one to push me forward. If I need clothes, or food or shelter, it is me alone that will find it. There is

no way to get out of this because there is no money and no way to get any. There is no exit. [At this point another man across the table said that the youth's real problem was that every time he got a little money he spent it all on women. The young man accepted these charges but provided the following excuse.] I have to have some human contact in life. My dream is simply to have money to give to my family, my sisters and brothers, and to God as well, because it is God who will help me out of this. I just want work, it doesn't matter what kind, just a job.

The number of young Abidjanais with jobs has plummeted in recent decades. While in 1979 43% of males below twenty-five were employed, by 1992 this had fallen to 17% (Le Pape 1997:90). I do not want to cast doubt upon the very real collapse of the economy and the increasingly limited opportunities available. Yet the longer I stayed in Treichville, the more I became convinced that legitimate sources of income were still available. If there had really been no jobs, Abidjan's rate of immigration would have been decreasing rather than increasing exponentially. After all, the economic downturn from which Abidjan has never recovered began in 1979 with the fall of the coffee and cocoa markets. Neighboring countries have had plenty of time to recognize this lack of productivity, but the flow of migrant labor to Côte d'Ivoire has continued practically unabated. In 1992, while only 43.6% of Ivoirian men over fifteen had some kind of work, 67.3% of the Burkinabe population were employed (Le Pape 1997:111).

I began to get a sense of this dynamic when a taxi driver started talking to me about the problems of xenophobia going on in the country. He told me he himself was 100% Burkinabe (this despite the fact that he had lived Côte d'Ivoire since he was fourteen—thus confirming the local perception of nationality as determined by descent rather than residence). He explained that "Ivoirians never drive cars for a living. You would never see them working on the street selling stuff for a living, driving a truck, or anything like that. Only immigrants do this, so the whole question of *Ivoirité* is ridiculous. There are four million Burkinabe in Côte d'Ivoire. Who would do all these jobs without us?" After this conversation, I began asking all my taxi drivers about their nationality. While the majority were immigrants, I did meet a significant number of Ivoirian taxi drivers. However, the following Ivoirian driver's comments can be taken as representative:

There are lots of Ivoirians who do this now. But the only problem is the structure of it. You get no respect. What is good is that you get lots of money. I take out 2,000 [$2.75][2] every day for my family, 3,000 or 6,000 a day for cigarettes, 800 a day for a meal of my favorite food, and all that is before you take account of my salary, and you multiply that by thirty days too. You know there is money in it. Not even government officials from Plateau get money like that. I mean, who do you know that can spend 150,000 [$200] in the month like that? So it's really good, at least if you have your own car [many drivers rent their cars from taxi owners]. But then people look down on you; they won't even talk to you sometimes. They don't think of you as a human being. My neighbor never even says hello since I took this job. It's like you are nothing. That's what is not good about being a driver. Otherwise it's a pretty good job. I just took it because I had to get by somehow. There are no good jobs here, none in which you get respect, anyway.

To provide context for these sums, a common salary at the time for those with regular jobs in Treichville was around 50,000 CFA ($70). So I began to ask myself what Abidjanais really meant when they said they couldn't find a job. The answer seemed to be expressed in a popular song by the Garagistes, in which the chorus chanted: "Ivoiriens comptent en bureau" (Ivoirians count on an office). My friends laughingly explained that Ivoirians were holding out for a proper job at a desk in an office. Interestingly, the band that wrote this song was made up mostly of youths with Burkinabe parents, and two of them actually worked as mechanics until they became a successful band. Although the social critique came from what many Abidjanais would consider to be "outsiders," the popularity of the song attested to a public recognition of these attitudes.

The issue was not the work itself, but rather that such work could not be done in front of others without losing face. Thus, Luc and Christophe, my neighbors from France-Amérique, explained:

Ivoirians are too proud, too self-inflated. Here one can not sweep the streets, drive taxis, sell food. All that is shameful for an Ivoirian. No, there is no way I could go clean things off the street. Work for the town hall? [The town paid garbage removers.] No, I prefer to stay at home. All those jobs like that, they're for foreigners, people from Mali, Burkina, places like that. It's the same for them. Do you think you would see them working jobs like that in their own country? No, it's shameful for them too. They come here to do that, to earn money, and afterward they will go back to their own country. We Ivoirians like to work in an office, seated properly. It's like the Garagistes sing, "Ivoirien compent en bureau." [Ivoirians] like to be seated somewhere, writing, and the money comes to them. They just sit there and count their money. For example, I could not drive a taxi, but owning a rental car agency, that I could do. Being a manager of a *maquis* is good, but working in a *maquis* is not.

Thus, Abidjanais viewed labor not only as an index of class hierarchy, but, more importantly, also as an index of cultural hierarchy, and their own national identity was framed within this evaluative schema. They perceived physical labor as an indication of a lack of development, a missing modernity. Many urban Ivoirians seemed to think of the world as a geographically dispersed scale of social evolution. They saw their own nation, and themselves as individuals, taking up specific locations along this hierarchical order. Most Abidjanais placed the United States at the top of this global order, with a variety of European nations in descending order. Côte d'Ivoire had a mediating position between these "pays des blancs" and the rest of West Africa (if not Africa as a whole). An old saying declared: "Abidjan is convenient to Africa," meaning that it was the part of Europe closest to Africa. Urban Ivoirians saw themselves in this light as well, as more European than their African counterparts, as further along this imagined path of modernity. Yet while they imagined themselves as superior to other West Africans, they accepted their inferiority vis-à-vis Europe and the U.S. Therefore, they admitted freely to being able to do physical labor in these more developed countries, for such work would be an accurate depiction of their social status there. I will delve much further into this cosmology in chapters 4 and 5.

However, this logic surrounding labor and social hierarchy could be twisted around to serve as a justification for xenophobia. The idea that Ivoirians were xenophobes was a hot-button topic at the time, as resentment was building between those who believed in *Ivoirité* and those feeling excluded by the concept. Henri, the college student, explained Ivoirian hostility to *les étrangers* in the following terms:

Yes, maybe you can say that Ivoirians have become xenophobic, but it is a *xenophobie provoké*. No one can say that we haven't really been one of the most welcoming countries ever, accepting so many immigrants. Africans are naturally hospitable, that is our culture; I mean, you have felt welcome here haven't you? But maybe as we have become more . . . [his uncle yelled out, "civilized!"] developed, more modernized, we have forgotten some of that. It is not that we are no longer Africans, but we have accepted some of the ways of the Occident; we are no longer what we used to be. But we are not the only country to become xenophobic. Everyone is, really, just to different degrees. Just look at World War II. That was caused by Hitler because the Jews had taken all the jobs, they were making all the money, and it was anger over that that made him kill them all. And then in Paris, when Africans first arrived there, the French were still in the mindset of "We want to elevate these people and make them like the French," so they let anyone who had been in their colonies come [to France] no problem. It was only afterward, when they found that the level of unemployment was growing and French people were having trouble finding work, that they changed there policy and stopped letting people in. Because Africans are willing to do all kinds of work, whatever you will give them money for, they don't care. And there are jobs that the French don't want to do, that it is shameful to do, and so all those kind of jobs, sweeping the streets, garbage, etc., went to Africans. People are willing to do anything to make money in another country because that is what they came for, whereas in their own country they are ashamed. Like here, it is the foreigners who take all the demeaning jobs, that Ivoirians won't do, but when Ivoirians go to France, they do the same set of jobs. But so when France kicks people out, creates this whole story of *sans-papiers* [illegal immigrants], everyone accepts that as normal; it's only when we do it that people call us xenophobic. Also it is a question of poverty. Anyway, it is when people get poor that they get angry. So long as Côte d'Ivoire was the wealthiest country around, one of the most successful countries in Africa, we were happy to welcome everybody here, but now that there is no more money and people have trouble making enough for a single meal, we don't want all these extra people. So our xenophobia does not come naturally to us; it is provoked.

This critical commentary demonstrates several points simultaneously. First, it clearly illustrates a parallel set of oppositions concerning national identity, migration, and labor:

West African immigrants : Ivoirians :: Ivoirian immigrants : French

Second, Henri's analogy demonstrates that Ivoirians had no problem doing demeaning work, so long as it reflected their social position as immigrants in a host society.[3] In their own society, this kind of work was meant for people below them on the Ivoirian cosmology of "cultural evolution," the *gaous*. In turn, the Burkinabes and other immigrants were thought to be content to do this labor in Côte d'Ivoire for the same reasons that Ivoirians would work in Europe: they did not lose face while in a foreign society. Ostensibly, they were there to make money and return to their home countries.[4] Third, Henri justified the rise in xenophobia, unflinchingly comparing the Ivoirian position to that of Nazi Germany in relation the Jewish population. While he argued that people were economically led to drive away immigrants because of the lack of work, this argument did not reflect the reality of the job market. I regularly saw Ivoirians reject available job openings out of pride, while immigrants continually complained that they found it impossible to get any decent jobs because of their nationality. Finally, it is a clear account of the Ivoirian "cosmological order of nations" (Malkki 1995) through which Ivoirians understand their place in the world and their access to power within it.

Kinship, Economy, and Gendered Sociality

In order to understand how resources are socially distributed, it is important to come to terms with the ways in which ideas of kinship structure social relations and exchange. As we shall see, gender is a key aspect of how kinship manifests itself in these urban exchange networks. Analyzing how domestic relationships are transformed in the urban setting, Vidal (1991) argued in her article "Guerre des sexes à Abidjan" that men and women find themselves in structurally antagonistic roles in a struggle over control of the economic resources of the household. Her fieldwork took place during the heyday of capitalist expansion of the 1970s, when a growing middle class was able to redefine itself in urban domestic spaces.[5] While women were no longer necessarily the principal laborers, as in the agricultural system (Etienne 1983, 1997), urban husbands expected their wives to hand over their monthly profits, following village norms of cash crop agriculture, and women were reluctant to give up their only source of autonomy. To further complicate the matter, many men felt that, ideally, they would prefer that their wives stay home and take charge of the household, leaving them to provide and control all financial income: "When the husband's revenue is enough to maintain the household, it is not rare for him to forbid his wife or wives to work" (Vidal 1991:135). Abidjan's domestic spaces were thus modeled upon an imagined European ideal, even as they often continued to conform to rural Ivoirian systems. Urban men hoped to be the "breadwinners" of the family complemented by homebound housewives, but women resisted such attempts to cut off their access to external wages, and most families couldn't afford to limit themselves to a single income.

For lower-class men economic success depended heavily upon informal peer networks spread across the city to gain access to the profits of the second economy. These were conduits for both information and wealth and required maintenance through regular exchange and acts of generosity, and they expanded upon the basis of reputation or "fame" in Munn's sense (1986). Income generated from this shadow economy was filtered through a hierarchical and flexible patron-client system of *vieuxpères* and *fistons*, modeled on the relationship between fathers and sons. *Fistons* regularly passed portions of their profits to their metaphorical fathers, the *vieux-pères*, who in turn gave them assignments from which they could generate more profit. Actors also built up egalitarian ties of mutual aid and carefully established trust over the long term—rare sources of stability in a social world where betrayal was expected. These ties were built and maintained through small exchanges and moments of collective waste, in which large sums were spent all at once. Such relationships were often characterized with the Nouchi words *frésang* and *bramogo*. *Frésang* is clearly taken from the French *frère sang* or "blood brother," thus making an explicit biological reference in a non kin relationship, while *bramogo* was said to be related to the Dioula word for "kin." Denot writes that Abidjanais youth networks are mechanisms of dependence and fidelity modeled upon kinship. "Brothers" share everything: "food, sometimes earnings, medical costs, various savings or collective pools of money, etc. . . . The groups are characterized by a spirit of fraternity." Furthermore, Denot describes the rituals surrounding entrance into the criminal network, saying that "the new arrival submits to an initiation which works both to reinforce the cohesion of the group and to attribute a street name like Khadafi" (1990:136). One of these initiations was portrayed in De Latour's ethno-fiction film based on Abidjan youth called *Bronx-Barbès* (2000). When the protagonist completes his first real criminal job, his *vieuxpère* buys him a brand-new outfit and brings him back to their *ghetto*, where the other *fistons* circle around him and chant his new name, Solo de Grand B. The idiom of kinship is further asserted in the *nouchi* funeral, which might take place with the actual corpse present in a *ghetto*, as a ritual separate from and parallel to the actual family funeral. Thus, the criminal network was a space of intimacy, of personal ties based on trust and fictive blood, the vulnerable connections of which are kept concealed in so far as it is possible.

In contrast to this constructed kinship, women remained embedded within what appeared as "real" kin networks. However, this was not the classic picture of unilineal kinship structure with corporate groups that anthropologists once found everywhere they turned. In villages, where these institutions remained principal social institutions (see, for example, Guerry 1975; Dozon 1985; and Gottlieb 1992), urban residents retained affiliation with these larger kinship structures from a distance, but within the city kinship was organized in much the same fashion as men's peer groups.

Figure 4. A group of *frésangs* on their way to buy palm wine. *Left to right*: Luc, Solo, Christophe, and Mory. The large boulevard Giscard d'Estaing cuts off France-Amérique from the rest of Treichville.

Relatives traced their connections through loose networks that were maintained through informal patterns of exchange and mutual support. Urban marriage had less to do with relationships between lineages or securing rights to children and was increasingly a kind of luxury, a *rite de prestige* proving one's modernity, financial stability, and ability to free oneself from dependence on kin. Vidal (1991) argues that the wealthier a man was the less likely he he was to allow his wife to work, because her deviation from the modern housewife role was seen as compensating for some lack in his own productive ability. Furthermore, Etienne has pointed out that marriage was not in many women's interests, because younger men "tended to perceive the role of wife in terms of the European model, expecting her to be constantly attentive to her husband's needs, serving him, his children and frequent visitors to the home. Such a husband may also be oriented towards the model of the nuclear family . . . unwilling to maintain a wife's junior kin" (1983:315). While Etienne describes traditional Baoulé kinship patterns as providing complementary gender roles in which women had economic independence, this model has become less and less common for conjugal relationships in Abidjan. Nor should this be reduced to the husband's desires. As Luc, who aimed to become a mechanic, explained, "Usually you can't get married even if you want to, because the parents will only let a girl get married to someone who has money, a job, and a way to support them both. It is the man who needs to get a house for them to live in too." Thus, it was a devotion to the letter of European marriage ideology that hindered marriage rather than a rejection of its values. Most men and women engaged in polyamorous sexual relations instead, often resulting in children, and this was considered normal well into one's thirties. Childcare for single mothers was typically shared by the woman's extended urban kin network, and so children were not perceived as a limitation on a woman's capacity for income or an obstacle to her desirability. Luc continued:

> Everyone has children without worrying about it. The woman keeps the children and lives with her parents and the guy sends money to help support them, but they are not connected unless they want to be. Most men also have multiple girlfriends, some have as many as eight. And then when a man dies it gets really complicated to work out the inheritance. Everyone is trying to get their share. But for all those he's lost interest in or who live far away, forget it, out of luck.

The man did not always accept paternity; he expressed his fatherhood through recurring gifts to the children and family that took care of them. Even inheritance patterns, which were once dominated by more formal kin relations, had become influenced by informal relations expressed through exchange. A child would only be able to claim inheritance from his father if the latter had recognized him through unregulated gift exchange during his lifetime. This was the more practiced form of urban kin alliance, and like most network relations, it was informal and voluntary.

The argument that urban kinship works more like voluntary personal networks was made much earlier by Boswell, writing about Lusaka:

> Generally speaking bonds of kinship are enduring but actual relationships may become dormant and only be resuscitated at certain stages in the life cycle or in particular situations . . . [and] which connections are actuated and which are left dormant result from the reactions of the parties concerned. Usually only fragments of the kinship universe are present in any one town, and the members may even then be widely scattered and in different occupations. . . . Whether putative or real these kinship connections are optative in as far as they are actuated. It is up to the individuals to decide which contacts to use and which to ignore. (Boswell 1969:288)

In this way, kinship can be construed as a crucial force in urban life, but one that was "actuated" according to the same principles of the personal network—that is, the voluntary exchange of information, services, and gifts. It is in this sense that its power to structure relationships was decentralized, even though the bonds of kinship were technically permanent and involuntary. The argument is important, because it is crucial to understanding the extent to which social relationships in Abidjan were mediated by material exchanges under an ethos of moral economy.

Women, as the de facto line of descent in urban Ivoirian society, were more invested than men in the kin networks that supported their children. They spent more time than men maintaining distant kin relations, traveling around the city and even to their parents' villages on a regular basis. This kin network formed their primary source of financial support. In addition, because they were not shamed by taking on menial labor, they were far more likely to have a steady income, even though they were unlikely to bring in windfall sums the way men did with the informal economy. Since the fall of the Ivoirian economy, women have increasingly found work (up to 47% in 1992 from 38% in 1979) (Le Pape 1997:90). The number of economically active women almost doubled in Côte d'Ivoire between 1996 and 2006, going from 1,722,000 to 3,290,000 (African Development Bank Group 2007) though such enumeration cannot possibly take into account all of the income generated by women, since they too make significant earnings in the informal sector. I am here primarily interested in the kinds of work taken on by young women between fifteen and thirty-five. While older women were just as likely to be involved in petty commerce, there were also significant numbers of older women who became proprietors of small businesses like *maquis* or hair salons, and dominant market women who had accumulated significant wealth.

Women had a variety of "legitimate" jobs available to them, working as maids, as seamstresses, or in hair salons—none of these well remunerated. Small-scale commerce was probably the most common source of income: running stalls in the market, selling street food, or working as *marchandes ambulantes*, selling *pagnes* (print textiles), water, fruit, or other sundries. Le Pape also described "illegal" women's commerce, his principal example being the sale of palm wine, or *bangi* (Le Pape 1997). Other examples would be selling *koutoukou* (homemade liquor) or running the ubiquitous, suspiciously low-rate cell phone stands.

Much more profit was available to women willing to work in a *maquis*, where they were paid relatively well and earned occasional tips, free meals, and drinks from men attempting to seduce them. Indeed, even female clientele profited by accepting gifts in exchange for varying degrees of sexual attention, and this can be seen here as a principal way through which women gained access to the profits of the criminal economy. The overlap between bargirls and practices of "transactional sex" connects to a longstanding and growing ethnographic literature suggesting that women's acceptance of money or gifts for sexual favors often does not typically carry the same kind of stigma that one finds in North Atlantic societies, even if sex itself very well might (Dinnan 1983; Hunter 2002; Wojcicki 2002; Chernoff 2003; Cole 2004; Undie and Benaya 2006). As Cornwall describes for Ado-Ado, Nigeria, "Many talk of money as productive, rather than expressive, of love: money can buy love, at least until the cash runs out" (2002:977). In either instance, money is not the antithesis of sentiment, but an integral part of it, and therefore it would be a projection of Euro-American values to describe "transactional sex" in urban Africa as the result of a process of commodification.

However, women in *maquis* were also looked down upon as *godraps* by more "proper" women and had more difficulty maintaining long-term relationships with men, because they were constantly under suspicion of cheating and impropriety. *Godraps* were distinguished from prostitutes by *nouchi*, even though both groups were promiscuous and both expected money in exchange for sex, because the *godrap* chose her relationships and where and when she might have sex, while a prostitute simply sat at her doorstep waiting for passersby (see Cornwall 2002 and Wojcicki 2002 for comparison). A prostitute was a professional, while a *godrap* simply enjoyed nightlife, nice clothes, and having a good time and used men to pay for these things. According to Chernoff, the *ashawos* (Ghanaian versions of the Ivoirian *godraps*) were disrespected neither for their promiscuity nor for their reliance upon money from sex; their controversiality derived from their freedom from familial and patriarchal control (2003:74). *Godraps* were at once scorned by "proper" women (especially married women or daughters in wealthier families) yet appreciated more generally for their wit, free-spirited lifestyle, and pragmatic, streetwise independence. As Cole writes of Madagascar,

> All girls who engage in the game of sex for money are constantly involved in a politics of reputation. They balance precariously between a basic cultural acceptance of youthful sexuality and a strong sense that after a short period of searching, young women should be married off and in the home. Although the idea of women married and in the home has always been more relevant to middle class than lower class notions of adult femininity, it is an ideal that many urbanites seek to achieve, even if financial circumstances prevent most people from doing so. (Cole 2004:9)

Similarly, women in Abidjan had to balance between the pride of economic success and independent streetwise survival they could get through the sexual economy and their failure to follow normative standards beyond their reach. Furthermore, as in writings by Hunter (2002) and Cornwall (2002), women often needed the income from sexual relationships with men in order to afford the clothes that provided them with the ability to bluff in the first place.

A perfect example of the two-sided nature of Ivoirian perspectives on femininity can be found in the advice column printed in *Gbich!*. The column was called "Courrier Drap," and it always included two responses to the letter it printed, one from a character named Godra and the other called Madouce (my sweet). The woman writing in February 2001 explained that she had been having an affair with a married forty-year-old man for four years. She was a university student living on campus, and he had furnished her room with such luxuries as a television, refrigerator, and cookstove. However, when she mentioned her desire to get married, he not only broke up with her, but also took back, without warning, everything he had given her. While Madouce accused the girl of being materialistic and told her to leave this married man to his guilt and move on and find a nice unattached man, Godra had a different perspective:

> If he hasn't already taken the bed, tell him to come and take that too! What does he think this is? You gave him four years good and loyal service and this is how he thanks you? Why can't they even change a little? My dear, you must threaten him. Wherever he put those things, he has to bring them back as soon as possible or you will go and *djafoule* [make a scene, scream][6] at his wife's house. He has cheated on her with you all this time, and he doesn't even have shame at his age. My dear, he didn't build you a house. He didn't buy a car for you. You gave him your body, and in exchange, he bought you all these things. He better go bring it back pronto! ("Courrier Drap" 2001:10)

Godrap is a catchall term covering everything from materialistic party girls to women that had left their families to those that survived through "transactional sex" (Hunter 2002). Paradoxically, while being *godrap* signified a form of financial independence, it ironically also referred to their reliance upon sexual relationships with men. At the same time, however, women served as "gatekeepers" between men and the resources of the kin networks they maintained. As we shall see in the next chapter, women were more successful at drawing on such kin resources because these formed their primary social network, and so they managed transactions between men and kin networks, allowed men access to more distant kin networks, and pressured men to contribute to organizations and life cycle events (funerals, marriages, baptisms, etc.). Thus, there was a kind of complementarity between the resources and rhythms of gendered social networks, though the transfers between these networks were fractious in spirit.

Bizness

Since there was so little acceptable labor available during the time of my fieldwork, most Ivoirian men earned their income through other means, often of dubious legality. These forms of income all fell under the term *bizness*, a Francophone African term used strictly for nefarious exchanges. I learned this term after I insulted a Congolese man in Paris selling CDs on the street. When I asked him how his *bizness* was going, he exclaimed: "I don't do *bizness*! I am a legitimate entrepreneur." Another French word frequently used by Ivoirians in this context is *se debrouiller*, meaning in so-called Standard French to "to manage" or "to make do." Literally, it means "to disentangle oneself." Ivoirians used this term to refer obliquely to all the illicit activities through which they ensured their survival. *Bizness* was the business par excellence of the average male resident of Abidjan's *quartier populaire*. It was my impression that a relatively small number of the people I knew engaged in the more violent crimes like armed robbery, mugging, breaking and entering, and drug dealing (though it was of course impossible to be sure, since such information was not typically given out freely). But almost everyone I knew under the age of forty (and many above) were connected indirectly to this realm. In one way or another, their income derived from the circle of exchange and distribution built around these initial acts of crime.

Frustrated at the difficulties of urban ethnography, I once told Dedy that I wanted to follow some acquaintances on their daily errands and activities. He laughed and said this was completely impossible.

> Youths like that [my acquaintances] may dress well during the day, but at night they are hoodlums. If you ask them what kind of work they do, they will tell you they don't have work. Many, many youths in Abidjan are out of work. They will say that life is hard, but they *se debrouillent* to live. They are what the Nouchi call *chercheurs*, they hunt for any kind of *bizness* to make money to live on. If you ask them what they do, they will never specify. It is too dangerous, because anyone can name them and they go to prison.

A *chercheur* was a sort of hunter, a man seeking money by any means possible. Men without fixed income spent their days gathering leads and information to the various scams, robberies, and deals going on, hoping to pick up some percentage of it. Most of the time, the *chercheur* made money as a middleman, profiting from the discrepancy of information between two people in an exchange. A key aspect of the *chercheur*'s skill was his ability to deceive the relevant parties in order to get a larger portion of the profit, and in this way the art of the bluff was tellingly linked to the skills necessary for economic productivity. A perfect example is found in one of *Gbich!*'s regular cartoons. It follows the adventures of a character called Cauphy Gombo, whose last name means both an okra stew and a deal. Beneath his name runs a description: "Cauphy Gombo, a businessman . . . is first of all a *chercheur* (*il se cherche*). Considering himself merciless and without scruple, his motto is 'NO PITY IN BIZNESS.' For him, every occasion is good for earning money. He wants to 'eat' something from everything."

The following is a brief list of the kinds of *bizness* activities upon which urban *guerriers* (warriors) made their living:

gardien (security guard): A form of employment typically chosen by *loubards* was to work as a guard. This was one of the most legal forms of employment available. It could involve anything from protecting politicians to standing guard at banks or working as a nightclub bouncer. However, the most important income from such jobs typically came from the subsidiary activities they allowed (examples include taking a cut of the entrance fee, directing customers to drug dealers or prostitutes, and picking the pockets of drunk clients).

djossieur de nama (car watcher): Young *nouchi* kids often made money watching over parked cars for tips—a kind of extortion, since refusal to tip could invite violence. This was especially profitable at nightclubs, since the clientele was wealthier and could be very generous. Access to these jobs was controlled by an older leader, often a *loubard*, who took a cut of the profits.

zero-zero (phone fraud): Phones, especially cell phones, presented an entire gamut of legitimate and illegitimate sources of income. Since cell phone owners could receive calls for free in Côte d'Ivoire, while calling people was expensive, people set up competitively priced cell phone booths all over town, selling call time at lower-than-usual rates. These rates were achieved by setting up accounts under false names and not paying the bills, stealing the accounts or SIM cards of others, or working out an under-the-counter deal with a phone employee. A stolen European phone would be used for cheap international calls until its owner was able to shut down the account. Landlines were also vulnerable, and *nouchi* would branch a victim's phone line late at night, run it into their own home or office, and set up shop selling cheap international calls. Some were only open for *bizness* at night and detached the wires in the day to avoid detection.

camoracien (forger): Forging papers was an extremely profitable career specialty. The most sought-after papers were passports and visas for Europe or the United States, papers that were practically impossible to attain through proper channels, requiring bribes, connections, and luck. *Camoraciens* considered these documents unforgeable, but stolen documents could be doctored successfully at enormous profit. They could find more steady income through the forgery of all the paperwork surrounding these principal documents: identification, attestations of work for the last three years, a statement from the boss permitting a vacation, and bank statements demonstrating sufficient funding for the voyage. Another *bizness* was the forgery of visa stamps for other African countries, to make the client look well traveled, since this improved the chances of getting a visa. Less honest forgers sometimes asked for money up front to get access to certain documents, saying they would bring the whole portfolio when it was ready, and then ran off with the money, disappearing into another quarter.

chantage (extortion, blackmail): While there were many forms of this activity, the one I often heard about was the impersonation of police officers to exact bribes from criminals caught in the act. Dedy had a military issue belt that he used to convince people he was undercover. A variant of this was to work in collusion with real police officers. Sometimes Dedy walked up to a site of suspicious activity while dialing the police on his cell phone, threatening to explain the situation. If he came across a large-scale activity, he might bring in a couple of officers he knew personally in exchange for a cut of whatever they confiscated. Because this threatened the moral boundaries of the *nouchi* networks, it was an extremely dangerous activity.

keneur (dealer): By far the most common source of income were *kens*, or deals. According to my informants, the origins of the word stem from the character Caine, played by David Carradine in the *Kung Fu* television series. The *keneur* acted as a middleman, selling stolen goods on the street. This could work several ways. One could purchase the object from the thief at a low price and sell it to someone else. A more common arrangement was to work for the thief, selling the object and taking a percentage of the profit, or selling the object at a higher prince than the thief specified and keeping the extra. Alternatively, one could find clients and bring them into contact with *rese* (resellers, fences) and exact a finder's fee. The symbolic relationship of masculinity, economy, and sex is revealed by the word *ken* also referring to a sexual exchange with a woman.

These are a selection of the most frequent kinds of roles people assumed in the "informal" economic sphere, but there are endless varieties and innovations based on these themes.

When I first asked Dedy what he did for a living, since he had no job, he described the classic *keneur* scenario: "Voilà. I do numerous things. I often hear that someone is trying to sell something, and then I find a buyer who is willing to pay a bit more, or I get the first guy to diminish their price, and I take the difference. Thus, the other day when I greeted the guy and I asked, 'Il y a quel manzements?' I was asking if he had anything for me to sell." However, he went on to describe a great variety of activities. For example, he worked as a kind of lawyer, mixing himself up in any kind of dispute, verbal or physical, and fighting for the defense of one side. One couple in which the boyfriend beat his girlfriend often used Dedy as an intermediary, and from time to time they gave him tips. As Dedy put it, "Sometimes when there are accidents or fights I intervene or help sort things out, and people give me something in return. I work like a hero in American films. If there is a burning building I can go in and save people. Only I don't usually get very much in return." This was a twenty-four-hour on-call job. People came to him at any time asking for his help in one matter or another, and he always had his eyes and ears open for something to do. As I got to know him better, I realized that he dabbled in crime as well. He was an expert in *chantage*, using an old security card from a former job and a police officer's belt he had acquired at some point as his proof of identification.[7] He did indeed enter a burning building when the Belleville market caught fire, but while working to protect stores from thieves he grabbed a few things of his own. To my knowledge, he no longer participated in armed robbery, though he admitted to having done this in his youth. I did find out about an incident in which he broke into someone's apartment, and it is quite possible that he stole several cell phones people accused him of taking (sometimes using me as a cover without my knowledge). He also occasionally worked as a police informer with people outside Treichville. Finally, he specialized in befriending Europeans who for whatever reasons found themselves in Treichville. He very rarely demanded money directly, but he always got something out of these relationships (including the one he had with me, of course).

There was no economic security in such forms of labor, and each day was a hunt for *manzements*. Like Dedy, most of the people I knew did not limit themselves to any one of these roles, even if they had more expertise in some than others. They dabbled in whatever they could find, trying to catch any potential *manzements* before anyone else in a very competitive field. Indeed, I suspect that a great deal more people worked "real" part time jobs than were willing to admit it. As I got to know people better, I found that they sometimes worked as apprentices to tailors, in coffee shops, as cell phone booth attendants, in the port painting boats, or in road construction. They simply lied about where they had been, saying they had been napping all day, or out drinking, rather than admit they had taken jobs they were not proud of. Nevertheless, even with the importance of reputation at stake, it is hard to understand how *bizness* made sound financial sense.

Early on in my study, confused over the daily economics of Abidjan, I asked an acquaintance named Eric how so many people in Abidjan managed to survive without work. His explanation for the success of *bizness* was rather surprising:

> *Bizness*! In fact, many Ivoirians prefer not to work. When you have a job your life is often harder than without, so people prefer to *se debrouiller*. This way they get 20,000 here, 5,000 there, they make do, they celebrate. In any case someone with a job will usually spend the whole month's paycheck in the first week and have to *se debrouiller* for the rest of the time. I myself tend to find that I often make more money if I stay home than if I go to work. And people often feel that it is better to live this way than to have a salary of 100,000. Because if you have a good job your whole family will expect you to get a big house for all of them, then you have your wife to take care of, and you can no longer ask other people for money because they know you have money. Everyone comes to you for help. So in the end you have even less money and more problems. If you stay at the house with your parents and find *bizness* no one will harass you. So many people choose this way. And you have to also understand that people here live in groups. This is my group here, at P.J. [a *maquis* named after the former job of the owner, an abbreviation of Police Judiciare]. I know that when I have money I will take them out and buy food and drink, and vice versa. We take care of each other and we live the good life. It is the Ivoirian way. We have nothing, but we are happy; we always enjoy ourselves.

In other words, the social obligation to share with kin and close friends was so strong that having a real job was too high profile. Everyone was aware how much money you had and the exact day you received your paycheck. The situation is comparable to that of U.S. urban poverty in Bourgois's *In Search of Respect* (2002) or Stack's *All Our Kin* (1997), where any visible money that entered into the social network was immediately siphoned off into maintaining social relations and paying preexisting debts. In Abidjan it was impossible to refuse money to family; such a breach of kinship was likely to bring on attacks of witchcraft. Friends were almost as hard to refuse, particularly when they knew you had the money. Because these urban "gangs" were like surrogate families, similar principles of exchange and dispersal reigned. Like many Abidjan residents, Eric lived with his parents even though he was in his midthirties. He no longer had a job, and he made his living though all sorts of petty exchange on the fringe of the criminal network. Thus, the secrecy of dealings within the networks also provided a screen through which to limit the social obligations of a moral economy where wealth should be shared—this was often asserted as a reason why it was better to make money illegitimately than have a job.

The Productivity of Social Networks

These networks were not organized into clearly bounded gangs—they might even be completely unaware of the others' existence. Nor were *fistons* exclusively loyal to a single *vieuxpère*—they were likely to have several contacts they maintained through occasional exchanges, and their service could be easily secured through distribution. Because of this loose structure, whose bonds of loyalty were based on informal exchanges, those within the system could not possibly be aware of the entire structure of relations or even sure of their positions within it. The greater the mystery of this network, the more imagined possibilities for power lay within it, and the fewer opportunities actors provided their friends to duplicitously profit from them by manipulating insecurities in the network. This network was thus a vast system of exchange through which information, goods, and prestige were circulated, but most actors didn't know the origins or destinations of the objects of exchange. Their ability to profit depended upon their mastery of the social network and who knew whom.

For a middleman, the amount of money one could skim off the top relied on finding the right sellers and buyers, on a detailed knowledge of the social position and connections of each participant in the deal, and on the ability to deceive those involved as to the "real" value of the exchange. This was precisely the source of prestige of the successful *keneur*; he boasted that he was more *yere* than his peers, able to outmaneuver sellers, buyers, police, and the victims searching for their stolen goods. He was claiming superior urban sensibility, which translated as a higher degree of practical social knowledge.

The Brick was a tall, somewhat portly figure who spent most of his time at the *ghetto* next to the cinema and had a wide network of *fistons* working beneath him. He told me he was the King of Thieves, though I never met anyone else who agreed with the designation. He explained gleefully how a *vieuxpère* could live without even stealing a thing, by gleaning information, knowing "everything that happens." He elaborated:

> For example, with the *reses* [fences] you can do *chantage*. When you get your hands on a stolen phone, you have one of your *petits* sell the phone, then a couple of hours later, *on les bombe* [you catch the buyers]. I tell them there is *drap dessus* [the real owner has found out about the deal] and I will beat them up if they don't give it back. Then I give it to some other youths, who sell it to someone else. Sometimes I sell the same phone ten times in this way, and each time I get a cut of the action.

To accomplish this kind of con clearly required acute knowledge of the social network linking the various actors in each deal. If ever stolen property passed into the hands of someone who knew the victim, or should the victim of a *chantage* learn of the scam pulled on him, the Brick and his associates could find themselves in serious trouble. Thus, the critical avenue to success in this realm was the accumulation of *fistons*, followers who respected your street credibility enough to pass you information, goods, and profit. The status of *vieuxpère* could only be achieved by building up a name for oneself and gathering followers who would treat you as one. Furthermore, the strength of his position in the network guaranteed him a much higher degree of security than many of his victims.

In dialectical fashion, I would argue that these *bizness* deals took place precisely to maintain and reinforce personal networks. Although stolen objects should theoretically be sold much cheaper than new ones for the buyer, I was surprised to find that often, when all aspects were taken under consideration, the price was not so far removed. For example, a stolen Siemens C-25 cell phone was sold on the black market for approximately 30,000 CFA ($45). The card required to activate it would probably be sold separately for another 3,000–5,000 CFA. The charger would also need to be purchased, for another few thousand. Finally, in order to use the phone, the purchaser had to buy minutes from the cell phone company. When I bought my new phone of the same make and model, it cost 60,000 CFA, but it came with everything, including 20,000 CFA worth of minutes. In this way, the purchaser of a stolen phone only saved a few thousand CFA (a matter of several dollars). Furthermore, because the thieves could not safely sell the phone themselves, they relied on *chercheurs* to fence the product, who ended up with a significant portion of the profit. The *chercheurs* themselves typically ended up paying a finder's fee to yet another party, who brought them a buyer. The thief was obligated to part with another percentage to support his *vieuxpère* (who protected him and kept him informed of potential *manzements*). When all said and done, it was not uncommon for a thief to make only 10,000 CFA on the deal ($15). As I tried to understand the allure of this market, it occurred to me that *bizness* was worth so much effort because the money spent in these situations was reinvested in the network itself. Instead of spending the money on a brand-new product and supporting corporations, Treichville residents preferred to spend the money on people in their own community, simultaneously reinforcing social resources that could be drawn on again. Thus, *bizness* was not a more efficient economic system, but a more moral one, in the sense that it redistributed the benefits of exchange within the community of the actors engaging in it. Although a *keneur* with a personal network combining multiplex connections, span, and density was certainly more likely to produce successful *bizness*, that very *bizness* reciprocally supported the personal network surrounding a given social actor.

Indeed, a sociological study by Henry and Mars (1978) supports this claim, arguing that stolen goods are transferred to an "amateur trading sphere" which does not operate according to normal market principles. They suggest that within this sphere not only are trades regulated by sets of personal obligation, neighborhood, and kinship ties, but also, most importantly for my argument here, that these trades rarely make much profit. But the paradox of the Treichville moral economy is that while the entire economic structure of *bizness* depended on theft, theft threatened the very community that it sustained and was therefore an act interpreted as inherently antisocial and immoral. Like the mythical Ouroboros that eats its own tail, this is a self-consuming form of economic production. Ultimately, the prestige of the successful *chercheur* was built upon their flamboyant ability to manipulate their social connections for personal gain, and the gain they derived rested finally upon the victimization of others connected at least circumstantially to their network. Like the zero-sum game of Ivoirian witchcraft beliefs, in which personal gain was always at the expense of one's own kin, the *chercheur* became well known only by siphoning off the income of others in the community. Taken too far, the hierarchical principle of the criminal network was unstable and likely to self-implode, as the fame of success within this system could produce greater resentment than respect from the community that supported one's status. As I shall explore in the following chapter, such success must be balanced carefully by spectacular acts of redistribution.

There is a darker side to this portrait of urban economy however, and this is where the "morality" of the system breaks down. In marveling as I have at the importance of reciprocal exchange and mutual support in these networks, one should not forget that they relied on the often violent expropriation of wealth from those disconnected enough from the social networks to be incapable of retaliation. Those urban residents most often in this position were precisely those described as *gaous* by the *nouchi*, and this may well have contributed to the growing resentment and divisive identities that brought on the Ivoirian crisis in 2002.

The Normative Network

The characteristics of *bizness* described above gain comprehensibility when we shift our focus to the social networks underlying all economic activity. Indeed, it was within these networks that *value* was produced, expressed through the symbolic transfers of wealth that maintained social bonds.[8] I argue that these networks, flexible, mutating, overlapping, and unbounded though they might be, were nevertheless the central organizing principle of Treichville society, and even Abidjan as a whole. It was the interlocking web of these networks that produced at once a viable economic system, a moral order, and a form of social insurance in times of trouble.

I have described economic survival in Treichville as a hunt, a daily search for deals and scams of all varieties. Finding a *ken* and completing a transaction before anyone else meant having greater access to the information circulating in the *radio trottoir*. Maintaining and expanding one's set of social relations was therefore crucial to economic success. MacGaffey and Bazenguissa-Ganga (2000) have likewise argued that informal economy, particularly in African contexts, is dominated by networks of personal ties built upon trust and obligation. The longer I lived in Treichville, the more I realized how tightly interwoven these overlapping informal networks were. I found that my "snowball" technique increasingly led me in elaborate circles back to others I had already met. By no means did everybody know everybody else, as in the classic village scenario, but there were typically not very many degrees of separation between any two given people. In one memorable example, I was shocked to find that the France-Amérique gang on one side of the quarter was going to the same funeral as Dedy on the opposite side. Luc was hoping to seduce a woman who had lived in his village, a cousin of the deceased, and the deceased was a cousin of

Mimi, Dedy's girlfriend. On arriving at the funeral, I encountered a teenager from yet a third circle of acquaintances. Even though each network was built from egocentric social obligations, constantly shifting according to transformations in affiliation, there was a larger force binding the whole together in an abstract way. This larger entity could not be reckoned in terms of boundaries or membership, but only as a sense of belonging to a community (and such belonging was itself a matter of negotiation at any given moment). I would like to suggest that this network, however fluid, was actually a normative force, a source of moral order.

Indeed, Epstein (1992) argued in the Rhodes-Livingston reports that networks might well be the source of new urban norms. Demonstrating that in many areas traditional norms have been undermined, he also points out that new norms emerge in response to a specifically urban environment. But how are such norms produced and spread throughout the community? Epstein makes the fascinating argument that gossip is the medium through which such normative structures are disseminated: "The closer the bonds of relationship, the more intimate or even esoteric the gossip, and the more trite or meaningless it will appear to outsiders. For one of the functions of gossip for those who are party to it is to define or reaffirm the norms regulating behavior among themselves, and marking themselves off from others" (1992:95). Epstein was building up the work of Gluckman (1963), who argued that gossip is always an exclusive practice, marking both the subjects and recipients of the rumor as inside in opposition to those who are not party to the story at hand. These two forces go hand in hand: the emergence of a norm and the emergence of a boundary. But in the urban field it is never so simple, because there is no clear-cut group boundary, only overlapping personal networks. Thus, I especially highlight the medium of this emergence, the informal passage of information between a series of dyadic personal contacts. Gossip (or any other exchange of information) is a way of maintaining social relationships while excluding those from whom the information is withheld. Furthermore, gossip is only interesting when it concerns other people who *belong* to the same network of relations. But more importantly, the very nature of gossip is to discuss out-of-the-ordinary social activities, that is, activities that in some way breach the quotidian norms of behavior. When gossip is deprecatory, it challenges the membership of those who have in some way transgressed such norms. For example, Dedy was accused behind his back of stealing a cell phone from the owner of the *maquis* across the street from his *cour commune*. Up until that point he had frequented the *maquis* practically every day, but even though he protested his innocence and no proof was ever uncovered, he never returned to that *maquis* during the rest of my research. Everyone knew that Dedy was a thief; this in itself did not damage his reputation. Rather, the gossip surrounding the event focused upon the violation of the norm of community. He was accused of stealing from someone in his own neighborhood. Whether or not the story was true, it simultaneously reinforced the norms surrounding whom one could steal from and excluded Dedy from a section of his former social network. The norms Epstein refers to should not be confused with rules, which have greater rigidity and cohesiveness. Rather they exist as diffuse, unspoken sentiments, lying latent until they collide with a particular concrete event, around which the buzz of gossip produces a collective representation of moral reaction and, hence, a fleeting but real normative order. The group exists only in the set of people drawn around a particular conflict or life crisis event.

Le Pape vividly describes the drama of struggling against anonymity in Abidjan, and the necessity of a social network for self-preservation, particularly in moments of accusation:

> Constructing a good reputation obviously results from putting into practice [norms of behavior], but this alone is not enough, because it depends equally on the relationships maintained between each and his/her community of origin and with the urban networks issuing from this community. Not because "traditional" values continue to orient behavior, but because, in cases of danger, a *citadin*'s defense rests on the mobilization of support. This appears clearly in court cases, without revealing the "work" which preceded such mobilization. By contrast, one knows, from having witnessed it directly, what kinds of investments of time, money and energy underlie such collective support. . . . This [is a] necessity of urban life: the struggle against anonymity which menaces the weak, the anonymity which permits anybody to accuse you of doing anything, or of doing anything to you. (Le Pape 1997:47)

Here we clearly see precisely the interconnections between the maintenance of social ties and one's ability to negotiate social crises. A good reputation, though vital, is not enough, for without proper social support, a mere unfounded accusation can threaten one's entire social identity.

State Intervention/State Cooperation

Although Treichville residents took theft very seriously, to involve the police was considered a far greater betrayal than the theft itself. The greater the social distance between thief and victim, the more likely police would be involved; one could not call the police on someone within one's own sphere of social relations without bringing retribution upon oneself. Even those with relatively honest livings, like Moussa the tailor, were loath to call the police, for undoubtedly some of his friends were involved in more nefarious undertakings, and it was very dangerous to be known as a police collaborator.

Furthermore, policemen were themselves often incorporated into criminal networks. Like the *vieuxpères* who sent their *fistons* out to rob for them, a policeman was reported to be involved in Treichville carjacking, in exchange for a cut of the take. Even once a criminal was taken into custody, it was common knowledge that the police could always be paid off to let their charge go. Therefore, the police integrated with the *nouchi* networks at various points and could be considered part of the social system. And even at higher levels of the state, the informal economy structured relations. According to popular belief at least, Houphouët-Boigny actually subsidized the criminal network from the late 1980s until his death, paying gang leaders 50,000 CFA a month in exchange for their cooperation in his political projects—the most famous case being that of Thierry Zebié, who was lynched for his role in helping the military defeat the student demonstrations demanding multipartyism (Grebalé 2001).

Further bizarre overlappings are found in the way that former gangs worked as *grandfrères du quartier* to protect the neighborhood from the very crimes they were committing elsewhere. Thus, the *loubard* Gros Guerrier had been part of the gang named Ma Police, a name that highlights the strange ambiguity of these structures, which at once served to protect their neighborhoods and rob from their community. And indeed the state sometimes made use of this service from the criminal networks as well: the most interesting example of this was when an external security company partnered itself with Treichville's mayor and the gang organization to produce a neighborhood security force. In other words, the gangs were essentially hired to protect Treichville from themselves. The system fell apart after only a year however, from lack of funds. The mayor complained in one public meeting that he continued to be harassed by former gang members demanding continued compensation for their efforts. Dedy was very proud of his time in this security force and continued to use his official Sécurité card to frighten thieves into giving him their loot in exchange for their freedom.

Such ambiguous relationships between the state and criminal social organizations are increasingly widespread in postcolonial Africa generally

Figure 5. Sergent Deutogo's last name literally translates as "two 100 CFA coins," the equivalent of 25 U.S. cents. In his stories he is usually at a police checkpoint and he always finds a way to collects two *togos* from someone. He is utterly corrupt and values only his bribe. In this cartoon, a taxi stopped at the checkpoint has two robbers holding the driver at gunpoint. They tell the driver to pay the police officer without causing trouble. The driver nervously whispers to Sergeant Deutogo that there are robbers in the car, but he responds as follows: "And you want me to do what now? Who told you I was hot to catch thieves? Listen well, I am here collecting my coins. Apart from that, I couldn't give a shit. Speaking of which, where is yours? Hand it over now. Pal, you've got manage your problem on your own; I'm not getting involved." At the end, one of the robbers watching from the car remarks that Deutogo took the taxi driver's money. The second responds, "In the end, he and us, we're the same thing." (*Gbich!* 70, no. 6 [February 9–15, 2001].)

(Bayart 1993; Bayart, Ellis, and Hibou 1999; Mbembe 2001; Apter 2005; Comaroff and Comaroff 2006; Ferguson 2006). In Côte d'Ivoire, the police took part in activities of extortion but ironically were often isolated from the system of justice itself. Involving the police was likely to put the thief in jail, and the length of his or her stay could be extended arbitrarily and indefinitely. Condemning a member of one's own circle of relations to imprisonment created a dangerous rift between oneself and the thief's family and close friends, thus cutting off sections of one's network: as such it was a loss of social capital.

Theft within the neighborhood community, while ideologically forbidden, was a relatively common practice, and when made public, such events required careful negotiation (Newell 2006). Since the police were unavailable for mediation, both parties called upon their own social connections to investigate and argue their case, a process which started immediately and whose resolution could take anywhere from minutes to days or even weeks. I witnessed this firsthand several times, including when I myself was robbed early in my fieldwork. Although we located the thieves relatively quickly (an effort that was led by my friends at their own insistence), the matter was dropped when it turned out their network was too closely integrated with that of my friends: the cost of betraying them publicly was too high in comparison with the benefits of protecting me, a relative newcomer. In this way, reputation and public support were crucial to being a successful criminal, and in order to maintain such support criminals needed to be generous and fair with their personal ties.

Thus, whenever disruption of the moral order threatened, justice was negotiated through the network itself—not the network as some abstract principle of interconnected social bonds, but as the specific set of social relationships which radiated out from that event. As Le Pape writes of Abidjan, "Reputation [has] great importance, it acts like 'local regulation' in a context where denunciation is a constant; reputation is, after an event, appreciable, measurable in its effects: the fact of being able to mobilize witnesses (who support you) or at least avoid a coalition of negative witnesses; this is verifiable in all affairs concerning the private life where culpability remains uncertain" (1997:31). The very real fluidity and boundlessness of urban community was confined by the daily mapping of social relations by the actors themselves. When an incident threatening moral order occurred, those involved traced out their relationships in an attempt to sway the outcome. The actors who could prove themselves more embedded in the web of social relations were able to define the terms of discussion and thereby influence the collective representation of the event.

Hierarchical Relations

As the importance of reputation implies, such social influence was not merely a question of the number of contacts in the community, but also of the ways these relations were structured hierarchically. Originally the criminal organization was made up of bounded gangs, each with its own name and territory. By the time of my arrival, no one would admit that gangs existed anymore, though I saw some evidence for remnants of these more formal organizations and occasionally overheard hints that they were re-forming. The most common narrative for why the criminal organizations dissolved was that these well-paid gang leaders had used the surplus money to buy tickets to Paris and depart (this was at the beginning of the popular movement to emigrate that I describe in chap. 5). The other central explanation was that the remaining gang leaders, including Jon Pololo, who had gone to Europe and come back to continue his domination of the Abidjan crime scene, had been killed off after the coup d'état of December 1999, when Guëi promised to "sweep away" corruption. As gang life became more dangerous, large numbers of *loubards* took jobs in "security," working as bouncers in nightclubs or banks and even joining the police force.

These group-oriented gangs had been replaced by more fluid sets of affiliations, structured by hierarchical relations between *vieuxpère* and *fiston*. Since even *vieuxpères* had their *vieuxpères*, the network had a kind of overarching "big man" form of leadership, with encompassing spheres of social influence. I watched this structure play out in decisions over whether Dedy could return to his old market territory. During the time when Treichville organized its gangs into a security force, he had patrolled the market collecting fees from those who insisted on placing their stalls outside the official market area, and even after the town stopped paying them, the same gang continued to collect every Wednesday. Dedy had dropped out of this scene after his failed attempt to reach Europe, which he was to ashamed to admit to his comrades (he had been made a *gaou* by a friend he trusted, who stole his papers). Now he wanted to join the group again, claiming he had been one of the people to set up this *manzement* in the first place. Danny was the current *vieuxpère* of one of the groups patrolling the market, and he supported Dedy's reentry, but the group that controlled the other side objected and insisted the decision be put to a man named Dekets. Although the group insisted that Dekets was not their "chief," the fact that he never showed up and nevertheless received a large portion of the group's collection before it was divided up, and that they all deferred to his decision in the end, clearly points to his hierarchical superiority. Georges, a man from France-Amérique who opposed Dedy's inclusion, ran into me one day and described how the decision had taken place:

> Why didn't you come to the market yesterday? You would have seen that it wasn't my decision to block Dedy. My guy showed up, Dekets (the one who works at Gar de Bassam). I told everyone it wasn't me all along. I was just trying to vaccinate Dedy against the decision that I knew would be made.

Dekets said that we couldn't take Dedy in my group. Not acceptable. He said that Dedy needs to find another terrain in the market, where he can collect for himself. Times are hard right now. One of our guys went to France, that's all, otherwise we used to have six. Now the other group they were six, but didn't like one of the guys and kicked him out, then hired another to take his place, but who doesn't get full payment. Now just because they did that, why should we have to take another guy at full payment? [I then asked him why Dekets got to make the decision.] No he doesn't, we all make it together. Well, its not that he is chief, but Dekets, he is *vieuxpère* to all of us. He has been around longer than all of us and seen more than all of us. So we owe him respect, we have to listen to his opinions. Even Danny, the animal, who kept talking about what would happen if Dedy didn't get a place, threatening us, when he heard our *vieuxpère*'s opinion he went along with it. He is a traitor to Dedy [he snickered]. I was just trying to get Dedy to see reality. I wasn't doing anything behind his back.

Clearly, the decision-making process was a hierarchical one, and so social influence did not depend merely on the span of one's network, but also on the centrality (or "betweenness") of those situated within it. This is illustrated brilliantly in Kapferer's (1969) analysis of a dispute in a Zambian factory, which demonstrates how key figures (those with the most powerful network configurations) not involved in the dispute itself come to control the terms of the debate, often steering the discussion away from the more sensitive issues in order to maintain their own social relationships.

However, it is equally important to understand that such hierarchical predominance is more a function of one's reputation and social connections than it is an institutionalized position. The Brick describes the process through which one attains this kind of position:

To be chief, you don't need to fight. You can, but that's not what's important. Being a chief is about respect; it's about how many people you know, the ordeals you have undergone. The same is true for having a name for yourself. It may be true that you can *chante comme ça* ["sing like that," meaning to scam others well], but the real importance of having a name is that people talk about it to each other, and all the new *petits* of the group want to imitate you. You are known wherever you go. Me, I've done some things. Currently, I've kind of given it up, because I have a family now, and I want to be respected. Prison is not good. But it is through what I have done, the trials I have completed, that I have shown that I have a name. Everyone knows that the Brick has *grand cœur* [courage, fortitude].

All of the *nouchi* had street names—typically taken from Hollywood movies (real examples include Tupac, Scarface, Biggie, Brico, Rock, Gros de Police, DeGaulle, and Chef de Village Molokai). Such names functioned as masks—public identities to which everyone knew the referent, and yet the connection between public name and private person was loose enough to allow for slippage. The way to build up the value of one's name was through legendary acts of display, stories which would circulate through the networks as currency. Thus, in order to cement the strength of their reputation and build *fistons*, actors publicly flaunted their connection to these hidden intimate worlds through what Abidjanais call the bluff.

Social Accumulation

I propose, then, that as counterintuitive as it may seem, the Abidjanais second economy was not motivated by profit in the normal sense of the term. Transactions did not typically produce as much financial gain as one would imagine, and such profits tended to be immediately diffused back into the network in any case. Instead, the economy was dominated by social investments and the maintenance of social relations. The social networks—both male and female—such transactions built were both necessary for survival and the primary source of economic success. Indeed, social connections were so important, and moral obligations to share one's wealth so pervasive, that close friends not uncommonly stole from one another. Even when such crimes came to light, it was difficult to recuperate one's losses, because it was understood that such wealth should have been shared in the first place (Newell 2006). However, these networks were hierarchical, and by increasing one's position and widening one's effective network, it was possible to attain some real economic success. Such profits, as we learn from Jane Guyer (2004), as well as Launay's (1978) study of Ivoirian inter-ethnic transactional spheres, can be found at the points at which different scales of value confront each other and must be converted—in this case the points of contact between legitimate and informal markets. MacGaffey and Bazenguissa-Ganga (2000) found that in the Congolese Parisian informal economy sometimes stolen goods were sold for more than their value in stores, because their stolen character was taken as a guarantee of quality. My own work among Parisian Congolese confirms this, as one of my contacts would buy used name brand labels in the flea markets and sell them on the street for much higher prices. Those further up the hierarchy tended to be the ones in a position to better profit from these moments of conversion, as we saw in the Brick's narrative about reselling the same phone ten times. Furthermore, by exploiting the imperfect knowledge of different segments of their network, *vieuxpères* could avoid some of their obligation to redistribute. It was control over the flow of information (which could only come from a wider social network) that allowed the actor to "get ahead" in a system where all known wealth had to be reallocated.

This final example of one of these tales of glory really embodies the central themes of the chapter—the hierarchical structure of the social network and its relationship to dispersing money, the intimacy of blood brothers, and the importance of both concealment and display. At the same time it points to a dimension only hinted at in this chapter, the relationship between the bluff and modernity, and the ultimate act of consumption: to *monter* (to climb, to go Europe). Ignace, a young Treichville man I had only just met, was excited to introduce me to his "Parisian" friends who had recently returned from Europe to *faire le show*:

> Ousmane and I, we were always together. We suffered in poverty together. . . .
> We struggled to make a living. He found a little job at Grand Paris [a clothing store], and he began to hide money without telling anyone. Even me, his *frésang*, I wasn't kept in the loop. When he saved enough, he sought out a *vieuxpère*. He explained, "I need to flee. There is nothing for me here, I have suffered enough. I have money; it's just a problem of papers. The *vieuxpère* had a *vieuxpère* of his own, who knew how to get papers, so no problem. He prepared everything until, one night, he assembled all of his friends in a hidden corner, and they began to *faire le show*. *Il a gâté la table* [he wasted the table], and now he said: "My boys, I have something to say. I leave tomorrow to *monter*." So we *avons fait le show* until dawn, and at 9 p.m. he left for the airport.

Ousmane had since returned from Europe with a story about a German woman who wanted to marry him, and he now traveled in the more refined circles of the *bengistes* (migrants who had returned). Once a blood brother, Ignace was now clearly a *fiston*, circling his superior in hopes of whatever wealth might come his way.

This complicated and fluid relationship among hierarchy, moral economy, and deception is essential to my arguments in the chapters that follow. I argue that the bluff of success had performative efficacy (it produced real success) because it was at once a demonstration of the strength of one's network and deceptive skill *and* at the same time legitimated one's success through immediate redistribution in the form of food, drinks, and other gifts. Out of these moments, fame circulated along the same pathways as money and commodities and information about the next target of tomorrow's scam. Thus, it was through the intimate pathways of gossip within the criminal "family" that *nouchi* bandits attained a public reputation for success, proven in the performance through which they demonstrated their symbolic mastery of the bluff. Concealment of the public secret, the unarticulated knowledge that the bluff does not index real wealth, allowed the performative act through which *nouchi* transformed the symbolic capital of their street names into the social capital of *fistons*, producing real success behind the trick mirror of its imitation. The machinations of the bluff provided a symbolic solution to the paradox of reputation—at once demonstrating one's proficiency at deception while at the same time distributing wealth and goods to the significant members of one's network to demonstrate one's trustworthiness.

THREE

Faire le show: Masculinity and the Performative Success of Waste

> Consumption and destruction of goods really go beyond all bounds. In certain kinds of potlatch one must expend all one has, keeping nothing back. It is a competition to see who is richest and also the most extravagant. (Mauss [1923] 1990:37)

> Ivoirian capitalism develops at the antipodes of the Protestant Ethic.—Claudine Vidal (Bamba 1982:19)

To *faire le show* was to put together a sort of spectacle of wealth, inviting an inner circle of *frésang*, and often spending every last centime in a single night. Such display dialectically both indexed a strong network and produced social success by drawing younger acolytes into one's network. The more elaborate of these events often required weeks of strategizing and accumulation, calling to mind the travails of Ongka's preparations for his "big *moka*" among the Kawelka of Papua New Guinea (Nairn 1976). One who wished to *faire le show* needed the right authentic name brand clothes, the right shoes, a new haircut, perfume if possible, at least a pack of cigarettes (which on a daily basis were bought *en detail*, one or two at a time), and *un paquet* (package, sexual connotation intended) of cash which could be drawn from the pocket to the awe of any witnesses. The clothing alone, which ideally one should not yet have worn in public, often took as much as a year of payments to attain. The wad of money often represented multiple debts cashed in as well as loans from one's closest *bramogo*.

By distributing *enjaillement* to their peers, social actors were investing in social relations, building up a group of followers who would support them in times of need, simultaneously bolstering their position in the social hierarchy and investing in the security of the network upon which they depended. The *maquis* spectators took on the role of a public, a rare image of collectivity, in this potlatch-style event of public "waste." The *maquis* was the spatial site joining together the social dynamics of the network with the status-building practices of public performance. It was the central ritual locus of urban social reproduction, in which symbolic statements of identity, exchange, and social organization were bonded together in the moment of collective display.

These acts of waste were performative: they were spectacle as a form of speech act (language that "does something." But as J. L. Austin (1962) warns us, the perlocutionary success of an illocutionary act depends upon the uptake—upon the audience's interpretation of the performance. Bluffing in the space of the *maquis* was a kind of street theater in which the clientele were the audience or addressees of the *bluffeurs* in question. The bluff involved a kind of public secret, as Taussig (1999) defines it—something that everyone knows yet which cannot be articulated: everyone knows that this cannot be known. The principal audience of the bluff was the local *maquis*—the concrete public of the here-and-now crowd: these were neighbors who recognized where the actor lived, they lent him money when he didn't have enough to eat, they saw his comings and goings and moments of fortune and failure—an almost private form of public. So certainly they were not deceived. And yet, as Michael Warner (2002) suggests of theater audiences, they stood in for the larger public, the public totality; the *maquis* was inseparable from the street and so indexically connected to the whole network of streets as abstract public space. As the public at large, they stood as witnesses to the symbolic mastery through which *nouchi* youth demonstrated their success and attracted followers both through what Simmel (1950:330–79) refers to as the radiation of adornment and through the mystery of the secret sources of their dazzling (if temporary) wealth.

The actor as *bluffeur* both is and is no longer himself. Indeed, Schechner makes precisely this point in his consideration of the relationship between ritual and theatrical performances:

[The actor] performs in the field between a negative and a double negative. A field of limitless potential, free as it is from both the person (not) and the impersonated (not not). All effective performances share this "not-not not" quality: Olivier is not Hamlet, but also he is not not Hamlet: his performance is between a denial of being another (= I am me) and a denial of not being another (= I am Hamlet). Performer training focuses its techniques not on making one person into another but on permitting the performer to act in between identities; in this sense performing is a paradigm of liminality. (Schechner 1985:123)

Schechner compares different forms of theater and ritual in terms of trans-formation and transportation. In some performances (such as initiation rituals) certain actors are transformed by the experience, whereas others are transported away from the everyday and then reincorporated at the end where they started. This latter form of transportation is the model for both performer and audience in North Atlantic theater, in which the "suspen-sion of disbelief" allows for blurrings of truth and fiction and the kind of reflexivity Victor Turner attributes to liminality (1969:vii). However, I would argue that the transformational potency of ritual comes precisely from the ambiguous make-believe of an audience transported through the theatricality of performance, in which it is no longer clear which things are realistic fictions, and which are fictitious realities. Like masking ritu-als, in which the performer and the performed are one inseparable entity, it is from within this set-apart space of theater that the efficacy of bluffing makes sense. This chapter begins with a consideration of the *maquis* as a ritual space of performative waste and the production of temporary collec-tivity, then moves to a consideration of the hierarchical distributions and gendered performances that made up the microlevel performative state-ments, and finally takes on an analysis of the bluff as a theater of the real.

The *Maquis*: Public Space Par Excellence

The primary site of such display was the *maquis*, an outdoor bar and restau-rant with loud music and dancing and, most importantly, *ambience*, that is, an atmosphere of festivity.[1] I once asked someone what would happen if a political leader tried to close down all *maquis* in Côte d'Ivoire. In shock he replied that the *maquis* was *the* Ivoirian priority in life. "No, if a president tried to take the *maquis* away from Ivoirians you can forget it. They will make him jump [out of office] then and there. They would rise up, and nothing could keep him in that job. There is no way Ivoirians can go with-out a *maquis*."[2] These spaces were not just places to drink, but also sites of the public spectacle of consumption and display. Originally, most *maquis* were actually illegal and hidden within the *cour commune*, but by 2001 many of them were public and splayed out onto the street. Nevertheless, they were sites for illicit exchange and the social gatherings and displays of *nouchi* groups, and so they continue to harbor a quality of illegality. Like the Nouchi language, the popularity of *maquis* spread beyond the domain of those who could afford nothing else to become a site for prestige production among all classes.

Maquis were primarily outdoor spaces, often jutting out into the street. Makeshift tables and dilapidated wooden folding chairs or benches spread out from the interior space, on weekend nights sometimes completely blocking the street itself. Loudspeakers were propped up outside, the music blaring beyond their capacity to reproduce it clearly. People were packed in around the tables, mostly in groups of four or five, but sometimes the tables were strung together to accommodate much larger parties of fifteen or twenty. There was no dance floor per se; dancing took place in whatever open space was available, including the street itself.

It is worthwhile here to compare the *maquis* and the role of gender within it to the case of the Congolese *nganda* (MacGaffey and Bazenguissa-Ganga 2000). Like the *maquis*, the *nganda* had illicit origins, beginning as informal spaces within people's homes and gradually, responding to various forms of state regulation, becoming larger and more regular businesses catering to those who wanted to drink beyond designated times. Like the *maquis*, they were spaces that blurred public and private, where food was served as well as drink, and where clandestine business deals often took place. But also "the presence of women who are 'available' was an essential feature of the *nganda*" (MacGaffey and Bazenguissa-Ganga 2000:143), and they tended to be the owners, managers, and servers in both establishments. MacGaffey and Bazenguissa described the *nganda* as one of the principal opportunities for employment for women arriving in the city (as it continues to be for Congolese women arriving in Paris today). Such women were designated as *ndumba*, which has the connotation of *femme scandaleuse* (a woman of ill repute), but they were not only vilified for their sexual license. Men revered them, for "the relative wealth, independence, and lavish lifestyle that these women achieved made them appear a symbols of success and paragons of beauty" (2000:143). Likewise, the women of the *maquis* were at once sought after, respected, and abused. Their presence was essential not only to the success of the *maquis*, but also to the masculine projects of display and bluff that take place there. Perhaps most importantly, MacGaffey and Bazenguissa describe the *ngandas* as spaces in which a large portion of male income is funneled into the hands of female proprietors (not to mention the clientele), which goes a long way to explain how such consumption brings about further circulation of wealth as well as female forms of bluffing we will consider later.

Both the regular clientele and servers of a *maquis* tended to live within a couple of blocks of the establishment. Seeing each other outside the *maquis* sphere, clientele and staff had entirely amicable relations, but all this changed once a customer entered the space of the *maquis*. This discrepancy was another instance of the hierarchical associations of labor in the last chapter. To work was to lower oneself, to admit one's need for money and lower-class status. In the setting of the *maquis*, to be a customer was to transcend that category, to project the image of abundant wealth and the superiority of the consumer. In this context, sexual flirtations between the customer and server were by contrast forms of display, for the bluff included the art of seduction, the ability to persuade the woman by the attractive charm of clothing and wealth. It was another way of establishing the hierarchical consuming power of the client.

It was crucial that the boundaries of the *maquis* were permeable to the street, that they were open air, and that passersby became witnesses, a part of the collective crowd, thus extending the audience metonymically to the public at large. The local *maquis* was thus a double identity, a real neighborhood collectivity in the sense of a regular clientele with interwoven relationships of obligation, reciprocity, and acknowledged hierarchy, and of the more abstract public—the audience of the *radio trottoir*, where fame of one's exploits would spread through gossip circuits, building one's name beyond the limits of the local community. But both of these forms were iterations of the street—the public life of the city as open and unbounded, rejecting the exclusivity of walled, private spaces.

Imbibing Differentiation: Drinking Establishments and Disdain

To place the *maquis* in its proper context, it should be pointed out that there was a marked division of establishments for drinking and display. Abidjanais categorized these into three types: the *maquis*, the *bar climatisée* (air-conditioned bar), and the nightclub. The concept of bar was always modified by "air-conditioned," because it marked the difference between the open-air street consumption of the average Treichville resident and the sealed, enclosed world of the bar, to which only those of more established means normally gained access. Nightclubs, which had almost disappeared (except in the expat Zone Quatre) required a steep entrance fee and the purchase of at least one drink at truly exorbitant prices (5,000 CFA, or $8, a drink minimum, sometimes as high as $15), effectively denying all but the elite. Most lower-class youth were surprisingly scornful of these upper-class locations, however, critiquing them as stuck up, old fashioned, and boring. They especially resisted the dress codes many of these establishments enforced (leather shoes, no jeans, sometimes even a jacket and tie). From time to time Treichville youth did go to bars and nightclubs, and on such occasions, it was precisely the exorbitant prices they found attractive; the more they paid the better the story would be later. Thus, the high cost was not the reason for their ambivalence; rather, it was on grounds of taste and style that Treichville youth rejected these higher-class locales.

During my time in Treichville, a new bar established itself just down the street from P.J., and one of the women working there gave me an invitation card. It said:

> "The world likes Dicky's Raymsy, and you?"
> [A picture of a man in a suit responds] "It's because you must be well dressed to come to evenings at D. R." [A thought bubble emerges from his head] "My I am so charming"
> At the opening, find The Aesthetic, The Natural, The Real, and The *Gravissime*. Directed and managed by DJ Roland, The Shooting Star.

Reading this, I was excited by the possibility of finding people with the style of the Congolese *sapeurs* and brought Dedy and Leguen along to see what we would discover. At the door, a man who turned out to be the owner accosted us, telling Leguen that he could not enter in shorts, and Dedy that jeans were unacceptable. After much argument, they were allowed in but were warned that next time they should dress properly. But by this time both were incensed. Leguen argued: "He doesn't know how many people I could bring to this bar if I want to. This is Treichville. Here we like to wear jeans, we are not into all that fancy stuff. If he starts turning people away because they are wearing jeans, he will never succeed here. Is anyone here going to put up with that? This isn't the place for that kind of bar. It is not even a nightclub! All those rules about wearing a hat, no jeans, that kind of stuff does not please Ivoirians." Once inside, I was initially disappointed to find a motley scattering of some of the same people I had seen at various *maquis* throughout the evening. No one there was dressed up in the sense the card had implied (though in Treichville terms they were at the height of fashion). What immediately impressed me, however, was that the behavior of these individuals, including two of my closest friends, was entirely different in this context. Everyone ordered whiskey, whereas normally they drank nothing but beer. Rather than the occasional dancer standing in place and dancing or showing off in the aisle, everyone tended to dance, sometimes literally all customers at once. The music was also different, much more the genre of the romantic disco ballad à la Johnny

Hallyday. Most people were doing slow couple dancing, something I never saw in a *maquis*. The women working at the bar were all dressed in sexy European style and were extremely friendly with the clientele, often dancing and encouraging the customers to slow dance with them. Although the sexuality between clients and workers was not unlike the atmosphere in the *maquis*, the dynamic in which this took place was entirely opposed to the aggressive conflict of the *maquis*.

At the end of the weekend, one of the women from this bar came up to a group of us at a *maquis* and began to gossip about the bar. "Now the boss is letting people come in wearing jeans," she wanted everyone to know. "He was so upset about how few customers he has been getting that he cried the other night." One man began to tell a story of being rejected at the door of a nightclub because of his flip-flops, but that once he got in he ordered four bottles of liquor and stayed until ten the next morning. Everyone began talking about how ridiculous it was to expect people from Treichville to wear slacks. This identification of Treichville with dressing "simple" was fascinating, because as we shall see in the next chapter, in the same breath this very group of people would describe themselves as excellent dressers and point out the value of each item of their clothes. Indeed, only moments before this conversation, the man with the flip-flops had been arguing with an older man about who was the better dresser, asking me to feel the quality of his shirt and judge (since I was a *bengiste*, I would know, he said).

Contemporary Ivoirian nightclubs were populated primarily by the rich and fabulous. Their regular clientele consisted of celebrities (who also made the circuit of popular *maquis*), foreign expats (especially French soldiers from the local base), elite youth with money to burn, and *bengistes* showing off their newfound wealth and European tastes. Although Treichville youth spoke of nightclubs with the longing of unconsummated desire, those fortunate enough to have entered one would privately express dissatisfaction. Inside a club, men wore slacks, leather shoes, and tucked-in dress shirts. Women, who in Treichville usually wore tailored *pagne* (African print) fabric, wore slinky, tight pants and miniskirts—all store-bought, ready-to-wear items. As in the bar, the drink of choice was hard liquor. Treichville youth who managed to get into nightclubs found the experience daunting, for there was no performative aspect to the nightclub experience. The value in such an excursion lay in the tales one could tell upon return to the quarter.

However, only a few years before, when Rue 12 in Treichville was at its peak, *maquis* were still considered the place for low-class nobodies, while nightclubs were the center of the social scene. By 2000, the more successful *maquis* were bubbling over with people from all classes, spilling out onto the street, while nightclubs struggled to stay open at all. The transformation that produced the popularity of the *maquis* was clearly linked to the same movement that brought Nouchi speech into the realm of popular culture and transformed the style of popular dress. It was a kind of class culture war in which hierarchy built upon a single metric of taste was disrupted and upended. Dicky's Raymsy bar did not appeal to Treichville youth because while one could certainly spend money ostentatiously there, its exclusionary atmosphere made it impossible to perform the bluff in front of the right kind of audience. It was the equivalent of bluffing in front of the mirror: no one was there to see the performance.

"Gâte, on est ensemble": The Trope of Waste

The social interaction of a *maquis* was a silent competition in which the goal was to cover one's table with as many empty bottles as possible. "Gâte la table," they said, drinking beer after beer. The verb *gâter* means "to spoil," as in "to spoil a child," but also as in "spoiled fruit." It carries a connotation of excess, but it can mean "to destroy, ruin, or waste." Surprisingly, the cost of items consumed was carefully monitored, but only in order to prove the excess of the spenders. Smaller bottles cost more per centiliter, and so it was a more powerful statement to cover a table in small bottles than large ones. Locally produced Guinness cost almost twice as much as Flag (a local beer), and many people found its bitter, syrupy flavor unpleasant, but to *gâte la table* with Guinness trumped everyone around (only a bottle of whiskey or champagne could top it). It was essential that there be not only enough for everyone present, but too much. When food was ordered (another key part of the symbolism of a *maquis* in contrast to the bar), it too had to be in copious quantities. I once overheard a man at a party eating a giant pot of *sauce graine* (palm-nut stew) with crab, saying, "We *eat* in Côte d'Ivoire. They can destroy everything in our country, but we will eat well all the same." The *maquis* experience was one of feigning indifference to economic limitation while continually looking over one's shoulder to see whose table looked most impressive.

The trope of waste was pervasive in *maquis* expression. Not only was the activity described obviously a competitive destruction of wealth à la potlatch (with the same kind of scornful attitude to value), but *nouchi* explicitly referred to waste in their speech. "On va gâter les tables ce soir" (We're going to spoil the tables tonight), my friends would cry gleefully. One night

Figure 6. A group of *nouchi* in the act of *gâter la table*. They are drinking in the *maquis* P.J. (Police Judiciare), a classic example of the genre. The case below the table is full of more beer. This was early in the night, before the group headed to the funeral of a famous *nouchi*.

I went out with Leguen and Billy on a *camoracien* scam in another quarter (Leguen was a dance choreographer by day and *camoracien* by night). They were bringing their "mark" a fake statement of salary (necessary for a travel visa) they had forged on a computer, and demanded money in advance before they could procure the fake passport. They managed to get 10,000 CFA ($15) from their victim, and we went promptly to a famous *maquis* in the area. Leguen began buying beer, then a pack of luxury Dunhill cigarettes, then wine and soft drinks (mixing these together was popular). Billy kept encouraging Leguen to order another round, repeating each time, "*Gâte*, on est ensemble!" (Waste, we are together!). By drawing on the notion of collectivity Billy put Leguen in a position of obligation; to refuse was to deny the very bonds tying the three of us together. The expression highlights the dynamic at work in bluffing at the *maquis*—what appeared to be agonistic interpersonal competition was at the same time a production of collectivity through redistributive exchange. By the end of the night, Leguen told me he had spent the entire 10,000 CFA, all in a matter of hours.

When you came across a large sum of money, it was expected that you would share it with your friends, and the appropriate site for this distribution was the *maquis*. It was a well-rehearsed saying in Abidjan that *maquis* were busiest on the first weekend of the month, after those who worked got their paychecks. An issue of *Gbich!* was devoted to this topic, called "Ceux Qui Depensent Leur Salaires Dans les Maquis . . ." In their pseudojournalistic section, Enquêt Exprès, they described characters who at the first sign of money forgot their families, debts, and needs for the next month for a night of *le show*, only to find themselves the next day with 1,375 CFA ($2) in their pocket for the next month. Those who had nothing preached against wasting money on alcohol, *Gbich!* claimed, but as soon as they got their first paycheck, "under the far-fetched pretext of forgetting the misery they have survived, they rush straight into drinking." One man in a cartoon who has just received his paycheck asks his friend to take him to the bank so he can start an account; when they arrive it is a *maquis* named La Banque, and his friend says, "Yes, here the accounts open in cases" (Simplice 2001:8–9). Of course, few people I knew actually had paychecks, or if they did they, were so meager they still made most of their money from *bizness*. Nevertheless, the same logic applied when *nouchi* scored cash. As Dedy said, "In the bar when you saw the group of youths with the tables loaded with bottles, you have to know those are *nouchi*. They haven't earned that money, and that's the only way they can spend it so easily. That's what they do when they score a *coup* [pull off a successful scam]: they celebrate." This idiom of waste reappeared in the daydreams and glory stories which people liked to tell each other when they were sitting around with nothing to do. Christophe was a great dreamer and enjoyed telling tales about what he would like to do if he only had the money: "If I had 10,000, then I would go do a *ken* . . . no, then I would go to my job [which he didn't have], and when I finished work I would go to a *maquis*, drink ice-cold Flag until I was drunk. Sitting there in my Nike baseball cap, my white polo T-shirt, with 20,000 in my pocket, fly. The *gomi* [babes] will flock to me. I'd go to Adjamtale and drink . . . no to Marcory. Get *boungbassa* [wasted]." Another day Solo (one of Christophe's closest friends) told us about a dream he had had the night before, in which he had a brand-new Mercedes Benz, and the four friends were cruising around together. Christophe was driving, and they picked up Solo's girlfriend Selena. Then they went from *maquis* to *maquis*. Christophe was very excited by this story, repeating *insha allah* over and over (a Muslim expression meaning "by the will of god"; Christophe was not Muslim). Suddenly he launched into his own "dream":

> I had a dream too. This guy came in his car and came screeching up and said, want to *faire un show*? And I said yes, and we went screeching off and went to a bank and put the card in and 400,000 came out. Bang! . . . and this guy's pockets were stuffed full of money because he had his father's bank card,

and I didn't spend *un moro* [one cent]. We went to a nightclub in Zone Quatre before I could even yell out the window to my friends, where he ordered two bottles of whiskey. We just kept on drinking and dancing all night. Then my friend said, "Let's go find some prostitutes"; he knew a good place, and we went to this little place [he pointed toward the bridge]. Then he dropped me off at home, and he burned rubber as he headed off to Cocody.

The structure of such future-oriented daydreams mirrored very closely the form of nostalgic bragging over past excess. Both were acts of fantasy, of self-projection into an imagined space. Kwao, a man in his late forties, thought back proudly of a night of *le show* from a former year:

> When I had money, I used to go out on the town. One night I took out my girlfriend on her birthday with 200,000 [$285] in my pocket. We started at *Le Petit Coin* [the most popular local *maquis* in our neighborhood], where we drank for several hours. She brought along two friends from Koumassi. Then we went to a *maquis* in Koumassi, where we stayed until about three or four in the morning. There were many people there, but we were the biggest spenders. At the time, I only drank liquor, because that seemed classier, so the whole time the others were drinking beer, I was asking for whiskey and other expensive liquor. Finally we went and slept a few hours at her friend's house and then in the morning we went to Yopougon and drank some more. When I finally got home, I only had about 10,000 in my pocket . . . but it really was a great way to waste money.

On the basis of work by Appadurai (1991) and especially Weiss (2004), it is important to recognize that such fantasy is not mere representation but in fact social practice, a form of activity tightly tied to forces of globalization both material and cultural. Indeed, the relationship between representation and reality is not easily divided; fictions and fabrications are (and always have been) social facts. For Ivoirian urban youth the performance and representation of the bluff transformed those who partook in it; it was a socially productive form of consumption. In this sense, the representation of the bluff, even the imagination of it, was an activity with real-world consequences.

On a Saturday night in one of Abidjan's more renowned *maquis* of the moment, my friends and I saw a large group of people who were certainly putting on *le show*. Throughout the night the DJ showered with praise a particular table of *bengistes* who had just made their return. They stood up and danced as the DJ performed a rap about them, including "the dangerous George C, who speaks in French francs, the force of France. He will *gâte les tables* tonight, he does nothing but spend." Later the DJ announced that they were buying a bottle of champagne worth 58 French francs. Dedy was awed, saying that we could be sure they truly succeeded "over there."

Another common expression of waste in the *maquis* was to shout when someone was getting up to dance, "Va gaspiller! On te din" (Go waste! We are watching). Again, notions of collectivity, waste, and display were brought together, this time explicitly invoking the gaze of the audience and the relationship between performance and waste. The spectacle of waste thus served to reinforce group identity through the dispersal of wealth and collective consumption, while simultaneously differentiating the giver hierarchically in relation to the recipients.[3] The "host" was obligated to give because "on est ensemble," and the moment of collectivity was used as a concept legitimating waste. But in fact, I want to argue the inverse here as well, that waste produced a sense of the collective, because the act of wasting meant that the giver and his recipients "were together."

"Go Waste! We Are Watching": Dance and Display

Dance was also an important idiom of display through which the other elements of competition were symbolically condensed, expressed, and performed. The various gestures of *nouchi* dance formed a sort of sign language through which actors stated their superiority to others in the room, even insulting others through the motion of the dance. Ivoirian dance is a dynamic part of popular culture and is continually evolving, each new genre with a title of its own. At the peak of its popularity during my fieldwork, the *logobi* was a fast-motion dance, almost violent in nature, at once an imitation of fighting and a display of clothing and labels. The first time I saw it, I noticed four youths facing each other and going through the motions of a fistfight in perfect timing to the music; one would throw a punch, another duck, another block, all in coordination.

Fama, a young Muslim man from the north who had made his way in the criminal network and was *yere* both in clothing and mannerism, explained the context of the dance to me. He told me that in Nouchi *logo* means "bluff," and *logobi* is like the "danse des bluffeurs." One can't help wondering whether the morpheme *logo* is referencing brands, but like so many Nouchi words, it was a word whose origin no one could tell me. In any case, Fama continued:

> So the dance includes the showing off of clothes: the shirt, the shoes, the belt.
> You might stroke your beard to show how well it is cut, run your hand over

Figure 7. This young man is performing the *logobi*, a dance that combines movements representing physical violence with the display of the value of his clothing. He was baptized earlier that day, after the church rite, and there was a festival in the street to celebrate him (an example of the life cycle ceremonies to be discussed later in the chapter). Having changed from church clothes to a traditional chief's robe to his very best street clothes, the man kinetically demonstrates his worth and style through the *logobi*. In the background children are imitating the dances of the adults. On the wall behind him, someone has spray-painted the message "Urination forbidden, 500 CFA fine," a perfect example of the informal self-regulation of Treichville streets.

your hair. You pull the shirt out, lift your arm to show the watch. That is a big part of how the dance is constructed. Really it evolved out of some other dances: the *nyama-nyama* came first; it was a kind of *danse des loubards*, where people showed off their toughness, and this evolved into feinting and dodging as though in a fistfight. Out of this movement came the *zeguei*, which is a Nouchi word for *loubard* [*loubard* was originally a French word]. This was more refined and came at a time when the *loubard* began to work out and develop muscles. It was a dance in which one shows off one's strength by holding out one's arms. Another part of the *logobi* today includes the aspect of imitating a fight that is found in the *nyama-nyama*, but to a more advanced degree. Each one of these dances evolves from its predecessors, we are always trying to modernize. In fact, these dances are often taken from traditional dances from the village, but we adapt them in the urban environment; they are brought up to date, given the edge of the city.

Fama gives us a good idea of the historical transformations here, and it has particularly intriguing implications. The dance began as a display of fighting skill, transformed into a display of muscle control and sheer strength, and ended up as a display of style (mixed with fighting). Did this index a new kind of relationship between consumption and masculinity in Côte d'Ivoire? How did clothing transform *nouchi* hierarchies during this period? Why did the muscle-bound *loubard* give way to a new generation of wily dandies? Certainly not everyone was happy with the transformation. Gros Guerrier, the old school *loubard* and self-proclaimed father of Nouchi, told me that the *logobi* was just a bunch of *conneries* (stupidities) added to the *nyama-nyama*, a series of unnecessary arm motions. "It is a *faux danse*" (fake, worthless dance), he said.

Dom gives us a better idea of how display and consumption were built into the newer form of dance:

> The *danse de logobi* is about *misant les choses en valeur*. One displays the labels, the gold chains, the watch. The dance is composed of these gestures; it is very interesting even. Every gesture *mise en valeur* a part of the body or an item of clothing. The *zeguei*, which came before . . . was also a form of *mise en valeur*, but in that case it was the power of the body that was displayed. It was wonderful to see, because those who did it could control each of their muscles individually, so that it was the muscles that did the dance.

I find that this idea of *mise en valeur* is a key to understanding Ivoirian consumption. The actors were already there at the *maquis* in their finery, the *loubards* were already obviously muscle-bound, but it was necessary to perform and embody the consumption of these items for them to take on their true value. Dance was an arena in which each item could be placed before the public gaze for evaluation, transforming the object into a valuable. But it was Dedy with his gift for explication who best described the dance of the *logobi*:

> The dance of the *nouchi* is like Chinese martial arts; it is a dance of significa-
> tion; every move has meaning. So this [sliding one finger up and down across
> the neck] means you are dead, I will kill you. This [biting finger] means *"ar-
> racher"* [a double meaning, as *arracher* can be used for pulling teeth or for
> purse snatching]. [Sweeping his arm across the table and then a gesture of
> throwing away] means that the neighboring table is worth nothing, then you
> [makes a gesture of calling waiter] call the waiter, and [starts hand up in the
> air as if holding a tray, swirls and then brings it down, moving slowly across
> the table while making a sort of magic spell movement with the fingers] this
> means *"gâte la table."* There are many moves to show clothing. Turning the
> hat around is to show the label; the same is done with the shirt collar. The
> move of the *logobi* where one lifts the foot up is done to show off the shoes.
> Then [pulling collar open and gesturing with the other hand to his chest]
> you show your *sami* [chain] and gesture to say that it is gold. The movements
> with the wrists are to show off the watch and bracelets. [Turning head to one
> side, and making subtle chin movements like snobbery] means that the other
> is worthless, *tu vaux rien.* There is a gesture for *foutaise* [disrespect, bullshit].
> The dance of the *nouchi* is a language. One person may start dancing, then
> another will get up and signify that the other is a *bluffeur,* that he is nothing,
> and then the dancer will *mise en valeur* everything that he himself is wearing.

Indeed, these dances were a language through which the silent competition of consumption was performed. The phrase *mise en valeur* oddly echoes French colonial discourse, in which it was a euphemism for the exploitation of lands appropriated through empire, taking the raw materials and mixing them with the spirit of "civilization" to bring them to their full potential value. To "make valuable" colonial land was also to extract value from it. The same phrase was also used by Houphouët to reference the state's policy of bequeathing land to anyone (including both internal and external migrants) who developed it or "put it to use" (McGovern 2011). The phrase in the context of the *logobi* thus carries an ambiguity between the possibility of "placing value on" objects through the performance of the dance and drawing or expropriating value from the objects in a performance of self.

Figure 8. Dedy dances the *logobi*, sliding his finger across his throat in a gesture of scorn signifying that he "kills" you with style. Such an accusation sometimes leads to real violence. The group had invited the woman by his side to the table. She was in the bar alone in hopes of being picked up in this way, a behavior typically characterized as *godrap*.

Maquis dancing was almost always performed by individual dancers who took turns dominating the public eye, thus concentrating the communication of value to a single performative subject.[4] In contrast, women's dancing in a *maquis* had quite different ramifications. Although women were equally concerned about the value of their clothes, their dances were not about highlighting the value of such prestige objects. Women's dances were much closer (if not identical) to traditional dances "from the village" and were usually oriented around the display of the body. The most famous women's dance of the moment was the *mapouka*, which actually had its own musical genre.[5] While it had specific ethnic origins, it was a generic Ivoirian dance by the time of my arrival. A woman performed the *mapouka* by placing her weight on her toes and rhythmically lifting her heels in alternation to the music in such a way that her buttocks "danced." Very slowly, her back to the audience, she bent down until her hands practically touched the ground, so that her jiggling posterior became the unquestioned center of attention. In contrast to the men, women often performed this dance in groups, lined up in an evenly spaced row. Occasionally, at the height of the dance, a man jumped up, grabbed a woman's hips, and joined the dance in an imitation of copulation. Despite its explicit eroticism, however, the *mapouka* carried little connotation of immorality. Everyone from elderly women to little girls performed this dance with equal aplomb. Once again we see that it was not sexuality per se that was linked to scandal, but the relationship to the public gaze of the street.

There was a clear symbolic opposition between men, who individually *misent en valeur* their possessions and fighting skills in the public sphere, and women, who collectively "placed value" on their sexual potency, most often in an occasion hosted by their family. Thus, like the "wasting" of display practices, the *gaspiller* of dancing was a form of self-production, a vaunting of personal power. Furthermore, the expression with which this section began, "Waste! We are watching," reminds us of the importance of the constitution of the appreciative audience for the efficacy of the performance. This brings us to a consideration of the micropolitics of exchange underlying the performance of waste that allows it to be productive rather than destructive of sociality.

The Gift of Bluffing: Exchanges Underlying the "Show"

Competition was not only between tables but was always at play within the interpersonal hierarchies at the table itself. Between a couple of close friends there could be a balanced reciprocity, each buying beer for the other like the luncheon clientele of Lévi-Strauss's famous wine exchange ([1949] 1969). However, in the presence of a larger group, one person often seemed to take on the role of the host, paying for everybody's food and drinks. Others seated at the table did sometimes buy drinks for the group or for one another, but such a gesture began a dangerous game, for what may have been intended as a kindly offer of reciprocation could just as easily have been interpreted as provocation to competitive challenge. But even as a passive recipient, one's job was by no means easy, for the host, in his attempts to outdo other tables, continually demanded that one drink repeatedly and quickly. Even though beer bottles themselves were collective resources poured into individual glasses, the speed with which one's glass required refilling was carefully monitored, and those who drank quickly and heavily drew the overt praise of the host.

A particularly apt example of this kind of aggressive hospitality can be found in Fidèle, a slightly overweight middle-aged man who spent a lot of time at P.J., a neighborhood *maquis*. His source of income was somewhat mysterious, though it was rumored that he had "connections" at CIE, the national electricity company, and that this made him wealthy. At any rate, he made it very clear that he had more money than his peers, a fact that seemed to separate him from them rather than strengthen any bonds. He had a regular group of drinking friends, however, which gathered around when he was in the buying mood. He became angry whenever he noticed other tables buying more than he was and tried to recruit anybody he knew to sit at his table. Once you were there, he had no qualms about shouting at you to drink more. The problem, however, was that once you sat down at a *maquis* table, you could no longer leave of your own free will but were bound to stay until the host ran out of money or could no longer drink himself. The struggle now was one of tolerance, which was another index of the masculine strength and endurance that *nouchi* constantly needed to demonstrate. To get up and leave before the others had finished was a mark of humiliation and weakness. Thus, the men I knew never said goodbye in such situations; when they left, they always acted as though they were coming right back, saying they were going to get cigarettes or go pee in the alley, and then disappeared. This excuse was so cliché that people often made fun of the man walking away behind his back, saying, "No, he's not coming back; he can't take it anymore." Nevertheless, these formulaic excuses were necessary, for it was an insult to the host to leave explicitly, even if one was too drunk to continue. "The host will say to himself that he has been wasting money on drinks for you," Dedy explained. I suspect that the successful bluff would be dashed should the table begin to lose its clientele, and the host wanted it to stay crowded until he himself called the act off. I once made the mistake of leaving early, thanking Fidèle for his generosity and excusing myself politely. For weeks to follow, he was so angry that he refused to acknowledge my presence.

Dedy told me that when Fidèle bought drinks in this way, "c'est pas cadeau" (it's not a gift, it's not free), rather it was "his fetish, his *médicament*" (literally, medicine, but in Francophone Africa it also means occult force, magic protection, or poison). It was precisely through this activity, Dedy argued, that Fidèle maintained his power. Of course, such asymmetrical exchange was an essential aspect of the bluff, a means of demonstrating one's superiority and success. The interesting thing was that in Fidèle's case, the power he maintained in this way was illegitimate. He may have successfully produced a group of apparent acolytes, but there was no sense of loyalty within these bonds. His failure to develop real social status must be attributed to his distance from the community in other terms. He did not participate in other kinds of exchanges, had no role in the *nouchi* network, and did not display a *yere* sensibility either in his fashion sense or in his interactions with *les nouchis*. It is also probable that his generosity and showy style were not appreciated precisely because he actually had money. The *nouchi* who bluffed attained the glory of overcoming their poverty, if only for a moment, in complete disregard of their actual financial situation. Fidèle's show had no power to impress because he was simply showing off his real wealth, not wasting a temporary accumulation in the exhibition of potential.

But Fidèle was an unusual case. People with positions of social (rather than merely economic) superiority, like the *vieuxpères*, could maintain nonreciprocal relations in all legitimacy. On a daily basis it was expected that your *vieuxpère* could demand money or beer from you at any time, and if you had the means, it was a good idea to concur. At a *maquis*, however, if the *vieuxpère* was present, it was appropriate that he took on the role of distributor. Unlike Fidèle's aggressive hospitality, the hospitality offered by a *vieuxpère* was not demeaning, but appropriate to accept. While Fidèle attempted to buy loyalty through economic superiority, the *vieuxpère* expressed his position of legitimate superiority by distributing his wealth among his *fistons*. Since this wealth was ultimately produced by the *fistons*, he was in fact redistributing; his dominance came in the form of controlling the flow of wealth rather than in wealth per se. Denot claims that "he who is affluent is called *grandfrère* or *tonton* [big brother or uncle], even by people who are older. The latter pay allegiance to the individual with the most material wealth, delegating their power in exchange for his protection, which manifests itself concretely in gifts" (1990:42). Thus, functions formerly fulfilled by kinship groups were partially or wholly replaced by more fluid affective networks. As Strathern writes, whereas in a commodity economy those who dominate can determine the manner in which surplus wealth is appropriated, "in a gift economy, we might argue that those who dominate are those who determine the connections and disconnections created by the circulation of objects" (1988:167). Thus, a *vieuxpère* expressed superiority by demanding valuables when he saw fit and distributing goods when and to whom he chose.

But to *faire le show* was always a declaration of the superiority of both the giver in relation to the group, and the group in relation to others at the *maquis*. Here one often entered into more flexible systems of competition, in which peers attempted to outperform each other by giving more than anyone else. When this was combined with careful maintenance of the social ties involved, the giver could earn greater respect in the community and potentially develop a set of *fistons*, thereby ensuring a superior position in the social hierarchy. So there were three forms of exchange relations that took place at the *maquis*: (1) the most common, an egalitarian alternation of "hosts," such that ultimately there was an at least perceived equivalence of relations, (2) a regular expression of a hierarchical relationship, in which the *vieuxpère* redistributed his wealth among his acolytes; and (3) the competitive performance of success, in which one tried to evade reciprocity by outbuying one's peers and climbing the social hierarchy. In all cases, the social actors playing the role of host and their audience were highly conscious of the social relations being expressed through exchange; they gave in accordance with their status in comparison to their peers, to the amount of money in their pockets, and to the sets of obligations and unreciprocated debts owed to members of the group at the table. Despite all the apparent politics and hierarchical calculations involved in *maquis* attendance, this effort to *faire le show* was ultimately a collective one. When the "host" didn't have enough money to handle the costs, peers would willingly and nonreprovingly loan their friend money, and it was not uncommon for friends to pool their money together at the beginning of the evening so that the "host" could display a larger bundle of currency when he paid for drinks. Everyone expected this money to be gone by the end of the night. Even though in such situations one person took on the role of host, the honor of the entire table was at stake.

However, in suggesting that the bluff had performative efficacy I beg the question: who is the audience for all this conspicuous consumption? In this chapter, I locate the sense of collectivity needed for a transformation of a person to take place within the *maquis*, a site constituted by precisely the forms of competitive distribution outlined above. Each *maquis* developed its own group of regulars, and more successful *maquis* became the social center for a whole neighborhood. When I didn't find someone at home, the next stop was always their favorite local *maquis*. Leguen told me that "every *maquis* has its own group." He claimed to be part of the group that frequented the P.J. *maquis*, and during the time that I knew him, this was certainly his spot. P.J. was the first place where I became known, and I could count on finding somebody there I knew at practically any hour of the day. The men and women who visited or worked there regularly almost all lived in the immediate neighborhood, and those who didn't, like Fidèle, had family nearby. They were not all friends and certainly did not all drink together, but the crowd was made up of familiar faces, and separate tables often taunted each other, or called out in greeting to someone they knew across the room. One subsection of the P.J. regulars also frequented a *maquis* across the street named Baraka. Early on, before I knew Leguen well, I often saw him drinking there, so I asked him if this was also his group. He responded vaguely that that *maquis* was attached to his family's *cour commune*. Dedy explained later that Leguen never went to that *maquis* anymore because "he has been walking with you. His family thinks he should have lots of money because he walks with a white, and there have been a lot of fights since he isn't sharing his money with them." Because Leguen did not distribute his money as generously as they believed he should, his connections with them were severed. Later, Leguen disappeared from that area entirely, and people at P.J. would ask me if I knew where he was. A rumor began to circulate that he had pulled off a very large false-papers scam and had run away to avoid having to give away portions of the money. Thus, the explanation for his disappearance was a denial of collective redistribution. It would seem then that urban Ivoirians interpreted the act of "wasting" money on one's friends as a sort of declaration of collectivity. When Billy kept repeating the phrase "*Gâte, on est ensemble!*" I asked him what he meant. He responded, "Everything we do, positive or negative, we are together." Correspondingly, the refusal to spend money one had procured (by whatever means) was seen as a rejection of the social bonds linking the group together.

This explains the focus on the local *maquis* in most acts of bluffing. Only if their audience recognized them would the effort of *gâter la table* gain them the reputation they desired. And so people were very loyal to their local *maquis*: the site people went to see *their* peers show off or fail to impress, a place to gossip about them when they were not present. Abidjanais needed to frame all of their show within their own network, in the place in which they were already known, where their theatrical "transportation" could also constitute a transformation of reputation through the circulation of their exploits. It is worth noting here, in the context of framing, that another Francophone term for *faire le show* is to *frime*, which also means "frame."

Out on "La Rue"

Despite the importance of the local *maquis* as the constitutive audience and base of *radio trottoir* from which one's reputation could be built, when urban youths really wanted to *faire le show*, a small group of friends would travel outside their quarter to one or more of the more famous *maquis*. Such voyages often began and almost always ended back at the local *maquis*, so that the group could regale the crowd with their stories of money spent, alcohol consumed, sexual exploits, and most of all the locations they had experienced. It was on these occasions that clothing became of crucial importance, so that even before they had told anyone, those gathered in the local *maquis* would know that this well-dressed group was going to *faire le show* that night. Everything was conducted in luxury; at such moments money became no object. Whereas normally the guys from France-Amérique would walk miles rather than spend 150 CFA (the price of a cooked meal) on a collective taxi, on these special outings they would hire a private taxi for a price as high as 1,500 CFA. People who hardly ever had enough money to buy their own beer would suddenly offer several to acquaintances, or to women they had never seen before. Unlike performance in the local *quartier*, such voyages of consumption closely paralleled the symbolic structure of migration, a topic to be taken up in chapter 5. The experience was transformative and liminal, and its principal value was only attained on the return home, when the actor was reincorporated into the group, circulating stories of fantastic spending adventures.

These trips outside the quarter were elaborately planned beforehand. Christophe and Solo were intent on impressing a certain girl named Caroline by flaunting their sartorial and spendthrift skills. They would have to undertake this in another quarter; otherwise too many *kôkôs* (beggars) would show up (their best friends would be especially unavoidable). Earlier that month they had completed payments on some new shoes and shirts, which they had hidden in my apartment so no one would know they had plans. Periodically Christophe had come by to visit and look at his purchases in pride, though recently he had decided he was not pleased with the new shirt (a polo shirt with the words DELUX written in capitals across it) because he suspected it was a fake. They had also worked hard to build up enough money for the event, through some sort of schemes they did not disclose in addition to Solo's work as an apprentice tailor and Christophe's work as a *djossieur de nama*.

On the big day, Christophe had his new blue Dockside shoes (all the rage in Abidjan), and the DELUX shirt and a gold chain with Jesus on it he had had custom made by a jeweler friend *en bizness*. Solo was wearing Façonnables jeans he borrowed without permission from Olivier, a white T-shirt and silver chain, and leather shoes of no particular value (he told me he had plans for some 70,000 CFA ones [$100], which he really did buy later). Over that he wore an unbuttoned dress shirt. The two emerged from their room in the new garb and the whole *cour commune* was awed. Someone mentioned that they looked like they had just stepped off the plane: "On dirait *bengistes*" (They look like they are from the land of the whites). Solo kept pulling a big wad of money out of his pocket to show off, talking about how when women saw that "leur cœur est mort" (their heart will stop).

We hailed an official taxi and drove to Adjame. On the way, they explained that they once lived in that quarter, and their old friends from there now thought they were very rich. All of the money was consolidated with Christophe; since the purpose of the trip was for him to impress Caroline, he would play host throughout the evening. When we arrived we made the rounds of several compounds where all the women "oohed" and "ahhed" over Christophe and Solo, their clothes and white friend. Their old friend Julien, dressed up in a Nautica shirt and with a Converse star shaved into the back of his head, joined us along with a couple of others. They bought three packs of cigarettes and stood around in the street showing off. Christophe repeatedly asked to borrow my cell phone so he could pretend to talk on it. He also had to give a couple of thousand CFA to a couple of young guys that wanted to tag along in order get them to leave us alone. From there we took a second taxi to Yopougon, where we visited more relatives, including Christophe's cousin Sylvester, who was apparently a rival for the elusive Caroline and was expecting to see her as well that day.

We stopped in another section of Yopougon at the *maquis* Le Point Finale and took tables outside under the open sky. Christophe pulled out his "packet" of money, headed into the bar, and brought out a case and a half of Flaguettes (the smaller, more expensive bottles). At the demands of our rumbling stomachs, he also bought snack food on several occasions. When we finished the beer a couple of hours later, Christophe announced that "le poulet est mort" (the chicken is dead), the Nouchi expression for "the money has run out." The pressure was then on Sylvester to perform, and he nervously went inside and brought out three Grand Flags for us all to share. The tension was really mounting between him and Christophe by this point. Caroline had still not shown up, and Christophe suspected that Sylvester had had a hand in keeping her away (to prevent her from seeing his display of success, which Sylvester could not compete with). Several times Christophe took Solo aside and spoke to him privately. In fact, Christophe had begun the trip with 30,000 CFA, and taking all expenses into account, he still had around 10,000 left. Clearly he had stopped because the target audience of his performance was not present. Nevertheless, before heading home, we traveled back to Adjame for one last round in another part of town.

Christophe stopped by my apartment a couple of days later and began to talk nostalgically about the day of glory. He told me that when he had pulled out the "packet" of money at the *maquis* in Yopougon (an action he had fantasized about for a couple of weeks beforehand), his cousin Sylvester had asked, "Are you guys bandits or what? You guys from Treichville always have money." He was proud that he had produced such an effect on Sylvester. It was unimportant that Sylvester thought he was more of a crook than he really was, the point was that Sylvester thought he was wealthy. Of course, he followed this story by asking to borrow money from me. Apparently he and Solo had dispensed with the rest of his cash after I had gone to sleep, particularly as Solo had passed out on the street and someone had emptied his pockets. So, having had 30,000 in his pocket only a couple of days before, Christophe now needed to borrow 1,000 CFA just to have something to eat through the next week.

The ideal place for this kind of night of reckless spending was La Rue Princesse, or as it was more commonly referred to, simply "La Rue" (The Street). On La Rue, Abidjanais of all backgrounds told me, it was always Friday night. On La Rue there was no first weekend of the month. One could hardly distinguish between night and day. All of these statements point toward a state of liminality. Just to get there was an epic journey, for one had to cross at least two police checkpoints and circumnavigate the lagoon from almost any other part of town. Even without police interruption, it could be a forty-five-minute trip. Furthermore, it was located in the middle of the largest district of town (so large that one Treichville resident tried to convince me in all sincerity that it was larger than Gambia), a quarter without grid structure or street signs, in which taxi drivers regularly got lost. Upon arrival, one was immediately thrown into the midst of an almost perpetual carnivalesque atmosphere. The *maquis* lined the street on either side, one adjoining another, with such names as The Godfather, Paradis Terrestre (Earthly Paradise), G-10, Le Pouvoir (The Power), Le Kosovo, Le Presidence, Venus, and Le Must. As in Treichville, the *maquis* consisted of a small interior space and large open-air spaces for the tables and chairs, only here the street was very wide, and the seating areas were massive. These establishments hired the top DJs in the country and blasted music at top volume out of stacks of powerful speakers, resulting in utter cacophony along the middle of the street. Women along the street sold grilled fish and chicken and tended stands with packets of tissue, cigarettes, and candy, and walking vendors passed with odd assortments of items like tweezer kits. Adding to the note of celebration and otherworldliness, Ivoirian pop celebrities regularly attended these *maquis*, and the DJs announced their presence as though they were nobility.

More recently, these *maquis* became stages for the arrival of the Jet Set, the entourage that developed around Douk Saga, who transformed the popular music scene and street style in Côte d'Ivoire with the creation of *coupé-décalé*. When the Jet Set arrived, they came in luxury vehicles like convertible sports cars and piled out with oversized cigars and outlandish haute couture outfits.[6] The DJ announced their presence one by one as they marched down the length of tables as a makeshift runway displaying their presence and often showering bystanders with money (a mixture of international currencies). They were known to pour champagne over their thick gold chains and $1,000 Weston shoes.

"All the pleasures of life are to be found on La Rue," I was frequently informed, though the speaker often continued, "and everything bad can be found there too." Leguen took me there for my first visit, and on arrival he said, "Yopougon is the capital of joy. It is another world, no?" For Abidjanais, the mere mention of La Rue was sure to raise eyebrows or provoke whistles or sighs of longing. Sitting in a very popular and equally loud *maquis* on the other side of town one night, a teenager next to me (whom I had never met) leaned over to me and said, "C'est pas *gaté* [It's not wasted]; when I get my paycheck we will go to the Rue Princesse." La Rue existed in Abidjanais' worldview as a symbolic center for decadent consumption, and for the youth of Treichville, one could only transcend the pleasures of such a *paradis terrestre* by escaping the confining boundaries of their quarter. The journey to La Rue corresponds to pilgrimage à la Victor Turner (1976), a journey out of quotidian social order and into the liminal sphere of antistructure. Such an experience was transformative; a night on La Rue was the pinnacle of local symbolic success. In miniature form, such events parallel the journeys to the "otherworld" made by youths who achieved the ultimate voyage to Europe or the United States: the stories of abundance they tell, the return home in style, the prestige accumulated from the experience.

The Dangers of Display

Given the criminal tendencies of the society I am describing, it is not surprising that despite the pressures to exhibit copious wealth, actors were also cautious in some circumstances, for such display also could turn dangerous. If witnesses to the "show" decided there was enough money to justify reallocation by force, they might try to take advantage of your drunken state and the late hour to mug you. This happened to Fidèle and a group of friends after they left a *maquis* outside his usual orbit one night. He was buying drinks for five tables at once, and some youths nearby felt insulted. Five guys followed them to a dark spot in the street and jumped them with knives, seriously wounding three of them. This kind of danger was always present. One man told me about watching a pickup truck pull up to a *maquis* with the back full of machetes and guns. The group had clearly just finished robbing someplace and wanted to live it up. In several cases newspapers reported such armed gangs robbing whole *maquis* at once.

On top of the physical dangers associated with conspicuous consumption, there were more prevalent negative social repercussions concerning reputation. One day the France-Amérique group learned that it was expected to pay the electricity bill that month. Olivier started giving Solo advice, saying that "if you didn't spend so much time in *maquis*, maybe the landlord would understand that you have no money. But when you are always in the *maquis*, the guy thinks, hey, Solo is doing well, he's got dough, and the man has no pity for you." Solo pointed out that since that whole week was elections, he didn't have to pay for a single beer, or to eat most of the time: everything was given to him by campaign people. Olivier responded, "still, you are producing the image of wealth, he sees that you are happy and well off, so he doesn't believe you need money." Solo, angry now, said, "You don't even understand the problem. The guy is mean, he only wants money." Olivier continued to argue that no matter how greedy the guy was, it couldn't help to let yourself be seen in *maquis* when you were trying to "joue au pauvre" (play the poor guy). Thus, while the goal of such performance was precisely to impress people with one's abundant wealth, the moment a social actor carried off such a charade with any degree of success, everyone and their kin group would show up asking for money. The spectacle of the bluff could generate negative and ambivalent ramifications, particularly when it was not carried out with proper delicacy and attention to social relationships at hand.

In the next chapter, I describe a similar dynamic at play in clothing. People admired the elite, envied their wealth, and did everything in their power to convince others of their own, but at the same time they refused to dress in suits, because they said people would think they were rich, that they were *les bosses*. The same issue was at play in Nouchi, whose speakers doggedly rejected the formalities of French and the social hierarchy it implied in favor of their own street hierarchical evaluation. Thus, there was a slippage between wealth and class, such that *nouchi* youth resisted eliteness per se only to reproduce it in their own neighborhood. As we saw in the last chapter, actors relied upon their network connections in order to produce wealth and reputation, yet the culminative performance of this success could undermine these same social ties. Therefore, there was a kind of normative conflict producing ambivalence over this triumphant exhibition. However, the *nouchi* tried to mitigate this problem by distributing their "wealth" to their primary community at the very moment they consumed it, in this way confirming collective sociality along with individual differentiation. Actors had to carefully balance their obligations to share resources with their ability to display wealth in order to gain prestige.

Street Rituals: Urban Life Cycle Ceremonies and the *Maquis*

The ability to overcome the dangers of display through the production of collectivity depended upon the maquis as a site in which conflicting norms could be resolved through ritual transcendence. In order to understand how ritual spaces are created in the largely secular arena of the urban streets, I want to briefly examine the frequent kin-dominated life cycle rituals such as funerals, baptisms, weddings, birthdays, and religious holidays. The fact that such productions literally stopped traffic by stretching tents across the street to create a public ceremonial site points to the centrality of the street as social space. All of these rituals were examples of *bricolage*, in which elements of "tradition" were melded with Christian or Muslim symbolism and urban norms. These rituals were extremely consistent across ethnic and religious lines and seemed to constitute a form of urban popular culture in their own right, despite the fact that they were the only events in which ethnic traditions and language were publicly invoked.[7] They made up the moments in which urban kinship networks coalesced and defined their internal structure through economic contribution and display.

Such events involved extreme expenditure for the families. In every case, a tent had to be rented, a DJ hired, copious amounts of beer, soft drinks, and coffee made available, and enough food to feed anywhere from fifty to several hundred people prepared. It was a matter of family honor that everything be as lavish as possible, and that all guests be received with generous hospitality. The bigger the tent, the more meat and beer distributed to the guests, the better the family name. Since the celebration took place in the street outside the *cour commune* of the family member concerned, it was available to the public inspection of all passersby, all of whom were likely to be invited to join. I occasionally came across truly grandiose productions, in which whole town squares were taken up with large stages, famous live performers, choreographed dancing, and concert-sized crowds. In order to fund such events, therefore, families had to pool their resources; every family member and affine was expected to contribute as much as possible, and guests of any social proximity tended to come with offerings as well. Of course, like the hosts at *maquis* display performances, families practiced a kind of competitive reciprocity, as each tried to provide a more bountiful ceremony than the last. Considering the relationship of these ceremonies to the visual, the ostentatious spending of resources culled from the entire kinship network, and their location in the public space of the street, there seems to be a strong parallel with the role of the *maquis* as a public space with the potential for ritual transformation.

While in the life cycle rituals the kin network drew on its members for resources and placed itself collectively on display by giving food and drink freely to the neighborhood, in the ritual of *maquis* consumption, individuals drew on their informal networks for help, then distributed to their table as a performance in front of the *maquis* public. Like life cycle rituals, the central dynamic of *maquis* display was the interaction between the principal actors and their immediate social groups (in the former the family, in the latter his personal network). In both cases, it was the theatrics of performance that produced a kind of efficacy, in which the social success of the giver was confirmed. The act of spending was confirmation in itself of the wealth of the actor, regardless of the origin of the money. People knew that a group of big spenders in the corner had undoubtedly just pulled off some kind of heist and were in the process of "wasting" all the money, but the fact that they were consuming in such a fashion was an efficacious act of self-production nonetheless. No one could question such a group's superiority without spending more themselves. As I shall argue in the next chapter, this legitimacy comes in part from a semiosis of consumption in which authentic value is transferred through metonymic contact, rather than the more familiar surface duplication of the original. But semiosis (even Austin's [1962] performative semiosis) is, after all, only as good as its ability to convince the proper audience of a coherent meaning. This was Mauss's (1972) critical insight into magic; his argument that Frazer's laws of sympathetic magic were really only the principal axes of language is followed by the Durkheimian principle that collective belief in signs with specific properties was the source of magical potency. Thus, it is performer's relationship to the collective pole of the audience that we must take account of here, before turning to the semiotics of power and style.

Potlatch and the Production of Audience

In order to think through *maquis* performances as a kind of ritual activity, it is worth exploring a comparison with the famous Kwakiutl potlatch. Graeber (2001) reinterprets Kwakiutl society as made up of surfaces lacking interiority, a series of titled individuals with no inherent internal connection, each descending from independent spiritual ancestors. Value for the Kwakiutl, then, came from the *giving* of massive quantities of generic objects. The person, he argues, was not embedded in the gift (like money, these objects resisted historical associations); rather, the giver constructed himself in the performance of giving, and in so doing established the collective group of the audience. He opposes this system to the Maori, for whom individuals all partook of the same interior force, such that differentiation and hierarchy could only happen through the appropriation of *singular* gifts containing the potency of the specific giver. Abidjanais *maquis* culture constructed personal value through competitive displays with clear parallels to the Kwakiutl potlatch. The valuables exchanged on these occasions, in accordance with Graeber's analysis, were correspondingly generic—it was the quantity of a generic substance consumed which produced the performative valuation of the person. The actor would theatrically cover the table in beer, food, and cigarettes. As Graeber points out, in order to have competitive gift giving, the objects presented must be easily comparable: otherwise there is no way to keep track of who has given more. The money itself was prominently exhibited, not hidden, in a *maquis* performance. Hierarchical reputation did not come from secret internal potency, but from persuasive display of potency. As we shall see in the next chapter, however, quite the reverse is the case for the brand name clothing being flaunted, whose announcement of authenticity masks the potency of the invisible histories upon which their value depends.

According to Graeber, the problem of Kwakiutl society is a cosmological theory of extreme polygenesis that renders individuality incommensurable. The urban situation for Ivoirians, in which individuals come from largely different ethnic and geographic backgrounds and are members of widely differing social networks and kinship groups, is in a strange way quite comparable to this dilemma. For both groups, it is the creation of society itself that forms a central cosmological problem. Graeber writes: "In this light, the potlatch was a mechanism for the endless re-creation of society: society defined . . . as a potential audience, the totality of those people whose assumptions matter to the social actor. Reproducing society is about assembling and having a dramatic effect on audience" (2001:217). This explains the recurring idiom of collectivity and waste in the context of the *maquis*. It was in the *maquis* that people as a group mattered and that a kind of collective recognition of the individual took place. This recognition was in itself constitutive of the group. The wanton destruction of wealth that so thrilled Abidjanais youth was a kind of moral technology for the production of urban Ivoirian collectivity, even if this collectivity only existed in the fleeting moment of the ritual. In making the *maquis* a space of ritual performance, they produced society in the form of an audience.

These acts of redistributing wealth paralleled historical Akan models of social reproduction, in which chiefs maintained their groups through carefully distributing wealth. The cognatic kinship system was flexible enough that groups could easily detach themselves from one chief and reattach themselves to another wealthier one, or even start their own village if they had enough wealth to attract members (Weiskel 1980). Furthermore, this pattern of authority production was both upheld and integrated into the system of the state, as Houphouët maintained a system of faithful support by disbursing state cocoa profits through personal networks, all the while making a show of the wealth of the state through magnificent ceremonies and the construction of monumental buildings.[8]

In a zero-sum system of moral economy, in which every success is at once praised and suspected of drawing its bounty through harm toward others, it would seem that the bluff would go against propriety, not only boasting about money your peers don't have but wasting it in a single night on consumables with no lasting material value. Instead, it formed the central mechanism in the regulation of personal networks and the establishment of personal success. The ritualized space of the *maquis* allowed for a kind of transcendence of normative contradiction that would be impossible in everyday contexts.

Reformulating classic theory on rites of passage, Terrence Turner (1976) emphasizes the role of ritual transcendence in allowing roles that conflict at the level of everyday social structure to coexist simultaneously. Taking the example of the roles "boy" and "man," Turner demonstrates that while in everyday life these are mutually exclusive categories, through transformative operation they can be made nonexclusive in a higher (or transcendent) level of the structure. Thus, "ritual behavior constitutes a means of dealing with this ambivalent and ambiguous relationship between the levels of a structure" (1976:65). Because the higher-level transformational aspect of structure has the power to alter any aspect of the lower-level structure of binary oppositions, it is both dangerous and powerful, and it is often symbolized by disorder and categorical confusion in the liminal phase of the ritual. Furthermore, the structure of the ritual is iconic of the very hierarchical structure of relations which gives it efficacy, while simultaneously representing the subjective experience of the social actor: "Ritual, in short, typically collapses sociocentric (i.e. relatively 'objective') and egocentric (i.e. 'subjective') levels of iconic representation within the same condensed symbolic vehicle" (T. Turner 1976:63). From the perspective of actors in the lower-level, quotidian realms, the transformative realm of ritual is seen as "the indispensable, generative ground of the system, a source of powers of a higher order," even as it embodies the danger of disorder and chaos (T. Turner 1976:58). Thus, social actors portray the efficacy of the system as external power from beyond, even as they are the ones producing it.

Applied to the sphere of the *maquis*, Terrence Turner's theory helps to explicate both the efficacy of the performance and its ability to combine the normally conflicting orders of individual self-promotion and collective distribution. In the dance of the *logobi*, the actors proclaimed their embodiment of modernity, combining dimensions of urban savvy with expertise over the authenticity of U.S. and European prestige goods and parading their ability to spend profusely. At the same time, this performance was combined with lavish distribution to their *frésangs*, during which the notion of collectivity was repeatedly invoked by the givers and recipients. In other words, the bluff had a real socioeconomic efficacy, because it allowed for a legitimate hierarchical transformation through the persuasive display of wealth (or the appearance of it) while simultaneously overcoming the immorality of economic differentiation through the reallocation of wealth within one's social sphere. As I discussed in the second chapter, the resulting expansion of social influence and increase in social network allowed for greater opportunity to perceive and safely profit from any *manzements* that might be in one's vicinity. Because of this transcendent power of *maquis* ritual, the bluff of success took on a kind of magical efficacy—the "social" of the audience provided the affirmation of the collective pole of belief that Lévi-Strauss (1963) tells us is necessary for the efficacy of sha-manic acts. Only in the *maquis* could the actor combine both the spheres of group identity and individual hierarchical superiority, generosity, and self-promotion.

Masculinity and the Dangerous Consumption of Women

If *maquis* ritual was capable of transcending normative conflict in the rela-tionships between men, such harmony was complicated by the ever-present threat of the women in their midst. For the dangers of display discussed earlier were not limited to male peer networks and disreputable clients at the same *maquis*: a far more salient fear shadowing the *bluffeurs* stemmed from the female members of the audience. *Nouchi* men felt that the most important element of seduction was the image of wealth and success, and indeed, the word *bluffer* also meant to cruise for women. Luc told me, "To seduce women one must get drunk, so that they will say you have money. That is why people like to sit in *maquis*; it is a way of saying 'money.'" Like-wise, *Gbich!* described the character of the *drageur* (playboy):

> Guy Martial Deubozieu [of-the-pretty-eyes] is a contractual employee some-where. Of middle class, he must manage his salary over the course of the month. Making 50,000 CFA a month [$75], he works his fingers to the bone just to hold on until they pay him. Without *dindin* [stopping to look] the man buys himself new clothes and shows up just as quickly in a *maquis* that he has had his eyes on. Calling the *go* [babe] that interests him to his side, he begins to order [drinks and food], all *pour la faire encaisser* [literally, to cash in on her]. The latter, who believes she has fallen on the chance of her life, does not hesitate to fall into his arms. She only loses her illusions when she sees him the next day completely broke taking the bus. (Simplice 2001:9)

On more than one occasion when telling this story, I have been asked by audience members if this was not a universal characteristic of gender rela-tions: men using wealth to seduce women. But as we saw in the last chapter concerning marriage, Abidjanais men were actually responding to a spe-cifically North Atlantic gender ideology in which men were supposed to be distributors of wealth and women consumers of it. This dovetailed with local values surrounding gender relations, which demanded that men ex-press their sentiments materially through gifts of money. To embody the new model of conjugality considered desirable in urban culture, men felt they had to exhibit wealth; the seductive image of modern attainment an urban Ivoirian man sought was caught up in a performance of masculinity as spending excessively. Any streetwise Ivoirian woman would be well aware he could not really afford such expenses, but both male and female seemed to collaborate in maintaining the fiction of his success.

Men cowered before women's acquisitive yearnings, fearing their capacity to reveal a fissure in the bluff. Mory, who made ends meet between work in an illegal cell phone booth, a coffee shop, and various "deals" on the side, had been planning a date with his girlfriend on the other side of the city for months, carefully saving his money. At the last minute he decided to cancel. Rather than explaining that he really wanted to be there but didn't have enough money, he told her that an important *ken* had come up and he needed to do business. I asked him why he didn't just tell her the truth, arguing she was probably much more insulted that he was prioritizing a deal over their date than if she knew he just hadn't received his money in time. Looking at me in desperation, he explained:

> She would leave me instantly. You don't know Ivoirian women. Maybe there is one in a thousand who is good enough to understand, but most of them are only interested in money, and as soon as they know you don't have it, they want nothing to do with you. In Côte d'Ivoire, you can't tell a girl you're poor. She will drop you like that. The moment she knows that you have a money problem she says to herself, "No, he's worthless; he's not interesting." That is why people will always pass money to the guy who is with a girl so that it looks like he is paying for everything.

The antagonism between the sexes is revealed by men's perceptions of women's limitless capacity for consumption. Abidjanais men represented women as creatures of insatiable appetite, whose only goal in life was to drain men of any income they had, then move on to another wealthier victim. Sitting in a *maquis*, I watched one man surreptitiously tell another who was flashing his money, "Damme tes pierres, bô . . . les gos va te din" (Hide your cash, man, the girls will see you). Again the ambivalence surrounding display emerges; the desire to show off one's wealth (often explicitly with the desire to attract women) mixed with the fear that others (especially women) will try to take advantage of your success. Despite all their talk of seduction and bluff, men felt powerless before the consuming demands of women in their life.

These ambiguities and anxieties are perhaps most clearly expressed in a pop song by Magic System entitled "Premier Gaou":

"Premier Gaou," by Magic System

It was in poverty that the girl Antou left me.
When I had a little, morning, noon, and night,
We were together on the Rue Princesse,
At Mille-Maquis, Sanfrofi, she was hanging out,
The money ran out, Antou changed sides,
Wari Bana ["broke" in Dioula] she changed boyfriends.

Thank God for me, I knew how to sing a little,
I made a cassette, you could see me on TV,
Morning, noon, and night it was me singing on the radio,
Antou saw that. She said, "The *gaou* [fool] has struck gold.
Hold on, I'll go scam him."

Chorus:
But, they say the first *gaou* is not *gaou*,
It's the second *gaou* that is *gnata* [The first time you are a fool, it's not
foolish, but the second time a fool, you're an idiot].

Sunday morning, knock knock, there is someone at my door,
To my great surprise, I see the girl Antou there.
Out of politeness I say, "It's been a long time."
She wants to lie to me. She says, "Dear, I was traveling,
now I have returned, and I belong to you.
Take me *cadeau* [free of obligation], whatever you want."

Chorus

So I said, "Darling, what would you like to eat?"
Without even hesitating she said, "Grilled chicken."
I said, "Darling, you want to eat chicken,
But a chicken is too small, it could not satisfy you.
A grilled alligator I'll give to you,
Stew of elephant, that's what you will eat."

She got mad, she said she's going back home,
But if she goes home, coagulation will kill me.
I asked for her forgiveness, and she accepted,
But a moment later, she ruined everything.

She gave up on chicken and started in on *alloko* [fried plantains].
"If you want *alloko*, it's no problem,
It is a plantation of bananas you will need to grill.
Instead of forks, they don't spear well enough,
It's with a pitchfork you will eat."
Chorus

(Magic System 2000)

In the song, Antou is a scheming gold digger who dumps the singer when he is poor and comes back when she hears he has made it big. When he tests her motives, she demands food, and the song emphasizes women's insatiable physical appetite, a superhuman ability to consume. But even as the chorus asserts men's ability to resist women, the protagonist does not send Antou away when he discovers her deception, for he fears that "co-agulation" will kill him. Urban Ivoirian men believed that if they did not have sex often enough, their semen would condense and become blocked, causing illness and even death. The song thus affirms men's vulnerability to women's seduction, even when they are aware of the beguilement.

One day walking on the street, Dedy and I ran into one of his many girl-friends, who invited us to her birthday party. In the same breath she asked Dedy for 5,000 CFA, since Easter was coming and she needed to get her hair done. As we walked away, he scowled: "Solange gives men too much crap. It's impossible to go to the party now; I'll have to say that I am sick. She says her hair needs to be done, she needs to go to the village for Easter. And my wife? Her hair isn't done either. How am I supposed to deal with that? It's like I walk in there with a pile of money on my head. The girl is used to all the grand types that go to the bar, she thinks I am one of them." Thus, men needed multiple women to prove their success to other men, but found themselves drained financially by these sexual connections. In private they complained about their inability to live up to the expectations of their female associates, even as publicly they threw their money around as though it were nothing. Even if women were aware of their boyfriends' limitations, they too needed to exploit these resources as best they could.

Luc told me about a group of women who lived on Avenue 19 called the *cleos* (a word that referred to guzzling straight out of the bottle):

They are clear-skinned like that, and they are always together.[9] People say that if you want to go out with one of these women, they send a spy to see if you have *pierres* [money]. Now, if you do, the woman accepts to go out with you. But they arrange the whole thing between themselves first. So when you arrive at the *maquis*, that same moment they all descend on your table. It is as though they had radar. You are obliged to pay for five or six women instead of one, and furthermore you have to make them *dai* [drunk], because they like to drink like that. If you really want the girl, you can easily spend 50,000 CFA like that without noticing it. They are dangerous, these girls.

Men were not alone in *yere* maneuvers of bluff and con. The *cleos* were the epitome of the *godrap*, feared for her ability to exploit men's resources even as men hoped to fool women into believing they were wealthy and worthy of attention (Newell 2009a).

As mentioned in the introduction, these dynamics, whether real or perceived, affected my own role as an ethnographer. At the beginning of my research, I often naively invited women from the neighborhood to join our table, or tried to set up appointments to talk to them. I did not realize the "danger" I was in until Dedy became angry with me for giving my phone number to a woman who had invited us to a nightclub. He said: "You have to understand that when a woman talks to you she is thinking primarily of money. When she sees white skin she thinks she has seen Jesus. So when Nicole invited us she was thinking that this would be great because *you* would be paying for her get into the club and buying her drinks. So it's just exploitation. You have to always pay attention to women here, they are dangerous." I was told that if I ever allowed a woman to know where I lived "it's all over," she would soon be living with me and cooking for me and I would never be able to get rid of her. Apparently I would be the exploited one in such a situation.

But how did women represent their own relationship to wealth and the bluff? I was often told women were even greater *bluffeurs* than men, though I think this was part and parcel of the same misogynistic perspective outlined above. Nevertheless, while some women dared to bluff with their boyfriends in the *maquis*, many who considered themselves too "proper" for such street displays still found a public site for the spectacle of consumption. A legitimate space for feminine display was in kin-dominated life cycle rituals discussed earlier, all of which were held in the street and so formed part of the public domain. In these spaces coded as under the control of kin, they were able to let go of propriety and perform with abandon. On such occasions women were the center of social space, dominating the dance floor and outshining the men in style and constructed self-presentation. They wore elaborate hairdos, expensive tailor-made dresses of African print material, and European shoes and purses. Here feminine competition came to the fore, as women examined each others' outfits carefully and evaluated them later in informal discussions with their peers. Women spent long hours preparing their appearance for such events, and any flaw or error was sure to be remarked upon. As described in the last chapter, women were crucial agents in the maintenance and organization of kinship networks and were thus in a much better position to acquire and control the funding for such events. Furthermore, women tended to benefit from the elaborate expenditures of men not only through compensation from informal sexual relations but also through their ownership of *maquis* and other sites vending food and liquor, and these funds cycled back into women's performative expenditures.

Women almost universally denied that they chose men based on material considerations but almost always continued by saying that they knew women like that, the ones that only considered money. More importantly, some women admitted to a kind of peer pressure between friends over the relative worth of the men they dated. Men themselves were a sort of accessory to the female bluff. Giselle went out with Raoul, a returned immigrant from the U.S. at least twenty years her senior and completely broke. His *Statois* (U.S.) identity made him a prestigious boyfriend for Giselle, but she became very upset when he talked about having no money: "You must not talk about problems of money in front of people. It's not good to talk

Figure 9. These women dance at a baptism celebrated under a tent in the street, shot through the bars of a gated entry to a *cour commune*. The whole street is blocked by the event. They wear clothes made from the same bolt of *pagne* cloth, a way in which families collected money to pay for these celebrations. The contrast between the style of the young woman on the left and the "proper" mother on the right demonstrates some of the variation in style possible.

about such things." I asked if women wanted men to lie about their wealth, and Giselle proclaimed that she herself desired the truth, but that some women preferred fantasies. "They don't like to hear about poverty. Women want their friends to think that her boyfriend is rich and powerful. This is a type of bluffing women do. They don't want their friends to think they would go out with a *vaut rien* [worthless guy]." Even though women were typically aware of the "real" state of their dates' finances, as a public secret, women were invested in the impenetrability of the man's illusion of wealth, for their reputation hung on male performance as well.

However, women did not only value men with wealth (or at least the appearance of it). *Godrap* girls did, in some cases, actively engage in taking what they could from their companions. Treichville was a community in which the ability to deceive others was highly esteemed, and perhaps one of the most socially acceptable ways for women to swindle people was to seduce men into giving them what they wanted. Sabine, the older and protective sister of the same Caroline we encountered earlier, muttered as Christophe and Solo walked away that those two were *draous*. She explained that girls used this word to refer to guys they didn't take seriously but whom they got to pay for everything. The linguistic relationship to the word *gaou* is obvious (in both sound and meaning), and the existence of this word used only by women points to women's active involvement in sex as a form of economic expropriation, as well as their creative role in the production of Nouchi (which men claimed women did not speak). A teenage girl from Luc and Solo's block once said to them, "Men think that they're the ones doing the whole *hohoho*, but why can't women be in the *mouvement* ['the informal economy,' but here 'movement' is clearly evocative in other ways]. You take me; I can take you. You can *mougu* [fuck]; I can *mougu* you too." This statement is at once a comment on the gender inequality of access to the informal economy on which men build their reputation as well as a comment about the structure of the sexual economy, in which men pretended to be the only agents. Gisele stated in no uncertain terms that in both realms, sometimes men were the ones getting screwed.

The day that Solange invited Dedy and me to her birthday party and demanded money, I asked Dedy about who celebrated birthdays. He told me that only women and children celebrated these:

> In any case, among adults, you never see guys celebrating their birthday; it's always girls. For women it is much easier to get money together; I think that is why. First, most women have at least three boyfriends, so she will go around and ask each of them to contribute. Then she is often able to find

a godfather or even a godmother. In any case, for girls, it's the facility of finance. . . . So she taps all these sources and pulls together a big party, with a tent, sound system, drinks, and everything. Often she doesn't spend a cent on the party, even though her guests are given free food and drink.

This picture appears to correspond well to the collective image of men as the suppliers of cash and women as the consumers. But in practice, men were not necessarily the sugar daddies that everyone pretended. For Dedy continued with a revealing conclusion: "That is why we guys often dream of having a girlfriend, because we feel it is easier to get things accomplished when you have a girl trying for you. We say, 'That which a woman wants, God wants.'" After all the stories of grasping, greedy *godraps*, it was women who had the "facility of finance" and provided for men in need! Precisely because they were allowed to ask for money from their boyfriends without shame, and could draw on kin resources more easily than men, women could get large sums of money together quickly. For this reason, despite male claims that "women are the greatest beggars of them all" and ample evidence of women's demands for money, men often relied on financial aid from women as well. Men's income was unpredictable and unstable but involved large lump sums interspersed with long droughts, while women tended to have jobs with steady incremental income. Furthermore, because men invested their energy and wealth primarily in nonkin networks, they could not demand very much from their weak kin ties, but intimate relationships with women allowed them a kind of access, a gateway, to those ultimately more reliable kin networks. The bluff was not only about building and securing intragender peer networks, then, but also about seducing across gender boundaries, thereby securing access to both the men's trade networks and women's kinship networks. The bluff was thus also a way of performing, producing, and reproducing kinship itself, or at least the urban social network form of it. Men seemed to speak of women as draining objects of prestige production, yet they depended upon women for financial stability. Women were feared for their ability to consume, but in reality there were social restrictions on women's access to arenas of display and public consumption as well as the profitable criminal economy. Women thus used men's reliance upon them as a central means of access to the space of bluff, prestige goods, and the benefits of the informal economy. In this way, women and men mutually constituted each other's productive social networks, performing their respective "modern" roles as male producer and female consumer, even as in practice these roles were somewhat reversed.

Gender and the Performativity of the Bluff

Sex itself was implicated in the economy of bluff: everyone was trying to *yere* someone else in Treichville, and perhaps nowhere more so than in the antagonistic relations between men and women, where every partner was a potential *gaou* ready to offer up their wealth along with their body. Such a relationship was hierarchical, an expression of the comparative modernity of the actors. I was told that women in villages were supposed to be attracted to *yere* men from the cities, but that when they arrived in cities they sought out the *gaou* men that they could "take for all their money." In the economy of the bluff, only those who mastered urban styles of life and the art of both tricking and avoiding being tricked would survive and prosper. This was the source of street hierarchy between men, but it was also a central tension between men and women, who attempted to outplay each other in the game of sexual exploitation. What I am interested in here is the way that sexual expression not only paralleled the economic model of urban life, but in fact was a dynamic part of that economy. The bluff was as much a means of making money by seducing one's victim as it was way of using money to seduce one's lover.

The bluff involved not only the Veblenesque conspicuous consumption of name brand sportswear and other prestige goods (Veblen 1899), nor simply the potlatch-style destruction of wealth around the table of beer,

Figure 10. The ideal type of the *bluffeur* and the effect he hopes to achieve. Notice the Mercedes pendant, the cell phone with earpiece, and the suggestion of labels on his clothes.

but also the performance of embodied gender identities of the "modern Other." I suggest that these competitive performances of otherness (what Butler calls "cross-identifications") can be compared to the performances of drag queens (Butler and Martin 1994; Butler 1990). Butler writes that "the transvestite, however, can do more than simply express the distinction between sex and gender, but challenges, at least implicitly, the distinction between appearance and reality that structures a good deal of popular thinking about gender identity" (1988:527). Drag undermines the distinction between mimesis and the original by demonstrating that the original is already a performance, an illusion: "In imitating gender, drag implicitly reveals the imitative structure of gender itself" (Butler 1990:187). In a passage that inspired Butler's theory of performative gender, Newton describes drag as a

> double inversion that says "appearance is an illusion." Drag says "my 'out-side' appearance is feminine, but my essence 'inside' is 'masculine.'" At the same time it symbolizes the opposite inversion; "my appearance 'outside' is masculine but my essence 'inside' is 'feminine.'" (1972:130)

Similarly, in the Ivoirian bluff, appearance indicated a modern and wealthy identity, while their "inside" continued to be an impoverished resident of the "global south." At the same time, the opposite: the *nouchi* youth's "outside" was known to be an unemployed urban hoodlum, but he was demonstrating that his cultural "inside" was that of a cosmopolitan man with the knowledge and wherewithal to equal any modern subject. In the economy of the bluff, embodied gender roles and the performance of modern identity coalesced into what constituted, for the *nouchi*, a symbolic (and real) transformation of the self. The urban Ivoirian actors were reveling in the illocutionary power of the performative, the ability to make real through appearance, if only temporarily, what was otherwise merely the reverie of desire. The bluff was more than simply the expression of the imaginary (Appadurai 1991; Gondola 1999; Weiss 2002, 2004); it was the projection of the fantastic onto the realm of the social.

However, Newton herself later critiqued Butler's work for taking the idea of parodic critique too far. As she wrote in 2000, "Drag and camp are not simply anti-essentialist performances that somehow undermine traditional gender dichotomy. . . . Both mundane and theatrical drag and camp are signification practices that cannot be separated from material conditions or from the intentions of actors and audiences who embody and interpret them" (66). Indeed, she writes, most drag performances "build on or reinforce" ideas of authenticity and essence rather than destabilizing them. Her analysis of lesbian transvestites' inability to take on the same kind of theatrical power as gay male actors leads to her request for more careful ethnographic analysis of power relations *within* the realm of the performance, rather than between the world of performers and the greater world of which they are a subculture. This distinction is crucial to understanding in what ways the bluff was at once a sort of conversion to the illusion of modernity offered by the "civilizing mission" narratives of the French and a form of resistance to it. The bluff was not, I would argue, the kind of playful, parodic camp described by Sontag (1964), even if it shared features of seduction and duplicity. Certainly the bluff, in its embrace of heightened theatricality, opened itself to multiple interpretations and play. However, it was not so much placing ironic quotation marks around the real, claiming life was theater, but rather the inverse: for the *bluffeurs*, the theater was life—it was a moment in which they could live as their "true" selves.

The double-edged performance of the bluff was more locally directed: it was a proclamation of modern identity that excluded all those in the audience that could not equal the performance while simultaneously undermining the semiotics of a political hierarchy that legitimated its class status through consumption of European luxury goods. The mimesis of African-American street style was at once a rejection of local class hierarchy based on elitist consumption of colonial symbols of power and a proclamation of superior cultural appropriation, since the U.S. was understood to be a site of greater contemporary power and modernity than Europe (Newell 2005). Thus, the bluff was neither a Fanonian postcolonial loss of authentic identity (Fanon 1967) nor an eye-winking slight of colonial whiteness, but a critique of local power and claim to superiority, utilizing the semiotic force of alterity.

The point can be illustrated through a comparison with the African-American drag balls of Livingston's film *Paris Is Burning* (1990). Throughout the film, background music focuses on the song "Got to be Real" by Cheryl Lynn, and the performers highlight the importance of being "real" or "natural" in their interviews. While the actors are concerned with masking sexuality in a heteronormative public, the categories performed at the ball speak to broader questions of identity, including soldiers, business executives, college students, and high-class models, as well as lower-class male and female heterosexual African-Americans. The ability to blend into "real" categories of life from which they are excluded is crucial—as well as the corresponding knowledge that doing so is *always* an act—but of almost equal importance is the fantasy of social importance, glamour, and wealth, all of which the actors feel they are entitled to. As Pepper LaBeija puts it, "I never felt comfortable being poor, I just don't. Or even middle class doesn't suit me. Seeing the riches, seeing the way people on *Dynasty* lived, these huge houses." Another performer adds, "A ball to us is as close to reality as we are going to get to all that: fame, fortune, and stardom and spotlights." A ball, they tell filmmaker Jennie Livingston, is a place where anything you want to be, you can be. And just as in the bluff, there is a crossover between this ritually produced space of fantasy and everyday life, as some of them dreamed of "making it for real" as models and dancers in the world of "actual" glamour.

Here it becomes quite clear that Newton's request for attention to the ethnographic complexity of local performance is not incompatible with Butler's approach to the semiotic challenge that performance raises for discourses of authenticity. For I agree that the drag queens at these balls are not actively trying to take down the hierarchies of class, race, or sexuality in their competitions (they are trying above all to bring down their competitors and gain status within local networks), and yet their boldfaced presentation of their ability to live—even if momentarily—like people in *Dynasty* does challenge the basis of "distinction" through which class legitimates its hierarchy.

I suggest that urban sexual antagonism in Côte d'Ivoire and beyond ought to be understood not simply in terms of domestic economic struggles, but also in terms of public acts of performative consumption, through which both men and women attempted to produce success through the creation of its illusion, and in the process made use of transnational gender roles they believed to embody modernity. Male and female genders were played to be read by their audience as Westernized, and since the bluff was a kind of seduction, desire itself was structured by the imagination of the modern Other. Through the performance of modernity, actors both seduced their lovers, secured their social networks, and challenged the symbolic (pseudocolonial) capital of the political elite. In the act of the bluff, the extravagant spending of money on the act of seduction was a kind of conversion from one sphere of exchange to another, producing social and sexual relations that were far more important to survival in the contemporary economic structure. Thus, as in the performance at a drag ball, the real and the imagined, the original and its imitation, the embodied and the superficial merged into indistinguishable social experience. Socially, for all intents and purposes, the *bluffeur* was wealthy, successful, and symbolically modern, and yet he was poor and powerless in the face of numerous symbolic and economic obligations from his network, lovers, and kin. In the urban Ivoirian imagination of modernity, women were consumers and men were providers, and for both sexes, the bluff became a dance of exploitation, in which seduction was money and money was sex, and the performance of gender produced social networks for urban survival.

FOUR

Fashioning Alterity: Masking, Metonymy, and Otherworld Origins

Toujours bien sapé . . . Toujours bien protégé [Always well dressed . . . Always well protected]. (An Ivoirian condom advertisement)

Adornment intensifies or enlarges the impression of the personality by operating as a sort of radiation emanating from it. . . . One may speak of human radioactivity in the sense that every individual is surrounded by a larger or smaller sphere of significance radiating from him; and everybody else, who deals with him, is immersed in this sphere. It is an inextricable mixture of physiological and psychic elements: the sensuously observable influences which issue from an individual in the direction of his environment also are, in some fashion, the vehicles of a spiritual fulguration. They operate as symbols of such a fulguration even where, in actuality, they are only external, where no suggestive power or significance of the personality flows through them. The radiations of adornment, the sensuous attention it provokes, supply the personality with such an enlargement or intensification of its sphere: the personality, so to speak, *is* more when it is adorned. (Simmel 1950:339)

A central figure in Abidjan social life was the *bluffeur*, that is, a master of the art of bluff, one who produced images of success regardless of real economic means. While theatrical displays of wealth in the *maquis* were of crucial importance to the efficacy of such imagery, the urban Ivoirian bluff was constructed primarily around the consumption of North Atlantic clothing and other prestige commodities. Unlike North Atlantic societies, which often fear clothing's potential to confuse social categories, Ivoirians did not see such "bluffing" negatively. Historically, in both Europe and the U.S. upper classes have sometimes even instituted sumptuary law to restrict such transgressions (Agnew 1986; White and White 1998), while contemporary U.S. youth culture scorns acts of faking it with the taunt of "poser."

Although Abidjanais recognized quite explicitly that many people who appeared wealthy were merely presenting a false front, they did not typically consider such acts inauthentic, superficial, or dishonest. Bamba writes that "to possess these imported goods seems to confer admiration on the individual, and even a certain power over others who find themselves in a position of inferiority" (1982:3). In Côte d'Ivoire the possession of commodities from *Beng* conferred immediate prestige upon the person in contact with them. Clothes really did make the man.

Abidjanais were proud of their ability to bluff, and the capacity to project an image of success was considered to be of primary importance by the wealthy and impoverished alike. It didn't seem to matter that the audience knew the actual limited economic circumstances of the actor, rather, it was the aptitude for artifice that was praised and evaluated. Such performances could produce real social transformations, increasing hierarchical superiority through reputation and, within criminal networks, greater access to knowledge and material exchange in the informal economy. But there was a kind of aporia with the bluff that I shall explore throughout this chapter: it was at once based on the idea of deception and the prestige of illusion, and at the same time no one was fooled—the audience was aware of the hoax before the show even began. And yet everyone acted as though the bluff were real. Indeed, the distinctions between artifice and the real, representation and misrepresentation, deception and self-deception broke down in the face of the bluff.

As in poker, the bluff was at once a misleading statement about one's success and an attempt to profit from others through that performance. In an economy of cons, the bluff refers to the skill of the actors in extracting wealth through deceit as well as their ability to climb the walls of social hierarchy through illusion. The bluff was an effort to produce that which it represented itself as already being (the winning hand, the successful man). It involved an intimate relationship with consumption, for it was an act of the embodiment of objects, a literal absorption of their value into the person through public performance. Thus, even though the bluff was inseparable from economic transaction, its impetus was in the realm of symbolic transformation.

The bluff expressed the urbanized cosmopolitan identity of the actor. Actors knew that their audience was well aware of their struggling financial reality; their aim was not to fool others into thinking they were rich, but rather to convince them that they knew *how* to be rich, how to embody the identity and lifestyle of those they aspired to become. I argue that urban Ivoirian consumption worked according to a kind of magical efficacy (though *bluffeurs* did not explicitly consider it in these terms), whereby according to semiotic connections of contiguity (metonymy), social actors possessing objects incorporated qualities of power drawn from the external into their personae. Obviously, this form of consumption involves metaphor as well, since they were explicitly imitating a "look" they associated with the U.S., but from an analytical perspective, all acts of consumption contain elements of metaphor and metonymy, as do all acts of magic. However, I am concerned with exploring the semiotic logic of evaluation through which those practicing consumption (or magic) located the source of causality. As Terrence Turner (1991) has argued, tropes cannot be looked at in isolation from the context of their use, but must be embedded in the cultural structures in which they are used. Despite their focus on appearances, I will show how Abidjanais consumption emphasized relations of metonymy in the evaluation of objects and persons. Metaphorical performance became a means of persuasion for the invisible metonymic links of authenticity.

Because modernity is a North Atlantic ideology legitimating global hierarchy, it makes a ready logic for Ivoirian appropriation as a language for thinking through power transfers and hierarchical scenarios. In this chapter, I elaborate the ways in which the conceptual apparatus of modernity has been imbricated with local logics of externality, metonymy, and materiality. By investigating this locally produced cosmology of cultural evolution, I hope to provide the basis for taking apart the assumptions of mimicry and superiority implicit in globalization theory.

The Centrality of the Sartorial

There was an adage in Abidjan that men prioritized first clothing, second women, then drinking. Bamba surveyed Ivoirians and found that 83% said that clothing was important in life (73% said "very" important), and he could find no correlation between these responses and the relative income of those questioned (1982:29). When I asked Luc and Christophe whether clothing was important for Ivoirians, they whistled in shock:

> This is what the Ivoirian does most. Everybody wants to follow the latest
> fashions. For example, there are American shoes, the Sebagos, which every-
> one wants to have now. But there are several varieties: at 25,000 CFA or at
> 50,000 [$35 and $70]. The expensive ones are real, the others are imitations,
> and you need to get the real ones. Another thing that is good are Dock-
> ers pants. With those you are good to go. We only want American brands,

Frame argument as a result of contextual information

French stuff we don't go for. Yes, the essential thing is *la frime*. There are *bluffeurs* here, dêh! . . . We are always searching to appear better than the next guy. Even if you don't have the means, you will go buy new sneakers or a shirt to show that you have what it takes, what is in fashion, more expensive than the other guy's, even if it breaks the bank account [neither of these guys had ever had access to a bank account].

This conversation combines a number of important themes which recur throughout this chapter: the importance of the brand, the importance of the cost, the irrelevance of income to appearance, and the fixation on authenticity and the origin of products. All of these were spheres of competition through which urban Ivoirians negotiated their identity in a war of appearances.

Simon, another carefully dressed youth in his twenties (one in the *nouchi* network), told me that

Africans adore dressing up! You must be "proper" if you want respect. Take a guy like the Brick, walking around in shorts and 300 CFA flip-flops. How can anyone expect to be respected wearing flip-flops? They could never dress like that in Europe, never. No, it's OK to dress like that when you're home, sure, *ça va*, but to go out on the streets? No, one must have a proper appearance. That brings respect.

This sentiment was echoed by Charles, another young man who walked with exaggerated style, wore fake glasses, and spoke in exceedingly mannered French:

I do like the *sape* [the art of dress] very much. It's true that it was a much stronger movement when the country was economically healthy, but there are still those who make an effort. Of course the rich have always dressed nicely and still do; they are unaffected, but I'm talking about people who are willing to make sacrifices for fashion. The *sape* is a way of presenting oneself to the world. When people see you, they know even before they talk to you that you are proper, that you are decent, and they make assumptions about your way of life.

A struggling clothing designer from a neighboring *quartier* explained that

Ivoirians love to dress. Everyone saves their money so that they can buy nice stuff. Dress is a way to get respect above your means, and in that sense it is good. It is a way of creating opportunities. When you see people dressed in a suit, you are afraid. But really they have nothing, they are just *bluffeurs*. There are a lot over in Plateau as well, they go to look at the clothing boutiques. Over there it is impossible to know if they are really a *boss* or not. But when they dress in their own *quartier*, everyone knows where they live and that they have nothing. There are people who live for appearance. I have a cousin who . . . will sleep for days at the clothing factory eating whatever he can get his hands on cheaply, just so that he can get the money together for more clothes. He saves his money so carefully that he has never had a girlfriend, because he can't spend the money on her to keep her. He can't work either, he doesn't have time. Everything is about getting more clothes.

The anthropologist reading these testaments to fashion must address the question of why clothing and appearance are so important to urban Ivoirians. How can it be that people without jobs, living in airless rooms with communal squat toilets and one shared water faucet, prioritize clothing over other elements of their life? The designer's statement described the value of appearing above one's "means" as good, *even though* everyone knew that the person in question had nothing. Appearance had value in and of itself.

When I asked Luc about all the rich people wearing suits in Plateau, he laughed and said that about half the people there were just *bluffeurs*. They told their neighbors they had jobs in Plateau, left the house in a suit with a briefcase, then walked all the way there, because they couldn't afford transportation. All that their briefcase held was their lunch, and they spent the day in the park gambling. But you could tell which ones were the real *bosses*, because a real *boss* would never be walking on the street; he would be riding in his air-conditioned Mercedes. A *Gbich!* cartoon satirized the complications engendered by these practices in a story called "Bluff Inutile" (Useless bluff). A man stands outside a building in a very nice suit and tie, as another explains how his new job as a chauffeur will work. Just then a childhood friend leaves the building, and the first man begins to bluff, telling his friend he is an accountant for a corporation waiting for his secretary. Only it turns out that he is to be the chauffeur for his old friend; the game is up. Abidjanais recognized the bluff as part of the artistry of social life and held respected such performances. However, if the bluff was publicly exposed, when the audience was made explicitly aware of false pretenses, the bluff brought great shame. In other words, the bluff did not fool anyone, but it was a public secret. Everyone knew *bluffeurs* had little but their name, but this knowledge could not be spoken without risking a great many social relationships.

Cell phones were continually used for such performances. In the Ivoirian cell phone system, it was possible to receive calls for free if you had a phone, and since cell phones were the staple trade of the criminal network, many people carried quite nice cell phones. Only they couldn't afford to call anyone. Therefore, it was not uncommon to see a man pull up in a Mercedes, step out of his car in all brand name clothing carrying the tiniest, hippest cell phone, and go to a phone booth to make his call. On the other hand, it was so prestigious to talk on one's phone that many people pretended to have conversations when no one was on the other line. Solo and Christophe never tired of borrowing my phone to walk around the street having such one-sided conversations. Christophe even wanted to make an arrangement to lend him the phone and then call him from a phone booth so that everyone would see him answer. Papis carried a broken cell phone, admitting openly it was just so he could bluff with it. In the same way, Ivoirians considered being seen with me a form of bluffing just because I was white. As I was standing and talking to one friend, a woman passed by and called out to him, "You think you can bluff talking to a white guy. But I have a white boss I can talk to, so I am unimpressed." Danny called back, "Where is this white boss? My white guy is right here."

As seen in a number of studies of photography in other African locales (Mustafa 2002; Behrend 2002), photographs were another way of showing off, and pictures were carefully constructed to display the subjects as though in a different world. When I tried to take pictures for a special occasion when some of my friends were particularly dressed up, everyone wondered whether the surroundings were not too "dirty," such that the proper effect would not be achieved. Some of my friends from the neighborhood had me take pictures of them in my room because they said it looked like a hotel room and they could tell people they had stayed in one. In the pictures, they carefully positioned themselves (always on the bed) with certain objects, like a bottle of whiskey and a Walkman, and asked me to make sure I included the magazine images I had taped to the wall. Despite being deathly afraid of cats (which could be agents for witches), Christophe even demanded a picture with a cat that had befriended me, because he said that it made him look more "European."

Absalam, a middle-class tailor and model (working for a well-known Ivoirian designer), analyzed Abidjanais practices of dress in terms of silent competition: "Yes, people want this kind of stuff for *la frime*. They will show up in a *maquis* and sit in just such a way that you will be forced to see the label and know that they paid more for their shirt than you did. . . . Ivoirian competition is a silent competition, a subtle competition in which

Figure 11. Christophe was afraid of cats because they were potential agents of witches. But knowing that Europeans like cats, he asked to pose in this photo with a neighborhood cat that stopped by my apartment.

one says nothing but shows nonetheless that one is better." Absalam's idea of silent competition helps to see the way in which clothing allowed people to say things without really saying them. If a man in Treichville were to brag about his wealth, people would tell him to his face that this was *blo* (bullshit). But to dress *as though* one were wealthy was another matter all together. The statement of superiority was implied and difficult to counter except on its own terms, that is, by dressing better oneself.

Dress was important for women as well, although the ramifications were somewhat different. As one tailor put it, "Women also compete, yes. . . . Some people spend all their time trying to follow the latest fashion. *Être à la page* [be on the page]. Especially women. Women keep track of all their friends' clothes. They know if she only has three outfits, or five. They know how often she wears each thing and catalog it, so a woman has to be well dressed all the time. Women always dress up to impress their *copines* [female friends]." Whereas men often said they dressed well in order to seduce women, women said they dressed in order to retain face in front of their female peers. In practice, this distinction was highly blurred: competition and seduction worked in both directions. While men competed with each other almost entirely through clothing from *Beng*, with the occasional local accessory, women's fashion was centered around the *pagne*. *Pagnes* are African-print materials imported from around the world and draped and tailored in an array of styles, many of them modeled on form-fitting European looks in contradistinction to the more traditional wraparound look worn by older women. Women also wore imported European clothes, or accessorized with high-heel shoes and leather purses, but the evaluation of women's fashion was dominated by the *pagne*. I shall explore the connections between male and female clothing semiotics later in the chapter.

The Bluff: Appearance and Economy

The paradox of urban Ivoirian consumption was that appearance and wealth did not correlate as one expected them to . . . and yet everyone acted as though they did. In other words, despite people's awareness that those around them were presenting mere illusions of wealth, they went on behaving as though clothing signified success. Somehow clothing retained a very real value, one that people challenged verbally from time to time, but very rarely in their actions. That is, while some Abidjanais might critique the bluff on principle, most still collaborated both in their own image and in the reception of others'.

Dedy perhaps said it best in a classic analysis of Treichville life. We were sitting in an illegal *maquis*, set up temporarily in the middle of the street (and taken apart by dawn), surrounded by what were apparently some of the hippest youth in Treichville. They were slouching on their chairs, mostly dressed in basketball shirts, T-shirts, baseball hats, shorts, and baggy pants. I was just beginning to realize that they were in the height of style. Dedy commented:

> People who dress really well, you can be sure that they don't really have a good job, that they don't work. To afford clothes like that you have to steal for a living. A person with a real job can't spend money earned through hard work on clothes. When a new clothing store comes into town it is dangerous, because the *nouchi* will try extra hard to steal money so they can go buy stuff.

Figure 12. Solo bluffs at the *bangidrome*. Despite the poverty of his surroundings, he maintains his pose. He has borrowed my Walkman in order to augment the effect.

Thus, within the *quartier populaire*, there would seem to be an almost inverse correlation between wealth and nice clothing.[1] From Dedy's perspective, at any rate, to dress well was evidence of criminal inclinations, of the lack of a job. But thieving was not inherently disrespectable, indeed, for the *nouchi*, it represented a more respectable way of life than the menial labor of the foreign *gaous*.

Raoul, freshly returned after a twenty-year absence, was continually surprised by the disparity between wealth and appearance, despite having grown up in Côte d'Ivoire:

> I am always shocked to see girls dressed up in fancy clothes, high heels, made up, rolling their ass, coming out of a smelly, ugly, dirty *cour commune*. I couldn't believe the girl I slept with in Dabou. When I met her I would never have known that she slept on the floor in a little room in a *cour commune*. She had no furniture, just about five suitcases of clothes. . . . She looked so perfectly put together and wealthy so long as she was separated from her house.

Coming from an outsider perspective, Raoul was shocked, but most Abidjanais did not see this disparity in the same way. Unlike Andie in *Pretty in*

Pink, who asks to be dropped off several blocks from her house in order to hide her poverty, an Ivoirian woman would not necessarily feel shame at being seen strutting out of her communal courtyard in her high heels.

The lack of correlation between income and appearance was further supported by Absalam the tailor, who invoked the opposition between Ivoirians and the immigrant population which "does all the work":

> True Ivoirians love competition, *la frime*. That is all they do, in fact. Ivoirians are not workers. We depend on immigrants for all the dirty work. Nothing would get done without them, because we prefer to sit around showing off. We are too proud to work as a taxi driver or sell *garba* [cheap Ivoirian staple food]. But the guys who sell *garba* make money! They build houses with it. When you visit them you know they are doing well. This is where Côte d'Ivoire's problems come from. All these foreigners come here and work and we just consume. And they make money, and instead of investing it here, they take it back to their country with them. If only we were doing the work, we would be better off. We are too busy making ourselves look successful.

The recurring expression "true Ivoirians" is of great importance for understanding the links between a *yere* sense of style and an emergent form of national identity. Of course, to look successful, from a *nouchi* perspective, meant precisely to not work. Not working was a kind of display in its own right and was simply one more element of the bluff. By the same token, as I will discuss further on, those who did work, by default "untrue" Ivoirians or immigrants, could have plenty of money, but they didn't know how to dress properly. As demonstrated by Fidèle, wealth in itself, divorced from cultural legitimacy, did not confer prestige.

Olivier, who had grown up in the family of a wealthy *fonctionnaire* (prestigious civil servant) but been left to his own devices when his father died (he was the son of a different mother from the rest and hence in a matrilineal system not part of the family), lived with his friend Solo's family in France-Amérique, scrounging pennies to get enough to eat. After watching a man in a suit and tie walk by, he turned me and complained:

> I can't believe how Ivoirians have no money but they go ahead and wear expensive clothes anyway. If I see five guys go by, I can be sure at least one of them is wearing jeans or some other expensive item of clothing. And yet he will tell you he doesn't have any money. I take this as a sign of not being very mature, very wise. If they weren't so caught up in getting the pleasure of the moment, they would save the money and invest it in something, and

then they would have enough money to be at ease, and have the clothes they want. OK, sure they need the clothes to attract girls, but if they can just wait a little while they can have it all. If with 70,000 I spend 50,000 on Sebago, I only have 20,000 left. But if I use this money to buy embroidered cloth and sell it, and keep using the money I gain to do various little businesses, I would have like two million by the end of the year. Then I could spend one million on clothes and have plenty left over for other things. But Ivoirians don't think like that.

Although very serious minded, Olivier was as much a *bluffeur* as any of his peers, as can be seen by the final phase of his economic plan, in which he would spend half his profit, one million CFA ($1,500), on clothing. Perhaps targeting me with a demonstration of his own "cultured" identity (another level of bluff), he critiqued the lack of correspondence between appearance and wealth, wondering about the ways that "Ivoirians" prioritized.

In fact, for those *dedans le mouvement* (in the criminal scene), money was not really all that necessary for acquiring clothing, as Dedy indicated. There were many ways to attain good clothes through social networks. Dedy's older brother Danny explained that:

> People have many ways of getting clothes, especially through contacts. Even if you don't steal you can dress well with little money. For example, if you can make friends with *un enfant de Cocody* [a rich kid from the most prestigious quarter], they put little value on their clothes, for them clothes come easy. Whereas we on the street in Treichville know the real value. The kid might be willing to sell a shirt worth 50,000 for just 5,000, because he wants something to drink. He didn't pay for the shirt himself; what does he care? Another system is to borrow the clothes. Because if you are a *yere* in Treichville there is a lot of pressure to always have new clothes. Because if you come out in the same ensemble too often, people will begin to talk, to scorn you, saying, "Him, he goes out in old things." So you have to work your contacts to always have something new.

Exchanges within social networks provided the necessary goods, and in this way, not only was clothing an invalid indicator of wealth, but also, in a place like Treichville, wealth was largely irrelevant to one's ability to *frime*. On the other hand, fine attire might more accurately measure one's social connectivity.

Somewhat paradoxically, Abidjanais never failed to be impressed by the monetary value of an item of clothing. As we prepared to go to Solo's brother's funeral, Solo and Christophe stepped out of their ten-by-ten-foot windowless room (shared by five people) into the public eye of the court-yard, wearing their finest attire. Henri's father (a renowned miser), smiled at them sardonically, before lauding them: "These youths aren't just amus-ing themselves. That is money, eh! They are walking on 150,000 CFA right now, like that." Though Solo and Christophe were proudly displaying their clothes that day, only weeks before they had carefully hidden them in my apartment to keep anyone from knowing about the new purchases until they had occasion to flaunt them. On their arrival, they excitedly tried on the new goods, all the while checking out the window to make sure their friend Luc outside was not going to come in. They told me that Luc and Mory never spent their money, and they were always chiding the rest of the group for squandering all their money on alcohol. "Well, they will see who's smart now, who has fun *and* looks good," Christophe gloated. Their secrecy stemmed from the questioning of their financial *sagesse* (wisdom, maturity). It was important that they unveil their prestigious purchases in such a way as to silence the criticism of their peers with the power of appearance.

Like the displays of wealth in the *maquis*, dressing too well could have negative repercussions as well. Paradoxically, while everyone wanted to look "successful," it was dangerous to convey an image of too much wealth. This was the explanation the members of the France-Amérique group of-fered for why they and their generation were generally not interested in suits: "Most people don't like to wear suits, because then everyone thinks they have a lot of money. They don't want to give the impression of a *boss*." Likewise, when I noticed the young tailor (as a migrant, he was unembar-rassed to work publicly) across the street totally dressed up in dress shoes, and slacks, with his shirt tucked in, and wearing a tie and glasses, I asked him why. He responded:

> Some days you just have to get out of the ordinary. I'm in the clothes of the *boss* today, no? Well, I just felt that if I was going to run a *couture* shop I had better show that I know what clothing is about. But I don't like to dress this way very often because people will say I am doing well for myself, that "lui, il est malin" [him, he is cunning]. If they see you like that twice in a row, they will say that "non, vraiment il est trop malin" [no, truly he is too clever]. Three times and they won't be your friend anymore. It's not so much that they are jealous as that they are *aigre* [sour, bitter]. Africans are too bitter, man!

Here we run into the dynamic of moral economy encountered in chapter 2, as well as the dangers of display discussed in chapter 3. If one too frequently *fait le show* with more success than one's friends, they would think you were holding out on them, not sharing your wealth with those who were most important to you. You risked being robbed or, worse yet, cut off from their network. Even though everyone in the quarter knew that this tailor was just that, an underpaid tailor (after all, he was standing on the street ironing clothes when I encountered him), they would begin to suspect him of claiming a superior standing to their own if he were to dress up too often.

In all of these stories then, we encounter a strange disjuncture between the appearance produced by prestigious clothing and the financial means of those producing the appearance. The conceptual link between the sartorial representation and "real" success was by no means a straightforward semiotic communication; the message seemed rather to function *as if* clothing indicated success, even while Abidjanais continually critiqued the validity of the symbol. This was the essence of the bluff. Even while urban Ivoirians recognized clothing as histrionic, they valued the act of performance itself, the successful image as an image. In fact, whether the "signified" of clothing's "signifier" had a true or false relationship to economic reality was irrelevant to its evaluation. Instead, Abidjanais seemed interested in how "true" the imitation was to the original, of how accurate the copy was—much as Vann (2006) found in Vietnamese consumers' evaluation of "mimic goods." As I shall argue in the sections to follow, the bluff was really a demonstration of *cultural* rather than economic superiority. It was the demonstration of the knowledge and taste acquired by the self-proclaimed modern urban social actor.

Elite Consumption: Following the French

Until the 1990s, urban Ivoirians ranked each other according to a common standard: the French.[2] Ever since the first educated *évolués* began to wear suits to their colonial jobs, the suit has had important symbolic resonance in Côte d'Ivoire. The ability to match this ideal appearance of elegance (shined leather shoes, a tailored suit, necktie and shirt, gold watch, briefcase, and glasses) became an iconic scale of prestige and power in urban Ivoirian society.

Although clothing was probably the most concrete manifestation of this emulation, the Ivoirian government and the elite cadre that populated it held a much broader project of cultural evolution in mind: the imposi-

france provision on fashion influenced the youth

tion of French culture as the model for development. Such standardization projects were not limited to language but encompassed all realms of self-presentation, such as manners, the aesthetics of the body, eating habits, and, of course, dress. The Ivoirian secretary of state pronounced in 1973: "The fact that culture will henceforth take its place in this country's plan of development is the best proof of [our] evolution. . . . Culture, in effect . . . is henceforth perceived by the authorities as the support, the dynamic of all development, because economic development alone does not suffice to determine a country's degree of evolution" (Touré 1981:24). This was an *Ivoirian* concept of cultural evolution, one that had been appropriated and localized, integrated into the local cosmology of cultural hierarchy, and versions of it refracted through all urban socioeconomic groups to some extent. By no means simply the product of elite education, this conceptual framework was regularly employed by urban Ivoirians of many different backgrounds.

Touré's book *La Civilisation Quotidienne en Côte d'Ivoire: Procès d'Occidentalisation* (1981) is an excellent analysis of elite discourse and consumption practices, treating everything from textbooks, advertisements, and restaurants to kinship patterns and political speeches. One of his sites of criticism is the advertisements for Le Toit d'Abidjan (The Roof of Abidjan), Abidjan's most prestigious restaurant at the time, more or less directly modeled on the Tour d'Argent in Paris: "The Roof of Abidjan. Dine at the summit. A prestigious restaurant where you can, close to the stars in a refined setting, appreciate a dinner *à la française* with candles and music" (Touré 1981:38). The restaurant was at the top of a twenty-four-story tower of Côte d'Ivoire's most deluxe hotel, which had a bowling alley, an ice skating rink, a pizza parlor, a casino, several swimming pools, and a fake Disneyesque village populated by "real" indigenes. As Touré puts it, "One must have visited this place at least once in life to not die a *dago* [an old slang word for *gaou*, or ignoramus]" (1981:40). Although my own visit to the establishment revealed a decrepit building, most of whose supplementary attractions had long been shut down, the Hotel Ivoire remained a focus of Ivoirian images of wealth. I heard several stories about Treichville youth dressing up in suits and wandering around the grounds as though they were customers. Those who won the lottery or *bengistes* trying to prove their new wealth upon returning from Europe often stayed a couple of nights at the Hotel Ivoire. For them it had lost none of its glamour, and when they told their friends back in the quarter of their exploits, they carried a bit of the sheen of the Ivoire with them. In this sense, the hotel's explicit exclusivity was speaking to more than its rich clientele's desire for luxury; it also described an Ivoirian ideal of proximity to French culture. Indeed it was here that the Jeunes Patriotes staged their defiance against French tanks in 2004, demanding the departure of all French citizens from their soil, and here that Outtara lived while waiting for Gbagbo to give up power in 2011.

Another of Touré's most interesting observations focuses on the "modernization" of the body. He treats a number of beauty advertisements directed at Ivoirian women. In many cases such adds depict white women, inviting comparison by asking why "you, too" can't have this shapely silhouette. The products themselves are often designed to mute racial signifiers by straightening hair or lightening skin. In other cases the ads stress the origins of the product or method, claiming that it utilizes the latest treatment developed in the U.S., or that a hairdresser has had three years of training "in Paris." Value, Touré surmises, comes from the Occident, not from the skill of the hairdresser herself or evidence of a given product's efficacy. It is the origin that is emphasized. Arguing that Côte d'Ivoire's many diverse ethnic groups each had their own canons of beauty, but that these have been undermined by "occidentalization," Touré writes:

> For the project of constructing the Ivoirian nation is also theoretically a project of uniformity: beyond the diverse ethnic canons [of beauty], there are henceforth canons for all and everyone. But this does not signify that there is equality in the actualization of these new models, but merely that multiplicity has been replaced by bipolarity: the differences between ethnic groups are negligible in comparison to that which separates the new upper class from the rest of society. It is therefore the civilization-modernization of the body that we have participated in since colonization, because modernization haunts this class especially. (Touré 1981:146)

Notice that the process of creating a national uniformity was modeled upon aesthetic norms appropriated from *outside* Côte d'Ivoire, and that it was precisely their external origin that was emphasized. Just as Standard French was imported as a tool for uniting the nation and simultaneously imposed as a universal signifier for social hierarchy, differential adaptation to European norms of beauty served to signify relations of superiority and inferiority. But unlike the models Bourdieu constructs for language (1991) and the distinction of taste (1984), here the model for standardization and hierarchical evaluation was imported from outside the society itself. In such a situation the elites themselves were forced into a relationship of imitation: they too were *bluffeurs*, competing at another level.

This was particularly true after the country fell on hard times (after crashes in the cocoa and coffee markets in 1979 and 1987), forcing even the wealthy to tighten their belts. The wealthy family I stayed with in Abidjan's Riviera my first month presented a surface of pure success. The father drove a recent-model BMW, dressed in nice clothes, and lived in a large house in a walled-in compound. His children were all in upper levels of education, and his wife studied at a university in the United States. But upon closer inspection, many aspects of his wealth were superficial. His once-beautiful house was in serious disrepair, with leaking plumbing, broken stairs, torn curtains, and broken air conditioning, and populated by rats. Although a satellite dish graced his yard, it was no longer connected to anything, and he was barely able to receive the two Ivoirian television stations. When his car was stolen at gunpoint, he couldn't afford to replace it and relied on public transportation for the rest of the time I was in the country. His story was by no means unique. Raoul, the returned migrant, told me about a couple that he met who lived in a fantastic house in Riviera with several maids and a fancy car. I had seen them visiting Raoul in his parents' *maquis* in Treichville, a fly-infested courtyard with only low wooden benches to sit on. He explained that despite their apparent wealth, they had visited him in order ask for a loan of 50,000 CFA ($70) for a business venture. When he refused (he didn't have the money), they asked for 5,000 CFA ($7) for gas for their car so they could get home.

Bamba argues that "the value of a university student depends less on their academic success than the appearance they present, their material attributes" (1982:31). Of those he interviewed 92% said that they "necessarily" gave respect and admiration to richly dressed people (31), even though, in response to another question, some complained that "one does not know who is who" (51). One sociology student that lived on my block told me that there were even university classes for would-be *fonctionnaires* on how to dress in a suitable fashion for such a position. He compared people who dressed in such a manner to con artists, calling it *la traffique d'influence*. The students scorned "traditional" clothing and "modern" clothes made locally, 75% arguing that foreign clothes were of better quality. Students tended to vaunt the cost of their clothing, and so many stores in Plateau found it beneficial to raise their prices extravagantly in order to draw interest away from competitors (Bamba 1982:39). Asked why clothing was so important, one student said, "We live in a society of *tape à l'oeil* [literally, hits the eye]. One must declare oneself to be seen" (Bamba 1982:30). As one of Bamba's female interviewees put it, one must follow fashion in order to avoid "falling behind evolution, being *gaou*, that is to say, a peasant" (1982:32). Again, the value of the product was related to its foreign origin, an origin that students linked to an idea of civilization.

However, bluffing did not stop at the level of the elite, but continued up into the state apparatus itself—unsurprisingly, since as Bayart (1993) so thoroughly demonstrates in his work on the "politics of the belly," the state and the economic elite not only overlapped, but constituted practically one and the same economic system in many African countries. That is to say, the dominant class tended to get its income either directly from the state or indirectly through the manipulation of state systems to produce income. As Apter (2005) demonstrates in the Nigerian case, the state parasitically takes on the model of the 419 scam, presenting itself as a state in order to drain the resources of its hapless citizens. To provide just a single example from Côte d'Ivoire of the profits obtained in this greatest of all cons, Bayart contrasts the difference between the cost of one kilometer of road in 1987 and what it would have been during the 1970s, before Houphouët initiated a crackdown on road construction "inefficiency": 70 million CFA versus 120 million, respectively (Bayart 1993:79). Bayart implies that Houphouët only took such an interest in corruption in this particular case because the profit was going to his political rivals.

But if the state was *yere* to a population of *gaous*, we should not overlook how, under the careful direction of Houphouët the Ram, it went about the act of *faire le show*. Houphouët, by all accounts, was a master of the surface. But his coup de grâce came with the construction of Yammousoukro. In the 1970s Houphouët secretly transformed his grandmother's village into a new capital city, completed with state-of-the-art monumental buildings to house the various branches of government, including a palatial one for himself. He laid out a grid of large boulevards abundant with streetlights, even though most of them continued to light only the cow pastures on either side. He gave one enormous building called the Fondation Félix Houphouët-Boigny pour la Recherche de la Paix to UNESCO. Finally, in a mere three years, he built a 300-million-dollar basilica (which he claimed was built entirely from his personal funds), which including the gold cross at the top stands taller than St. Peter's, making it the largest Catholic church in the world. After including himself as an angel in the stained glass windows, he gave this monument to the pope. How else to interpret these vast expenditures, built primarily upon the large-scale loans offered to the country on the basis of its "miraculous" profits from cocoa, if not as a bluff of global scale? As Ferguson (2006) has suggested, African mimesis should be taken seriously as an attempt at membership in the modern world, and Houphouët was determined that Côte d'Ivoire would achieve recognition not only as the foremost nation in Africa, but also as a nation of international renown. Unfortunately, by the time construction on the basilica was completed in 1990, his country's economy was faltering toward ruin, and disgruntled university students under the tutelage of history professor Laurent Gbagbo were rioting for more representative politics. Côte d'Ivoire's status as an African Miracle was no longer more than a bluff.

Yere Consumers and Urban Symbols of Modernity

Lower-class urban youth followed an evolutionary structure of thought and practice similar to that of the elite, a hierarchy expressed as we have seen in the slang terms *yere* and *gaou*. The crucial factor in lower-class presentation was to establish one's identity as a *citadin*, an urban resident, and therefore to differentiate oneself from those *qui viens d'arriver* (who have just arrived). The distinction therefore corresponded to an idea of cultural evolution. Urban Ivoirians understood migration as a kind of geographic ladder of modernity, such that "peasant" West Africans traveled to Abidjan to become more "civilized," while Abidjan residents made the voyage to Europe seeking further cultural transformation. This alternative cultural geography strongly corresponds to Wyatt MacGaffey's work on Kongolese conceptions of the West (1968, 1972). MacGaffey describes a map, drawn in the sand by an informant, in which a mound floats above a surface of water, mirrored by an identical mound below the water. He was told that he himself was from the land on the other side of the water. MacGaffey's work traces versions of this cosmology back to the earliest encounters with the Portuguese in the 1490s, as well as explaining many of the terms for whites, such as *amindele* (whales) used to this day by Kongolese. In Kongo cosmology, the otherworld or land of the dead had a parallel mapping, such that the world of the spirits could be accessed through mirrors and water as well as direct contact with dirt from graves. Thus, the kinds of mirroring processes De Boeck has written about in his insightful work on Kinshasa (De Boeck and Plissart 2006), where the everyday was mirrored by both the imagined West and the imagined spirit world, had an established pedigree in cosmological thinking of the region. From this "otherworld" flowed the life force, or *ngolo*, Friedman (1994) describes as the underlying logic of the *sapeurs*. In a very similar way, *nouchi* cosmology surrounding modernity also overlapped with ideas of otherworldly forces.

According to urban Ivoirians I spoke with, uncivilized qualities were easy to spot merely by the clothing someone with a "peasant" mentality would wear. One day I was walking down a familiar street wearing admittedly somewhat ugly bright green pants and flip-flops, when an acquaintance named Charles called me over and began to ask me about the U.S., talking about how cool it had to be over there and how well he would dress if only he could get there.

> But when we see you, we don't understand how you can dress all *gaou* like that, you who are American. . . . [Intrigued, I asked him to explain what it meant to dress *gaou*, and he pointed out several *gaou* people on the street, including a man pushing a cart.] People who push carts are always *gaous*. They come from Nigeria, Burkina Faso. *Gaous* are always people who come from outside the country. But not Americans. That is what we don't understand. You are who we imitate here, those of us who are *yere*. Jeans, baggy pants, things like that, that is what Americans wear. But you, you can't really wear that over there, can you?

He also pointed out a man walking by in a *pagne* shirt and jeans, and a woman selling oranges tricked out in a velvet hat, tight fitting grey pants and button-down blouse, defining both of these as *yere*. For Charles, clothing should be a transparent indicator of modernity. It was impossible that someone as "civilized" as myself (being from the U.S.) could dress like someone who did not understand urban sartorial norms. He was not really talking about class here (for the woman making a living selling oranges was *yere* despite her occupation), but rather a kind of cultural development.

Danny had great expertise on Ivoirian fashion and loved to talk about it. When he heard that I was studying the subject, he got very excited and began with the following topic:

> This is true, people really like to dress up here, there is a style, and you can tell who is *yere* by virtue of it. Even someone from the village who comes to the city, if he is able to inform himself about the latest fashion in the city, if his father is a big plantation owner, he might have the money to buy [the proper clothes]. He will hear that he needs Façonnables pants, a polo, Sebagos. But by the way he carries himself, his mannerisms, those who are *yere* will know that *il vien d'arriver*. For example, he will be overly concerned about his clothing. He just spent a lot of money on it and doesn't want anyone to damage it. Whereas someone who is in *le mouvement* doesn't care. He knows that he can replace his clothes through one means or another; he can give them away if he wants.

So even if a *gaou* could imitate the style of a *yere*, he would never get it quite right—someone truly "in the know" would be able to see through the bluff. This suggests that the "knowledge" allowing an Ivoirian to distinguish between who was *yere* and who *gaou* was at least as crucial as, if not more so than, the ability to dress well in the first place. Here we begin to see the importance of what I refer to as symbolic mastery—to be *yere* was to precisely control the effects of one's own performance and to detect any missing authenticity in the performance of others.

Urban youth applied the term *yere* to the modern; to be *yere* was to display a sense of what it meant to have civilized taste in comparison to the *gaou*. Likewise, commodities and clothing from *Beng* were *yere* in relation to Ivoirian-made products (and U.S. clothes were more *yere* than French ones), while Ivoirian products were often superior to those made in other African countries. By consequence, the countries from which immigrants derived, Côte d'Ivoire itself, and the countries to which people emigrated were all arranged hierarchically according to distinctions of relative *yere*-ness. Thus, the cosmological understanding of geography and origin corresponded to a hierarchical schema of modernity. Increasingly, the *yere* urban identity of the *citadin* overlapped with an emergent national identity of *citoyen*, while the *gaous* who just didn't get it were rejected as foreign impostors.

If *yere* constituted a kind of openness that allowed connectivity with the external or invisible, it was also a means of seeing the "truth" of things. The invisible is a space of imagination once dominated by the dead but now shared with the technological apparatus of modernity and the mysterious value form of commodities. Like the second world of the occult, the urban world anxiously combines deceptive illusions and invisible authenticity. It is a space of unseen causality that can only be understood by those with the special eyes to see it.

A young man in his twenties working at a Treichville clothing store called *Petit Paris* told me that "the importance of clothing in life is evolution. One must look good in order for evolution to take place. Suits are even more important, more in fashion now than ever before, because it is now completely essential when you have a job to be in full suit and tie. Our society is evolving." To look good could actually produce the "evolution" of the person. This connection between cultural evolution and clothing is borrowed directly from the language of colonialism. Within the French colonies, the class of Africans first educated and brought into the bureaucratic apparatus of the state, *les evolués*, was treated as a group apart from the indigenes they "left behind." Of course, as Martin (1994) has argued for the Congo, and Bhabha (1994) more generally, the very look which colonists encouraged for those in their employ was seen as threatening to the colonial order once it began to be appropriated outside the contexts of their own control.

Bruno told me that "when you dress well you are treated differently. If I go to the hospital in a nice suit, I get to skip the line. A *minister* [as in 'high government official'] wearing jeans and a T-shirt might have to wait while I go ahead, because I have an air of importance." Likewise, Maitre Seka, an old alcoholic renowned for his illustrious youth, when he was a well-known dancer and esteemed dresser, told me:

> When I walk around this quarter well dressed, everybody claps and looks from wherever they are. . . . You should see me in my *dernier cri*, the best suit in my wardrobe. Ahhh. No one can resist me when I dress up. If I sit in a bar, the women will approach me, they will destroy my clothes pulling on me. Here look, they pulled this button off of my pants. Even my older brother over there, he is afraid of me. It is true that I am afraid of him too, but he is even more afraid of me. Because in matters of dress, we are very strong.

Stories like this were common. Abidjanais felt that when well dressed, they possessed a kind of internal force which produced an irresistible impression on those around them. As I shall explain in the book's conclusion, this idea of an internal force corresponded to an Ivoirian cosmology of the double, a component of the person that mediated between the material and metaphysical.

Eliane de Latour's movie *Bronx-Barbès* (2000) arrived in theaters during my fieldwork. Named after real *ghettos* in Abidjan, the film used real *nouchi* to act and correct the script. It was an enormous hit in Treichville, and on opening night one had to know the *loubard* bouncers to get in, as a seething crowd mobbed the entrance. The fictional movie describes two young men who gradually become incorporated into a criminal network and rise up in the ranks, and at the very end one of them stows away on a ship to Europe. The scene that produced the greatest reaction from the crowd was that of the sartorial transformation of the hero after he makes his first successful robbery and attains his street name (Solo de Grand B). Up until that point in the movie, the main character has always worn the same grungy *boubou*. From a *nouchi* perspective, these robes are associated with poverty and Muslims, though to many West Africans they are not religiously coded and can be made from luxurious and expensive materials. His *vieuxpère* takes him to one of the "Lebanese" clothing shops on Rue 12 (near Petit Paris) and buys him an entirely new outfit, all in white: Seba-gos, jeans, a Façonnables shirt, and a baseball hat. The audience roared in appreciation at the transformation from *gaou* to *yere*, and even afterward my friends from France-Amérique discussed how good this scene was. For them this scene did not represent merely the culmination of the hero's de-sires, but the principal moment in the action of the story, a moment in which the protagonist became something other than what he had been before.

I had many occasions to witness the excitement such moments of dress-ing up produced, but one of the most remarkable events was when several friends (all in their late twenties or early thirties) were invited to an elite wedding in Cocody (one of them was a distant cousin of the groom, whose father was French). First I met Dom, who was wearing leather dress shoes (wingtips), slacks, and a subtly shiny, blue, long-sleeve shirt, with a hand-kerchief tucked into his pocket, and gold-rimmed glasses (normally he did not wear glasses). His hair and beard were freshly trimmed. He said, "You barely recognized me, no?" He then told me my *pagne* shirt wasn't good enough, that I should put on a long-sleeve shirt. Dom said he had consid-ered wearing a tie and jacket, but the weather was too hot and he didn't like "all those trappings" anyway (in fact, I did not think he owned these items). Then Marcus showed up in a four-button jacket, a tie with a gold tie clip, slacks, and brown dress shoes. Dom cried out in astonishment, "Look at that *bluffeur*. You'd think it was him getting married. People will con-fuse him for the groom when we get there." At this point other people on the street began calling out to us in wonder. Dom decided we both needed a tie and jacket after all, and I lent him the necessary items. At Ibrahim's house Dom began to get really excited at his borrowed regalia and stare at himself in the mirror, pretending to smoke his cigarette and taking up various poses. There was a giddiness in the air. Neighbors began coming by and admiring us and demanding to know where we were going and why they hadn't been invited. As we walked, they kept exclaiming: "Ça va chauffer la-bas dêh!" (It is going to heat up there, man). Marcus said, "They are going to ask, 'But who are these guys?' The women will fall all over us." At first Ibrahim carried a cell phone prominently in his hand, but he later decided it was too large (low prestige in those pre-smartphone days) and asked me to carry it in my bag. At the wedding, they paid a photographer to take our picture and talked about how good this picture would be all the way home. They said that we looked like models, remarking repeatedly that we had really changed our look. Returning to the Treichville that night, Marcus refused to change back into regular clothing, saying he wanted to walk around the quarter bluffing. This kind of identity transformation, I suggest, is an example of the magical efficacy of clothing.

Suits versus Hip-Hop: Taste and Social Hierarchy

As the youth working at Petit Paris indicated, any position of authority in urban Ivoirian society required appropriate dress, that is, a suit and tie for men, or an equivalent business outfit for women, looks that were strongly connected to France and French colonial power in the Ivoirian imagination. On television, the newscasters were the height of elegance, the politicians were rarely seen in anything but expensive haute couture, and even game show hosts would be considered dandies by U.S. standards.[3] However, despite the proliferation of the suit in prestigious positions, and the widespread recognition of its associations with power, lower-class youth had recently come to reject its symbolism for themselves. The dismissal was ambivalent, for many still dreamed of becoming *un boss* and, as in the previous section, were thrilled to find themselves in suits and ties. But as we saw in chapter 3, Treichville residents were angered by dress codes that asked them to dress in slacks and dress shoes, saying this was not how people in Treichville dressed. Instead, they look to U.S. hip-hop and sports styles for inspiration: *le style Statois*. Pop music stars adopted these styles and propagated them, dispersing the look across the television screen in music videos. Much as Nouchi can be seen as a grassroots reorientation of linguistic values, I believe these lower-class transformations in taste represented a challenge to the authority of the governing elite. It is important to note that this challenge continued to draw its legitimacy from externality rather than local sources of prestige. Treichville youth viewed the U.S. as an alternative cultural center outside Côte d'Ivoire from which power and prestige could be absorbed and appropriated. Likewise, the first time I asked Solo about what kind of style he liked, he said: "I have the rap style, I am a *rappeur ambulant* [a play on *marchand ambulant*, a walking salesman]. With style I am always ahead. We dress *en Statois*."

Pierre, a young man from the streets of Treichville who was now studying to be a judge, explained the stylistic difference in terms of class dichotomy: "In Cocody they try to be like Europeans, wearing all French imported clothes, eating fancy foods, nice cars, they *faire le show* with lots of cash, and go to Europe just for tourism. In Treichville, by contrast, people want to imitate American black culture. Their idols are basketball players and rappers. They want to show that they struggle to survive in the ghetto too. They identify with the problems of poverty in the urban environment."

However, it is clear that a stylistic shift in value was at work. I talked with another tailor who was trying to make his living selling suits. He was in despair: "I have the impression the world is upside down. Nothing is working. The country is *gâté* [destroyed]. I haven't worked in days, our couture shop is for classic style and now everyone wants American stuff, name brands, jeans. It is the change in style from suits to this new casual look that is ruining our business. People don't want stuff made here anymore." Likewise, I questioned a young guy named Koffi who was seated at my table in a *maquis*. Unlike the rest of his peers, dressed in Calvin Klein T-shirts and the like, he was wearing a black suit jacket a size too small and a white dress shirt, and I wanted to know why. He responded: "I wear a suit because I like to dress like the former generation. I deplore modern taste. I don't like this hip-hop." I questioned one of his friends about this response, and he too made no mention of the imitation of France; rather, he interpreted Koffi's style as a "respect for tradition." For some *nouchi* youth, at least, suits were so embedded in Ivoirian national identity that they were considered traditional garb rather than a reference to French authority. Indeed, the France-Amérique gang told me that "suits are only for old people. We want things that are new, that are young." For Koffi, the suit referenced the past. But he too explained that people were afraid to wear suits because others would think they were rich. He had found his jacket for not much money, however, and he hoped that he could change the prevalent attitude.

Again, for the *nouchi*, the suit was tied to class and wealth *within* Côte d'Ivoire while hip-hop clothes were connected to U.S. externality. Here, because Koffi was an unusual character wanting to show his "respect for tradition," the hierarchy was reversed. He wore the suit to show his support of local Ivoirian identity in opposition to imitation of the U.S. Notice the pattern whereby foreign influences were incorporated and appropriated into the hierarchical order as vehicles of status, only to be naturalized as part of the local ("traditional") system itself (and thereby losing their transformative potential).

But just as French language could be too *choco*, the suit maintained an ambivalent authority among these youth. They recognized the power the *boss* held in society, even if they chose not to imitate it. A music video entitled "La Doubleuse" by the Marabouts reveals this ambivalence.[4] The video follows the story of a young *nouchi* man whose girlfriend is stolen away in a *maquis* by another man in a suit. He tracks them down in a *bar climatisé*, only to be physically tossed aside as the girlfriend looks on calmly. The *boss* wins the girl.

Whiteness and the Otherworld:
A Local Cosmology of Externality

There is also the question of race at work here. We must consider the possibility that Ivoirian men were identifying with African-American style in opposition to the whiteness of the French colonist, a transatlantic racial solidarity. However, it is crucial to avoid exporting a U.S. concept of race (which does not even correspond perfectly to that found in France) outside its appropriate context. Certainly Ivoirians were aware of the existence of black Americans and identified with the imagery of "ghetto fabulous" in African-American hip-hop, which used images of luxury and gangsta power comparable to the bluff (Mukherjee 2006). However, given the strong association of whiteness with Europe and the U.S. as spaces of modernity, I do not believe that they were identifying with "black" style in opposition to "white," but rather with the images of lower-class transformative acts of consumption depicted in hip-hop videos. If "whiteness" for Abidjanais was more about symbolic power than skin color, U.S. blacks were the "whites" with whom *nouchi* youth could most easily identify. The U.S. was imagined as a space of endless bounty in which no one was truly poor, and I often argued about the presence of racism and poverty to their continual disbelief. Thus, the blackness of African-American hip-hop stars was subsumed within the whiteness of U.S. modernity and wealth displayed within the images urban Ivoirians consumed. We must here follow the lead of Bashkow (2006) in thinking about the construction of race from local perspectives. Because races are not biological but cultural constructions built upon phenotypical differentiation, the fact that many Ivoirians evaluated perceived racial qualities hierarchically did not mean this would correspond to a U.S. understanding of racial categories. Indeed, Bashkow finds that the Orokaiva see whiteness as inhering in particular kinds of objects and encouraging particular forms of social relationships; the fact that whites had been to the moon was iconic of their ability to travel obscenely long distances, ignoring the kinds of social obligations that keep Orokaiva tethered to local spaces. Wyatt MacGaffey (1968) likewise investigated Kongolese perceptions of whiteness. He was told that whites were the spirits of the dead and former ancestors, and African-Americans were said to be ancestors who had not yet transformed fully to white spirits. Indeed, the slave trade was understood as a terrible form of witchcraft that displaced large portions of the living into the land of the dead, where the transformation to whiteness took place. These examples demonstrate the flexibility of racial constructs in cross-cultural contexts.

The Baoulé, an Akan ethnic group from the center of Côte d'Ivoire, consider the source of mystical powers affecting causation in the world of the living to be *blolo*, a parallel or second world where all forms of spirits and shades can be found.[5] The king was the most important intermediary, though ritual experts such as marabouts, *féticheurs*, and witches also had access to the otherworld, and anyone could find means of connection through spirit possession or the use of ritual objects like "fetishes." Although *blolo* is not in a definite location (Guerry 1975), there is a kind of spatial understanding of it, for Wiredu writes that "access to the *post mortem* world is believed to be by land travel during which there is a river crossing involving payment of a toll" (1996:107), bringing to mind the expression *derrière l'eau* as reflective of both the space of death and the space of otherness: *Beng*. At the same time it is imbricated with the quotidian. As Amon d'Aby writes,

> The world of the spirits is a reality which surrounds the human being and which, by reason of its incredible proximity, confounds itself at every moment with quotidian life, in such a way that the distinction between a purely profane act and a religious one is not always easily made in the comportment of an individual or group. Often, in effect, a gesture of completely natural appearance is nevertheless attached, in the final analysis, to a bundle of religious precepts lost in the mists of time. (d'Aby 1960:62)

In other words, while eminently Other, the spirit world is so enmeshed in everyday life that the actions of social actors are often unconsciously motivated by this cosmological structures. It is simultaneously present and absent in social gesture, and social actors themselves are not always certain whether they are interacting with such forces or not.

De Boeck argues that in Kinshasa the second world of the occult is a kind of mirror coexisting with the real: "In this second world, the dimension of the marvelous combines with the dimension of terror to form the tain, the back of the mirror that reflects these qualities back into the daily life experience of the Kinois" (De Boeck and Plissart 2006:57). To put it differently, it is through an understanding of the occult that people *imagine* their reality, and it is through that imagination that reality is culturally produced. But more importantly, for the Kinois, this second world is, if anything, more real than the first. As one Kinois told De Boeck, "The second world is the world of the invisible and those who live in it and know are those who have four eyes, those who see clearly both during the day and during the night. Their eyes are a mirror. A man with two eyes only cannot know this world. The second world is a world that is superior to ours. The second world rules the first world" (De Boeck and Plissart 2006:58). This provocative statement points us toward an understanding of the interrelationship between the invisible and the visible more generally. This idea of having eyes that see the invisible is important to the concept of *yere* modernity.

In Baoulé the word *blolo* comes from the word *blo*, meaning "to claim, to praise, to vaunt," and the suffix *lo*, which designates a place. Its most direct translation therefore, is "the place that is vaunted" (Ravenhill 1996:1). It is fascinating, therefore, that the Nouchi word *blo* has come to mean "bullshit," that is, unwarranted vaunting, and is used to denounce those who promote themselves illegitimately, thereby linking the second economy of the con with the occult. Still more intriguing, the Baoulé word for a white person is *blofwe*, *fwe* being a suffix designating a person. Thus, whites are called "the people that are vaunted," bringing them into semiotic proximity to *blolo*, the location of social power and the world of the dead. Such a connection corresponds to that found in Gottlieb's description of the Beng (a West Ivoirian ethnic group, not the Nouchi concept for "land of modernity") understanding of whites:

> Beng classify whites as people who are *kalε*. This term can be translated roughly as "powerful," given a metaphysical foundation to power. . . . The range of African people, deities and objects that the Beng consider *kalε* is wide and includes twins, witches, diviners, great hunters, medicinal plants, and political leaders (village and clan chiefs, kings and queens, and country presidents), as well as the forest spirits they worship. Indeed, most (though not all) *kalε* people are said to derive their *kalε*-ness from an association with forest spirits. (Gottlieb 1992:126)

Gottlieb goes on to describe the ways in which whites are equated with forest spirits, and how it took months for she and her husband to be removed from the spirit category for most of the Beng in their village. I suggest that the connection between whiteness and power comes from a cosmology that locates power in externality; it is the transcendence of having origins beyond simple human intervention that gives chiefs and prophets alike the authority to wield political power. The emergence of peoples from "beyond the water" with claims to still greater forms of authority does not need to be interpreted as a deification of whiteness so much as a cosmological classification of power from beyond.

All of these words involving acts of "claiming" and "praising" implicitly call into question the relationship between the visible appearance and the underlying reality. Just as the belief in the world of the spirits "claims" there are invisible forces that affect visible appearances, to be *bien zango* (well dressed), I would argue, is a "claim" about the invisible forces underlying the power of the appearance: the sartorial performance is really an argument about "other" forces, be they from *blolo* (the world of the dead) or *blofwe* (the white man). Guerry writes that Baoulé describe *blolo* as "the village of truth" in contrast to the village on earth, that world of pretense where one never gets to the bottom of things, where men live in lies and deceive one another. As soon as one enters this better world, truth is revealed, and one can no longer be deceived (Guerry 1975:138). Notice that this idea of worldly deception and appearance is precisely that referred to in the hierarchical distinction of *yere* and *gaou*. To be *yere* is to "see clearly," to see through the deceptions of others so that one cannot be deceived. Ivoirians use the French expression *les yeux claires* (clear vision) to describe the occult abilities of those who can see into the "truth" of the spirit world to detect witchcraft. Thus, there is an apparent connection between proximity to the spirit world and the social hierarchy of the civilized described by the binary pair *yere* and *gaou*. One's regular eyes therefore are likely to detect only the deceptive illusions of life, it is to see the "invisible," the place from which underlying causes emerge, that "opens" the *yere* actor to truth. But not only people are *yere; nouchi* youth also spoke of *yere* objects and demonstrated a great concern with the authenticity of the brands they consumed.

Evaluating Objects: The Modernity of Brands

For both men and women, the label was prominently displayed as proof of authenticity; the brand of the clothing was crucial to the success of one's public appearance. In this way, Abidjanais were concerned with more than the image they produced. I believe that in their emphasis upon the authenticity and origin of objects, there was a glimpse of an answer to the question underlying this chapter. That is, within the urban Ivoirian evaluation of objects in terms of their origin lies the transformative efficacy of consumption.

On Christmas day (a particularly important day to dress well), I was at Dedy's house, waiting for his girlfriend Mimi to finish dressing. To all appearances she was very ready; I had never seen her so dressed up. Her hair had just been done (12,000 CFA, Dedy told me regretfully), and she wore a brand-new *pagne* outfit with an elaborately embroidered top and new high-heel shoes. She carried a leather purse and wore heavy makeup. But she kept hesitating in front of the mirror, and I had a sense that she was simply looking for excuses to delay. As she stepped out the door, all eyes in the *cour commune* fixed on her. When we got into the taxi to leave, she said angrily of one of the women we had passed, "She couldn't even look me in the eyes. All she was interested in was looking at my hem to see the quality of my *pagne*, I forgot to get this sewn up so that it wasn't in sight. I didn't even want to leave for that reason. I am so sick of that *cour commune*." The *pagne* label was printed along the hemline. Although Mimi was extremely well dressed, her *pagne* was only of medium quality, and because she had not sewn the hem up, it showed. Because Mimi was obviously putting on her best for Christmas day, it was important to her to overwhelm her neighbors with her appearance; she could not leave any fault for them to critique. Of course, had she owned an appropriately prestigious brand of *pagne*, Mimi would have purposefully displayed her hemline.

The *pagne* is an impossible combination of "traditional" and "modern" elements, a perfect illustration of Piot's (1999) explorations of the modern embedded within the most traditional and historically ingrained of African practices. The *pagne* is not really a traditional fabric at all, nor is the style of wearing the fabric related to any specific Ivoirian ethnic group. The fabric itself is mostly imported from other countries, including Benin,

Figure 13. Mimi dressed in her best Christmas outfit. The bag, purse, and hairstyle were all expensive luxuries, and this was the only time I ever saw her this dressed up. Still, she was ashamed at the quality of her *pagne*, which did not hold up to the scrutiny of her neighbors, despite the poverty of the courtyard as a whole.

Togo, India, England, the Netherlands, and more recently China. In a wonderfully complex "biography" of the *pagne*, Sylvanus (2007) explores how the cloth mimics wax batik that was originally made in Java and brought to Africa for trade by the Dutch. The colors and designs have been made by European producers to meet African consumer criteria since the nineteenth century. To this day prints of "genuine wax" process originating in the Netherlands are the most prized. Strangely for a fabric that signifies "Africanity," the patterns themselves often depict objects of modernity: airplanes, computers, cell phones, sewing machines, and automobiles.[6] The designs change every year, and in this way women know whether their peer is wearing new material or an outmoded *pagne*, regardless of the cut of her dress.

The "traditional" look for urban Ivoirian women was made up of *pagne* cloth wrapped around them in several layers, but contemporary urban women often had the cloth sewn to precise measurements to produce a form-fitting effect with elaborate and creative embroidery and hemlines. There was enormous variation and creativity in these patterns, which the tailors said women usually designed themselves or picked from images published in posters demonstrating a variety of the latest styles, but many of them were inspired by North Atlantic dress silhouettes. The "traditional" *pagne* look covered the legs entirely, wrapping around the hips several times and adding bulk to the figure. Another piece of fabric wrapped around the top (or was sewn into a blouse), while a third was used as a headpiece. The shape of the body was largely hidden in the folds of fabric, though the belly was sometimes bare. In contrast, *pagne* tailoring could be far more revealing, with short, leg-exposing hemlines or suggestive slits, shoulders bare, and the silhouette clearly displayed by the body-hugging cut.

The *pagne*'s value was determined primarily by its origin, which was clearly displayed along the edges of the fabric. I asked an older woman selling *pagnes* in the market to explain their pricing to me, and she said the value was determined by the cloth itself. She informed me that "Wax Aurlandais" (imported from the Netherlands) was the kind of *pagne* material most sought after. After this came a series of other countries including England, Benin, and India. The designs printed on the fabric were not so important, she said. The prices ranged from as much as 30,000 CFA for three meters of "Aurlandais" to as little as 3,000 CFA for the lowly "Fancy." According to the vendor, Ivoirian *pagnes* were more valuable than other West African examples, but less valued than European ones. *Pagnes* made in India were among the least valued, and the emergence of Chinese "fakes" of the prized "genuine wax" *pagnes* had caused panics over authenticity in other parts of West Africa (Sylvanus 2007). While social actors had a great deal of freedom in expressing their relationship to the modernity-tradition continuum through the design of the cut of their dress and choice of print, the evaluation of the worth of their appearance was inextricably tied to the authentic origins of fabric.

Men too were constantly comparing labels and often tucked in part of their T-shirt to reveal the label on their pants. When I asked about the importance of clothing, I usually received a list of brand names in return, but the way in which such labels were considered hierarchically only became clear to me after a certain conversation on my usual corner with the neighborhood gang. Jacques was showing off his watch, and everyone examined it respectfully, checking the brand in particular. I asked what the most sought after-brand of watch was, and several people confidently responded Swatch. Solo, however, added, "But there are some other brands still more *yere* than Swatch." My ears pricked up. "So objects can be *yere* and *gaou* as well?" Certainly, they assured me: "People often point out that one person's label is more *yere* than another's." This meant that an object, like a person, could be more *civilized* than another. Objects themselves were incorporated into the hierarchical schematization of modernity, such that a Swatch was more evolved, more urban, more savvy than a nameless watch off the street. Furthermore, by virtue of owning such an object, the person themselves took on the qualities of the object, they too become more *yere* than their peers.

The group explained that there was not really a fixed hierarchy of brands, or, at least, such a hierarchy was always contentious. Solo tried to make a list anyway: "Nike is best, no, now it is Façonnable that is really strong." Jacques interrupted, "Kappa is really good," and everyone immediately groaned.[7] A debate proceeded over the relative hierarchy of a variety of brands, and no agreement was solidified among them. Although such evaluation of objects was open for discussion, the social intensity of such negotiation was an indicator of the evaluative significance of labels. Dialectically, one's knowledge of the hierarchy of brands was both supported by and formative of one's position in the social hierarchy. Arguments over the worth of a particular object or brand were not anecdotal; rather, they were expressions of struggles over social superiority.

So, when Jacques's older cousin Henri criticized him for being a *gaou* by spending 70,000 on a pair of shoes, when you could get the same thing made by the Ghanaians around the corner, Jacques responded that even if Henri had one million, he would still not have better clothes, because he didn't know how to tell the difference. Henri pointed out his own Ghanaian

Figure 14. Luc makes sure to pose in such a way to reveal his Dockers label. Notice also the chain and blue glasses. His shirt is another example of *pagne* material.

leather shoes and tried to argue that they were just as good as Jacques's, at which point the whole group started laughing. Incensed, Henri claimed that he would prove to people that he knew how to dress, and that from now on he would only wear nice things. Later Jacques came over to my apartment still fuming. He said:

> Henri was trying to tell me that black shiny shoes are better than Sebago. But he doesn't know anything. . . . Now Souba [a friend of Henri's from the university], there is a different story. He knows how to dress properly. When you see him, he is always in shoes, long pants, long-sleeve shirts, a watch, a chain, a nice haircut. He looks responsible, like he could already be a doctor. Look at the clothes Henri wears, his worthless shoes. Me, I appreciate real brands: Sony, Samsung, Philips. For cars, it's BMW, Benz. If the brand is powerful and expensive, if it's authentic, then it is for me. But you see that I don't work. I have struggled for myself.

Although Henri and Jacques were arguing about superior knowledge of the evaluation of clothing, the discussion turned on an understanding of the authenticity of objects, an ability to distinguish an object which is "powerful" from one which is "worthless." This anxious contention over origin and authenticity raises the question: why should Abidjanais worry so much about the authenticity of clothing, when they were so ready to overlook the authenticity of the image of wealth a person produces?

Authentic Imitations, Metonymic Transformations

The authenticity of the product seemed to be central to the transformative efficacy of clothing. A social actor could become the Other, a more "culturally evolved" being, only by wearing a legitimate object from the Occident. Thus, the efficacy of the bluff lay in this power of the object which originated in the external.

The guys from my neighborhood explained that to wear a fake label showed that you were a *gaou*, that someone was able to *yere* (scam) you into spending money on a worthless object. Luc said that it was very dangerous to buy clothes at stores like Petit Paris because they had so many imitation labels:

> The majority of the stuff there are false things, *griffes colés* [labels "stuck on" to inferior products]. They will tell you it is an original, but if you buy it they will say afterward, "We *yere*'d him, we cheated a *gaou*." But if it's us,

we know, we say, "I can't pay for that, because it is not the original." It can look very close to the real thing. They hire people to make the labels and everything. You need to have a connection there; that is the only safe way, a trusted friend who will get you the real stuff. When I bought my Sebagos, I went with a friend who knew how to differentiate. It was at one of those Arab stores. They handed us one pair and said it was 50,000. My friend said no, that's not the real thing (because there are three kinds, from the U.S., from France, and from Morocco). They sat there and swore up and down it was real, straight from America. But when we said we were leaving, the store owner said, "I think I can find what you're looking for," and came out of the back with the real shoes. "Now," my friend said, "can you see the difference?" One was a little brighter than the other, and the leather was harder in the back, stiff, whereas the Moroccan ones were already soft, you could tell they were not as well made.

For this reason Luc preferred to go to Le Black (the city's biggest black market) where you could find all sorts of used clothing that you knew was real. The fact that such clothes were worn out and discarded by somebody already seemed to make no difference to their value, it was their authentic origin that concerned the people I knew. The moment of purchase was another test of the urban savvy of consumers, of their ability to differentiate the real from imitation, and therefore another source of hierarchy.

These obsessions with fake labels were not unwarranted paranoia. I spent some time with Dalbé, the local tailor that specialized in *griffes colés*. He bragged that he could make you any brand of clothing you liked and had imitation Façonnables complete with embroidered flags displayed prominently on his walls. While I was talking to him in his shop, a man came in with a plastic bag full of labels he had stolen from somewhere. Dalbé examined them carefully, praising them as "beautiful," but in the end did not purchase them. He told the man they were worthless because they did not form a complete set. There were some for the back collar and some for the front pocket, but they did not match. "I sell my products to clothing boutiques and they need to look completely real," he explained.

In a world pervaded by counterfeit products, people sought legitimate sources in things brought directly from their supposed authentic site of origin. Danny explained that when the *bengistes* return from Europe they bring many things to sell:

Already they are sending things down here that they will sell later, so you know they will arrive soon. They are bringing the *oridji* [original]. All kinds of stuff. Westons for example.[8] . . . In the old days those were what everyone wanted, but the Moroccans made so many fakes that people became really skeptical. They were afraid to spend any money on fakes. So if you bring the real thing [back from Europe] you need to get some local connoisseurs to validate their authenticity. If two or three people legitimate the shoes, you will have people running behind you to buy them.

Bengistes were important sources of "real" objects, because they had a direct connection to the country of origin. Nevertheless, even their wares had to be legitimated by connoisseurs, and this issue of semiotic mastery is crucial to understanding both the efficacy of the bluff and dangers it contained for ethnic division. I will examine this further in chapter 6, but here I stress the importance of indexical origins in the evaluation of objects. Bamba writes: "The Ivoirian does not like to consume locally. . . . [They] manifest a particular attachment to all that comes from the Occident, especially Europe and North America. In this sense one often sees that an Ivoirian who has returned from France or the United States is the object of particular attention from his friends and family, who confer a great deal prestige on him" (1982:2). It is precisely the externality of the object which imbues it with value, and the "authentic" label is merely a sign documenting the object's origin in the world of the foreign.

The Nouchi terms for evaluating objects are clear indicators of externality as the source of urban Ivoirian value. Danny used the word *oridji* above, an abbreviation of "original," but one could also say that an item came from *derrière l'eau* (behind the water) or that it was *natation* (swimming). Ivoirians commonly referred to *derrière l'eau*, a concept I can only designate as "the land of the whites," revealing a sense of geography more influenced by hierarchical conceptions of power than cartography (W. Mac-Gaffey 1972). Not that Ivoirians were ignorant of maps; indeed, maps were cherished and gazed at reverentially, and I once even saw a teenager studying Parisian Metro maps (see Gondola 1999 for comparison). Rather, by using the phrase *derrière l'eau* I suggest that Abidjanais place *Beng* in a conceptual category of otherworldliness. Following Wyatt MacGaffey's work in the Congo, I believe that the opposition between Côte d'Ivoire and *derrière l'eau* was structurally homologous with the opposition between this world and the next. In this way, for Abidjanais the Occident represented the symbolic Other, a source of external power from which value is drawn. The word *natation* was merely a more oblique way of saying the same thing, seemingly implying that the object *swam* across the water dividing Côte d'Ivoire from the Occident, perhaps referencing the clandestine nature of the migration process itself (often achieved by stowing away on ships, or dangerous night crossings of the Mediterranean). I am arguing that an abstractly conceived *Beng* came to stand in a parallel symbolic position to the otherworld, as the source of the force of value itself, which urban Ivoirians discussed in terms of what they called modernity. If to be *yere* was to be open to the external and invisible, proximity to the external world and its transformative potential was a supremely valuable achievement.

If this is so, Abidjanais consumption was really about bringing the consumer into contact with the "modernizing" power of the symbolic West. Objects could be *gaou* and *yere* because they embodied the transformative force of modernity on which that distinction was based. I suggest that to consume such an object was to become that much closer to the Occident itself, a kind of partial migration (and migration could likewise be considered the ultimate act of consumption, which I explore in chap. 5). Modernity was transferred metonymically from the object to the person, so that by wearing U.S. clothing, urban Ivoirians transformed themselves into more potent social beings. In this contemporary Ivoirian cosmology, modernity acted as a kind of force or quality which inhered in places, objects, and people, rather than a state of development, as it is typically defined in academic discussion. In this sense, the Abidjanais discourse on modernity and social evolution was an idiom for the explanation of social hierarchy, an idiom structured according to a local cosmology of the power from the otherworld. The efficacy of urban Ivoirian fashion stemmed from its metonymic mediation between the social identity of the person and the externality of power. We must thus consider the possibility of a semiotics of consumption in which relationships of contact are as important as those of metaphoric appearance with which we are accustomed to evaluating messages of consumer activity.

Ivoirian Masquerades and *Yere* Vision

If *yere* constitutes a kind of openness that allows connectivity with the external and invisible, it is also a means of seeing the "truth" of things. The invisible is a space of imagination once dominated by the dead but now shared with the technological apparatus of modernity and the mysterious value form of commodities. It is the space of unseen causality that can only be understood by those with the special (occult) eyes to see it.[9] The urban world is paradoxically then a space of both surface illusion and underlying authenticity. It is a space that in this sense parallels the logic of the masking ritual, in which the deception of visual performance references the invisible and authentic presence for those who have the knowledge to see beyond the illusion. As Phillip Ravenhill puts it, "The visible functions to keep the invisible invisible" (Nooter 1993:24).

Masking rituals are one of the most widely distributed cultural practices in Côte d'Ivoire, to the extent that one of the government's failed efforts to produce national identity was entitled Festimask, bringing together the various ethnic traditions of masking onto a single stage in a celebration of Ivoirian artisanship and tradition intended to produce at once a spectacle of unity and a tourist attraction (Steiner 1992b). According to Steiner it was a failure on both accounts. As Picton (1990) has brilliantly demonstrated, masking is a complicated and culturally specific practice that cannot be taken for granted. Of greatest importance is to escape the Eurocentric cultural predilection for understanding masking as deceit, a covering to hide underlying authenticity (a perception closely tied to the fixation of North Atlantic subjectivity upon deceptive appearance in general). Picton describes the Nigerian Ebira tradition of masking as one in which "faith and deceit" are strangely but inseparably conjoined. Male maskers sometimes claim that the whole affair is a trick to get money out of women, and gleefully tell

> anecdotes about famous performers outwitting women intent upon discovering how their deceased husbands or fathers would be manifested as masquerade. These stores reinforce the idea of trickery while at the same time also presenting the theory of masquerade as ancestral presence: the problem is that women are not to be trusted with the knowledge of how this is achieved. For the most part, men seem convinced of that presence even though one cannot see it. The whole enterprise is riddled with puzzle and paradox; it works yet it is a deceit. (Picton 1990:196).

While the article's attempt to classify different masking types may create more puzzles than it solves, Picton's concept of "power mediated by deceit" seems an important clue to understanding the bluff, especially when combined with rituals that constitute the performance of masculinity in front of female audiences.

Simmel (1950) brings us a long way toward understanding this paradox in his essay linking secrecy with adornment. He suggests that secrecy, like adornment, is really a kind of display drawing the attention of the audience to the social actor, a form of social attraction that enlarges the sphere of the individual like a form of radiation. As Simmel argues, the "secret produces an immense enlargement of life . . . the possibility of a second world alongside the manifest world; and the latter is decisively influenced by the former" (1950:330). In the context of Côte d'Ivoire, such a phrase immediately leads us back to *blolo* and the invisible second world of the spirits, the site of hidden causality influencing the manifest world. The secret is an "adorning possession" made more potent because its exact nature is unknown. Thus, the content of the secret is less important than the fact of its concealed existence, the attraction of its invisible presence. But the flip side of the coin has been relatively ignored—consumption and display may be more contingent upon the ambiguous potency of secrecy than we typically recognize. As Simmel puts it, "The secret produces an immense enlargement of life," offering "a second world alongside the manifest world" (1950:330). Secrecy offers all of the potency of the invisible that lurks just on the other side of the visible, present but out of sight. It is this potency that the surfaces of display rely on in order to convey value. After all, value is a matter of social convention; it is by nature invisible. Like Picton's maskers who even with their masks off retain the powers of the ancestors they perform as long as women don't see them, the *bluffeur* both is and is no longer himself.

However, we must not lose track of the mix of faith with deceit, of the ability of deceit to mediate real, authentic power. It is the mediation of the appearance with its connection to the "space of death," the conceptual second world of liminality, transcendence, and otherness, that brings "presence" to life in the masquerade: a connection of metonymy that guarantees the real. As Simmel writes in the same rich essay, the attraction of the "genuine" is in its being more than its mere appearance (which is identical with its counterfeit):

> Unlike its falsification, it is not something isolated; it has its roots in a soil that lies beyond its mere appearance, while the unauthentic is only what it can be taken for at the moment. The "genuine" individual, thus, is the person on whom one can rely even when he is out of one's sight. In the case of jewelry, this more-than-appearance is its *value*, which cannot be guessed by being looked at, but is something that, in contrast to skilled forgery, is *added* to appearance. (Simmel 1950:343)

Thus, it is metonymic ties of the thing beyond its appearance that make it more than a counterfeit, and in the deceit of masking, it is the real contact with the space of liminal otherness that brings power to the performance.

Bluffing and masking have parallel figurative logics in which the visible makes present the invisible. The mimesis of North Atlantic identity practices was thus not simply the consumption of the image of modernity, but, much more importantly, through the indexicality of brand name goods that physically came from *Beng*, urban Ivoirians discursively controlled the invisible and mysterious forces of modern capitalist success; the invisible hand was revealed in their embodied commodities. Modernity was in-scribed within and through a local semiotics of power, in which indexical connections to invisible forces were visually referenced, at once revealing and concealing that force behind a dramaturgy of externality (the presence of otherness). And as Kramer's (1993) insightful if ethnographically de-contextualized work tells us, there is a constant overlap in African represen-tations between the space of death and the space of the foreign, such that masks with European characteristics are common finds throughout Africa.

Thus, the bluff of success, while calling attention to itself as an artful per-formance, is anchored in the authenticity of the objects themselves, which must have legitimate origins in order to make the performance efficacious and build the reputation of the actor. The magic of mimesis through which *bluffeurs* demonstrate their success is given force by the "real" of the objects in the performance. It is not only the magic of similarity at work in the image, but also the tactile magic of contact (Frazer 1950; Taussig 1993). Ultimately, it is the belief of the audience that must be secured around the value of the objects through a performance of urban identity. Thus, the per-formance is not usually "unmasked" by exposing the poverty of the actor—everybody knows that wealth is an illusion even if it cannot be admitted, but a more serious danger lies in the exposure of artifice in the objects the performer displays—only a *gaou*, an untrue Ivoirian, would have made the error of purchasing a fake. At the same time, in the world of counterfeits, where the veracity of the brand may be privately doubted, a convincing performance of modern urban identity is needed to anchor the always un-certain evaluation of the label. There is a dialectic between the performers' ability to convince the audience of the brands' authenticity and the power of the label to grant performers their status as modern subjects. In turn, the youth culture upon which these distinctions were built increasingly em-phasized the opposition between *yere* and *gaou* not only to exclude those unable to keep up with the demands of fashion from their urban subcul-ture, but also to exclude them from the emergent definition of citizenship.

FIVE

Paris Is Hard like a Rock: Migration and the Spatial Hierarchy of Global Relations

Paris has already captured me, just like our own genies do when they cast a spell over someone and remove their power of speech. Isn't that what's happening to me? I seem to be floating; I barely acknowledge anything or anyone. I tell you Paris must be a wicked city indeed; to be able to work that kind of magic from that great a distance means only one thing: the evil spirits there must definitely be stronger than ours, whom we abandon, and who in turn abandon us. (Dadié 1959:5)

C'est pas en France tu vas partir, c'est France qui va venir te trouver [You aren't going to France, France is going to come find you]. (A sorcerer's curse at the airport [Magic System 2000])

Bernard Dadié, an Ivoirian novelist, wrote *An African in Paris* on the eve of independence from French colonialism, describing the reverie that Paris produced upon West Africans as a magical force. Forty-one years later, the premier Ivoirian pop stars Magic System continued to sing about France's mystical hold on Ivoirian minds. To travel to Europe and return was the foremost desire of almost every Ivoirian I met. This desire crossed over the deepest social oppositions: gender, class, religion, and the pervasive north-south dichotomy that is currently tearing apart the country. At the same time, most Ivoirians were extremely proud of their national identity. The desire to emigrate was not one of permanent escape, but of personal transformation. The target of this migration was of course the land of *Beng*, and a migrant who succeeded in reaching this mythologized destination was thereafter known by friends and family as a *bengiste*, or sometimes more specifically as a *Parisien* or *Statois*. In the mythical narrative of the *bengiste*, an Ivoirian travels to a European country (or the U.S.) for several years, becomes very rich, and returns with enough money to build a large house for their family and sustain themselves and their family in a life of luxury happily ever after. Even though this story rarely came true for migrants in financial terms, they did undergo an important transformation. The returned travelers were no longer seen as merely Ivoirian. As *bengistes*, they seemed to exist on a different social plane than their peers, and they tended to move in an exclusive *bengiste* circle while publicly flaunting their newly refined palates and temporarily overstuffed wallets.

In practice, the dream of the *bengiste* very rarely came to fruition in an economic sense. Those few Abidjanais who successfully managed to cross the many obstacles between them and Europe or the U.S. did return bearing the appearance of wealth. They distributed gifts to family and friends and spent extravagantly at the best nightclubs and *maquis*. In reality, however, they were producing a temporary display of wealth that could not be sustained for long, and typically after a month or two of such conspicuous consumption, they disappeared again, returning to *Beng* for another few years. Rather than upsetting the myth of copious wealth available to the migrant, most Ivoirians remaining in their home country saw the *bengistes'* perennial return to Europe as proof positive that life in *Beng* was really as glorious as migrants tended to boast. Once someone had tasted the bounty of *Beng*, Abidjanais claimed, they forgot all about their origins.

This chapter is an exploration of the symbolic process of migration, the ways in which people reconstructed their identities through the transformative journey to *Beng*. Within the social field of Côte d'Ivoire, at least, such migrants had become Europeans, regardless of their lack of papers to prove it. In distinction to many theories of migration that focus upon hybrid identities, the destructuring of nations, and remittances from migrants to their home countries (Appadurai 1991; Rouse 1991; Basch, Schiller, and Blanc 1994; Clifford 1994; Kearney 1995; Hannerz 1996), I concentrate here on migration patterns from the perspective of the home country. This focus highlights the overlapping relationship between consumption and migration, symbolic processes paralleling and feeding into one another. At the same time, I examine the Abidjanais geographies of global hierarchy in relation to the local conception of modernity as a space of unseen powers and causality that I explored in the last chapter. This angle on the cosmology of migration complements the work of Gardner (1993) on the villages from which Bangladeshi migrant populations stem and of Goldring (1999), who argues that transmigrants maintain connections with their native community because only in the native community do they find a shared perspective in which their migratory act takes on value. My argument connects with the work of Ferguson (1999) on Zambian understandings of modernity and Malkki's (1995) exploration of the Hutu "cosmological order of nations."

But the migratory process is not merealy a passively received social act evaluated from the perspective of the homeland; the migrants are genuinely culturally transformed by their experience. My argument dovetails with the position outlined by Hahn and Klute (2007) in *Cultures of Migration*, in which they suggest that the process of migration itself forges new cultures, and that cultures themselves can be dialectically organized around the process of migration—thus further destabilizing the relationship between culture and territoriality as outlined by Gupta and Ferguson (1997). While Ivoirians had long been traveling to Paris and back, the surge in *popular* migration that began in the 1990s created a new migratory culture, one that reified the concept of Ivoirian nationality through the reflexive distance of travel.

Most "transnational" theory has focused upon the perspective of migrants *outside* their home country. But if we are to understand why migration happens in the first place, and how it perpetuates itself, it is important to examine the home communities from which migrants emerge. Anthropologists and other social theorists overwhelmingly assume that the motivation for the process is economic or political, the "aetiological tendency," as Hahn and Klute call it (2007:9). Such models almost inevitably portray the migrants as helplessly pushed and pulled by factors beyond their control; they are cogs on the periphery of the world system. By examining migratory acts as practices of consumption, we are better positioned to reveal the local evaluatory schema motivating these dangerous voyages. Koenig indicates that migration is a "positive social value" in itself for West Africans, apart from the political and economic factors outside observers have insisted upon. As in the Akan song she cites, "you don't get civilized if you do not travel" (Koenig 2005).

In this way, urban Ivoirians understood migration as a means to accessing a kind of geographic ladder of modernity, such that "peasant," or *gaou*, West Africans traveled to Abidjan to become more modern, while Abidjan residents made the voyage to Europe seeking further cultural transformation. As a young Cameroonian university student explained to me, "Many Ivoirians think they are already European. They think that they are already civilized, *évolué*. They think they are a superior race." And as described above, Abidjanais who succeeded in the dream of going to Europe came back transformed as *bengistes*, occupying a new social category considered inherently superior to those who had not yet left the country. Linguistically, the hierarchical conception of geography is expressed by the terms used to describe the journey to Europe: to have gone there is to have *monté* (climbed up) while the return voyage was called *le descent* (the descent), a terminology mirrored in the language of the Congolese *sapeurs* (Friedman 1994; Gondola 1999). The actual inhabitants of *Beng* were looked on with a great deal of ambivalence, but the "land of the whites" was revered as the source of power and prestige. In this way, urban Ivoirians seemed to distinguish between the power of a geographic location and the people who lived there. It was the place itself that imbued people, metonymically, with prestige and success.

In the last chapter I suggested that to consume imported goods was to become that much closer to the Occident itself; it was a kind of partial migration. In this chapter, I explore the reverse hypothesis: that for urban Ivoirians, migration itself was the ultimate act of consumption. If the bluff of modernity transformed the person, urban Ivoirians considered the voyage to the source of value itself to be an irreversible and total metamorphosis. For the *bengistes* had traveled beyond the bounds of the mundane and everyday, to the source of power itself; they had become like beings from another world. This was a transcendence of the social through entry into the set-apart space of the Durkheimian sacred: the origin of the modern.

Urban-Village Migration

Before exploring migration to Europe and the U.S., I want to look at the importance of migration within Côte d'Ivoire in order to demonstrate my argument that travel was conceived of according to a kind of nested hierarchy of cultural evolution. Antoine writes that in the villages he surveyed (all within eighty kilometers of Abidjan), urban migrants surpassed 20% among the 45–60-year-old age group, and more than 70% in the 15–25-year-old group (Antoine and Henry 1983:376). There was thus a continual influx of migrants into Abidjan, who arrived to find themselves at the bottom of the local social hierarchy. At the same time, they had already achieved greatness in the eyes of the families they left behind. As Christophe put it, "The people of the bush, their dream, their single greatest dream in life, is to arrive in Abidjan."

Even those who had grown up in the city, however, maintained their social contacts with their kin network in at least one village. They returned periodically (at least once a year if they could) to visit their kin, bringing an array of urban products to give away (Mayer 1962). They also hosted their kin who visited or migrated to the city. Typically the village with which they maintained contact was that of the parent to whose lineage they belonged. For Akan groups, this was usually the village in which their mother grew up (their mother's brother's village), although the Baoulé tended toward cognatic descent and so had more flexibility in the matter. Gouro groups are patrilineal: Dedy had often visited his father's village, but never his mother's. But the urban situation bred more complex kinship patterns; for example, Christophe had a Baoulé mother and an Atié father—and so he visited both villages. The obligation to visit the village was both continuous and diffuse. I often heard people mention their families outside Abidjan and how they owed them a visit, but people also spoke of the dangers of returning to the village, because the witches were strongest there, and they would be jealous of the newfound wealth and success of the urban *citadin*. Neither could they wait too long, or the witch might become angry at their lack of respect and come to find them in the city. On the other hand, they could not return "home" without a bounteous display of goods to distribute to their kin, and the journey itself cost thousands of CFA. Such an expensive act of social production was not lightly undertaken, and it is important to understand the motivations behind it.

In returning home, the *citadin* was immediately given a status superior to those who had never left. Denot (1990) writes that urban migrants are referred to in the village by terms of age respect (aunt or uncle, big sister or big brother, *vieux* [older one]) regardless of the relative age of the actors involved. In the following explanation by Mory, the kinds of hierarchical relationships that existed between villagers and *citadins* are further explored through the lens of gender.

> When we go there [to the village], we are superior to everyone else of our age group. The village girls want guys who are *yere*, who know the city. So we go and can pick the very youngest ones because that is what guys like. That's why when you see girls here all cute and little you think they are virgins for the taking, but then you find out they have already been plucked. But when the girls get to the city everything changes. They look for guys who are *gaou* because they are afraid of the *yere*. They can get what they want from a *gaou*, take him for all his money, whereas a *yere* will wriggle out of it.

Just as the *bengiste* in Abidjan, a visitor from the city in the village was considered a being from another world; he returned a different person from the one he was when he left. He was capable of seducing the woman of his choice with his urban charm. Likewise, a new arrival to the city was likely to find himself a victim of the guile of an urban seductress; he did not yet know how to defend himself from *yere* women. This same principle was paralleled in economic exchange. Dedy introduced me to an uncle of his, telling me afterward that this uncle was a liar. While in town, he bought up lots of watches and other items from the city, then went back to the village. He had children who were in Europe, so he told the villagers that all these goods were authentic European products sent by his sons, and they believed him. He did the same thing in the reverse direction, buying up masks in the village and selling them in Abidjan as authentic Ivoirian artifacts. He had been telling his family that his sons had just sent him eleven million CFA for some of these masks, but then he asked Dedy for 4,000 CFA travel money so he could get home. In this way, the uncle both boosted his own prestige in the village and used it to take advantage of the villagers for his own profit.

Most return migrations were less about taking from the village than about giving to one's family. Just as in the competitive consumption per-formances of the *maquis*, the returned *citadins* had to prove their superiority through display and distribution. They brought back clothing, technologi-cal products like radios, watches, and cell phones, and of course money. As Dedy explains,

> They dress up; they bring all kinds of things to give away. Typically you arrive with your suitcase full, and when you leave, it is empty. Dress is especially important for women. They have to be in a good *pagne*. If not, everyone will look at them and talk to them right to their face about how worthless they are. "Look at her, she lives in the city and yet she can't even get a *pagne* bet-ter than what we find here." The problem is that when you leave, they are going to expect you to give them most of the *pagnes* you bring with you, so you need to prepare with some regular *pagnes*. Mimi is planning to bring those necklaces I managed to steal during the market fire. Then Barbette . . . you know she has nothing here, but she has to show something, so she is sending a bag, a backpack. Many people can't go to the village unless they have gathered some money together. That is why it has been a long time since Mimi went to Bouaké. That is why those youths [my France-Amérique friends] can't go this year, they haven't pulled together the money.

Likewise, Christophe said of his own excursions:

> When I go to the village, all my town friends and I each pay for a case so we can sit around with our village cousins and drink all night. Especially my cousin in Adjame contributes a lot. I always bring presents when I go, because they have nothing and they are pleased with anything you can man-

age to leave them. I always give them some of my old clothes, even if they are a little torn—they don't care. I recently gave my old pair of Sebagos to a cousin because he had written and asked for a pair. And when my mom sent me a lot of shirts from France I gave them to the villagers because I don't like French clothing. The fabric is too fine. I prefer T-shirts.

So the return to the village was a serious affair, in which one's reputation in front of the extended kin network was at stake. And with the threat of witchcraft always hanging over their heads, people did not like to take too many risks.

Funerals served as the principal occasions for such migrations. With the exception of Muslims, for whom religion decreed immediate burial, Ivoirians preferred to be buried in their natal village (or at least the village to which they were most closely linked by kinship). As we saw in chapter 4, this entailed elaborate preparations and great expense. Typically, a formal wake had to be held in the city for friends and kin who could not afford to go to the village. This was taken just as seriously as the one to follow in the village, with live music, DJs, dancing, and distributions of food and drink. Afterward, another ceremony was held at the morgue, where the body was identified (this was also when the possibility of witchcraft was discussed). Finally, a caravan with hearse and charter bus accompanied the body to the village. The bus was adorned with palm fronds to let passing motorists and police checkpoints know that this was a funeral journey. I accompanied one of these funeral caravans when Mimi's cousin died and she was obligated to go to the village of her father (which she had never seen before).

The bus filled with kin and affines dressed in their finest. Many men and women wore the official funeral *pagne*, which had been picked out in advance and sold to help with expenses. Older men wore suits, while younger men dressed in the U.S. sportswear discussed in the preceding chapter. They wore sneakers, jeans, and T-shirts of course, but also a "Pippen 23" basketball shirt, another shirt with "hip hop" printed in repetitive pattern around the sleeves, a Boos Sport shirt, and many nylon tracksuits. Dedy even had on his best, a Nike T-shirt I had given him and his green Nike track pants. Many wore sunglasses as well. As we drove further north from the city, the youths continually remarked upon the transformations, at each change in environment exclaiming, "Now we are really in the village." There was a lot of talk about the *gaous* in the village and of what it was like living "in the bush." Such talk reinforced group identity as urban residents, legitimating their claims to superiority among themselves. They teased one of their group for having a Beninois parent. When he said wistfully that he was going home, someone snidely remarked, "To do that, you would have to cross the border!" While joking, such discussions pointed to a concern with marking social boundaries during this journey. Upon arrival, the urban migrants were kept separate from the villagers, and one by one we approached the elders and shook hands. Over the course of the weekend, the younger city men drank together in small groups, always dressed up, always exclusive. The villagers, for their part, were extremely concerned that their hospitality be appropriate, offering far more food than necessary and lodging for all of us and serving an endless supply of palm wine. Departures contained the most ambiguities around behavior, as the villagers approached those leaving and began demanding things they had seen their visitors wearing or using. Dedy had tried to ward off these demands by preemptive giving, as well as elusive answers about our departure, but a couple of aunts and one of Mimi's cousins were all able to take advantage of the moment to glean a bit more money from us. Migration is a complicated process in which participants negotiate transformation in the social hierarchy through rituals of exchange and display.

The importance of urban-rural migration is revealed by the Baoulé ritualization of the return migration process. Since Côte d'Ivoire's government has been dominated by Catholics, Easter is a national holiday. However, the event has developed a special relationship with the Baoulé, who consider it the central ritual event of the year, and many Ivoirians call it the *fête des Baoulés*. It is a time when all self-respecting Baoulé go "home" to their village. Luc told me: "By tomorrow you will not find a single Baoulé in town. If they say they are Baoulé, they are lying. A true, true Baoulé has to get to the village. I don't know when it started to be that way, but it has been that way as long as I have been conscious of the world around me." My surprise at this event was not because "Africans" took Easter seriously, for after all, many Ivoirians have been Catholic for generations. Rather, what is significant is that Easter has been appropriated by a particular ethnic group in order to dramatize and formalize the migration process. Some police officers in a *maquis* overheard me asking why the Baoulé "owned" Easter and volunteered the following explanation:

> The Baoulé are hard workers, and go all over the place to work, so that many
> of them don't live in their proper village. Many of them moved to the west,
> to work on plantations there. . . . So they profit from the vacation of Easter
> to go home and reunite with their family. . . . Then it has also become a
> time when we try to make improvements in the village. We meet and discuss

whether this year we can bring in electricity, etc. We have to bring money to contribute to that as well.

The Baoulé ethnicity, more than most other ethnic groups, had developed this migratory pattern because they were among the most involved in the internal migrations provoked by the *mise en valeur* schema of Houphouëtist policy, profiting from cocoa plantations in the west of the country.

Olivier went home to his village for Easter and asked a village elder about the origins of the holiday for me, bringing back the following description in his notebook:

> We are in April, when the father who takes care of everyone leaves his plantation to go back to the village and rest. For some urban *citadins*, who are working, they want to see their kin, because for many it has been more than a year, for some (like the *bengistes*) more than ten years. The students also have their Easter vacation. . . . Finally, everyone began by getting together haphazardly, but because there is a holiday close to this time, it became a celebration. Little by little, it has become a planned encounter and an important festival. . . . Little by little, with evolution, this festival became important for the Baoulé without even developing an understanding of its real [religious] significance. Today, it is the most important festival for the Baoulé.

The Christian significance of this date had little to do with the motivation for the Baoulé celebration. The Baoulé had adapted this holiday to meet their own community needs, and it had become the primary event of the year for both family and village politics. It was a testament to the central significance of migration and return as a social practice that this relatively recent festival could overshadow every other Baoulé ritual so quickly. Indeed, the day had taken on a fully elaborated ritual schedule of events, complete with formal dances and gift exchanges. The culmination of the event was a community meeting (alluded to by the police officers) in which the entire village and its migrant guests were arranged according to social hierarchy, and the future of the village was discussed. Those urban residents who had enjoyed real success made their financial contributions at this moment, offering to help build roads or bring electricity. And as with less formalized returns to the village, the occasion was understood as a time when the migrants prove their success. Again the village elder spoke:

> We are in April, and the university students, high school students, *fonctionnaires*, and other urban residents know that this is a moment when all the

old kin are in the village, and this is the moment where everyone can see
each other. And so they prepare themselves with new clothes, uniforms, and
money to *faire le show* in the village. Already, two weeks before the festival
people arrive and begin *le show*.

Since this book has largely focused on job-deprived youth, it is significant
that the elder included government officials in his description. The displays
I have described were not merely a function of the cockiness of youth, but
a part of the social fabric itself. Olivier described a *fonctionnaire* from the
Front Populaire Ivoirien (FPI)[1] who returned to the village for Easter. Because the Baoulé were customarily affiliated with the Parti Démocratique
de Côte d'Ivoire (PDCI), the party of President Houphouët-Boigny, this
particular minister had therefore never amounted to much in his village.
However, since Gbagbo, the founder of the FPI, had won the election mix-
up of 2000, the village politician had become very rich and earned the respect associated with a position of power. He returned to the village accompanied by bodyguards with a brand-new Mercedes and a Smartcar for
his wife. He took a prominent place in the village meetings. The *descent* to
the village incorporated the bluff regardless of age and placement in life.

In the Easter ritual of the Baoulé, migration is a ritual of transformation,
a ritual completed in the repeated return of the migrants to their "home." It
is crucial that this home itself becomes increasingly symbolic for most migrants. They no longer identify with the people from their village, nor do
they feel "at home" there, for a continual tension between *citadin* and villager was clearly evident during my funeral visit. Rather, the journey home
is the moment of legitimation in which their increased value is socially
recognized. These same patterns are repeated in even clearer forms in the
migrations to Europe and back. As I have argued, urban Ivoirians perceive
both internal and external migrations as processes of cultural evolution,
steps along a chain of personal transformations.

Migrating Dreams

The dream of travel was an obsession for many. Gondola (1999) describes
how Congolese youth experience France first of all from home in the space
of imagination, and these fantasies formed a key social practice for Abidjanais youth as well. It was Christophe's favorite subject of discussion,
and the following statements were collected from a series of conversations
with him over several months:

For the last two days I have felt like I am in France. I think about nothing else. It is like I am not really here. Even in my sleep, I dream I am there. [When an airplane passed overhead he pointed it out to me, looking at it lovingly and with an air significance. I said: "You're thinking of France." He nodded in pleasure.]

I'm sick of Côte d'Ivoire. All my friends have gone to *Beng*. I am a guy who likes cash, who lives with *pierres* [money]. I am not meant for this lifestyle. Right now everything annoys me here. I need to go join my mother in *Beng*, where I belong.

I am wasting my time here, achieving nothing. If I could only get to *Beng*, I could do some great things.

Others focused their dreams more specifically on what they would do once they arrived in *Beng*. I met two young thieves with the street names Biggie and Scarface, dressed to a T in Façonnables, Timberlands, Docksides, and jeans, who told me excitedly of their plans:

America is so great, life is sweet over there! All those cute little "chicks," they all drive cars over there. You cruise, listen to rap, you are satisfied. Yes it is good over there. When I go to America I'm going to sell cocaine. That sells well there, no? Yeahhh. But in order to last over there [not get caught] I will have a clothing store. Beautiful shirts that will sell for at least $50, and then I will put a little bag of coke in the pocket, like a present. I could do the same thing with shoes, hide a little baggie in them, you know.

Scarface explained that he was supposed to be in Paris by now, but he had been scammed. The guy who was supposed to sell him a visa gave him a fake and he was turned back at the border. He showed me where the police had unstuck the forgery from his passport, complaining that it had cost him 500,000 CFA ($715). In comparison, a middle-class salary was about 50,000 CFA a month, still much more than what most Treichville youth brought in through their day-to-day *bizness*.

Charles, another young thief, had similar plans:

No, I need to get myself to the States, I've got to do it. . . . I won't work there, though, I am going to "get by" there just like I do here. I want to sell drugs I think, because in a single day you can make sooo much. Drug gangs? No,

I'll be able to handle it, I won't be a *gaou* there because I know from my experience here how to get along. When I arrive in the airport, I will kick off my sandals while crossing the street and head straight for a nice clothing store . . . then go into a changing room like they have there, and put on some brand-new sneakers, a new hat, a nice jacket, and I'm out of there, man.

Notice that the most important element of this story for Charles was the transformation in his appearance. He had to rid himself of his demeaning flip-flops as soon as he was out of the airport (apparently he saw bare feet as less conspicuous). And he seemed to be offering this suggestion about his new clothing as an explanation of how he would avoid trouble with U.S. gangs.

The pressures to make such a voyage were not merely internal. People experienced social pressure from both family and friends to succeed in such an endeavor. Dedy had gotten as far as customs in Germany, but there his papers were identified as forgeries, and he was repatriated immediately. Since he had already told everyone he knew that he was going to Europe, he had dropped his old social circles. This had taken place in 1994, but even as late as 2001, when we ran into any of his old acquaintances, they often said, "Tiens, I thought you had *monté* [gone to Europe]." Dedy told me he wanted to "hide himself in shame" at such encounters, because all his old friends had already made the journey to Europe, some multiple times. Often he carefully let people believe he had actually been inside Germany (after all, he had been on German soil), saying, "but I didn't last long over there." Dedy felt not only that his own reputation depended on his one day really succeeding in reaching Europe, but that his whole family's reputation rested on this achievement.

Since I left Côte d'Ivoire, he has become involved at least twice in elaborate, yearlong schemes to get to Europe. In one case he arranged to get his photo affixed to a real French passport that had been stolen. It took all his savings and many forged documents to correspond to his new name, but he was turned away at the embassy: the missing passport had been reported and no longer worked.

Although Treichville men tended to rely principally upon their informal social network for day-to-day support (loans, food, gifts, and knowledge of where to find the next "deal"), most maintained ties with whatever kin they had in Abidjan. Older Treichville residents placed their hopes on their children. For them the myth of *Beng* for their children consisted of a dream of their own house in their natal village. They expected their children to return from Europe wealthy enough to support them through the rest of their lives. But even beyond this dream, becoming a *bengiste* was among the highest aspirations available to unemployed, undereducated youth. The returning *bengiste* was a source of pride to all who knew him, and produced prestige for the entire family. Thus, Dedy's father, who had helped Dedy raise funds for his first attempt to reach Europe, was desperate for him find the means to try again.

Michel was a university graduate working as a telephone repairman who considered himself to be more enlightened than his peers. His difference in opinion was not really an expression of class difference so much as a critical political stance, as many of his peers in the university system were as obsessed with Europe as the Treichville youth I focused on. He explained:

> It makes me sad. People just want to leave the country, they don't care. They have no respect for intelligence, it's travel only. For example, in a family where one son has a degree in engineering and another dropped out but went to *Beng*, it is the second son the family is more proud of. They don't care what he is doing there, don't even want to know, it is the fact of arrival that counts. Ivoirians are proud of this country in relation to other neighboring countries, but when it comes to Europe or America, they forget their origins gladly.

While Michel might be speaking hyperbolically here, the story of a family prioritizing travel over a degree in engineering gives us some idea of the importance travel to the metropole had in the urban Ivoirian understanding of personal success. Degrees were prestigious but relatively useless due to the collapsing economy. Ismaël Isaac, an Ivoirian Reggae singer, sang of how when you see a madman on the street it is probably a former university student whose overdeveloped brain burst under the pressure of not being able to find any use for the knowledge he had accumulated. Migration by contrast, provided the endless possibilities of economic success, adventure, prestige, and riches that only the unknown is capable of offering.

Migratory Practicalities

For many years, university students sent to further their education by wealthy families dominated travel to Europe. But in the early nineties a widespread popular change in taste commenced, such that Treichville youth, especially those connected to the criminal networks, began to dream of France as well. Some of the first street kids to achieve this dream were the musicians leading *zouglou*, who used their success at home to travel to

Paris and record their music. Their representations of Paris (both mystifying and demystifying) did much to spread lore of the bounty available in Europe. In the late 1980s, when Houphouët-Boigny began to sponsor the street criminal organizations in exchange for political support, the influx of money sent many of the gang leaders to Europe, to such an extent that formal hierarchical gang structure largely disintegrated. However, at the same time that migratory demand was increasing, it was becoming more and more difficult to penetrate European borders. France in particular severely restricted entrance to African immigrants during this time period. An Internet café owner named Keita described the difficulties involved today in gaining access to the appropriate paperwork:

> But visas, that is a difficult thing. It is not even possible to enter normally, one doesn't get in through legitimate means. . . . That's how it is now. I know a woman who took out loans, her parents borrowed on their retirement pension, plus she had worked and saved money, and went [to the embassy] and applied and was refused. She shook the white guy in there and cried, saying, "Kill me now, I can't go on . . ." Now she has given up, she put herself and family in debt in order to go to France and make money, and now there is no source of money.

According to Keita, the rate for a French visa was over $2,000, and a U.S. one was at least twice that. While corruption existed within the embassies themselves (an acquaintance who worked at the U.S. embassy claimed there were profiteers taking large bribes for visas), the space surrounding embassies became centers of *bizness* as well. The guards at the gate required bribes to allow access, and others who knew the guards could get you past the line for another fee.

As seen in chapter 2, an entire branch of the *nouchi* economy was devoted to document forgeries, with its own term for the profession: *camoracien*. The *camoracien* focused his activity on the peripheral documents required to get a visa: proof of work, a letter from the boss granting a vacation, proof of sufficient funds in a bank account, and so forth. Leguen and Billy had stolen stamps from local businesses and worked long hours in Internet cafés trying to imitate their letters. Stolen passports were among the most valuable items on the underground exchange networks. *Camoraciens* sometimes worked elaborate scams to con their clients, giving them all the peripheral documents and asking for a large advance to procure the passport and visa, then running off with the money. Because of these difficulties, many people chose more direct and dangerous methods, like bribing someone working on a ship bound for Europe to hide somewhere on board or trying to cross the Sahara to find a crossing point from Libya, both perilous and costly methods in their own right.

Much of the money needed for such a voyage had to be procured through success in the world of *bizness* or some kind of large theft, but unless an actor was fairly elevated in the hierarchy of thieves, this was not enough. As in Keita's description, the journey was usually the result of collective effort, pooled resources from close family and extended kin, as well as smaller contributions from friends. Many of those who helped saw such contributions as investments, as the *bengistes* would be forced to allocate their newfound wealth generously when they returned in order to prove their success. Family members hoped that their children would find success in Europe and provide for them and looked forward to the prestige of having a *bengiste* in their midst, while friends expected that their peers would "remember" them upon their return with some kind of valuable gift. Social networks, especially kin networks, were crucial to departure—the voyage was difficult to make without their support.

The Descent and the Bluff

The *bengiste* who makes his or her descent must continually display their superiority, in personal display, glorious stories, and finally massive distributions of wealth, goods, food, and drink. Michel described their arrival:

> Soon we are going to enter the season when the *bengistes* arrive. They come with their cars and their clothes, showing off what they have achieved, seducing girls by saying that they will find them a visa to bring them to France. There are even people who have only been hiding out in Burkina that show up later and say they were in *Beng*. Those who come back always talk about how wonderful it is. They never talk about what they did there. There is one who I know who has gone back and forth several times; he always comes back with lots of money. When you ask what he does, there he always says he is a businessman. But you have to understand the relationship of the CFA to other currencies. If you make 1,000 francs in France, it is 100,000 in Côte d'Ivoire. So who is going to challenge him? Even if someone comes and says that they saw him there as a crook or a prostitute, people are more likely to believe the adventurer. Because he is rich. How could he make that money otherwise? They come back and tell of the marvels of Europe, how they worked behind a desk in a big office building, how everyone is rich and how easy it is to get money.

There was always an air of excitement and anticipation around the recently arrived *bengistes*. One day, approaching the street corner on which my friends and I spent most evenings, Solo pointed out a *bengiste* standing by his somewhat battered Opel convertible, wearing pristinely clean sportswear of the highest-ranking U.S. and French labels. He was surrounded by a crowd of people, several of whom turned out to be other *bengistes*, the rest eager onlookers and old friends. Although to untrained eyes there was nothing unusual happening, the gathering had a keyed-up energy that indexed the extraordinary. Everyone was trying to talk to the man at once. Solo remarked, "His hand goes into his pocket, and it just keeps coming back out." Practically everyone who approached the man (named Ousmane) asked for money in one way or another. After awhile, Dedy also approached him, only to be chastised for having avoided him previously. Dedy explained to us afterward that he didn't like to be seen around Ousmane, because the latter used to be one of his *petits*. He didn't want anyone to think he was mooching money off a *petit*, nor would he want Ousmane to have that impression. The power of the *bengiste* identity was revealed here, for Ousmane had clearly transcended his former subordination to Dedy, such that even to be seen in his presence caused Dedy humiliation. The importance of distribution of wealth in establishing these hierarchical relations also emerges. So long as Dedy avoided receiving from Ousmane, he avoided confronting the transformation in the relationship. Ousmane's former equals, however, eagerly accepted his offerings, recognizing his now-superior social status (and the possibility of benefiting from it).

Other people described their anger at having been forgotten by their former friends. Mathilde, a university student working in a printing and photocopy booth, was excited to hear that I was from the United States and began to tell me how much she would like to get there herself: "It seems that over there life is sweet. There are good jobs. OK, maybe I couldn't get an important job, but one can find a little job, and when you return here the money becomes big like that." The dream of migration was just as prevalent among women, and there were increasing numbers of women who succeeded. During my fieldwork in 2009 in Paris there seemed to be as many women as men traveling to Europe, though in 2001 I had had the impression that this was a field dominated by men. Elections had been scheduled for November of 2009 in Côte d'Ivoire (they did not take place), and the peace accords of 2007 required that the entire Ivoirian population prove their citizenship and get national identity cards before voting. This gave me a chance to see a random sampling of the entire immigrant population of Paris (legal and illegal) lined up outside the embassy, and I was surprised to see that men and women seemed fairly equally represented. Furthermore, I met women whose age ranged from twenty-five to fifty-five, working such jobs as supermarket cashiers (this was a woman with proper paperwork from the elite district of Riviera in Abidjan), janitors, bartenders, and nannies (the latter jobs did not always require proper paperwork and were easier to attain).

Although migrants often attempted to cut off their former connections (and corresponding obligations) when they realized the very real difficulties of life in *Beng*, Mathilde made clear to what extent they were breaking cultural norms:

> But our brothers over there forget us quickly! When they return, we always ask them to bring us American clothes. We want jeans, Sebagos, Façonnables . . . but then often they bring us nothing. They lie to us, tell us the bag got lost at the airport, or that they haven't unpacked yet, and then a couple days later they are off to another part of town, and you never see them again. Often they are even ashamed to sleep in their own house where they grew up. They prefer to go sleep at the "Ivoire," at Ibis, like that. But what is certain is that when people come back they have money, and then they have gotten so fat, you can't imagine what they've been eating over there, really not. In any case, they get here and they forget about us immediately. They forget about their own family.

Evidence of the social dangers of transgressing such obligations could be found in *zouglou*. Unlike most *bengistes*, *zouglou* musicians were secure enough in their status to criticize their experience of Paris, and their lyrics often attempted to disrupt the myths of *Beng*. Nevertheless, observers pointed out that these musicians kept going back to Paris, despite all their complaints, and so were disinclined to put too much faith in such negative portraits. The following song by Fitini describes an ill-fated migrant to Paris named Gloglou. Note the family's reactions to his failure to live up to social obligation.

"Parigo," by Fitini

> Your parents build houses,
> While for the sake of a few coins you follow people all over,
> But you should stay home a bit, stay home.
> A youth from our quarter, who dreamed of going to Paris,
> Since his birth, he dreamed of going to Paris.

In the quarter, he gave us a lot of shit,
"I want to go *derriere l'eau* [behind the water, Europe], to seek my future."

"My brother Gloglou, France is not like Côte d'Ivoire.
Over here it is cold, problems with papers,
Individualist, every man for himself,
You have all the time you need to ask questions."
Example: Chez les Dioula "*Ani sogo ma* [salutations]
   Television *bei waa*? Are there *bei* radios? [Are their lots of televisions,
   radios?] Money *bei waa*? everybody has *bei*? [Is there lots of money?
   Does everybody have a lot?]"
Nevertheless, Gloglou wanted to know nothing.

"I want to go *derrière l'eau,* to seek my future."
It is at the base of a wall that you see the true house.
So we began to save money.
"Here is your money, go now *derrière l'eau,* but there is one condition.
As soon as things are going OK, you must bring Zouzoi over,
Zouzoi in his turn, will bring over Nyaware."

Certainly, right away Gloglou accepted, he went off to Paris.
Three months later, a letter arrived.
Gloglou has written, Mama, Gloglou has written.
All the youth of the *quartier* gathered around to read the letter
Gloglou has written, Mama, Gloglou has written!
My brother read us the letter.

"Truly things are not going well,
The cold will kill me, the white people ignore me,
Petit Yode was right, Paris is hard like a rock,
Come and bring me back, I sense that I will die."
He was really full of *donyere* [shit].

For the response, we didn't have to think long.
We also wrote a response: "Go ahead and die."
He screamed mama, He sobbed papa, *djebelekou* [cry of sadness].

                (Fitini 2000)

In the song, a youth dreams of going *derriere l'eau* to seek his fortune. Glo-glou's family reluctantly agrees to provide the money to send him to *Beng* so long as he will reciprocate by bringing over his brothers once he succeeds. When Gloglou fails to meet the expectations of the family's investment, they sever their connection with him and tell him he might as well be dead.

It is important here to consider the role of reciprocity (and lack thereof) in the migratory process. Mauss ([1923] 1990) describes material exchanges as both expressing and defining social relationships—exemplified by Treichville's moral economy in chapter 2. As Sahlins writes, "A material transaction is usually a momentary episode in a continuous social relation. The social relation exerts governance" (1972:186). At the same time, however, "the connection between material flow and social relations is reciprocal. A specific social relation may constrain a given movement of goods, but a specific transaction—"by the same token"—suggests a particular social relation. If friends make gifts, gifts make friends" (1972:186). Gifts and their reciprocation are obligatory acts for the maintenance of social relationships, but they also have the power to transform the nature of such relations. Both of these processes were at work in Ivoirian migration. Migrants were obligated to legitimate their "success" through extensive gift-giving practices. At one level, as I have suggested, such gift-giving can be understood as a reciprocal return for the economic support family and friends gave in helping initiate migration in the first place—it was a necessary expression of the bonds between migrants and their kin and friends. But such gifts were often in the form of objects unavailable to the recipients, or sums of money beyond the means of those who received it. In this sense the returning migrants gifts were marked by an unreciprocable surplus. Such asymmetrical exchange inevitably involves relations of social hierarchy and is often, as in this case, constitutive of them (or to put it another way, the equation is balanced by the prestige the donor acquires as a result of the gift) (Leach 1951). The massive distributions accompanying the return of the migrants could thus be understood both as a performative legitimation of their newfound identity and as an act of self-production through unreciprocated giving. As such, these return gift-giving performances conformed to relationships between authority and distribution already seen within the social networks of the informal economy, where older, more established criminals gave to their younger acolytes in order to maintain loyalty.

Bengiste Networks, Migrant Economies

But the economics of the *bengiste* lifestyle were somewhat mysterious. From my periodic research in the African immigrant community in Paris since 2000, as well as reports from older Ivoirians no longer concerned with their reputation, the reality of migration was quite different from the stories of success *bengistes* proliferated. Without proper papers (visa, passport, work permit, etc.), most immigrants could not get legitimate work in Europe. Their income tended to come from within the African immigrant community itself. Working in underground African bars and restaurants, selling black market goods smuggled in from other E.U. countries with lax borders, hawking drugs, prostitution: these were the sorts of occupations on which most of my acquaintances in Paris survived, a far cry from the office jobs of which Ivoirians dreamed. Their living conditions were often extremely difficult, four or five people sharing low-income one-room apartments with no hot water, no bathrooms, and sometimes even no electricity. In their work on the Congolese informal economy in Paris, MacGaffey and Bazenguissa-Ganga (2000) have described an entire market based on renting or selling squats to other immigrants, housing which gains value the longer it remains undiscovered by the authorities. However, because the French franc was worth a hundred times its value in Côte d'Ivoire, the meager savings immigrants accumulated over several years of these kinds of conditions were enough to spend a month or two of luxurious wealth back in their home country. Such displays were enough to uphold their identity as a person of success, a *bengiste*, and to bolster the prestige of their entire family in the eyes of the local community.

While migration literature has tended to focus upon remittances to the home country, urban Ivoirian migrants expressed transfers of wealth as gifts and were explicit about the prestige associated with such assymetrical exchange. Of course, these two practices are closely related, but they have different social and analytic ramifications. Remittances are largely understood as a means of accumulating capital in the homeland (people migrate for the purpose of bringing otherwise inaccessible income to their families), while an emphasis on gift exchange brings attention to the expression and transformation of social relationships. Thus, Lisa Cliggett (2005) argues that Zambian urban migrants did not engage in cash remittances, but rather brought gifts in order to maintain social relationships with their rural villages. I choose to call migrant Ivoirian economic distributions gifts rather than remittances because this better reflected the intentions and interpretations of the actors. Remittances are a means of maintaining relationships over distances of space and time; as in Munn's (1986) description of the *kula* in Melanesia, actors enhance their name across "spacetime" by sending material wealth. In contrast, Abidjanais seemed to be more concerned with face-to-face relations upon their return and with hierarchizing such relationships through gifts. Migrants often sustained only sporadic contact with family while away, and money was rarely sent. Families of Ivoirian migrants did expect remittances, but they were often disappointed and complained that their kin had forgotten them. Rather than extending one's name through "spacetime" with long-distance money wirings, *bengistes* employed in situ performative distribution of gifts in front of a home audience that built reputation. Urban Ivoirians gained prestige through the action of potlatch-style competitive exchanges: it was by doing, not having, that they produced names for themselves. Ultimately, migrants genuinely aspired to build in their communities and contribute to their families' welfare, but the social obligations for display often took precedence.

In reality, the *bengistes* economized in ways very similar to the youth in Abidjan. Just as the *nouchi* relied on informal criminal networks for their survival and income, the *bengistes* developed similar networks in their destination countries and even back in Côte d'Ivoire. In the same way that youth at home in Abidjan invested such income primarily in clothing and other forms of conspicuous consumption in order to build their reputations, *bengistes* used their limited savings in a grand exhibition of wealth and success upon their *descent*, and left home empty-handed to begin the process again. Upon arrival in Abidjan, they reentered the informal economy immediately, selling the prestige goods they had brought with them to support their luxurious lifestyle (often including *France au revoirs*, Nouchi for used, possibly stolen cars from Europe). In an unusually explicit description of the inner workings of *bengiste* networks, Christophe explained:

> In principle, guys who talk about going to France are full of shit. To go over there, if you have nobody there, you get repatriated fast. You have to have somebody to help you, to give you somewhere to stay for a while, all that. First someone from our *ghetto* has to get there and establish himself, then, others can come, little by little. *Bengistes* are like that, that is their system, their *manyerage* [way of manipulating the system]; they are together. Here, when they come, they have their kiosk, their bar. You wouldn't even believe that it is for them, because it is always in some forgotten corner, *coin façon* [messed up place], without a sign. You see them there figuring out their network. They are on the phone to France: "OK, he's coming in on the plane at such and such a time, then he will be in this place, and you will find him over here." They are all connected, the *bengiste* group.

According to Christophe, many *bengistes* had to commit crimes in order to get the money to leave; they were even more caught up in the criminal hierarchy than before (one wonders, given that he knew this, why he continued to imagine France as such a utopia). The point was that *bengistes* continued to operate within the same informal economy as the one they supposedly left behind when they migrated.

The difference was that they had jumped up the hierarchy within this system. In this way, Dedy was no longer superior to his former *petit* Ousmane, who now had whole circles of acolytes supporting him. Thus, the magical transformation of migration actually had real social effects; even if in economic terms the *bengistes* were not that much better off than when they left, they had far greater social influence. In an informal economy in which whom one knew was the difference between starvation and success, such influence and fame actually had real economic effects. However, in order to preserve this superior status, which was, after all, based on a kind of bluff, they spent much of their time within the delimited network they established in *Beng*. Among their own peers they could drop pretence, while the exclusivity they cultivated reinforced their perceived importance from the outside.

Demystification and Remythologizing Discourses

Abidjanais seemed to be increasingly confused by the disparity between the perceived wealth of the *bengiste* and the reality of migration, for despite the best efforts of many *bengistes* to perpetuate the myth of bounty upon which their prestige was based, more and more stories debunking these glorious images were circulating. The primary critiques came in *zouglou* pop songs, a whole genre of which discusses the difficulty of life in Paris. The first song to blow the whistle was Petit Yode and Enfant Siro's "Paris," and its chorus, "Paris est dur comme caillou," had taken on the status of an Ivoirian proverb (it was even quoted in the song by Fitini above).

"Paris," by Petit Yode and Enfant Siro

In Paris when you see a white, he is dirty but his house is proper. But when you see a black, he looks proper but his house is dirtyyy!

Alewan yan ze [when we speak to you, you don't understand]

Beng is hard:
Since we were little, they spoke to us of France as a country of dreams, a country of leisure, a paradise on earth. You yourself know, the white does not give a

name for nothing. If he calls you Sylvain the Black, you know that you are black. If it's François, you resemble a sheep. They called their country France, *franc* [money] is for the whites, and *souffrance* [suffering] is for the blacks.

Chorus:
Beng is hard, Paris is hard like a rock.
A black in Paris never says, "I am going to work"; he says, "je vais *djossi*" [menial labor]. That is why all the "Parisians" [from Côte d'Ivoire] have polished complexions, but their palms are rough.

The whites are clever, if you work for them, they will pay you well, but in the same way that they pay you, that is how you will spend.

Chorus

In Paris, the Arabs who have white skin take themselves for blacks, but Antillais, who have black skin, think they are whites. Oh, everything is mixed up.

Chorus

Petit Yode in Paris, had the intention of doing some deals, one step into the metro, there's a white in front of me, who says the following to me: "Sorry to disturb you during your voyage, I am an unemployed French youth, and I would like a franc or two to eat and sleep somewhere warm. For those who have nothing, a smile will suffice" [in perfect tonal imitation of a beggar on the Metro]. My mouth hung open in surprise at seeing a white begging from me, *Dja* [damn], a white person asking for money, a *moisi* [broke] white guy in his own country. My brother, Abidjan is better.

Chorus

In all countries there is a kind of food to *soutra* [sustain, help] the poor. At home in Côte d'Ivoire we have *garba*, but there in France, it is the *grec*, bread and fries, a little meat to the side, and some *quaker* [condiments]. Your Paris *a gagné* [is a success].

Chorus

"Dear African friends, I am going to Paris." Truly it is sweet in the mouth, but when you arrive on the ground, *Bô! C'est dûr, dêh!* [Dude, it's hard, man!].

A little economic advice: the money for the airplane ticket, use it to buy a taxi, or a small business. Now if you are mad and you really want to go: My friend, over there you will eat your totem. In Paris what makes a difference is that there are real *djosseurs* [workers].

Chorus

(Petit Yode and Enfant Siro 2000)

The song circled around a series of humorous structural reversals, drawing out a topsy-turvy picture of a world in which nothing is as it seems. One of the favorite jokes was the image of the poor white man begging in the subway, which many Abidjanais found to be nonsense and hard to believe. Despite knowing the words to the song by heart, however, many Abidjanais youth had trouble believing in them. If it is so bad over there, they would ask each other, why do Petit Yode and Enfant Siro keep going back?

With increasing pop songs critiquing Paris, and gradually spreading rumors about the reality of the *bengiste* experience in France, Abidjanais were becoming disillusioned with their long-standing Francophile orientation. But rather than drop the dream of migration, they had displaced it onto other European countries, and even more so onto the U.S. There were continual discussions about which countries were better, what each one was really like, how difficult it would be to find work. The following conversation is transcribed directly from a recording of a group of friends from my neighborhood:

OLIVIER: They say that life is hard there [in the U.S.], that one has to be a beggar to start out, that you shouldn't expect any more than that to start out, because really, it is difficult, eh?

CHRISTOPHE: But others, they say that, to get over there, that is hard, but once you arrive there, it's easy.

OLIVIER: There is where? Have you spoken with one person who's been over there?

MATHIEU: But over there, since there is already a mix between whites and blacks, they let people alone, whereas in France it's only white.

CHRISTOPHE: No, it's saturated there now.

MATHIEU: But when they see blacks in France . . .

CHRISTOPHE: No, it's saturated.

SOLO: Totally saturated. Malians, Senegalese, Burkinabes . . .

OLIVIER: But the Malians have their papers to be there.

MATHIEU: And the Senegalese, then?

SOLO: They have their papers on the table.

MATHIEU: Malians even, they must have come after the Senegalese, they learned all that from them. Isn't it in France that they have a whole quarter of blacks?

SOLO: Yeah, at Chateau Rouge.

Although Mathieu argued that it was easier to pass in the U.S. because of preexisting race dynamics, Christophe reacted to the representation of France as white. He and the rest of the group emphasized that France was "too black," that there were so many immigrants there that the country no longer had the opportunities it once had. Likewise, Abdou also wanted to go to Switzerland, claiming it had a smaller immigrant population and you could still find work. He told me that "France has too many Africans, so many that it is practically Africa itself." Here metonymy was working in reverse effect. So many Africans had arrived in France that it no longer carried the same otherworldly aura it once did; the brilliant shine of the metropole had been banalized. For this reason, the U.S. had increasingly taken center stage as the land of dreams, the *paradis terrestre*, as one *nouchi* put it. Few criticisms of the U.S. circulated at that time, and even when offered my own critical impressions, people were quick to deny their significance. When I suggested that there were many poor people in the U.S., Mory scoffed and said, "But in America the poor people all live in those houses that you pull behind cars, no? The movable houses." When I told an older man that some people search through dumpsters for food, he replied, "Yes, but over there the trash cans are clean. There you start a chicken but don't finish it, and throw it away like that. Then it is nicely wrapped in paper and plastic, so eating out of trash cans over there, it's good."

The representation of *Beng* as the source of value was not static, but continually influenced and adapted by the *bengistes* and Abidjanais as they accumulated rumors and representations of the "otherworld." The overall structure of this cultural geography of value remained the same, but the internal organization of its hierarchy was continually altered to match the experiences and practical realities of urban Ivoirians, just as the value of the brands they consumed was regularly rearranged. In this way, the United States had superseded France as the ultimate source of cosmological value. During the Ivoirian political crisis after 2002, this changing global representation played out in the demonstrations of the Jeunes Patriotes against French intervention, explicitly requesting U.S. military aid. Ivoirians from southern ethnic groups increasingly perceived France as closely linked with the northern rebels, who were associated with the "tradition" of *dozos* in their mystically charged hunting garb (though most rebel forces were not *dozo* and did not identify as such). The Jeunes Patriotes furthered their allegiance to this rearranged hierarchy by fashioning themselves after the *nouchi*, imitating U.S. hip-hop and sports styles rather than the "French" style of *les bosses* with their suits and ties.

The Mediation of the Otherworld: Migration as a Form of Consumption

Migration, I argue, can be considered a form of consumption that turns migrants into media for the distribution of alterity. Rather than migrating as an act of economic production, migrants seek the symbolic and social capital of personal transformation. In fact, according to my friend Michel, the popularity of migration was a recent phenomenon, which had emerged directly out of the collective importance formerly placed upon clothing fashions. While youth used to put all of their income and energy into achieving the proper style, the importance of clothing had greatly diminished in relation to the dream of travel. In a sense then, migration was itself a fashion, a form of consumption that had replaced earlier modes of self-production. In the eighties, Michel explained, everyone was trying to imitate the Congolese *sapeurs*, who dressed in European haute couture clothing:

> Everyone was trying to get suits and ties and labels. People would cut tags off shirts and stick them on the back of their pants. They would say, "Look, what are you wearing, that is nothing, not even labeled. My pants are such and such" and then they would point out the label. This was all over Abidjan in those days. . . . But in 1990 . . . after the economic crisis began, everyone who had money left for France, and then there was no money at all. Meanwhile, some of the people going to France were coming back filled with stories of how great life was there, of how the money was more powerful, and even if you were a prostitute there you could come back rich. By 1995, everyone wanted to go to France. If you put ten people in a row and asked them, nine out of ten would have said they wanted to go to France. "La voyage est devenu à la mode" [The voyage became the fashion]. This is how migration became so important. Even the pop music stars, some of the most famous and successful people in Côte d'Ivoire at the time, have left for France and never came back.

In this sense, migration was merely a continuation of an ongoing relationship to consuming otherness, to a fascination with the external. While consumption was itself the incorporation or metonymic absorption of otherness, the migration process became a total self-transformation, one which finished by both dramatically increasing one's social status and producing a Durkheimian "set apart" or sacred quality to the *bengistes*, who ended up congregating mainly among themselves. As we see in the pop song *Parigo*, cited above, Europe is referred to by *bengistes* themselves as *derrière l'eau*, recalling its symbolic parallels with the otherworld.

In conclusion, I believe that the urban Ivoirian consumption of North Atlantic goods and the migration to *Beng* are parallel symbolic operations. Migration was a more powerful and total version of the temporary transformation that the *bluffeur* achieved through clothing; the *bengiste* not only absorbed the "modernity" of the West, but became him or herself a *purveyor* of that modernity. This transformation took place at two levels: cosmologically, through migration the "adventurer" became someone from "the land of the whites," the ultimate source of value, while socially, this symbolic operation expanded the hierarchical position and social network of the actor. The prestige of the *bengistes* gave them new social influence within the informal networks that dominated the Treichville economy, allowing them opportunities and resources they would have had great difficulty achieving without leaving Côte d'Ivoire.

This parallel between consumption and migration as forms of magical transformation has important ramifications for our understanding of both spheres of social action. I follow the likes of Appadurai (1986), Kopytoff (1986), Daniel Miller (1987, 1995), and Friedman (1991, 1994) in theorizing consumption as personal symbolic action through which the categories of person and thing intermesh. At the same time, I insist with Douglas and Isherwood (1979) that consumption is ultimately a social and semiotic process through which goods make concrete the abstract categories of social life—that consumption works like a fixative to pin down the slipperiness of meaning (temporarily). However, by considering consumption a form of partial migration, I emphasize the importance of *contact* in the Abidjanais cosmology of persons, things, and places. Despite the importance of gift theory to the discipline, which from the beginning has emphasized the metonymic "person in the gift," scholarship on consumption has tended to focus on questions of appearance and imitation, neglecting the possibilities for indexical relations of contiguity as sources of value and symbolic transformation. At the same time, by examining migration as a form of consumption, we can investigate local constructions of the relationship between place and value, shedding light on the motivations underlying the migration process.

I suggest here that in neglecting the cosmological underpinnings of migration, anthropological accounts of transnationalism or diaspora often miss the crucial local effects of the process, effects that determine the motivations for migration in the first place. It is important for anthropologists to be sensitive to the ways in which the North Atlantic discourse of modernity can be appropriated and used within local cosmological systems. Thus, explanations of the postcolonial cultural hegemony of the metropole often rely upon a working misunderstanding between cultures, in which concepts like modernity and civilization produce quite different resonances and associations in the culture from which they came from those in that which has come to adopt them (Sahlins 1994). Indeed, by disrupting these coordinated misconceptions of global hierarchy, the space is opened up to interrogate North Atlantic cosmologies of modernity, value, and place, a direction I shall pursue further in the conclusion. For I suspect that modernity is imbued with just as much transformative power by the social actors directing the politics of global economies as it is by urban Ivoirian youth.

Migration and National Identity

"Ivoirians have an identity crisis: they do everything to look like they live in Paris. Some of them, if they weren't here, you would swear by the way they dress and talk that they were French, that they had spent their lives in France," Olivier told me. As has clearly been evident throughout this book, urban Ivoirians were profound imitators, focusing their gaze outward rather than inward in the search for personal identity. Olivier summed up this tendency negatively, arguing that Ivoirians did not have enough pride in themselves. And yet Dalbé, the tailor specializing in *griffes colés* referred to in the introduction, was proud of precisely this aspect of Ivoirian identity, saying that "when Ivoirians imitate, they don't do it at 50%, they imitate at 100%." Imitation could be a source of nationalist pride. There is an alterity within the construction of urban Ivoirian identity, for the incorporation of symbols from outside Côte d'Ivoire has become the foundation for a new national identity. In this section, I argue that the external migration process that became widespread in the early nineties was another key causal factor in the emergence of a popular construction of national identity.

I want to suggest that the migration process can be understood formally as an inversion of tourism. The value in this comparison lies in MacCannell's (1989) theory that tourism is in fact a central ritual of modern society, that it is our primary means of representing society to ourselves. Arguing that a constitutive problem of modern social life is the increasing differentiation and alienation of individuals (a lack of Durkheimian collectivity), he claims that "sightseeing is . . . a way of attempting to overcome the discontinuity of modernity, of incorporating its fragments into unified experience" (1989:13). MacCannell's book problematically assumes that preindustrial societies are actually "authentic" and have clear-cut collective identities unobscured by the complexities of internal diversity, and McCannell contrasts this with modern culture as one overcome by "spurious" duplication, where the representation and the original are so confused that the original is lost. However, both the representation of premodern society as stable and coherent and the idea of postmodernity's break with the past—a rupture of authenticity, stable boundaries, and system—are equally problematic. Societies of all varieties have always faced the problem of their own fluidity and potential for disintegration, have always needed a way to represent social differentiation and coherence simultaneously, and so the structure McCannell outlines for travel as a means of self-discovery is relevant for understanding Côte d'Ivoire as well.

The idea of McCannell's I want to apply here is of tourism as a ritual structure of self-representation, carried out by individuals but ultimately producing a collective sense of self. Because tourism is elaborately organized (through tourbooks, maps, tour groups, travel agencies, etc.), the process produces a collective sense of "places of value" and of the meanings each attraction has. MacCannell argues that in this way tourism is a kind of ceremony that sacralizes the site. Such sacralization is evidence of collective evaluation, and in that sense the tourist experience is also one of an interaction with the idea of society itself:

> In the establishment of modern society, the individual act of sightseeing is probably less important than the ceremonial ratification of authentic attractions as objects of ultimate value. . . . The actual act of communion between tourist and attraction is less important than the *image* or the *idea* of society that the collective act generates. . . . A specific act of sightseeing is, in itself, weightless *and*, at the same time, the ultimate reason for the orderly representation of the social structure of the modern society in the system of attractions. (MacCannell 1989:14–15)

In this way, individual journeys are not so important as the models of the world they both work from and help to produce, and these models in turn serve as the foil upon which a collective consciousness is forged. MacCannell discusses this in terms of a dialectics of authenticity, in which tourists persist in the search for forms of authenticity they no longer find in everyday life. The obsession of so-called modern subjects with authenticity is something I will treat in the conclusion, but here I want to emphasize the parallels with urban Ivoirians' own journeys to the metropole to bring back authentic objects with which to link them to the external. In this sense, the kind of migration Abijdanais engaged in can be understood as an alternate form of tourism, one that rather than seeking to encompass the world in a global (and imperial) vision of middle-class ideology, seeks to find the source of authenticity in the imagined center of the metropole.

But not everyone is a tourist. As common as tourism has become, there are still many who rarely even travel around the United States, much less the world. And this was still truer of urban Ivoirian migrants. As widespread as the dream to travel to *Beng* might have been, comparatively few actually achieved this, so how can we consider this to be at the roots of the production of national identity? MacCannell argues that the tourists are the activators of a more widespread process of self-representation, that the knowledge they disperse to their friends and family in their narratives and slideshows actually brings about group self-identification:

> It is the in act of sightseeing that the representation of the true society is formulated and refined. But this act is neither continuous nor participated in by everyone. It is merely the moment of greatest intensity in the operation of tourist attractions on the touristic consciousness. The tourists return home carrying souvenirs and talking of their experiences, spreading, wherever they go, a vicarious experience of the sight. It is the vicarious representations that are general and constant. Without the slideshows, travel talks, magazines, and other reminders, it would be almost impossible for the individual to represent to himself the differentiations of modern culture. (157)

Thus, employing the diverse depictions of the world outside brought to them by tourists or migants, people structure their universe and their own place within it by ordering these representations into a system of differentiations. Urban Ivoirian migrants went to the metropole and brought back representations of the source of value itself, and people used these in order to build, legitimate, and contest social hierarchy. But this continual appropriation and incorporation of alterity also served as a medium through which to integrate the diversity of Ivoirian ethnic identities into a new national Ivoirian identity. Ivoirians used the material of otherness to negotiate a dynamic self-production of collective identity. Rather than an acculturation toward European identity, urban Ivoirians used representations of European qualities to construct a sense of *Ivoirité*, converting these images into a local system of differentiation. Just as Nouchi uses the French language as a base through which Ivoirians adapt and reorder the diversity of ethnic languages into a coherent national language, so too have they transformed a collective representation of *Beng* into a medium through which to forge together the diversity of ethnic identities into a sense of hierarchically arranged commonality. This sense of collectivity was not universally accepted, especially since not all "Ivoirians" belonged equally to this new schema—some were implicitly *gaous*. In the following chapter, I will explain how the very process of negotiating this identity has torn the nation asunder, as the north and south each claim to have a more legitimate understanding of the meaning of being Ivoirian. The presence of a sense of collectivity can be more divisive than its absence.

SIX

Counterfeit Belongings:
Branding the Ivoirian Political Crisis

"Douk Saga en Fête," by Douk Saga

Come, Come, Dance! Douk Saga has arrived in the city!
Come, Come, Dance! Douk Saga has arrived in the city!

19 of September 2002,
Sadness came and hit Côte d'Ivoire.
Gun shots here, cannons there,
Everyone was surprised.
They announced the death of Boca,
Marcelin Yassé, and Général Guéi, oh.
Hundreds of people fell that night there.
We were shocked, We cried a lot.
It was pitiful, we were all beaten.

Like the messiah,
A young man will arrive,
With his battalion armed with joy and gaiety.

What is his name, oh?
Doukouré Stephane, oh [Douk Saga's real name].
What did he create?
Sagacité [sagacity, shrewdness, clairvoyance, but also Saga-ness].

They critiqued him.
They insulted him.
But in the end, everyone has Sagacité.

He put joy in our hearts, he made us forget our worries.
What did he create?
Sagacité.

(Douk Saga 2005)

On those rare occasions when stories of the Ivoirian civil war filter into the U.S. media, they are sculpted so as to correspond to our imagination of African ethnic struggles, in which ancient "tribal" tensions are exacerbated and turn into genocidal conflicts (often fraught with exoticized understandings of "primitive" magic, child soldiers, and "barbaric" acts of mutilation, rape, and cannibalism). I am not trying to claim that such representations are pure fiction—versions of these things can be found in the Ivoirian conflict—but rather that this story is too well packaged, too easily digested by television viewers as yet another African tragedy based on ethnic rivalry. In particular, it is this idea of ethnicities rooted in immemorial tension as the cause for violence and political instability that I wish to overturn here, for even the most cursory glance at the history of Côte d'Ivoire reveals that it does not fit comfortably into this narrative. Rather, it is the performative efficacy of discourses of autochthony—despite the underlying instability and fluidity of their meaning—that is cause for investigation (Geshiere and Jackson 2006; Marshall-Fratani 2006).

However, this chapter is also about examining how urban street fashion, a process of identity production associated less with ethnicity than with its abandonment, has contributed to the reification of ethnic categories that had little social relevance during my fieldwork in Abidjan in 2000 and 2001.[1] While the concept of the mutability of ethnicity is by no means novel, this chapter traces the connections between nascent nationalism and branding in the production of ethnic oppositions, demonstrating that the unstable semiotics of authenticity generate performative behaviors—including both consumption and violence—through which actors attempt to demonstrate the "real" of their identity. Finally, drawing on fieldwork during the years leading up to the failed coup d'état that sparked the Ivoirian political crisis, this chapter takes a step toward understanding how a country with a history of tolerance, diversity, and conflict avoidance transformed in less than a decade into one where gangs of youth wearing T-shirts with the word "xenophobe" proudly printed across their chests target their former neighbors as foreigners (Packer 2003).

I suggest that the emergence of the discourse of *Ivoirité* in the 1990s works according to a logic similar to that of brands. Nationality and brand value are both unstable semiotic forms that must continually perform their authenticity by policing, excluding, or destroying the doubles and counterfeits that threaten identity by mimicking the role of "real" citizens or products. In Côte d'Ivoire, these logics intersect in the performance of the *logobi*, where the mastery of authentic brand labels is also a demonstration of modern citizenship. But underlying the performative declaration of authenticity lies the lurking doubt of whether the objects to which one sacrificed half a year's income or the friends in whom one has invested trust are indeed really what they seem. As Geshiere and Jackson write, unintentionally invoking one of our central themes, "In practice, belonging turns out to be always relative: there is always the danger of being unmasked as 'not really' belonging, or even of being a 'fake' autochthon" (2006:1). Côte d'Ivoire's history of open-border policy for immigration means that many of those labeled Burkinabe or Malian in the present day are in fact second- or third-generation Ivoirians with few ties remaining to their supposed home, raising even further suspicions, just as those born in the city who reject the *nouchi* aesthetic to express their ethnic roots may not have a rural home to which to return.

Ethnicity, Postcoloniality, and National Identity

There are three prevalent explanations for the Ivoirian crisis. The first, as mentioned above, is that most commonly found in media representations of the Ivoirian crisis, that Côte d'Ivoire has fallen victim to a kind of primordial tribalism, as so many African nations have in the past. Obviously, such a narrative fits into a patronizing and racist narrative of Africans as incapable of rational political governance. Yet it is true that contemporary politicians and street pundits at the Sorbonne (a small square in Plateau in which self-proclaimed political experts lecture about current issues) have operationalized an essentialist discourse of autochthony, especially since Gbagbo's rise to power in 2000. Ruth Marshall-Fratani (2006) provides a wonderful history of discourses surrounding ethnicity and autochthony in Côte d'Ivoire's past, arguing that Ivoirian nationality has long been localized in specifically ethnic ideas of citizenship, constructed in opposition to the *étrangers* who later settled the land. Côte d'Ivoire does have a long history of importing labor, both for colonial plantations under the French and later during Houphouët's *mise en valeur* scheme to increase production by giving immigrants the land they worked. However, such identifications of *étrangers* remained at the level of localized ethnic resentment toward outsiders over land claims and were as likely to be directed at internal migrants as immigrants from beyond the national borders. There is little evidence for a sentiment of shared Ivoirian identity against those from outside the national borders, and indeed, during Houphouët's reign the border remained open to anyone who wanted to come and stay as long as they liked, no paperwork required. Houphouët's successor Bédié worked to promote the discourse of *Ivoirité*, but even he dared not date autochthonous origins before the colonial period: "The 10 March, 1893, at the moment the Côte d'Ivoire was born, the ancestors of all the great ethnic groups were already there" (Marshall-Fratani 2006:23). A shallow autochthony, if I have ever heard one.

A second common explanation is that greedy Ivoirian politicians manipulated the politically innocent population into xenophobia by employing ethnically divisive concepts such as *Ivoirité* in an attempt to block competitors and consolidate their own ethnic base of support. Without denying the existence of such irresponsible efforts at ethnic pandering, I question the way these explanations imply that Ivoirians were passive and naive victims. As Marc Le Pape and Claudine Vidal (2002) argued, even if politicians have exploited nationalism for personal gain, the concept of *Ivoirité* produced a mass movement of southern Ivoirians in opposition to a mass invasion from the north, and such large-scale collective transformation is too large to be the effect of political propaganda alone. An interpretation blaming the crisis on political greed denies the agency of Ivoirians themselves and treats them as gullible and manipulable instruments of power. Ivoirians sometimes employed this patronizing rhetoric against themselves; I was told on several occasions that Ivoirians were not *sage* (mature) enough for democracy, infantilizing themselves in relation to European models of citizenship and governance.

A third socioeconomic explanation is that Côte d'Ivoire's problems were inevitable, given Houphouët-Boigny's open-border policy. By inviting migrant laborers into the country without regulation, he produced the kind of economic pressure that breeds xenophobia in the competition for limited resources. While more nuanced than the former two explanations, this third line of argument assumes that the bounded map and census model of the nation-state (whose history, after all, is relatively recent) is the only possible successful model of governance, despite seemingly countless studies on transnationalism telling us that this model is in decline and ultimately untenable under the pressures of neoliberal globalization. After all, it was Houphouët's liberal policies on immigration that most hold responsible for the Ivoirian Miracle in the first place, and, rightly or wrongly, until quite recently Côte d'Ivoire was upheld as an icon of political stability, tolerance, and economic integration. Certainly his plan of giving all inhabitants, regardless of citizenship, the right to vote (even if, as his opposition claimed, it was designed to assure his victory in elections) is a revolutionary approach to democratic government in a transnational world. We must at least question the inevitability of the failure of this open-border model of nationality by investigating the reasons for its decline in the 1990s.

In contrast to the oft-assumed scenario of ethnic categories dominating African social life, Treichville residents did not typically group themselves according to ethnicity. Intermarriage was common between ethnicities, exchange networks were extremely diverse, and I witnessed firsthand the mixed quality of groups of friends and courtyards. For example, Serge, a sociology student who lived in my neighborhood, was Baoulé but lived off a shared courtyard with representatives from two other ethnic groups and a family from Benin. Leguen, a Bete, also lived with Anango, Senufos, Burkinabe, and Malians, all in the same *cour commune*, but he claimed it was like "one big family." Urban African ethnicity should be understood, in accordance with Mitchell's largely ignored arguments in the Kalela Dance (Mitchell 1956), as a form of popular culture stemming from urban locales rather than essentialist identities or primordial oppositions. Ethnicity is not a matter of "traditional" identity but a product (just as in the United States) of melting-pot scenarios in which it becomes a differentiating factor. It is a means to categorize diverse groups in order to navigate the confusing multicultural world of the African city.

As we have seen, Côte d'Ivoire's adoption of the French demarcation of a multitude of ethnic groups made it difficult for large-scale ethnic conflict to emerge. As David Guyer puts it, "Within the Ivory Coast, there was no one predominant tribe. For this reason, perhaps a blessing in disguise, political movements had to be deferential, pragmatic, and absorptive of other indigenous groups" (1970:78). Furthermore, despite all this diversity and some rankling over the lack of a multiparty system, Ivoirians were largely united in their support of (even reverence for) the former president Houphouët-Boigny until his death in 1993 (Toungara 1990), and the majority of Ivoirians continue to admire him to this day. This is not therefore a country with a history of ethnic tensions, even if resentment had been simmering in the west over the influx of Baoulé and Dioula migrants who claimed local land and profit through the *mise en valeur* cocoa plantation incentives Houphouët put in place (Chauveau and Bobo 2003; McGovern 2011). Indeed, from the so-called pacification of the Baoulé in 1915 until the elections of 2000, there were almost no violent incidents large enough to attract international attention. Even in the aftermath of these failed elections, which pitted the *gendarmerie* and one of the largest demonstrations in Ivoirian history against the national army and General Guéï's personal mercenaries at the center of the capital, Ivoirians told me that they would never have a war in Côte d'Ivoire, insisting that Ivoirians were too peaceful to fight each other.

McGovern (2011), however, has demonstrated in his insightful analysis of violence in Côte d'Ivoire that this has more historical continuity than is typically recognized. Because most scholarship on the region focuses on the period between 1920 and 1990, it has projected a "peace mirage," characterizing the current violence as an aberration. McGovern points to the precolonial period in which Samory Touré raged across the West African region in a state-building exercise legitimated by Islam, while in the stateless southern forested area local gerontocracies were often pillaged by youth who took power through violence. He also raises the specter of the largely forgotten antiforeign nationalist movement at the dawn of independence, though it is important to consider the resentment Ivoirians felt toward foreign African elites the French had brought in to fill colonial posts at the expense of Ivoirians. However, while the historical continuity of regional violence is a key to reframing regional identities, this should not be taken to imply that violence is the inevitable result of local culture. Cultural differences exist between north, center, west, and south in Côte d'Ivoire, but the reawakening of these as oppositional identities first required the collective imagination of their unity to take hold at a popular level.

Thus, I examine the novelty of Ivoirian nationalism as a grassroots fantasy of shared modernity, rather than a retreat into ethnicity. As Werbner argues, "The story of ethnic difference in Africa threatens to overwhelm the larger debate about postcolonial identity politics across the continent. It is as if an old narrative, once told in terms of tribe and now in terms of ethnicity and ethnogenesis, is still spellbinding. Yet ethnic identities are merely a small fraction of the many identities mobilized in the postcolonial politics of everyday life" (1996:1). Postcolonial identity dynamics encompass those of ethnicity, and it is to the larger problems of symbolic struggles over representations of national identity and its political, economic, social, and cultural relationships to the colonial metropole that we should turn in order to understand the issue of ethnicity.

Following theories of nationality by Bourdieu (1991) and Anderson (1991), anthropologists tend to think of nation building as a hegemonic, top-down process. The state in this model forces cultural assimilation and identification through standardized education (especially linguistic standardization) and bureaucratization, as well as the production of print media, maps, museums, monuments, and other state-controlled social representations. Indeed, analyzing how France built national identity within its own borders, Eugen Weber argues that there is little difference between the top-down homogenizing processes of nation formation and the process of colonialism itself:

> We are talking about the process of acculturation: the civilization of the French by urban France, the disintegration of local cultures by modernity and their absorption into the dominant civilization of Paris and the schools. Left largely to their own devices until their promotion to citizenship, the unassimilated rural masses had to be integrated into the dominant culture as they had been integrated into an administrative entity. What happened was akin to colonization, and may be easier to understand if one bears that in mind. (Weber 1976:615)

Arif Dirlik (2002) takes one further step, arguing that struggles for liberation from colonialism were forced to reproduce methods of colonialism in the form of nation building: founders of new nations had to adopt a European model of social organization and impose it upon their people. Only by declaring themselves an independent nation could they claim autonomous status, and thus, independence became a form of self-colonization. Using this model of the nation-state as a form of internal colonialism, I now explore the context of Ivoirian postcolonial dynamics in order to come to terms with how the emergence of *nouchi* identity and the efflorescence of popular culture that accompanied it had such profound effects on the production of Ivoirian identity as a whole.

Ivoirian Models of Nationality: French versus Nouchi

In this chapter then, I argue that a mostly overlooked key to understanding the failure of the Ivoirian state can be found outside the realms of economics and state politics, in the amorphous and slippery realm of popular culture: the popular imagination of the nation. I suggest that until the 1990s, most Ivoirians did not really think of themselves through a lens of nationalist identity, but rather primarily either as bounded by their regional ethnic enclaves (those outside urban contexts) or in terms of their relative proximity to French culture. There was no unifying national culture that could be labeled by the concept of *Ivoirité*—indeed, *Ivoirité* was no more than a state dream for national unification, an attempt to build a new identity, but there was no popular movement behind which a politician could rally support. Toungara writes that "the ethnic factor remains a divisive and disturbing theme in the country's internal political struggles. Since independence in 1960, there has been little change in the way the peoples of this small West African nation perceive themselves. Foremost in their psyches is their identity as members of regional extended-family and corporate kin groups competing with others for their share of scarce economic resources and political clout" (2001:64). For these reasons, the Houphouët regime needed to find ways of producing a sense of shared national identity to prevent the fracturing of his new nation, and the only ethnically neutral culture with which Ivoirians had any experience was that of the French. Thus, not only were these policies top down; their content was also for the most part empty of indigenous cultural content. Since all local culture was ethnically marked, it was difficult to draw on any symbols of Ivoirian identity without being accused of tribal favoritism. In this way, the Ivoirian state self-imposed precisely the kinds of nation-building strategies described above, replicating French colonial institutional structures and ushering in an explicitly Francocentric worldview in which many central social distinctions oriented around proximity to the standard of French culture. Under such a cultural system, in which value and identity were continually measured against a foreign standard, a national identity in the usual sense is hard to envision. *Ivoirité* in the Houphouët period could only be considered French culture, once removed.

According to Dembélé, "despite the affirmation of its independence, the creation of a national territory, and a strong idea of the nation, Côte d'Ivoire did not appeal to citizenship as a mode of national social construction until thirty years later, starting in 1990" (2002:157). In fact, in the early days of independence, immigrants from surrounding West African nations were no more *étrangers* than the flood of Ivoirian migrants (as likely to be Baoulé as Dioula) encouraged to help develop new cocoa plantations. Under Houphouët, autochthony was downplayed and neighborly fraternalism emphasized under the banner of economic productivity. The *mise en valeur* scheme took this logic to its extreme; in Houphouët's words, "La terre appartient a celui qui la cultive" (The land belongs to those who cultivate it). *Mise en valeur* policy invited nationals and immigrants alike to settle wherever they liked, a scheme explicitly (and perhaps ill-advisedly) designed to foster national integration by allowing people to feel at home wherever they lived. It was also a key strategy of economic development, bringing the labor necessary to maximize cocoa production and through it the income of the Abidjan's political elite (McGovern 2011).

I suggest that it was nascent urban popular culture that allowed for a sense of shared belonging among citizens themselves, developed on urban terrain that both colonists and the Ivoirian state had enforced as ethnically neutral or "extraterritorial" (Dembélé 2002:139). As I argue in chapter 1, in the 1990s a new grassroots sense of national identity was forged by lower-class urban youth in search of a new model for identity. This was the moment in which Nouchi speakers began to self-identify their register, but language was only one among many new signs of Ivoirian national identity emerging at this time. After years of imitating other African styles like those of the Congolese *sapeurs*, Ivoirian youth invented a look of their own involving torn jeans with handkerchiefs tied around their legs and shirts, and in the late 1990s African *pagne* material cut in a contemporary Euro-American style gained popularity in youth culture. Young women abandoned both the traditional wraparounds of their mothers and store-bought miniskirts for *pagne* dresses cut in daring and creative patterns associated with *Beng*. It was also in 1990 that the movement for multipartyism succeeded, strongly aided by the well-organized demonstrations of the student political organization FESCI (Féderation Estudiantine et Scolaire de Côte d'Ivoire). At the same time independence of the press was granted, beginning a period dubbed the "springtime of the press" because of the sprouting of literally hundreds of new publications. Didier Bilé, a university student caught up in the politics of the multipartyism movement, started *zouglou* in 1990, starting a revolution in stylistic and musical innovation. As Dedy explained to me:

> Suddenly in 1990 Côte d'Ivoire went through big changes. This was when multipartyism started. Everybody was thinking about politics. . . . Youth culture was focused on the students and the FESCI organization. And suddenly there was a new music, an Ivoirian music: *zouglou*, which talked about political problems, about the difficulties in the life of students. . . . Didier Bilé began it. In fact, a new style of dress came about too, based on the student style. Jeans, Docksides, T-shirts or polos. . . . This is the epoch when they tied foulards around their legs. . . . It was music of self-liberation, of self-expression. The songs of *zouglou* were there to explain the problems in social life. Music we had heard before was always about love and killing, but this was about what was going on in society, the issues of everyday life.

Indeed, *zouglou* was not simply a political pop music, but a music of liberation and unification and a statement about Ivoirian culture. One did not say, "I am going to dance *zouglou*," but rather, "Je libère en *zouglou*" (I liberate in *zouglou*) (Konate 2002:783). Yacouba Konate, an Ivoirian ethno-musicologist, describes the way in which *zouglou* brought groups of people together in a new understanding of Ivoirian identity:

> *Zouglou* caused a kind of return to the source; it brought together students, an acculturated and elite social group in power, and the little people without hope, the shoe repairers and the car parkers. Everyone acknowledged that its preferred language, Nouchi, made it accessible to all the national communities, and furthermore, escaped from "ethno-strategy." . . . [It] reproduced in some way the conjunction between the uncertainty of future elites and the disillusionment of those excluded from the system. Politicians continued to invite them to return to the land, which is to say the village. Not only did politicians not seem to believe this themselves, but they didn't seem to realize that, while for parents and grandparents the notion of the village retained its sense of value, for the majority of these youth, the village was the town, the quarter. (Konate 2002:778–79)

Konate goes on to suggest that the "real culture" of Côte d'Ivoire was born in the 1990s, and its motor was not in Abidjan's center, but rather in the *quartiers populaires* around its periphery. This seems to have been a cultural revolution of sorts, overthrowing the elite hegemonic cultural dominance based on the superior imitation of French culture in favor of new, self-proclaimed sources of legitimacy. And though these cultural phenomena had their origin in the urban lower class, they have quickly spread throughout the country and even into upper-class culture. *Zouglou*'s descendant *coupé-décalé* has even gained popularity across Francophone Africa and now counts as a legitimate cultural export.

It seems significant that *coupé-décalé* replaced *zouglou* in the midst of political crisis. Strangely, *zouglou* is a much more explicitly political genre, while the lyrics of *coupé-décalé* rarely contain a real message. Indeed, the manifesto of Douk Saga would seem to be contained within the lyrics with which this chapter began. He came as the messiah, to bring joy and gaiety to the people. His was a message of national unity, but a unity of excess, in which acts of production and work (*travail*) were inverted and turned into spending money and dancing. In the same song, Douk Saga calls out that he is "strong, very, very strong. One is not president for nothing. To be president you must be strong. Since the age of five, since the age of six, I have been strong." Proclaiming himself president and an icon of national unity by virtue of inherent internal force, Saga responded to the civil conflict through symbolic negation. As the figurehead for the efficacy of symbolic production, Saga's own history was a powerful example to his followers. Though it is not known from whence the wealth of Saga and his Jet Set derived, the *radio trottoir* spoke of nefarious dealings in Europe, something Saga never denied (and the fact that the music style he invented is called "scam and scram" would also seem to support this rumor). However, his real success and international fame came through his music, which he promoted by going to African nightclubs in Paris and London and bribing DJs to play his song while he showered dancers with money. Just as he produced his own fame through a bluff of wealth, his music was a fantasy of gaiety and limitless resources that sought to overcome the strife of Ivoirian reality.

Diouf (2003) argues for the significance of the category of youth in contemporary Africa, particularly as a site for the redefinition of citizenship. Blocked from the success falsely promised by failed states and never given adult legitimacy by outmoded initiation rituals, youths struggled not only to find a space and narrative in which to exist, but to create public spaces for themselves, often in the streets of the cities in which they gathered. The motivations behind Abidjan's popular youth movement did not concern nationalism in a direct way, but rather a class struggle against the elitist hierarchy based on differential access to symbols of French civilization. As this book outlines, they attempted to supersede this system by emphasizing their lower-class identity while legitimizing it through the appropriation of African-American fashion, linguistic style, and music. Because these representations were from a cultural source considered even more powerful than the French, such appropriations challenged the superiority of elite consumption practices. At the same time, because this new value system celebrated the incorporation of influences from a wide variety of local ethnic groups, these cultural products formed the basis for an understanding of "Ivoirianess" that could not have existed before. Just as the prestige of speaking Nouchi became a mark of Ivoirian identity despite its hodgepodge origins, the efflorescence of popular culture at this time created new ways of thinking Ivoirian, cultural modes that were not the mass-mediated groupthink of Anderson's print capitalism and therefore largely outside the state's reach. These were localized street hegemonies of people attempting to define themselves as modern Ivoirians in opposition to West African immigrants on one side and elite followers of state-imposed Francophilism on the other.

The elite *fonctionnaires* of the state and the lower-class *bluffeurs* are united in a shared cultural frame: that of social evolution. They both oppose themselves to all that is less civilized; they disparage the villager who has not yet learned how to dress or eat or walk properly or even survive in the urban landscape such youth have mastered. What appears in the global media to be an ethnic and religious opposition is primarily, from the perspective of *nouchi* youth, an opposition of cultural hierarchy between urban sophistication and perceived rural naivety, a hierarchy based on an urban Ivoirian cosmological understanding of modernity. It is this hierarchical opposition that oriented new understandings of national identity, driving a wedge between urban Ivoirians and the inhabitants of the rural hinterlands, who recognized their exclusion and refused to suffer it in silence.

It is necessary to point out that (as anywhere else) this dichotomy does not adequately portray the complexity of crosscutting Ivoirian identities. Most of the south is rural, and urban centers have as many northern residents and immigrants as southerners. The Nouchi language and culture are shaped by Dioula as much as Baoulé. But as the *nouchi* worldview became politicized, such that *yere* increasingly implied "Ivoirian" and *gaou* foreigner, the concept of Dioula crystallized around the style of the *boubou* robe (though it was no more an authentic example of Dioula culture than the *pagne* is Bete). Dioula and *nouchi* were increasingly stereotyped in opposition to one another in ways that did not correspond to the mixed ethnic reality of urban social networks, but rather to a stylistic opposition between *yere* and *gaou*. The opposition contains still further contradiction, because, as Cutolo writes, since the 1990s the state had increasingly associated Dioula with the criminality of the gangs of which they were demonstrably a part (2010:545). These were precisely the Dioula whose *nouchi* stylistic adoption made them *yere* from the perspective of the street, their Dioula characteristics invisible to those employing the stereotypic image of the *boubou*. Some of the *nouchi* portrayed in this book, including Brico and Papis, as well as style mavens like Dalbé and Absalam, were of Dioula origin. They did not deny their identity, but neither were they targeted for it in the time I knew them.

Although it is tempting to explain the emergent xenophobia in terms of economic pressures and competition for jobs, what urban youth more often spoke of was the way that labor migrants blithely ignored the street hierarchy of cultural distinction, rejecting its terms in favor of the pragmatic accumulation of financial capital. As McGovern argues, Mande from the northern savannah take a great deal of pride in having a "higher level of civilization" than their forest-dwelling southern neighbors, due to the large state formations of their recent history and earlier conversion to monotheism (2011:60). Thus, urban *nouchi* were not always wrong to sense that northern migrants rejected urban self-legitimation through modernity. This racialized stylistic divide was expressed politically in the division of FESCI into two camps, one led by the *nouchi*-styled Blé Goudé, a Gbagbo follower of Bete origin, the other by Guillaume Soro, a Senufo who supported Ouattara and who increasingly represented himself as a fellow northerner, even though he was Catholic and came from the same urban culture as Goudé. These two students, once close friends and even roommates, became epicenters of the conflict, going on to lead the Jeunes Patriotes militia and the Forces Nouvelles (New Forces) rebel army against each other.

The Death of Houphouët and the Emergence of *Ivoirité*

In my ensuing efforts to synthesize a convoluted political history, I will necessarily glide over many shifting alliances and oppositions and elide contentious debates over historical fact to present a concise interpretation of political transformation. Former president Félix Houphouët-Boigny became a national representative in the French parliament in 1945 and continued to control national politics until his death in 1993. Although an autocrat of sorts, he was considered relatively benign by those outside the country and revered by the great majority of Ivoirians.[2] Technically, he was a democratically elected president, but as the semideified head of the only political party, with a payoff system of loyalty and the aid of criminal organizations, he was firmly entrenched as a kind of chief—a role he explicitly referred to (Toungara 1990; David 2000). As Amondji bitterly remarks of Houphouët's legend, "The head of state tends to be represented with the qualities of an inspired prophet prudently leading a docile, happy, and appreciative people toward a kind of terrestrial paradise" (1984:15).

Unfortunately, Houphouët's most lasting legacy to the country may be his refusal to choose a successor, arguing that according to Baoulé tradition, "no one may know the identity" of the chief's successor while he is alive (Chappell 1989:671).[3] "My legitimacy is intransmissable" he claimed, all too prophetically (David 2000:43). When Houphouët died, there were two major contenders for his "throne": Henri Bédié, another Baoulé, and President of the National Assembly, and Alassane Ouattara, the prime minister, a Muslim from the north of Dioula ethnicity, who had worked in the International Monetary Fund (IMF). Bédié, quickly nicknamed *Dauphin* (Prince) won the remainder of Houphouët's term according to a clause in the constitution, but he only had two years before the next elections to solidify his power. In order to combat the threatening popularity of Ouattara, Bédié cast aspersions on the legitimacy of his main competitor by suggesting that he was born of foreign parents. And so the crisis began with a neologism: *Ivoirité*.

Ouattara is Muslim and from the Dioula ethnic group, from a region where families tend to straddle the border between Côte d'Ivoire and Burkina Faso. He was favored to win because of his international reputation as deputy managing director of the IMF from 1994 to 1999 and national reputation for his success in temporarily turning the economy around in the 1990s (by selling off national services like telephone and water to the highest international bidders). In practical terms, Bédié proposed that in the interests of *Ivoirité*, no child of an immigrant parent should be capable of becoming president. Bédié claimed that at least one of Ouattara's parents was Burkinabe and so declared that his competitor was not a legitimate candidate.[4] In principle, not only did the concept of *Ivoirité* symbolically challenge the citizenship of large numbers of immigrants who had chosen to spend their lives in Côte d'Ivoire, but, more importantly, it also extended to an uncounted number of children of immigrant residents who had never lived anywhere else. Many, like Ouattara's parents, were of an age to have arrived when Côte d'Ivoire and Upper Volta counted as colonial provinces of France. In effect, the entire northeast region of country, predominantly Muslim and sharing Mande ethnicity with bordering Mali and Burkina Faso, became suspected of illegal immigrant status (Bassett 2004). Having a name of northern origin or wearing clothing associated with Muslim identity became a sign of foreignness (despite Islam's being the most demographically significant religion).

The media increasingly focused on the large numbers of immigrants in the country and wondered whether Ouattara's popularity originated from such *étrangers*—could it be a false popularity, the newspapers asked? Newspaper headlines from my time in the field include these:

THE RDR PREPARES A REBEL ATTACK: WITH THE AID OF BURKINA FASO, MALI, TOGO, AND THE UNITED STATES (*Le J.D.*, October 13, 2000)

AFTER THE VALIDATION OF THE CANDIDATURE OF ADO BY THE CNE [the electoral commission]: A VERITABLE DANGER HOVERS OVER CÔTE D'IVOIRE (*Le Regard*, November 27, 2000)

EXCESSIVE AMBITION: THE ADO [Ouattara] COUPLE WANT TO BUY A COUNTRY (*L'Aire du Temps*, December 5, 2000)

A typical prewar urban Ivoirian opinion is represented by the following editorial from *Le Regard*:

> The truth is that Ivoirians want to break with the past, a past made up of lax-
> ness, of *laissez-faire*. . . . The truth is that Ivoirians want to retake their country
> in hand, and refuse to continue to manage with the foreigners that they have
> welcomed, who have benefited from their hospitality. . . . [Ouattara is popular,
> it's true], but popular among a population made up essentially of immigrants,
> composed of fathers, sons, and their kin. This popularity that his followers
> gargle about only proves one thing, the exaggerated number of foreigners
> and their descendants [in our country]. (*Le Regard*, November 27, 2000)

It was at this time that the *rafles* became a regular part of daily life, forcing people to carry identification papers at all times, to be able to prove their citizenship or their visa. Thus, as Ceuppens and Geschiere write, "In the Ivory Coast [autochthony] refers to efforts to redefine or even 'save' the nation" (2005:393). They trace this ideology as one implying that autochthony belongs solely to the southern Ivoirians, "a purified community of 'real' Ivoirians" (394). Such a discourse was new in a place where, under Houphouët, immigrants had been encouraged to come and go as they liked, to work, become landholders, and think of themselves as Ivoirians. As McGovern (2011) argues, the focus on autochthony corresponds to a fantasy of "turning the clock back to zero"[5] to an imagined time when all people lived where they were supposed to, when spatial and ethnic relations were mapped onto one another.

Counterdiscursive measures were iniated from Ouattara's party, the Rassemblement des Républicains, and one of the papers supporting him led with the headline "Are Ivoirians Xenophobic?" (*l'Aurore*, no. 213 [February 1, 2001]). The corresponding front-page photo depicted youths marching with placards, one of which depicted a map of Côte d'Ivoire with the words "Malians," "Guineans," "Burkinabe," and "Babylonians" written across it, each with arrows pointing outside the border. Alongside were scrawled the words "On vous voit donc quittez dans ça" (We see you so stop it/get out of that). One of Houphouët's former government ministers, Ahmadou Yacouba Sylla, the son of a Malian immigrant, had the following to say in a 2007 newspaper interview:

> Explaining the causes of the crisis, some have quickly branded the concept
> of *Ivoirité*. And yet we don't need to have such a complex with the concept of

> *Ivoirité. Ivoirité*, it is [the same as] Francité, Marocanité, la Burkinabité. Why should Ivoirians have a complex about calling ourselves Ivoirian? . . . It is true that at a certain moment, we got fixated with Alassane Ouattara. Afterward, certain agents of the state began to consider an Ivoirian who calls himself Sylla [a northern first name] is not a Koffi [a southern first name], that a Koudou [a southern name] is not a Coulibaly [a northern name], and for that he is outrageously *indexé*. ("Ahmadou Yacouba Sylla Crache ses Vérités à Gbagbo" 2007)

Ivoirité then, became a mark for a new concept of Ivoirian citizenship, one purified of members whose belonging was considered questionable. In a sense, *Ivoirité* was a new trademark for redefining the values of authentic citizenship. As Harrison (2002) suggests, such trademarking of identity has dangerous effects, for ethnic strife most often occurs because of underlying similarities rather than age-old differences, it is the desire to destroy the dopplegänger, the impostor, the counterfeit who infringes on one's own identity. It is the classic Hegelian duel for self-recognition.

In December 1999, General Guéï increased these growing tensions by leading a military coup d'état to oust President Henri Bédié from power, accusing him of trying to rig the elections and embezzle state finances.[6] It was the first coup d'état in Ivoirian history, but Guéï claimed that he would "sweep away" all the corruption in the government and then step down from power once proper elections had been held. His symbol became the broom. But, by midsummer, Guéï had decided that he would run for president as well, representing his newly created party, the UDPCI, and proceeded to initiate the same politics of *Ivoirité* as his predecessor, including a national referendum which established that one could not be president unless both parents were Ivoirian.[7] On the day of the presidential election in October of 2000, when Guéï started to lose, he put a hold on the count and claimed victory. This sparked the largest public political demonstration in Ivoirian history, as people from all parts of Abidjan marched toward the capital demanding that the votes be counted. By the end of the day Guéï had been forced to flee from the capital. Gbagbo, founder of the first rival party to Houphouët's PDCI, declared himself the winner of the election, with over 60% of the vote. A socialist history professor and activist for multipartyism, he would probably not have had the clout to win if the poll hadn't been reduced from seventeen candidates to five by the ruling of a judge whom many suspected of being under the pay of General Guéï. Alassane Ouattara, who had asked his party (the RDR) to boycott the elections after he was ejected from the race, demanded new elections in which everyone could take part, and Gbagbo refused—with the support of many southern Ivoirians who were fed up with political instability. Two days of brutal violence ensued between Muslims and Christians, including mosque and church burnings, until Ouattara backed down.

While part of this story would suggest that the ethnic divide was produced by conniving politicians for personal gain, this does not explain why the concept of *Ivoirité* clearly fell on such fertile ground. I suggest that the logic of authenticity underlying the Ivoirian crisis is not so much one of some perceived ancient and original autochthony as one of the brands urban Ivoirians consume—that is, *Ivoirité* built upon an urban Ivoirian conception of true citizenship as *modernity*.

Boubous and the Politics of Exclusion

Boubous are robes worn throughout West Africa; they are simple and loose in shape, though they are often embroidered with elaborate patterns. In Côte d'Ivoire, however, while the robes were not exclusively worn by Muslims (I knew several Christian young men that wore them because of their comfort in the sticky city heat), they have developed a strong association with Muslim identity as well as with ethnic groups and immigrants from the north. *Boubous* are perceived to signify an antimodern, parochial attitutde, and *nouchi* saw them as embodying foreign tradition. Although these robes were not Ivoirian in origin, they became associated with what Ferguson (1999) would call "localist" style. There is in fact almost no equivalent everyday dress worn by ethnic groups from the southern region of the country to represent what Ferguson (1999) called a "localist" perspective. Remember the story of Koffi and his suit from chapter 4—who, in contrast to all of his peers in Adidas and Façonnable, was going for the traditional look out of respect for his elders. Women do wear wraparound *pagne* cloth with African prints, sometimes in a "traditional" style, but as we have seen, the most valuable kinds are produced in Europe. Only chiefs continue to wear the garb signifying their rank, and even this is typically only seen on ceremonial occasions. Thus, for urban residents, the *boubou* not only symbolizes Muslim identity, but also a past they feel they have left behind. At the same time, because the *boubou* is worn all over West Africa, especially by the dominant immigrant groups from Burkina Faso and Mali, it is easily associated with the wrong kind of foreignness. These immigrants have typically come merely to make some money and go back home, whereas Ivoirian migrants from the village are more likely to integrate into urban society and adopt the styles of the *nouchi* or the elite.

The *boubou* therefore symbolized many of the same categories lumped together in both the political discourse of *Ivoirité* and the street hierarchy of *yere* and *gaou*. Because it condensed the polyvalent associations of both the nationalist political discourse of the politicians and the preexisting hierarchical schema of cultural evolution on which that discourse was built, the *boubou* became a powerfully resonant symbol for exclusion. For example, I often bought *garba* down the street from where I lived, and the man who ran the place wore very nice, high-quality *boubous*. Invented by immigrants, *garba* is a food that could be sold cheaper than the food prepared by Ivoirian female street vendors and that became so popular across ethnic boundaries that it is now associated with Ivoirian identity itself as a kind of national cuisine. Paradoxically, its preparation and sale are looked down upon and associated with Dioula immigrants. When I referred to a particular *garbadrome* as the one who wore the nice *boubou*, Dedy replied, "Could there even be one Dioula that wears nice *boubous*? No, they are all too dirty." For Dedy and his peers, the *boubou* was thus the ideal typical apparel of the *gaou*, something which could not look good, for it was by definition culturally inferior.

Thus, as political tensions mounted, the *boubou* became more and more pronounced as a symbol not only of cultural inferiority, but also of immigrant status, of political insurrection, of support for Ouattara, who was increasingly looked upon by urban *nouchi* as a foreign usurper trying to steal control of the country. I mentioned to some Muslim friends of mine who ran an Internet café that I had been told that there could be no xenophobia in Côte d'Ivoire, because "no true Ivoirian could support Ouattara." Keita responded angrily:

> I was never for the RDR [Ouattara's party] in the beginning even though I am Muslim and a northerner. But people began to group around Ouattara, especially once it became a question of whether he was really Ivoirian, and said that he represented us people from the north. And then it became this thing where everyone who has a certain name or wears a *boubou* must be RDR. I had nothing to do with it in the beginning, but as they began burning mosques and harassing me and everything I realized I really didn't have a choice.

Cutolo clarifies the condensation of foreigner and northern Ivoirian in "Dioula" identity by arguing that the Houphouët *mise en valeur* policy led to the production of a subaltern category of migrant laborer that came to be despised by the state as parasitic and prone to crime. The Bédié-inspired discourse of *Ivoirité* used this category as the foil to its vision of modern citizenship—Dioula representing the part of the country that was lagging behind the rest: "Anti-modernity, allochthony and extraneousness were made to coincide with subalternity as Dyula and 'strangers' were merged" (Cutolo 2010:545).

In 2002, the crisis officially began with the attempted coup d'état of the rebel Forces Nouvelles but was stopped by the Ivoirian army in Bouaké (the center of the country), and the country was reduced to a five-year standoff enforced by U.N. peacekeeping troops and a sizable force of the French military. Meanwhile, Abidjan's street gangs, which had always been responsible for maintaining social order even as they disrupted it, either merged into or were replaced by localized militias, which fulfilled essentially the same social functions but now with an orientation to the purification of citizenship.

Like the former criminal groups, the Jeunes Patriotes were made up largely of unemployed men whose income came almost entirely from shaking down or demanding bribes from those of northern origin at roadblocks or collecting "protection" fees from local populations. While the degree to which former gangs were incorporated into these militias is unclear, the heavy involvement of the *nouchi* in formal and informal "security" work would have been an easy segue into the new militia. What is certainly clear is that the leaders of the Jeunes Patriotes were the kind of university students we discussed in chapter 1; they styled themselves after the *nouchi* youth and proclaimed their affiliation with the United States. Like the *nouchi*, they adopted pseudonyms, though with a militaristic theme— Che, Sankoh, Kabila—and were organized according to a flexible patronage system in which one sought to be the loyal *bon petit* of a superior in the system (Human Rights Watch 2008:34–35). They were led by a charismatic man named Blé Goudé, who took on the street name Machete. From 1999 to 2001 Blé Goudé was president of FESCI, the same student movement for multipartyism that Gbagbo had helped get started in the late 1980s. During the height of its efforts to demonstrate for democracy, the movement had been infiltrated by street thugs hired by Houphouët to cause disruption, start riots, and discredit the group's political undertakings. Anger against these *loubards* had led to the lynching of Thierry Zebié, the "chef des loubards etudiants" in June of 1990, following the military's brutal attack (led by the very same General Guéï who would later take over the country) on the campus, in which many students were reportedly injured and raped (Grebalé 2001). But after Gbagbo's election to power, the FESCI student movement split between its president, Blé Goudé, and his friend,

Figure 15. This cartoon chronicles the transformation of the style of students between the 1970s and 2000. (1) Student Sweet was Sweet. (2) Student My Country Has Fallen. "I am bitter, very bitter." (3) Student Zouglou. (4) Student Machete, Butcher, Terrorist. Here we see the development of the *zouglou* style at the university as a reaction to economic decline and its subsequent transmogrification into the style of the *nouchi* hoodlum and Jeune Patriote militia member. (*Gbich!* 79, no. 9 [April 13–19, 2001].)

former roommate, and fellow English major, ex-president Guillaume Soro. The latter supported Ouattara and wanted FESCI to organize in support of the legitimacy of his candidacy. When Blé Goudé resisted, the university campus was reduced to a bloody machete war between factions, in which no student was allowed to remain neutral, and classes were shut down for most of the semester. After the coup d'état of 2002, Guillaume Soro became the leader of the Forces Nouvelles. Meanwhile the Jeunes Patriotes were increasingly accused of being paid to do the unofficial dirty work of Gbagbo. Thus, the principal opposition in the Ivoirian crisis, as well as the leadership of two of the most significant military forces, had its roots in urban youth culture.

The Structure of the North-South Divide in Popular Culture

The ideological divide between "north" and "south" was often framed in terms of cultural superiority and education as opposed to the ignorance, childishness, and animalistic tendencies of the other. These themes show up even in online chat room debates between Ivoirian university students. From one debate in which a Dioula student accused the government of murdering his ethnic group, I have taken the following excerpts:

[October 21, 2002, after the northern rebellion began]

DEVANDOUGOU: My condolences to your whole family. If all the Dioula are dead in cities and towns, there is only one thing left to do. . . . It's to pound them down to the last living baby!!! You should know that violence does not belong to any particular ethnicity or region. You tried in Bouaké, we just cut up a certain number, and already you talk of "genocide." . . . What's keeping you from trying again? Which will drive you to your extermination, band of pathetic xenophobes.

GUESSWHAT? Who is this Devandougou? . . . Your reflection is in a precarious and infantile state. What age are you? You represent the shame of Ivoirians, because you know nothing of your history or origins, which could be from Ghana, Liberia, Benin, or even Mali, Burkina, or Guinea, and maybe even from France. Or maybe you think your ancestors lived in the Atlantic Ocean or the Ebrié Lagoon? Barbarian!!! . . . You act like an ass and think like a monkey. . . . [in English] *Get some helps!!!!!*

DEVANDOUGOU: Hahaha!!! I am very happy with my posting. I hit so hard and justly that the damage is inestimable. The proof: Guess what is in an unequivocal demented hysteria. Instead of discussing the truth that I suggested, he prefers an animalistic and gregarious reaction. And as I do not understand the language of animals, I prefer to laugh at this exotic comedy. . . . LONG LIVE THE PREZ! THE PEOPLE SUPPORT YOU. IN FRONT FOR THE STRUGGLE AGAINST ISLAMIC TERRORISM. IT IS A GLOBAL BATTLE OF EVOLVED NATIONS AND CIVILIZATIONS AGAINST THOSE WHO SWIM IN OBSCURITY AND ISLAMIST EXTREMISM. WE ARE ALWAYS IN FRONT . . . IN DISLIKE OF THE BITTER AND THE JEALOUS AND ALL KINDS WITH THE AIR OF YESTERDAY.

In another debate from the same day, after someone had denigrated the intelligence of the north, another post responded by accusing the south of a loss of culture and colonized mentality:

Educate yourself well and closely about your own miserable kin before coming to show your intellectual and cultural merit here. "In the south, it is progress towards the twenty-second century." Do you know what you are talking about? Stop masturbating intellectually. Your country cannot even defend itself against a little group of "bandits," and you speak of progress towards the twenty-second century (skipping *of course* [in English] the twenty-first century). Is that your big insight? . . . Even a CM1 student [equivalent to fourth grade] could do better. You say that the north constitutes a "caste"!!! Have you ever set foot in your village (do you even know where to find your village)? Bastard "street" kid from the "city." . . . Truly a true pitiable—*déraciné* [loss of racial identity, loss of roots]—"slave of the white man" because he represents your "lord" of progress. It's probably at his house that you are writing these *chiffoneries* [crumpled papers, throwaway lines].

This was followed by a vicious retort against the north:

> If Mamadou Koulibaly [an important member of Gbagbo's regime with a Dioula name] were not already [in the government], he would be in the bush today with the Zaga-Zaga, busy shooting at Ivoirians. That is why Houphouët required all his children to be educated, but when it came to your mother-fucking kin in dirty *boubous*, he preferred that their children accompanied them to the fields every morning, or specialize in arms smuggling, or used tires, or cigarettes and stolen cars. I repeat, our problem in CI, it is this re-tarded region of the north, tribalist, illiterate, and antiprogress.

In this way, each side accused the other of being less Ivoirian. From the southern perspective, the northerners were recent arrivals with question-able ties to the country, who had not yet developed the "modern Ivoir-ian mentality," while from the northern perspective, the southerners had so sacrificed their own culture to the gleaming lights of urban European identity that they had lost their "roots" in Côte d'Ivoire. The final southern statement of course symbolizes the entire north by representing them in "dirty *boubous*."

Ble Goudé and his militia embraced the *nouchi* aesthetic, strutting and posturing in track suits and gold chains, through which they displayed their anti-French politics. Packer (2003) writes of their admiration for American boxing and basketball, idealization of American rappers, and general appreciation for African-American popular culture. English was of-ten incorporated into political speeches. The stylistic convergence of *nouchi* networks and contemporary youth militias seeking out *gaous* to oust from the country clearly points to the role these style hierarchies have played in shaping Ivoirian identity and the contemporary understanding of citizen-ship. Like the *nouchi*, the Jeunes Patriotes explicitly rejected France, calling Radio France International "Radio Fraud Intentionel." Anti-French senti-ment culminated November 6, 2004, when France somewhat unwisely bombed the Ivoirian Air Force, causing most French ex-pats to be evacu-ated as the Jeunes Patriotes looted their houses and farms. But sentiments such as these had been growing for years among urban street youth, who saw France not only as a symbol of colonial domination, but perhaps more saliently as a symbol of the contemporary domination of Ivoirian elites, who modeled themselves on the French and enriched themselves with the backing of contemporary French neocolonial economic and military policies. Many young Ivoirians blamed the entire Ivoirian struggle on French schemes to control the country themselves, accusing France of being the "godfather of the rebellion." As one member of the Jeunes Patriotes told the BBC, "Whenever I see Chirac, I see a colonizer. He is using an army of occupation here." Jeunes Patriotes rallied their crowds by speaking to them in English. They marched with signs demanding that the United States drive the French out. Blé Goudé himself said that "even if the United States didn't colonize our country, they should come to our assistance. Ivory Coast is a land to be taken. . . . Above all, the generation today has been educated in the American spirit. The American spirit is freedom. The American spirit is integrity in action" (Packer 2003:68). This was a fascinating take on colonialism, responsibility, and postcolonial identity. Goudé suggested that America was still responsible for taking care of Ivoirians because Ivoirians had adopted the "American spirit." He claimed a kind of membership in and loyalty to American culture that he felt the United States should recognize, regardless of colonial history. His sense of international relations paralleled the patron-client model in which loyalty should be met by protection and support.

In contrast, Guillaume Soro and other leaders of the Forces Nouvelles sometimes sought to legitimize their connection to the north through an appropriation of symbols of traditional authority. Although Soro normally wore *pagne* shirts or suits, he sometimes wore a *boubou* and stood beneath an umbrella like West African chiefs of the past, as in figure 15. Likewise Ousmane Chérif, leader of the Leopards, one of the four principal armies of the Forces Nouvelles, has been photographed in the magical garb of the *dozos*, who were often been accused of being in service to the northern forces (Hellweg 2004). The Forces Nouvelles were thus explicit in drawing their symbolism and legitimacy from the semiotics of "traditional" authority and mystical forces in clear opposition to the semiotics of modernity. The fact that Soro was Christian, was university educated, and had lived in Abidjan for many years, as well as two years in France, only makes the importance of this stylistic opposition clearer. In a surprising reverse appropriation, the urban Soro had to *bluff* his genuine northern affiliation and traditional authority by wearing a *boubou*, which in the incident pictured is clearly thrown over his more typical attire of jeans and matching jean shirt.

Figure 16. This photograph by Réné-Jacques Lique depicts Guillaume Soro in a
boubou beneath an umbrella, bluffing the traditional authority of those communities
he has come to lead. The photographer describes the setting thus: "This photograph was taken
in February of 2003. All the rebel chiefs, of the MPCI, the MPIGO, and the MJP, had called a
meeting to explain the Marcoussis accords, a meeting that sent them successively to Korhogo,
Bouaké, Man, and Danané." Notice that Soro's *boubou* covers up the kind of all-jeans
outfit he was more known for wearing. (© R-J Lique.)

This stylistic opposition between Goudé's *nouchi* modernity and Soro's
bluff of traditional authority was symbolically negated in the 2007 reconciliation, in which Gbagbo agreed to name Soro the country's prime minister and create a new position for Goudé: the "president of youth." When
the two old friends at last shook hands again, both reflected their unity and
connection to the state by wearing the symbol of political authority Koffi
described as "tradition": the suit.

In the geographic mapping of power relations through which Ivoirians
understand global politics, Ivoirian youth replaced France with the U.S. as
the apex of modernity, but this shift was not merely an external reorientation; it had vast effects on the internal social hierarchy, Ivoirian politics,
and Ivoirian identity. The appeal of Gbagbo himself as a leader for Ivoirian youth stemmed partly from his break with elitist French style—he was
the first president to wear *pagne* shirts. *Gbich!* commemorated his style in
a weekly cartoon entitled "Les Habits Neufs du Président" (The president's
new clothes), dramatizing his sneaky desire to wear *pagne* shirts against the
wishes of his advisers. Sometime during his ten-year reign, the cartoon was
renamed "Les Vieux Habits du Président" (The president's old clothes).

The point here is that these "global cultural flows" of U.S. style not only
are incorporated into local cultures, but can also be instrumental in the

production of local nationalist identities. Neither the model of fracturing identities à la Appadurai (1990), on the one hand, nor that of hybrid identities, on the other (Bhabha 1994), is well equipped to talk about the ways in which "deterritorialized" cultural material (Basch, Schiller, and Blanc 1994) can be used specifically for the territorialization of identity. Indeed, precisely the same disgruntled youth who tried to drive the French peacekeeping forces from the country in the name of Ivoirian sovereignty dreamed of traveling to Europe or the U.S.—transforming into *bengistes* on their return home. These were not anticolonialists (indeed, they invited the U.S. to move in), nor were they merely colonized passive mentalities accepting the hegemonic power structure they were fed by those dominant over them. They were actively attempting to manipulate the symbolic schemes of power in their favor, and in so doing, they constructed a new collective vision of shared identity. Such a thesis dovetails nicely with one of the key arguments of McGovern's (2011) analysis of the Ivoirian crisis: that the war has largely been a form of play, actions taking place in a secondary social frame in which young men with no productive outlet try their hand at war. They were motivated less by the ideological stakes typical of ethnic violence (the evil, inhuman enemy) than by the opportunity to escape.

Thus, the origins of ethnic violence, in Côte d'Ivoire, at least, seem to be located in the symbolic resonances of the consumption of "Western" material culture with an emergent urban culture, a mix with powerful potential for the production of national identity. These ethnic categories developed contemporary salience precisely because a different boundary took on greater significance for the first time: the national boundary. This was no longer merely an arbitrary border handed down from the French and defended by the inheritors of the French legacy, the *evolués*. Ivoirian culture came to mean something besides the imitation of the French or a collection of separate ethnic traditions, but in developing a self-determined meaning, it also produced a violent exclusionary politics based on the hierarchical understanding of space and citizenship. What upset many contemporary urban Ivoirians, I suspect, was not that people migrated to their city and took their jobs, but rather that some migrants refused to adopt the urban mannerisms that marked Abidjan's "superiority," thereby rejecting the cosmological schema according to which Ivoirian urban youth understood the world and their place within it.

Thus, the opposition between *yere* and *gaou* masked a more dangerous divergence between "true" Ivoirians and those deemed "false," those who rejected the new imagination of Ivoirian in favor of their rural or religious identity. The competitive display of the bluff was not simply a display of money and foreign goods, but also a display of the cultural mastery of the symbols of modern identity, allowing *bluffeurs* to differentiate themselves from untrue Ivoirians incapable of making such distinctions. Absalam told me: "A true Ivoirian prefers brands from America especially. We like this kind of clothing and will without thinking about it spend 180,000 CFA [$250] for a pair of sneakers with Jordan written on them rather than a suit for the same price. Just because it says Jordan on it. And there are sneakers just as good made in Côte d'Ivoire, but nobody wants that." The fact that Absalam was a middle-class Muslim makes his use of the common characterization of "true Ivoirian" all the more important to my argument that *yere* and *gaou* were more about modernity and its connection to nationality than religion or ethnic origin. For many, the shifting polysemous term *gaou* came to characterize Dioula and Muslims, but the opposition was not primarily about these things. Employing that ultimate mark of distinction in which only renowned connoisseurs can safely indulge, the ironic display of bad taste, after my departure Abidjanais youth developed the *Soirée Gaou*. At such social events, young people dressed up in imagery of traditional chiefdom, of loin-clothed eccentricity, of the slipper-shod Islamic, and wore poorly counterfeited goods, all in a competition of antistyle for the prize of worst dressed—further emphasizing their symbolic mastery through negation.[8] There were many ways to be *gaou*: to wear ugly clothes, to be the target of a crime, to practice the Muslim religion, or to be rural, uneducated, or awkward—and all of them posed a question mark above one's "true" Ivoirian status. The spectacle of the bluff with which this book has been primarily concerned was thus a confirmation of one's connection to external otherness and a production of local, national identity.

Branding the Nation: Cultural Mastery and the Unstable Signification of Authenticity

There is an old Ivoirian joke in which a contingent of the Gouro ethnic group approached Houphouët-Boigny and complained that all the products in Côte d'Ivoire had Dioula names. They cited such brands as Awa bottled water and Fanta orange soda, both of which are common Dioula first names. Houphouët looked at them in puzzlement and replied, "But you have BiFiol toothpaste!" (The morpheme *bi* in Gouro dialect signifies "son of" and is used in all Gouro names before the patronym). The story's significance is clearer when one considers the ethnic stereotype involved. "Dioula," a word whose etymological origin is "trader," designates a particular ethnic group from the north, but this has been extended to include all those who look or sound as though they come from the north (especially if they wear clothes understood to signify Muslim identity in Côte d'Ivoire, such as the *boubou*). Stereotyped as greedy merchants who believe in nothing but money, the Dioula were commonly thought to have undue control of products in Côte d'Ivoire, and according to the interlocutor of the joke, many Ivoirians still believed that Fanta was a local Dioula product. Like most jokes, this is impossible to tell well outside its cultural context, but the story is relevant for our purposes here since it signals a connection between Ivoirian investment in brand names and the opposition between northern and southern identities in the construction of Ivoirian national identity. As the Comaroffs have recently argued, the logic of branding has extended beyond products to ethnic identity and the nation itself, as cultural identities are packaged and marketed as products while nationalism is practiced through consumption (Comaroff and Comaroff 2009). I focus on this intersection here to emphasize that the instability of the connection between brand and product (the possibility of the counterfeit) parallels the anxieties surrounding citizenship and its impostors.

In a country where bribery made up for the state's inability to support its own institutions and workers, no document's validity could be taken for granted. To repeat the scandalous 2001 headline from *La Bombe* quoted in the introduction, "ALL THE FOREIGNERS WILL HAVE IVOIRIAN I.D.: CÔTE D'IVOIRE IS IN DANGER" ("Tous les Étrangers Auront des Pièces d'Identité Ivoiriennes" 2001). Indeed, the question of papers proving identity sparked by the concept of *Ivoirité* only increased in importance after the time of my fieldwork.[9] Proving one's citizenship became a daily necessity for many, who even to get to work might need to pass several checkpoints requiring papers along with bribes. Movements to reclaim the land migrants had attained through the *mise en valeur* policy brought with them more questions and suspicions regarding authentic paperwork and contracts. Police routinely rounded up residents in *rafles*, forcing them to document their Ivoirian identity or pay a bribe to avoid prison. Even as early as 2000, police sometimes tore up or confiscated the documents of persons they suspected of being foreign. The more pressing problem in recent years surrounded the determination of who would be allowed to vote, a genuine problem that was manipulated to delay the election several times over and to discredit the election of 2010 when it finally took place. In Paris in 2009, when I interviewed Ivoirian immigrants waiting to declare their identity, many reported having stood in line for over twenty-four hours. Within the line rumors circulated that Dioula who had already gotten their papers

were standing in line again to prevent southern citizens from voting. Paranoia over Burkina Faso's desire to annex Côte d'Ivoire continued unabated,
and in a January 30 headline from 2010, the *Conservateur* reported, "CÔTE
D'IVOIRE HAS BECOME A COLONY OF BURKINA FASO: 500 SOLDIERS
FROM BURKINA WILL SECURE THE ELECTIONS." Gbagbo's administra-
tion accused the president of the electoral commission of falsely including
over 429,000 names on the list of legitimate voters and requested his arrest
(Agence-France Presse2010). The *New York Times* reported on February 7
that there were close to one million people "whose identities have fallen
under official suspicion," their names and photos posted up in each town
for public scrutiny: "At the elections offices, each voter's national identity
is minutely scrutinized, and if a person has not been found on previous
lists—an old elections list, or a list of pensioners, for example—it may
make voting difficult. 'I gave them everything, but they won't let me vote,'
said Lancina Soumahoro, a welder in Yopougon, a working-class district
here. 'If you come from the north, there are big problems'" (Nossiter and
Coulibaly 2010:A8). All too predictably, these issues of "faking" citizenship and other forms of governance were invoked when the elections at last
took place in December of 2010. Gbagbo refused to accept the authenticity
of election results, describing the process as a masquerade to illegitimately
oust him from power. He had the results from all of the northern provinces
annulled, claiming that their had been too much fraudulent behavior to
count those votes. Although the international community refused to accept
his claims, the damage was done, for many Ivoirians continued to believe
even as Ouattara took power in the spring of 2011 that he was an impostor
who had used his neocolonial foreign allies to gain power in a country that
was not his own.

Such anxieties around false claims to citizenship mirror the anxiety
nouchi felt about the "real" origins of their brand name products, as explored in the fourth chapter. Actors attempted to overcome the possibility of the fake through a performance of culturally mastery, persuading
their audience of the authenticity of their commodities. The relationship
between nationality and authentic citizenship is constructed around a set
of issues similar to those of brands and "true" products, thereby shedding
new light on the semiotic structure underlying each. I suggest that in Côte
d'Ivoire the parallels between these two concerns over authenticity were
not merely coincidental, or even just symbolically reflective of one another,
but that Ivoirian anxiety about the authenticity of brands was connected
to anxieties over the authentic modernity of Ivoirian citizens. This modernity was demonstrated and embodied (and therefore proven) in the dance

of the *logobi* (the dance of brands), through which actors displayed their knowledge of U.S. clothing, taste, and lifestyle. In this sense, the ability to detect the difference between the genuine article and the imitation was considered to be a particular purview of Ivoirian nationality, something of which the immigrant population was believed incapable. In this context of counterfeit goods and illicit immigrants all loudly proclaiming their legitimacy, the bluff was as much a verification of national identity as it was a performance of the authenticity of one's brand name goods.

In both cases, it was a masked performance in which the visible signs concealed invisible identities that might or might not be authentic, but whose power stemmed from their ability to make one believe that they were. In a world of counterfeits, in which one's modern status and national identity could only be verified through the capacity to distinguish the real from the fake, the logic of the masquerade coalesces with the bluff: the categories of real and fake are subsumed within the power of the discursive language of images to produce social reality. Thus, only those with the capability to convincingly perform the authenticity of their brand name objects could anchor their national identity in the shifting phantasmagoria of Abidjan. The visual semiotics of masking, in which the public secret protects the unstable connection between the signifying image and its signified potency, allows the performer to overcome the gap between illusion and reality. The *yere* was someone capable of seeing behind the mask, and grappling with the invisible forces that lay therein, and for that reason, no one could doubt the authenticity of their bluff.

Throughout this book I have been exploring two parallel processes of authentication, both of which were meant to produce Ivoirian nationality. In the one case, urban youth constructed themselves as modern Ivoirian citizens in opposition to foreigners through their ability to consume authentic (as opposed to fake) brands. At the same time, the politics of the Ivoirian nation shifted to exclude those within its boundaries who did not conform to this new idea of "Ivoirianess." I believe that the coordination of these two efforts took place as part of one and the same cultural process, built out of the production of pan-ethnic urban culture based upon the mastery of signs of modernity. How are we to understand these processes in terms of the semiotics of value and the literature relating originals to their copies?

Following Robert Moore's insightful commentary on the unstable semiotic combination underlying the brand, I want to think of brands as composites of "tangible, material things (products, commodities) with 'immaterial' forms of value (brand names, logos, images)" (2003:4). A branded product, he suggests, is partly a thing and partly language, and the connections between them are under constant negotiation. Indeed, following the work of Strasser (1989) and Klein (2002), we should consider the development of the brand a response to the mass-produced object, a commodity inherently duplicated an unthinkable numbers of times, its production and distribution rendered invisible. It is not simply a guarantee of origins, but also the fabrication of a kind of artificial Maussian *hau* to replace the personhood in the alienated object (Mazzarella 2003:192–95). Personhood is enregistered at various levels—in the fictional characters (Aunt Jemima, Tony the Tiger) or celebrities (Michael Jordan) attached to brands (McCracken 2005), in corporations, which are represented as embodying personal qualities, and in their consumers, who adopt the brands as part of their identities. Brands function as Peircian qualisigns, becoming "lovemarks" rather than mere trademarks (Callon, Méadel, and Rabeharisoa 2002; Foster 2007; Manning 2010). Abstract, largely immaterial images of "people" thus replace the social relations once held between producer and consumer, as well as the local shopkeepers who once stood as a personal guarantor of quality (Klein 2002:8). As the materiality of the object is reduced to a copy in mass production, its qualitative uniqueness must be reasserted at the level of the brand. In a similar way, localized communities of personal relations have been increasingly mediated by the concept of a larger impersonal community governed by the state, where due to scale community must be both imagined and continuously represented.

Indeed, as corporations increasingly produce their goods in distant parts of the globe in order to profit from cheap labor, the brand of the product is increasingly distanced from the site of production. In Yanagisako (2008) and Reinach's (2009) research on Italian brands that manufacture their goods in China, Italian representatives of an undisclosed fashion label are sent to train Chinese workers how to make—that is, to fake—Italian goods, providing authenticity by virtue of their *Italianata* (their Italian national identity). They ship the finished products back to Italy in order to add the label "Made in Italy," and then ship them back to China to be sold in one of their fastest growing consumer markets. Thus, we find a fundamental instability in the link between the materiality of the object (including its authentic indexical connections to the place of production) and its iconic symbolic content (the meaning or "spirit" of the brand, and its ability to transfer such associations to the consumer). The performance of value and identity through the display of material objects derives much of its power from the ambiguous relationship between iconicity and indexicality in the branded good. The "image-object" (Mazzarella 2003) consists of an unstable slippage between the constructed surface image of the thing, labeled and discursively produced, and the inescapable but invisible realness of the object—its tactile presence and the historical chain of contiguities that establishes its "authenticity." As Mazzarella indicates, these two aspects can either complement or contradict one another—this is the gap in the commodity form. As Gupta and Ferguson reveal (1997), the relationship between culture and locality is equally slippery; there is a gap between the idea of the nation (typically understood to be monolithic and sharing language, values, and history) and the experienced reality of constantly shifting populations of differing background, divergent understandings of community, and transforming values. As with commodities, this is a slippage that must be governed, and the link between idea and locality must be continuously restated. Anderson's final chapter, "Census, Map, Museum" (1991), describes the ways in which the state performs nationhood, or, more appropriately, we could speak of how it *brands* nationhood. Such nation branding is an effort to iterate what the nation is, and through such illocution to make it true.

It only takes the briefest of glances behind the curtain of production to realize that the brand does not really guarantee, or even say, anything about the product, even when we consider "the real thing" (as Coca-Cola likes to refer to itself). Manning (2010) argues that brands have increasingly lost their intended role as rigid and unmanipulable indicators of the origin of their products. As they have morphed into transferrable forms of property, it has become increasingly debatable whether they can still indicate source or even act as guarantees of quality at all. Manning cites Beebe: "The modern trademark does not function to identify the true origin of goods. It functions to obscure that origin, to cover it with a *myth* of origin" (Manning 2010:37). The need to police this authenticity by eliminating counterfeits and insuring "authentic" production overseas through the brand management of production also corresponds to the problems nations are experiencing in their attempts to insure the authentic citizenship of their members. Here again, "nationality" is an abstract, symbolic label referring to diffuse cultural characteristics, linked in an unstable manner to the materiality of place. Just as brands do not necessarily originate from the location they signify, people within the physical borders of a country do not necessarily share the cultural or legal components of nationality. And it is increasingly difficult to trademark that authenticity in a world of false paperwork and mimesis, where self-proclaimed experts at forging visas, the *camoraciens*, are loafing about on every corner.

In turn, from the perspective of consumers, mastery of the signs index-

ing the difference between "reals" and "fakes" becomes the key to legitimizing claims of identity—as with the connoisseur who displays the "naturalized" ability to distinguish quality (Keane 2003). In the urban Ivoirian
context, the performance of this naturalized ability is a key claim to the
authentic citizenship of *Ivoirité*. Thus, the relationship between nationality
and comsumption cuts both ways, each guaranteeing the authenticity of
the other in different contexts, each masking the underlying duplicity of
mimicry underlying that authenticity. The bluff of modernity motivating
Ivoirité, then, is one in which the performance of cultural mastery gives potentially counterfeit goods the legitimacy of expert approval, while everyone acts as though the transformative authentic origins of the brand name
product carried the qualitative nationality of the goods to the consumer.

Modernity as Bluff

The wonder of mimesis lies in the copy drawing on the character and power of the original, to the point whereby the representation may even assume that character and that power. (Taussig 1993:xii)

The truths of metaphysics are the truths of masks. (Wilde 1969:432)

The central question raised by the bluff is the role of the fake in social life, especially as a part of the postcolonial dynamics of the mimesis of modernity. It has been my aim throughout this work to use the Ivoirian concept of the bluff to think through the ways in which masking activities are not mere deceptions but rather performances that produce meaningful fictions, and since our very social reality is a fabric of such everyday fictions, our truths are masks. In these concluding pages I would like to consider the role of the fake in modernity and the hidden world of performative magic continually denied in the daily quest for authentic self-production.

Oscar Wilde's willful contrariness aside, the Oxford English Dictionary makes quite clear that masking in the English language is almost always about covering up some underlying truth: "To go about in disguise, to hide one's true form or character behind an outward show, to conceal the real nature or meaning of, to obscure the true character of, to hide from view, etc." But if we look at the origins of the word, masking only takes on this sense of disguise in the 1500s, the earliest use of the term in writing cited as 1533, and the bulk of the uses coming toward the very end of the century. Indeed, three of the first uses of the word "mask" derive from Shakespeare, the very same master of disguise to whom Oscar Wilde refers in his argument about costume containing truth. Earlier uses of the term came from the mesh of nets (circa 1329) and as an alternative word for the "mascles," or heraldic symbols (circa 1460).[1] In this sense, the concept of the mask would appear to be a transformation of the word for the symbols of aristocracy (brands, if you will), thereby hinting at the very forms of mimesis that drove the fear of artificial imitation at the heart of modern subjectivity. Delving further back, we find that "mask" is probably connected to the latin *masca*, meaning "evil spirit" or "specter," which points to the authenticity of representation in earlier uses of the word. Although these historical connnections are far from definitive, I describe them in order to suggest that the anxiety surrounding the image in our society is a historical cultural product, closely linked to the rise of capitalism and the fluidity of social hierarchy it created. Before considering the relationship between mimesis and postcoloniality, therefore, we must delve further into the relationships among value, image, and copies in modern subjectivity.

On the Nature of "Western" Imitation

Gabriel de Tarde argued that imitation was a fundamental principle of social life, paired with innovation as twin motors of social change. Tarde envisioned society as a water tower: "Invention can start from the lower ranks of the people, but its extension depends upon the existence of some lofty social elevation, a kind of social water tower, whence a continuous waterfall of imitation may descend" (1903:221). In other words, innovation happens everywhere, but only with the help of hierarchy is it accompanied by replication. From Tarde's perspective, imitation is always directed upward. Simmel's (1957) model of fashion is typically accused of the same "trickle-down" structure, but a careful reading reveals a much more subtle and flexible interplay of imitation and differentiation, in which those copying others drive the copied to seek new symbols of identity in order to maintain social boundaries or individual status. While his primary model of fashion is one in which the upper elite are continually producing new fashions that are imitated in turn through the ranks, it is important to recognize that they are driven to do so by the continual social pressures for membership on all sides. They are not in control but rather in perpetual flight from those that seek their identity. Once these forces are in play, each drives the other onward: "Just as soon as the lower classes begin to copy their style, thereby crossing the line of demarcation the upper classes have drawn and destroying the uniformity of their coherence, the upper classes turn away from this style and adopt a new one, which in its turn differentiates them from the masses; and thus the game goes merrily on" (Simmel 1957:545). This creates a "fashion system," a dynamic in which the symbols of social representation are constantly and systematically shifted in a perpetual struggle between the maintenance and penetration of cultural boundaries.

But the fashion system is not some eternal universal; it is a historical fact connected to specific social dynamics. Lipovetsky (1994) connects the emergence of fashion as a system of collective change with the rise of individualism and democracy. But it is Agnew's (1986) surprising history of the relationship between the rise of the market and the theater in seventeenth century England that allows us to understand the emergence of the European fear of masking as deception. As the feudal system organized around nobility (ascribed status: hierarchy as sacred, unchallengeable, order) was replaced by emerging hierarchies based on money and industry (achieved status: hierarchy as a ladder with those at the top kicking the climbers), personhood itself was transformed into something more malleable and suspicious. This was a movement away from "ritual, kin, and prescriptive bonds toward contractual, commutable, and convertible forms" (Agnew 1986:8). The qualities of liminality and liquidity inherent in the "free" market were extremely destructive in a society based on prescribed rather than achieved status, for social relations themselves became commodifiable. Personhood could be manipulated, bought, and performed, and "since these confusions included serious questions about the character and authority of the 'self' on whose behalf these anxieties were expressed . . . these sentiments [were] structured around problems of *representation*" (1986:10).

The difficulty of this period arose from the fact that people could no longer interpret social identity through appearance: the semiotic communication of objects (such as heraldic imagery) was no longer reliable. The market spread from a bounded ritual space on the outskirts of communities to the established center of town, its influence flowing unheeded outward into society. Radiating from the architectural center, market values became insinuated in the most intimate, sacred, and powerful relationships. Thus, Agnew argues that it is no coincidence that it was during the Elizabethan period that the *theatrum mundi* metaphor became so powerful. Although the metaphor has ancient Greek origins, where it referred to the concept of people as actors of divine will, its meaning transformed into the fear that people are all actors hiding an inner identity beneath a social mask. There seems to be an emergent divide between apparent surface and truth, as if one can only discover reality by stripping away the outer layers. The theater was looked upon with extreme suspicion as the symbol of the problems with contemporary society, for it embodied the principle of imitation and simulation through which surface illusion could disrupt "proper" patterns of social relations. Therefore, Agnew's transition became a search for "emblematic forms" (1986:10), or paradigmatic metaphors, to define the positions of social actors. Agnew stops there, but one can immediately see how this would lead to what Simmel describes as a "fashion system," as each category strives for self-determination even as its signs are being appropriated by others seeking to draw on the value of their association.

The development of the capitalist system in Europe led to a destabilization of the symbolic articulation of social stratification, producing a new system of flux and, more importantly for the present purposes, performance. This new "fashion system" led to a strange paradox whereby all were forced to take part, and yet none could admit the parts they played. Identity and consumption were closely tied, as people tried to demarcate boundaries of taste and symbolic mastery with which to shut out impostors to their class brackets. The concept of performance was something to be despised, for it implied imitation, falseness, and the attempt to enter social circles to which one did not rightly belong. Such a conception of authentic (but invisible) selfhood corresponds to an ideology of true, individual self-expression, of communication as an outpouring of the hidden insides, as opposed to the interpersonal reciprocal dependency of "dividuals" described by Strathern (1988). The Protestant stripping of ritual forms in the search for true unmediated inner spiritual connections with the divine goes along with this hypertrophy of the image as deceiver.

Dangerous fakery shows up again in the mid-nineteenth-century American obsessions with confidence men, as documented by Melville's novel *The Confidence-Man*, in which no character's appearance can be taken for granted. Much like the *nouchi*, the confidence men were thought to prey particularly on young men arriving in the city fresh from the country (Halttunen 1986). It is precisely the innocent's trust in the correspondence between surface appearances and underlying truth from which the con artist draws his sustenance. Imitation and performance, therefore, in North Atlantic societies, became closely aligned with the fake, with inauthenticity, and with the danger of social instability. In this sense, Homi Bhabha's (1994) formulation that colonizers were trying to keep the colonized down by disparaging Europeanization as mimicry is only part of the narrative. It is not only colonial mimesis that produces such ambivalence, but imitation in general.

How fascinating, then, that so many critiques of modernity have been caught up with society's mimetic facilities! It is Horkheimer and Adorno who argue that proper mimesis has been replaced under Western civilization by the "organized control of mimesis" (1987:180), and Benjamin (1976), of course, who laments the diminishment of the aura in the age of reproduction. As the aura withers, so too the role of the image as a magical or ritual technique. It would seem that magical production has been replaced by industrial reproduction. But Williams puts the magic back into industry in nefarious form, arguing that the mere consumption of objects is not in itself enough to keep the industrial system going, so that advertising fills the gap through fantasy, validating the act of consumption through association with other values like "social respect, discrimination, health, beauty, success, power to control your environment" (1980:189). In essence industry itself takes on the deceitful charm of the confidence man in the guise of a shaman: a modern Quesalid (Lévi-Strauss 1963). Williams writes: "The short description of the pattern we have is magic: a highly organized and professional system of magical inducements and satisfactions, functionally very similar to magical systems in simpler societies, but rather strangely coexistent with a highly developed scientific technology" (1980:185). Thus, the "organized control of mimesis" is a new form of industrial magic. Disneyland, for example, is a temple and destination for pilgrimage to such organized mimesis. As Baudrillard says, "The Disneyland imaginary is neither true nor false: it is a deterrence machine set up in order to rejuvenate in reverse the fiction of the real" (1998:175). In other words, Disneyland, "the magic kingdom" and "happiest place on earth" is a space of mechanical liminality meant to promise the real beyond its gates through symbolic opposition, denying the omnipresence of the fake in everyday life. The fake is the pariah of Western culture, even as (or because) it pervades every realm of society.

Orson Welles's brilliant documentary *F for Fake* (1973) disrupts our sense of reality by undermining its own authority at every turn, but at the same time it highlights the layers upon layers of uncertainty running through social narratives of value. The film portrays De Hory, the painter of counterfeits who did not make copies of stolen art but rather created originals in the style of Picasso, Modigliani, and Matisse, claiming they were genuine works from his personal collection. Even art dealers who began to suspect his seemingly endless supply of never-before-seen paintings were profiting so much from them that the fakery continued unabated, until his forgeries hung in museums throughout the world. As we watch footage of De Hory forging plausible Matisse after Matisse and burning them in the fire, the question of the value of art, its Benjaminian aura, rises inevitably to the surface.

Bluffing does not merely inflate the art market, but has also come to structure capitalism itself within the epicenter of modernity, as high-paced abstracted trading—much of it run virtually through computers whose processers move more quickly than human reactions—inflates the value of the economy far beyond any sense of on-the-ground production. As doubt pierced the bubble of confidence—a self-assurance preyed upon by genuine confidence men like Bernie Madoff—the collapsing of Wall Street under the weight of the real echoed throughout the world, shaking faith in the neoliberal vision that had torn away the restraints upon the economic fictions at the heart of social value. This deceptive mask of success through which huge corporations maintain their place in the economy is the performative magic at the foundation of late capitalist production.

On the Character of (Alternative?) Modernity

It is one thing to think of Simmel's fashion system in terms of the interplay of imitation and differentiation up and down the class structure, but it is another altogether to apply it to the dynamics going on when actors imitate across cultural boundaries, and still another when they are imitating their former colonizers (the latter being breachers of boundaries par excellence). If one of the characteristics of so-called modernity is the reorganization of mimesis, then what does it mean when modernity itself is imitated? Is there really a way to tell the difference between counterfeit and original, when the original consists of the production of counterfeits?

The recent anthropological gaze on postcolonial modernity gets bogged down in questions of the authenticity of such newly produced modernities. Anthropology is obligated to combat pervasive developmental models that place cultures on scales of relative modernity, a teleological perspective of "convergence" (Taylor 2001). In order to do so, however, many have stressed the continued authenticity of local culture, which is merely employing symbols of modernity for its own semiotic purposes. As Ferguson warned us vis-à-vis Friedman in the introduction, this is at the peril of reifying "traditional" cultures in some kind of static isolation. The opposite approach, of granting the status of "alternative" modernities, claiming that we must leave room for other cultural versions of modernity (Gaonkar 2001), obfuscates our ability to analyze the power relations between so-called modern countries and "the rest" in exchange for the weak symbolic equality of anthropological representation. The concept of modernity is an exclusive force, one that uses its mythmaking power of representation both to convert and to keep others at bay (Ferguson 1999). Indeed, following Pratt (2002), we can best understand modernity as a flexible ideology of dichotomy, where "we" (whoever that may be) are always modern and "the others" are by definition not. To cite a Comaroffian classic, "Such binary contrasts, we would argue, are a widespread trope of ideology-in-the-making; they reduce complex continuities and contradictions to the aesthetics of nice oppositions" (Comaroff and Comaroff 1993:xii). While a very real set of historical transformations has taken place, it is the way Europe represented these transformations to itself that places it at the center and the rest of world around it, and the details of such a representation are always changing in order to keep that structure in place. Thus, alternative modernities do little to help us out of the bind of global inequality—simply by being alternative, they continue to be, as Bhabha puts it "almost, but not quite" (1994:86)—which is to say, counterfeit.

Postcolonial Mimesis and the Crisis of Signification

In turning to postcolonial modernities and Comaroff and Comaroff's challenge to think through the relationship to the counterfeit, we must keep this practice of exclusion in the forefront, for the relationship between modernity itself and its obsessions with authenticity has always been organized around the exclusion of those who aspired to claim membership. To be fake is to not belong—an idea that might clarify the abundance of fakery within the postcolony.

Apter (2005) provides us with a wonderful picture of the "419" economy of Nigeria, where value forms become empty forms of value. He traces the origins of this culture of counterfeit to the oil boom era, in which money was produced as if by magic from hidden sources under the ground. Tracing the rise and fall of the petro-nation, Apter argues that Nigerian culture was vastly affected by the emergence of money and wealth so suddenly and with no productive labor, ushering forth a worldview in which it seemed possible to make money from nothing, magically. It is no wonder, Apter suggests, that when the economy faltered it became dominated by get-rich-quick schemes, forged documents, and counterfeit money:

> The value forms that emerged during the boom years detached from the value of oil itself to become forms of value and sources of illicit profit unto themselves. The letters of credit, bank drafts, official signatures, and corporate logos that previously legitimated and authorized the international instruments of purchase and sale began to circulate like "floating signifiers," devoid of any real monetary or institutional referent—until, quite literally, they hit their mark, a credulous dupe who went for the bait, losing his or her shirt by giving something for nothing. (Apter 2005:254)

For Apter, employing the metaphor of the *mis-en-abîme* (two mirrors reflecting one another on and on), this is not merely an economic shift, but one that has destabilized social and political credibility in all realms, such that both the state and civil society have collapsed into dissimulations of themselves. It makes for an interesting comparison with Côte d'Ivoire, whose economy went through a similar if less dramatic boom and bust, and whose government became so entangled in the second economy that the head of state was said to have paid gang leaders a regular salary to keep them under his control. As in the Nigerian concept of money magic portrayed by Apter, Ivoirians have many stories about the occult production of money, most notably through the technique of burying an earthen pot filled with blood or human body parts and money and digging it up later to find that the money inside has vastly multiplied (Newell 2007).

This overlap between magic, the second economy, and the collapse of signification can also be found in De Boeck's groundbreaking *Kinshasa* (De Boeck and Plissart 2006), where he argues that the second world of the occult has overshadowed the real just as the second economy has overtaken the more visible second world. When the world of the dead merges with the living,

> symbolization, in other words, no longer takes place, or more precisely, the qualities of the structuring of symbolization have changed. Thus, the linkages among the orders of imaginary, symbolic and real, have lost their simultaneity, they have disappeared or weakened, and can no longer be trusted or taken for granted. Today, the two sides of the mirror have not only become entangled, but they have radically collapsed into each other. It is at this very point that the mirror has lost its power of reflection. (De Boeck and Plissart 2006:207)

I have been arguing throughout this book that the bluff is precisely this, at once real and imaginary, counterfeit and effective. For De Boeck, it is precisely this failure of reality to hold its own that causes the hypertrophy of the surface that allows phenomenon such as La Sape to thrive. But must this mean that symbolization itself is failing, that the relationship between the lived world and the imagined has collapsed into a sea of floating signifiers? Is this the postcolonial condition—meaninglessness?

The answer to this question might be found in critical theories of modernity itself, for they make the same claim about the collapse of meaning into itself as the corrosion of imitations undermines true meaning. Debord ([1967] 1994) and later Baudrillard (1998) have argued that the spectacle subsumes the real within its phantasmagoric play of images, leaving nothing but empty signs in its wake. Debord's scathing remarks remind me of the way in which many people react to the concept of the bluff:

> The individual, though condemned to a passive existence of an alien everyday reality, is thus driven into a form of madness in which, by resorting to magical devices, he entertains the illusion that he is reacting to this fate. The recognition and consumption of commodities are at the core of this pseudo-response to a communication to which no response is possible. The need to imitate that the consumer experiences is indeed a truly infantile need. (Debord [1967] 1994:153)

Once again we are faced—this time in the form of high-theory self-flagellation over the modern condition—with the scorn for the artificial. In Baudrillard (1998) too we find a collapse of signification and reality, such that representation (in which the sign corresponds in some imperfect way to the real) is overcome by simulation (in which the sign presumes an equivalence between itself and reality, erasing the distinction). His example of simulated illness, in which a patient takes on real symptoms of the illness he or she is faking, thereby actually becoming sick, perfectly illustrates the impossibility of distinguishing the performance from the effect. Such is magic, the performative production of reality, in which signs bring about their referent—the simulation of sickness is a self-imposed "voodoo death" (Siegel 2006). It would seem then, that the postcolonial mimesis of modernity *is in fact modernity*: the copy is indistinguishable from the original, because the underlying reality is one already based upon the production of copies, counterfeits of itself.

I hope to show that imitative performance does not need to initiate the collapse of signification. If so-called moderns and their postcolonial "mimics" are united in conjuring an illusion of modern authenticity, this need not mean that there is no sense to culture. Rather, it is in the successful con, when the floating signifier meets its mark, that meaning is sparked. Indeed, this is how meaning has always been produced: in those moments when more than one person forges consensus in the exchange of incommensurable values, each thinking the other was duped into receiving less than he or she gave. The concept of culture as harmonious shared meaning is an idealization long vilified in critical anthropology, one we should not allow our faith in words to maintain. By thinking of culture and communication as acts of bluffing, in which we con(vince) others into accepting our interpretation, our discursively produced reality, we are closer to an actor-centered model through which collective representations are built as well as destroyed.

Signifiers are notoriously unstable creatures, and it would take more hegemony than any regime has ever managed to muster to actually manage to pin them down. The death of signification, I would argue, is found in the unrealized extreme of perfect totalitarianism rather than the "hyperreal" of unmoored signifiers. These flirtations with semiotic apocalypse stem from an exaggeration of the importance of the metaphoric realm of images in social theory, a tendency to neglect the other axis of meaning. Signs do not exist unmoored, but rather in context, which is to say, in *contact* with other signs. And it is here, in the realm of contiguity and contagion, that other branch of magic, that we must turn if we are to come to terms with the role of mimesis in postcolonial Côte d'Ivoire.

Incommensurability: Fetishes, Doubles, and the Fake

The European reinvention of itself did not take place in isolation (Wallerstein 1975; Mintz 1986); its performance had a target audience from the beginning, for capitalism had to convince its periphery of its superiority as well as the superiority of its valuables in order to harness the flow of resources that allowed for the consolidation of wealth. The so-called periphery—for it is only a periphery from within the perspective produced by the bluff of modernity—has always been a zone of performativity, in which value is produced on the fly in a situation in which no actor has firm control of the conversation (Sahlins 1994). In other words Western identity is itself a magic sign that produces its own superiority—this is, after all, the message of Orientalism, in which knowledge of the difference of otherness produces otherness. My claim here is simply that such oppositions between societies have always been a form of bluffing, one that mimics the very means by which upper echelons of society within North Atlantic cultures keep others out—by accusing them of not understanding proper taste and value (Bourdieu 1984). The legendary "purchase" of Manhattan for a string of beads is a classic tale of the con, but the tale also excludes the *gaou* who didn't know any better from membership in modernity. Bluffing thus establishes real hierarchy through the masking of value, hiding the underlying incommensurability of otherness behind the performative declaration of superior, encompassing identity.

As Jane Guyer (2004) describes it, incommensurable systems of exchange are brought together at particular, conventionalized thresholds of connection, a problem particularly relevant to the history of West Africa, in which slavery, fetishism, and commodity fetishism intersected in nefarious and unpredictable ways. People and inalienable (personified) things were transformed into European commodities whose value was determined by liquid transactions of currency, but currency whose own value was always in flux. One of my favorite examples of such competing scales of value is Apter's description of a nineteenth-century antislavery treaty signed between the representatives of the British queen and the Nigerian king Obi as his war canoes outfitted with British flags looked on. When the British emissaries insisted on a ceremony asking blessing from the Almighty for the signed treaty, the king trembled and quickly had his own "fetish" brought in order to counteract their magic and protect his end of the deal with his own spiritual forces (Apter 2005:144–47). Each side insisted on controlling and sealing the contract with supernatural force—the confrontation between European and African models of exchange took place through the "hybrid idiom of the fetish" (2005:147). Such exchanges were not egalitarian, as neoliberal models would predict, but explicitly asymmetrical and sensitive to regional geographies, hierarchies, and established authority. Pietz's (1987, 1988) intellectual history of the fetish revolves around European misunderstandings of local value systems; the word "fetish" itself is a pidgin Portuguese word used by European explorers to describe the puzzling behavior of many West Africans in relation to material things. It is fascinating that the word "Guinea" was originally used for both Africa itself and for the first manufactured gold coins, bringing together a European connection between exotic otherness and value. The word has gone on to be applied to exotic otherness worldwide, including guinea pigs and Papua New Guinea (Pietz 1988:105). But while Pietz's account is wonderful in its point that the fetish is the product of intercultural space where incommensurable systems converge, he does not ever provide a clear perspective of how local ideas of fetishism were constructed and what this meant for cross-cultural transactions.

Wyatt MacGaffey's (1977, 1994) exploration of Kongo fetishes remains one of the most useful ways of thinking through relations of personhood and value, and it is applicable far beyond the Kongolese cosmology he describes. Citing De Heusch, MacGaffey writes:

> They always include two series of objects, metaphoric and metonymic. The metaphoric group, including in this instance the shell, the ginger, the squash seeds and the cricket, give concrete expression to the end in view. The met-

onymic elements, in this instance the white and red earths, unlike the others do not evoke a desired state of affairs; they establish a link between the powerful dead, the charm itself, and the client, giving him the illusion that he controls an effective force: "spirits of the dead metonymically caught in a metaphorical trap." (MacGaffey 1977:174)

Metaphoric signs are used to represent the spirit supplicated and/or the intended beneficiary or victim of the act, but also the hoped-for effect of the ritual actions. At the same time, each object has a receptacle into which the sorcerer places ingredients. Usually the hair or fingernails of the victim or recipient are included along with the *mpemba* clay, thus metonymically establishing a link between the world of the dead, the *nkisi*, and the recipient. Thus, the fetish combines principles of metaphor and metonymy, drawing upon relationships of genuine contiguity with the power of the dead for magical efficacy while using metaphoric appearance to direct the effects.

MacGaffey argues that these *nkisi* objects are not fundamentally different from other means of connecting to the world of the spirits, such as chiefs, magicians, witches, or graves: "The fundamental concepts are the immortality of the personality and the relationship of that personality, or soul, and its visible container, by means of which it enters into social relationships" (1977:181). All human bodies contain spirit doubles, which continue their existence in the second world but can be brought back into relation with the living through the mediation of chiefs, priests (witches), and *nkisi* objects. The crucial point for us here is that Bakongo do not make any radical distinction between these different kinds of "containers." Thus, "All powers are exerted by enduring personalities, or souls, varying in their age (the length of their existence in the universe) and in the circumstances of their incorporation in various kinds of body, or container. *Among containers BaKongo do not distinguish as clearly as might be expected between human bodies, fabricated objects.*" (1977:182; emphasis added). MacGaffey provides us with a radical critique of the North Atlantic conception of the relationship between people and objects, the material and immaterial worlds. According to this conceptualization of the fetish, there is not a significant distinction between people and objects; both are merely containers for the spirit world to occupy; both are animated by the spirit within them. In this sense, the body is a container which absorbs power metonymically from other things and people—it is at once a cosmology of personhood and material value understood as recipients for spirit value (Maussian *mana*).

MacGaffey's treatment (like that of the relevance of *derrière l'eau*) is remarkably applicable to cosmologies at play in Côte d'Ivoire, where the concept of the double was widely held, and as in the Kongo, it was believed to apply to both people and things. The Ivoirian historian d'Aby writes of the Agni ethnic group:

> One could say that in a general sense for the Agni all bodies, be they animate or not, that surround us are provided with doubles or *woa-woè*. This interpretation stems from the fact that offerings made to the spirits, accepted and consumed by them, remain materially intact, and that all bodies, no matter what they are, can incarnate a spirit. In these examples, the *woa-woè* is at once nourishment for the spirits and a catalyst in the soul-body complex. (d'Aby 1960:20)

Thus, when spirits consume their sacrificial offerings, they only consume the double of those offerings. All material things are vessels for the spirits, and all have a double in the spirit world that nourishes those spirits. This idea of consuming doubles appears again in Ivoirian understandings of witchcraft, where death is typically caused by witches feasting upon one's double in nefarious nocturnal gatherings.

The double in Akan thought originates in the semen of the father: "The father's semen is held to give rise to something in a person that accounts for the degree of impact which that individual makes upon others by his sheer presence. Both the inner cause and outer effect are called *sunsum* [*wao-woè* in Baoulé] in Akan" (Wiredu 1996:108). As in so many matrilineal systems, the kinship role of the person is provided by the mother along with the physical substance of the body, while the father establishes the adornment, the social presence, the persona (Weiner 1976:121–30). But in this concept of the double we find the outer appearance of the person conceptually connected to a spiritual being who is "other" than the person himself or herself. "Both the inner cause and outer effect" are combined in the double (Wiredu 1996:128). And yet the double cannot be reconciled to a mere reflection of the self. It is the double who leaves in dreams and roams about unfettered by the self, sometimes engaging in malicious acts of witchcraft which the self has little or no control over in its waking life. In this sense the double is at once the internal other and the external self. It represents the invisible social forces that dictate from within and the mask of the outer social self, both of which invade the space of the individual self.

Furthermore, many Ivoirians believed that those who truly succeeded in life were bound to reflect their accomplishment through the physical transformation of the body. Wiredu writes that "of a person with a strong *sunsum* [double] the Akans say: *Ne sunsum ye dure*, literally, 'His *sunsum* is heavy'" (1996:109). The double is "quasimaterial," in that it is considered heavier or lighter according to its perceived strength (1996:107). Consumption was seen as a literal process of incorporation, and Ivoirians used the verb *se grossir* (to grow or fatten) to describe the process of accumulating wealth. When I asked the France-Amérique group whether people gained weight because they were wealthy, they laughed in affirmation: "It is true. Ivoirians always gain weight when they have money, and you really can tell if someone is gaining money by how heavy they are." The relationship between persons and objects (the relationship of consumption) is in this perspective one of "eating" and absorbing the value of those things one brings into semiotic or physical contact with the person or body. The mask is thus more comprehensible as an image that metaphorically describes the invisible spirit contained and performed by the dancer.

Bluffing and masking are similar kinds of semiotic acts in which deceit is a true mediation of power—a performance that produces the effect of its representation—because both interconnect metaphoric mimesis with metonymic connections to otherworld sources of power. From such a perspective the bluff of modernity has an authentic indexical connection with the causal force of the modern. It is an illusive deceit combined with real presence, just as the mask was a performance of spiritual presence in which the performer was no longer himself—an ambiguous imbrication of "faith and deceit" (Picton 1990).

What I am suggesting here is that "faking it" is a culturally specific process that should not be subsumed within the capitalist trauma over authenticity even if it is inevitably in dialogue with it. Vann's (2006) explorations of Vietnamese understandings of counterfeit products reveals that while real and fake products are differentiated, their evaluation does not correspond to the logic of authenticity that social theory often assumes to be universal. Authorship is not the issue at all, but rather the quality of the product. Thus, many of the counterfeit products available on the market are understood to to have mimicked not only the appearance of the brand but the quality as well, producing a market of differing levels of fakeness. Vietnamese thus differentiates among model goods (the original), mimic goods (high quality but illegitimate duplications), and fake goods (copies that deceive the customer into purchase but have little value). The distinction between real and fake is thus culturally constructed—the difference between the counterfeit and the original is not objectively transparent but requires ethnographic investigation.

Siegel (1998) likewise found that Indonesian society was overrun with things *palsu* (from "false" in English), but that falsity had an entirely different ring to it. Things *palsu* were as much "almost valid" as they were counterfeit: "In the Indonesian press, what works is valid. It is why the rector of Unidu [who sells false diplomas] thinks he has done nothing wrong, rather the contrary. People want university degrees and it is acceptability that matters. The swirl of false documents, false shoes, counterfeit monies, is not necessarily outrageous; it rather testifies to the creative abilities of the counterfeiters" (1998:57). Siegel goes on to demonstrate that the same principle is at work among the magic men who cure or produce money, as well as the state, which seeks to control and magnify rather than abolish the power of *palsu*. While the press is full of accounts exposing such fakery, Siegel tells us that the narratives resemble ghost stories more than exposés: narratives in which one thought they were interacting with the real, only to discover at a later point that it was spectral. It is with a sense of wonder rather than indignation that readers learn of others' ability to produce value from nothing. If it works, it is valid; only upon discovery does it become fake.

In this sense, a semiotics of masking in which authentic presence is invoked through the deceit of adornment allows us to see beyond the North Atlantic bluff of modernity that always relegates the postcolony to its not-quite-modern status. For Ivoirians, the bluff is an art, an achievement that at once publicly authenticates their ability to make a living by duping their peers with imagery and establishes their reputation as legitimately modern urban citizens. The modernity bluff therefore is neither fake nor real, but rather the ability to produce the real through manipulation of the imaginary. The imaginary, or second world, is produced through masking, an act that displays the presence of power without while concealing the power itself. It presents a face which everyone knows is not real, suggesting the presence of a subsurface authenticity, even if that authenticity cannot be verified. Ultimately, our unmasking of the bluff exposes not the mimicry of the postcolonial subject, but rather the fantastic performance through which the North Atlantic continues to manufacture the illusion that modernity exists, thereby ideologically supporting the global system of exclusion through which wealth is concentrated in the so-called center. For the very brands upon which contemporary value is built—increasingly our own only source of legal authenticity—are counterfeit copies of themselves, performative labels declaring an underlying value that is ultimately indistinguishable from its counterfeit. Such is the modern condition.

NOTES

INTRODUCTION

1. All names in this text have been changed to protect the identity of the real persons this book describes, even though many of them gave me permission to use their real names.

2. I have chosen to use the abbreviation U.S. to replace the term America or American in this book, following the style guidelines of the American Anthropological Association, since the latter terms also apply to the much wider region of the continents. I do use "American" when citing my informants.

3. The curious can see a slice of Abidjan's nightlife at the fabulous www.abidjanshow.net.

4. To see Douk Saga in action, view some of his videos on You Tube: *Sagacité* (http://www.youtube.com/watch?v=TwBJ8_V0_TE), *Héros National* (http://www.youtube.com/watch?v=YCXciozT0Y4), and *Douk Saga en Fête* (http://www.youtube.com/watch?v=ozxOTqBNG7g).

5. There seems to be a generalized phenomenon here, certainly throughout sub-Saharan Africa, as documented extensively in works by De Boeck in Kinshasa (De Boeck and Plissart 2006), Ferguson in the Copperbelt and beyond (1999, 2006), and Apter in Nigeria (2005), studies of the *sapeurs* of Brazzaville (Gandoulou 1984, 1989; Friedman 1994; Gondola 1999; MacGaffey and Bazenguisa-Ganga 2000), and Smith's rethinking of development in Kenya (2008), but also in postcolonies more generally, as revealed in works starting with Fanon's *Black Skins, White Masks* (1967) and including the rich literature on cargo cults in Melanesia (Worsely 1957; Lawrence 1989) and Taussig's work in Colombia (1993). Could it be a product of two systems of value colliding, rendering reality less stable and more illusory as the social actor jumps back and forth between one vision of the world and the other? But what is the role of coloniality?

6. According to Rouch, in 1961, the children of immigrants who married local women were looked down upon by Ivoirian and immigrant populations alike. Technically part of their father's patrilineage as well as their mother's matrilineage, they were often rejected by both and ended up forming voluntary associations of their own called *goumbe*. This was no longer the case during my time, although the politics of *Ivoirité* were making it an issue once again (Rouch 1961: 300–304).

7. I have taken the term "externality" from Ekholm-Friedman's work on Congolese understandings of social hierarchy and cosmological power (Ekholm-Friedman 1991). Lifeforce and value itself were drawn from that which was external to the social system. The foreign and the spiritual overlap in the realm of externality.

8. I follow Van Binsbergen (2001) in using this concretely geographic designation to describe a zone typically referred to symbolically. While having the downside of stylistic awkwardness, it emphasizes a geographically demarcated social group (as complex and internally differentiated as Africa) rather than the ideologically constituted one of "the West."

9. There are multiple ironies here. The urban Ivoirians who characterize themselves as *yere* frame Dioula identity as the epitome of the *gaou*, whose eyes are closed to the forces of causality that surround them in the urban sphere. And yet Dioula identity itself emerged from the urban environment and is of relatively recent origin (Launay 1982), and it is precisely their influence that shapes the urban sphere and their lingua franca at the origin of Nouchi speech and many of its words, including *yere*.

10. Kongo with a *K* refers to the ethnic group that ranges from northern Angola to the People's Republic of the Congo to the Democratic Republic of the Congo. This group once controlled an enormous kingdom spanning this region. Congolese with a *C* refers to the nationality of the latter two countries.

11. All translations within the text, unless noted in the bibliography, are my own.

12. Congo here refers to the ex-French Congo rather than the ex-Belgian colony, both of which now go by the name of Congo, even though for many years the ex-Belgian country referred to itself as Zaire. Like Angola both countries had significant segments that were under the control of the vast Kingdom of the Kongo when Europeans arrived in 1491 (Balandier 1968; W. MacGaffey 1986; Thornton 1988). For this reason there is a great deal of shared culture between them. However, it was in Brazzaville, the capital of the ex-French country that La Sape originated. Later the pop singer Papa Wemba from Kinshasa, the capital of the ex-Belgian colony which sits directly across the river from Brazzaville, adopted the style of the Sape and spread the style throughout Francophone Africa on the wings of his widely appreciated music. However, the original Brazzavillean *sapeurs* despised this version of the Sape as pure commodity consumption, an attraction to expensive brands without the taste to properly harmonize their attire.

13. Ferguson's resistance to the use of culture is understandable given his important struggle against the culture concept as a bounded, holistic, geographically fixed, and systematic object. My defense of the role of culture in mimesis should not be taken as a defense of the culture concept per se. Rather, I think that the strength of the culture concept lies—and has always lain—in its indeterminability. Anthropology *is* the debate over what culture is.

14. This article is by Rémy Bazenguissa-Ganga, but in this early publication he employed a different spelling (Bazanquisa) and had not yet added the hyphenated name.

15. To see these objects outside the ritual context of display was potentially lethal. However, this was an example not of accessing power visually, but of mystical punishment for the breach of the moral proscription against seeing masks outside of their performed state (Vogel 1997).

CHAPTER ONE

1. I follow the French here and write Dioula, but in many Anglophone contexts it is written as Dyula, part of the Mande family of languages.

2. Nouchi is Pronounced [nuʃi]. The orthography of Nouchi is quite complex, since it is largely based on French orthography, but, as with other elements, has been purposely "deformed" to reflect its distinct identity. Thus, "qui" [ki] is often written as "ki" in Nouchi. Of course, such spelling is not standardized and quite idiosyncratic. Nevertheless, my own spelling here attempts to mimic Nouchi orthography as much as possible.

3. To differentiate between Nouchi as a kind of speech and *nouchi* as a figure in urban life (whether it be an identity or alterity), I capitalize the former and italicize the latter whenever it is found in the text.

4. The fact that Abdou associates *nouchi* as a negative identity associated with northern immigrants (of whom he is a representative) demonstrates the mirroring possibilities of such identities, since *nouchi* is more typically an urban identity that rejects northern immigrants as unfit for survival in the city.

5. In "Standard" French, these terms are used as familiar expressions between father and son, but in Côte d'Ivoire they have been adapted to refer specifically to gang relationships.

6. In fact, this trade language itself is an amalgam of Ivoirian languages forged onto a Dioula linguistic structure and is sometimes called Tabusi-kan (which can be glossed as "nonnative speech") by northerners and immigrants who speak "purer" Mandingue dialects (Tera 1986). This vehicular Dioula has even borrowed heavily from French. As Tera points out, both Ivoirian French and vehicular Dioula are urban languages associated with "modern activities." He writes, "The influence is therefore reciprocal, for of all the Ivoirian languages, the influence of Dioula on *Français Populaire d'Abidjan* is by far the most complete" (1986: 16). There would seem to be a continuum between popular French and vehicular Dioula. Lafage gives phonetically transcribed examples of four sentences meaning, as she phrased it, *il faut déplacer le véhicule* (or *n'a qu'a pousser camion*):

    na ka puse kamjō
    a ka puse mobili
    aka kā ka mobili puse
    aka kā ka mobili nyoni (1978: 63–64)

    According to Lafage's surveys, while the first two were recognized as Français Populaire Ivoirien, the second two were considered Dioula. Thus, the two languages developed in mutually constitutive competition throughout the urban centers of Côte d'Ivoire, especially Abidjan. While both languages can be understood in this way as products of colonialism and urbanization, they have received dramatically different symbolic valences, particularly as the political opposition between north and south emerged around 2000.

7. Senghor uses the word "noosphere" to refer to a kind of "sphere of mind," from the Greek *noos* or "spirit" (see C. Miller 1990: 184).

8. According to the CIA factbook, accessed in May 2011.

9. The Ebony Coast.

10. Though Lafage's early work exhibited some of these problems, her numerous analyses have become increasingly nuanced and reflect the linguistic situation more clearly. A more recent work concludes that *Français Populaire Ivoirien* may be an integrative force in Côte d'Ivoire. However, even here she maintains an objectivist stance, constantly differentiating one form of speech from another, such as the difference between "français de les rues" and Nouchi (Lafage 1998).

11. This image was reproduced in Newell 2009a.

12. See Irvine and Gal for a discussion of iconization and indexical icons (2000:27)

13. See fig. 14 in chap. 6, but also check fig. 1 in Newell 2009b.

14. Images of from these publications corresponding to this description can be found in figs. 2, 3, and 4 in Newell 2009b.

15. I did not meet many Ivoirians except university students who used computers, but computer literacy has been on the increase, given my Ivoirian friends' increasing interest in corresponding by e-mail and instant messaging.

16. Interestingly enough, this site is run by Ivoirian expats in the midwestern United States (Karen Morris, personal communication).

CHAPTER TWO

1. In reality they often stole from the immigrant community, which, as "strangers," didn't count as members of the community in the same way.

2. I have converted CFA francs approximately according to their rate in 2001, which fluctuated around 750 CFA to the dollar. Throughout the text I mimic the Ivoirian speakers who leave out the "francs" and refer to number of CFA (pronounced *sayfa*), though technically the currency is in CFA francs.

3. Actually, my own research in Paris conflicts with Henri's statement. I found that similar hierarchies exist among Africans in Paris. Thus, the Congolese often refused potential sources of income (such as streetsweeping) because they claimed that this kind of work was for the Senegalese or Beninois. They preferred black market exchange profits as a more honorable occupation. See also (Gandoulou 1984).

4. To what extent immigrants accepted the Ivoirian understanding of foreign immigrants as culturally inferior is difficult to say. There was certainly a lot of resentment about Ivoirian xenophobia, and to a more limited extent, I did hear immigrants complain that Ivoirians were "stuck up." On the other hand, I often heard immigrants praise Abidjan's modernity and degree of development.

5. For a wonderful account of the middle-class district of Yopougon in the 1970s, see the *Aya* graphic novel series, by Marguerite Abouet and Clément Oubrerie.

6. Literally translated as "death-crowd." The probably origin is screaming at the scene of a crime to bring a crowd, not infrequently resulting in mob justice killings of the accused.

7. He also used these as a means to get out of trouble with the police. Several times when I was being hassled by the police for overloading a taxi or not having my passport with me, he would flash his belt (kept under his shirt) and the policeman would salute him and let us go.

8. Networks could very literally form the basis of income. Some *loubards* could actually sustain themselves for long periods of time simply by requesting small amounts of money from everyone they knew in their network. Their sheer physical bulk and reputation for violence was influence enough for most people to dig up some money, but these were also important people to keep on your side, as they could use this same influence on someone else for your benefit.

CHAPTER THREE

1. The French word *maquis* originally meant a sort of impenetrable briar patch (or the "bush") but later was used metaphorically to refer to the hideouts of Corsican gangsters. The French also applied the term during World War II to the "secret army" resisting German occupation (Morrisson 1980:3). Ironically, still later the word was

apparently applied to Vietnamese forces resisting French occupation. So it is particularly intriguing that Ivoirians use this term—symbolizing secrecy, impenetrability, gangsters, and resistance movements—to describe these outdoor bars.

2. The *maquis* was considered to be an Ivoirian national institution not limited to any particular class. In practice, however, while all Ivoirians talked about *maquis*, different classes often meant something different when they used the word. Thus, the father of the elite family I stayed with referred to one of the most expensive restaurants in Treichville as a *maquis*, though it was a fully enclosed establishment with guards and expensive cars parked outside.

3. This is a far cry from Guy Debord's spectacle ([1967] 1994), which serves primarily to negate society (though it inverts reality in a similar way). But I will discuss this comparison further in the conclusion.

4. Men did dance in groups on other kinds of occasions, however, especially funerals, in which everyone present was invited to dance at once. There were also traditional men's dances performed by groups, but these would never take place at a *maquis* (which was seen as site of "civilization" in opposition to "village" lifestyle).

5. Although I label this a women's dance, it could technically be performed by men as well, and from time to time one did see them (particularly in formal performances). However, the idea of men doing this dance was always ridiculed. "Who wants to see that?" was a frequent comment.

6. For a video of this behavior see these You Tube clips: http://www.youtube.com/watch?v=mI_f0J2DyGg and http://www.youtube.com/watch?v=Y0SFg3Jr1uI&feature=related.

7. Only when they crossed religious boundaries did one come across obvious differences (for example, Muslims had to bury the dead before sundown, whereas the Christian groups had the liberty to follow village traditions and keep the body around for viewing for as long as they had the means to preserve it).

8. The cocoa *filière*, the state fund produced by taxing all cocoa sales, was worth the value of about 25% of the world's cocoa in any given year (McGovern 2011:136). Ostensibly it was designed to protect farmers from price fluctuation, but in actuality McGovern demonstrates its use as political instrument and source of personal wealth for a series of Ivoirian politicians.

9. The French word *claire* is often used by Ivoirians (and Francophone Africans in general) to describe lighter skin tones. This is usually seen as a positive quality, a mark of greater beauty.

CHAPTER FOUR

1. Of course, *les bosses* also had both wealth and nice clothes, and Treichville residents were well aware of this. But when they saw "one of their own" in nice clothes, they did not assume actual wealth.

2. Such a statement does require at least two rather large caveats: (1) Muslim populations have always been somewhat more resistant to assimilation to French values, probably because they are already oriented in relation to a powerful culture of externality. Nevertheless, important Muslim figures in politics or business often wear suits rather than *boubous*. (2) Of course, the majority of the Ivoirian population living in villages still have indigenous forms of prestigious dress, and "traditional" chiefs continue to legitimate their power in these forms, at least on ceremonial occasions. Nevertheless, many villagers covet items of Western dress, and these are the most sought-after gifts from urban residents returning to their natal village.

3. President Laurent Gbagbo was an exception to this rule among politicians. Although he often dressed in suits, he was equally likely to wear *pagne* shirts cut in the style of a suit jacket, a style now associated with old men, in an intentional effort to play up his Africanity. However, he was also ridiculed for this habit, both in informal conversation and in the press, and even accused of being *gaou*.

4. http://www.youtube.com/watch?v=lI10MCoZjq8.

5. The Agni, an ethnic group from southeast Côte d'Ivoire, also use the concept of *blolo*, referring to it as *ebolo*.

6. They were by no means limited to such themes, however. There were many with political themes, abstract patterns, animals, trees, and a continuing phantasmagoria of images. Sylvanus (2007: 211) demonstrates how many of the prints also contain hidden themes of Western culture within them, such as monogamous conjugal fidelity.

7. *Nouchi* were not only interested in American brands, though they spoke about the U.S. with far more enthusiasm than Europe. However, it was hard to be sure of the actual origin of their inspiration. For example, Façonnable, while originally French, exploded in the American market in the 1990s and was purchased by Nordstrom's around the time my research began. I had never seen Americans wearing the multicolored Sebago Docksides shoes the *nouchi* drooled over, but I have since seen them for sale in elite stores in Mississippi, and their Web site claims they were the rage on the 1980s college campuses.

8. J. M. Westons are French-made formal shoes that cost over $1,000 a pair. They have long been the Holy Grail of Congolese *sapeurs*, for whom no outfit has reached its apex without them. During the civil war in the late 1990s young men were said to be burying their shoes in the forest to keep them from being stolen. Danny is here referring to the late 1980s (the time when he had a reputation as a style maven), when Ivoirians were imitating the Congolese and even received Djo Ballard, the *sapeur* who best exploited media interest in the movement to project his own fame. By 2000, none of the lower-class youth I knew aspired to Westons; they were much more interested in sneakers than dress shoes. However, by 2005 Douk Saga had brought Congolese influence back to Côte d'Ivoire, and Westons and Italian brands were again the rage.

9. To see "clearly" was to see into the invisible world. Witches of course had this ability, but also *féticheurs*, marabouts, pastors, and twins, among others with occult powers.

CHAPTER FIVE

1. This is not the same FPI as the linguistic denotation for Français Populaire Ivoirien.

CHAPTER SIX

1. By this I mean that while people used ethnic categories and stereotypes to navigate urban space, they did not typically organize sociality along ethnic lines. I originally intended to choose an ethnic group to affiliate with in the city and learn the language, but this proved useless if I was to follow on-the-ground social interactions. However, people did attach particular stereotyped characteristics to each group: Dioula only care about money; Bete like to fight; Ati are intelligent. Nationality played a much bigger role in terms of social groupings and occupation.

2. This is not to say Houphouët didn't have his critics, or that he was necessarily as benign as his reputation. Stories circulate about the disappearance or arrest of various

figures that opposed him, and there is the question of his refusal to share power or how he became rich enough to build the largest church in the world with his personal funds. Nevertheless, he was most successful at maintaining control through the encompassment of his competitors within his party (in other words, buying them off) rather than through violence (Bayart 1993).

3. Indeed, while under pressure from the international community he promised to put in place a vice president in the 1985 elections, but at the last minute changed his mind, dubiously referencing Akan traditions surrounding chiefship. (Grebalé 2001; Toungara 1990:23–54)

4. The idea of a presidential candidate's authentic citizenship status being repeatedly called into question even after submitting official documents to the courts should no longer take U.S. citizens by surprise, given repeated challenges to Barack Obama's citizenship by public figures such as Donald Trump.

5. McGovern borrows the phrase from the title of an unpublished manuscript of Chauveau's from 2000.

6. Guéï was a former general who had lost his power after an embarrassing incident in which his soldiers were accused of raping and killing university students in a raid targeting militants for multipartyism. Bédié was responsible for demoting him to minister of sports, and some considered this coup revenge. Furthermore, according to *Radio Trottoir*, Guéï was only brought in after the fact to head the resistance. The initial trouble started when Bédié failed to pay the military who had worked as U.N. peacekeepers in the Central African Republic. When they protested, Bédié told them it was his Christmas vacation and he would talk to them about it later. The next thing he knew, he was fleeing the country and Guéï had taken power.

7. That year Fitini had a great *zouglou* hit entitled "Le 'Et' le 'Ou'" (The "And" the "Or"). Because of a change in the necessary qualifications for presidential candidates from "father OR mother" to "father AND mother," many Ivoirians were characterizing each other as "Ets" and "Ous," meaning children of two Ivoirian parents versus children of one Ivoirian and one foreigner. Fitini's song criticized the divisiveness of this language and warned Ivoirians to be careful of this kind of politics. Despite the popularity of his song, the warning was in vain.

8. Some masking ceremonies incorporate antiaesthetic performance in a similar way. The Gongole in the masking ritual of Sande women's society (the female corollary to the Poro) is played by a male performer as a grotesque, clownish parody of the graceful dance and beautiful adornment of the female masqueraders. His clowning highlights the girls' beauty through a kind of inverse mirroring.

9. Ironically, Ouattara, now the representative of the excluded "north," bears the responsibility of introducing the *carte de sejours*, which documents the status of all immigrants in the country.

CONCLUSION

1. The etymology splits here, with the mask as a net or heraldic symbol being traced to the Latin *mascula* (mesh) while the mask as a face covering stems from Italian *mascara* (circa 1390), which is probably linked to the Arabic root *mskr* (to make fun of). On the other hand, there would also seem to be a link to the Latin *masca* (evil spirit).

GLOSSARY

bakroman: A homeless person.

Beng: The land of the whites.

bengistes: People who have returned from the land of the whites (either Europeans, Americans, or Ivoirian migrants).

bizness: The illicit or "second" economy.

blo: Bullshit.

bluffeur: Someone who dresses well or makes a show of his or her wealth, especially in an attempt to gain prestige.

boss: A member of the elite.

boubou: A robe worn across West Africa, increasingly associated with Muslim identity in Côte d'Ivoire.

bramogo: A trusted friend, said to have originated from a Dioula word for "kin" mixed with "arm" from French.

camoracien: A forger of documents.

chantage: A scam in which one pretends to be a member of the police force in order to collect the bribe.

chercheur: A hunter, a seeker of income of all varieties.

choco: Greasy (opposed to *sec*). The word is used to describe the speaking style of native French speakers.

citadin: An urban resident.

(se) debrouiller: To manage, make do, to survive by means of informal economy. Literally, "to disentangle."

coup: A successful scam.

coupé-décalé: A new musical style that originated in the Ivoirian diaspora in Paris during the early 2000s. Literally, "scam and scram." Inspired by *zouglou* and samples of Congolese dance music with lyrics sung in Nouchi, *coupé-décalé* has become a dominant music genre in Africa.

cour commune: A lower-class architecture reproducing "village" social organization in the city: a series of tiny apartments surrounding a shared courtyard in which "facilities" for water, bathing, and cooking are located. Ivoirians often state that their *cour* is like a family.

derrière l'eau: A synonym for *Beng*. It also denotes the cosmological location of the land of the dead. Literally, "behind the water."

djossieur de nama: A car watcher: a security job within the informal economy in which one watched people's parked cars for a tip, given in advance. Should you refuse payment, your guard would become the robber, and the car would be damaged and any valuables taken.

dozo: Traditional hunters of northern ethnic origin who are infamous for powerful bulletproof magic.

drageur: A playboy.

enjaillement: Fun, a turn-on, something exciting. The word derives from English *enjoy* and French *jaillir*, to launch a jet of liquid.

évolué: The educated upper class, elite. Literally, "evolved."

faire le show: To show off, particularly through conspicuous drinking and dancing in *maquis*, wearing expensive clothes.

féticheur: Someone capable of harnessing occult forces, for good or for evil purpose.

fiston: A hierarchical inferior in the criminal network (see *vieuxpère*).

fonctionnaire: A prestigious civil servant.

Forces Nouvelles: The consolidated term for the rebel armies that attempted a coup d'état in 2002 and ran the northern half of the country until the reconciliation of 2007.

FPI: (1) Front Populaire Ivoirien, the political party started by Laurent Gbagbo and the first opposition party to the PDCI. (2) A linguistic term for the French spoken by the Ivoirian lower class, *Français Populaire Ivoirien*.

frésang: A trusted friend. The word derives from the French *frère sang*, "blood brother," and is a synonym for *bramogo*.

frime: To frame, to show off, but used in Côte d'Ivoire in a positive sense.

gaou: A victim of a crime, idiot, hick, or peasant; primitive, unstylish.

garba: Cheap Ivoirian staple food, sold primarily by migrants from northern Côte d'Ivoire and beyond.

gaspiller: To waste.

gendarme: A military branch of the police based on the French system.

ghetto: A criminal hangout—often found in abandoned buildings, the spaces underneath bridges, the alleyway next to the cinema, etc.

godrap: A shameful woman who causes problems or has them herself.

glôglô: A dark alleyway, a criminal territory.

grandfrères du quartier: Responsible youths who gain respect for their wisdom and advice and who protect the people in their neighborhood. Literally, "big brothers of the zone."

graté: A whitey. The word apparently comes from the idea of shaving off the skin to reveal the white beneath (as with a *kola* nut).

griffes colés: Labels "stuck on" to inferior products.

gros-gros Français: French as spoken by the elites (high-falutin').

Ivoirité: Ivoirianess, the quality of being Ivoirian, a contentious term popularized by President Bédié in hopes of winning the election.

Jeunes Patriotes: Young Patriots—the youth militias that informally supported Gbagbo, enforced the exclusion of "foreigners," and rejected the influence of France on local politics.

keneur: A dealer.

kôkô: A beggar (onomatopoetic, from the sound of knocking on the door).

logobi: A dance in which the *bluffeurs* display the labels of their clothing, their watches, and their gold chains. It also includes some imitation of fistfighting (as in the *danse des loubards*; see *nyama-nyama*), but the *logobi* is mainly about *mise en valeur*.

loubard: A gangster who makes his living through physical force and proves himself through muscle display and public fighting. *Loubards* seem to control top positions in the criminal network.

maquis: A semilegal outdoor bar and/or restaurant, the site of most social display.

manzements: Any source of income. Literally, "something to eat."

médicament: Occult force, magic protection, or poison. Literally "medicine."

mise en valeur: To give things value, to place value on them.

mouvement: The criminal scene.

natation: A word used to characterize objects from the West (see *derrière l'eau*). Literally, "swimming," in French.

Nouchi: An Ivoirian urban slang language.

nouchi: (1) A bandit. (2) A speaker of the eponymous slang language.

nyama-nyama: The *danse des loubards*, in whichpeople show off their toughness, which has evolved into feinting and dodging, as though in a fistfight.

pagne: African printed fabric, usually manufactured abroad and imported. Most women's clothing, formal and informal, is made from it, and many men wear shirts tailored from it as well.

panoman: A pickpocket.

PDCI: Parti Démocratique de la Côte d'Ivoire, the political party started by Houphouët-Boigny and the only party until 1990.

peau gras: A whitey. Literally, "skin of fat."

petit moussa (also *petit negre*): The dimunitive expression for Ivoirian popular French, or FPI.

pierres (also *pia*): Money, cash. Literally, "stones."

quartier populaire: The lower-class district of a city.

radio trottoir: Gossip, information disseminated through the street network. Literally, "sidewalk radio."

RDR: Rassemblement des Républicains, the party started by Alasanne Ouattara to run against Henri Bédie after Houphouët-Boigny's death.

rese: A location known for selling stolen merchandise (short for "reseller").

sec: The way language sounds when someone can't speak the language well. Literally, "dry."

tchung: To sell, to sell out, to snitch.

travailler: Publicly giving money to dancers, a practice popularized by Douk Saga and widely imitated throughout Côte d'Ivoire and the diaspora.

UDPCI: Union pour la Democratie et pour la Paix en Côte d'Ivoire, the party supporting Robert Guéï.

verlan: A French street language in which syllables are reversed.

vieuxpère: Hierarchical superior in the criminal network; a criminal term of respect in all social relations (literally, "old father," paired with *fiston*, a diminutive informal term a father calls his son as a child).

yere: (1) To rob, scam, or trick someone. Literally, "to see clearly." (2) Urban, civilized, hip, smart, stylish, in the know.

zeguei: A *danse des loubards* involving the rhythmic isolation of muscles in fixed poses to *mise en valeur* the body.

zouglou: An Ivoirian pop music created by university students in the 1990s. It eventually evolved into *coupé-décalé*.

REFERENCES

Adams, Monni. 1988. "Village Masking in Canton Boo, Ivory Coast." *Art Journal* 47 (2): 95–102.

Adegbija, Eforosibina. 2000. "Language Attitudes in West Africa." *International Journal of the Sociology of Language* 141:75–100.

Adopo, François, Reine Caummaueth, Simone Ehivet, and Kalilou Tera. 1986. "Langue d'Enseignement, Langue Officielle, et Langue Vernaculaire dans les Systemes Educatifs: Le Cas de la Côte d'Ivoire." *Cahiers Ivoiriens des Recherches Linguistiques* 19:80–95.

African Development Bank Group. 2007. *African Statistical Yearbook*. Denmark: Scanprint.

Agence-France Presse. 2010. "Liste Électorale Ivoirienne: La Justice Dénonce des 'Fraudes,' Climat Tendu." February 6.

Agha, Asif. 2007. *Language and Social Relations*. Cambridge: Cambridge University Press.

Agnew, Jean-Cristophe. 1986. *Worlds Apart: The Market and the Theater in Anglo-American Thought, 1550–1750*. Cambridge: Cambridge University Press.

"Ahmadou Yacouba Sylla Crache ses Vérités à Gbagbo." 2007. *Inter*, August 17.

Amondji, Marcel. 1984. *Félix Houphouët et la Côte d'Ivoire: L'Envers d'une Legende*. Paris: Editions Karthala.

Anderson, Benedict. 1991. *Imagined Communities*. London: Verso.

Antoine, Philippe, and Claude Henry. 1983. "La Population d'Abidjan dans ses Murs: Dynamiques Urbaine et Evolution des Structures Démographiques entre 1955 et 1978." In "Abidjan au Coin de la Rue: Eléments de la Vie Citadine dans la Métropole Ivoirienne," ed. P. Haeringer, special issue, *Cahiers O.R.S.T.O.M., Série Sciences Humaines* 19, no. 4: 171–196.

Appadurai, Arjun, ed. 1986. *The Social Life of Things: Commodities in Cultural Perspective*. Cambridge: Cambridge University Press.

———. 1990. "Disjuncture and Difference in the Global Cultural Economy." *Theory Culture Society* 7:295–310.

———. 1991. "Global Ethnoscapes: Notes and Queries for a Transnational Anthropology." In *Recapturing Anthropology: Working in the Present*, ed. R. Fox, pp. 191–210. Santa Fe, NM: School of American Research Press.

Apter, Andrew. 2005. *The Pan-African Nation: Oil and the Spectacle of Culture in Nigeria*. Chicago: University of Chicago Press.

Argenti, Nicolas. 2007. *The Intestines of the State: Youth, Violence, and Belated Histories in the Cameroon Grassfields*. Chicago: University of Chicago Press.

Austen, Ralph A. 1993. "The Moral Economy of Witchcraft: An Essay in Comparative History." In *Modernity and Its Malcontents: Ritual and Power in Postcolonial Africa*, ed. J. Comaroff and J. Comaroff, pp. 89–110. Chicago: University of Chicago Press.

Austin, J. L. 1962. *How to Do Things with Words*. Cambridge, MA: Harvard University Press.

Balandier, Georges. 1968. *Daily Life in the Kingdom of the Kongo: From the Sixteenth to the Eighteenth Century*. Trans. Helen Weaver. New York: Meridian Books.

Bamba, Karim. 1982. "L'Importe des Produits d'Importation Occidentale sur la Vie Socio-economique des Ivoiriens à Abidjan." Mémoire de Maîtrise, Department de Sociologie, Université Nationale de Côte d'Ivoire-Abidjan.

Basch, Linda, Nina Glick Schiller, and Cristina Szanton Blanc, eds. 1994. *Nations Unbound: Transnational Projects, Postcolonial Predicaments, and Deterritorialized Nation-States*. London: Gordon and Breach Publishers.

Bashkow, Ira. 2006. *The Meaning of White Men*. Chicago: University of Chicago Press.

Bassett, Thomas J. 2004. "Containing the Donzow: The Politics of Scale in Côte d'Ivoire." *Africa Today* 50 (4): 31–49.

Baudrillard, Jean. 1998. "Simulacra and Simulations." In *Selected Writings*, ed. Marc Poster, pp. 166–84. Stanford, CA: Stanford University Press.

Bauman, Richard, and Charles L. Briggs. 2008. *Voices of Modernity: Language Ideologies and the Politics of Inequality*. Cambridge: Cambridge University Press.

Bayart, Jean-François. 1993. *The State in Africa: The Politics of the Belly*. Trans. Mary Harper. London: Longman Group.

Bayart, Jean-François, Stephen Ellis, and Béatrice Hibou. 1999. *The Criminalization of the State in Africa*. Bloomington: Indiana University Press.

Bazanquisa, Rémy. 1992. "La Sape et la Politique au Congo." *Journal des Africanistes* 62 (1): 151–57.

Behrend, Heike. 2002. "'I Am like a Movie Star in My Street': Photographic Self-Creation in Postcolonial Kenya." In *Postcolonial Subjectivities in Africa*, ed. Richard Werbner, pp. 44–62. New York: Zed Books.

Bellman, Beryl. 1984. *The Language of Secrecy: Symbols and Metaphors in Poro Culture*. New Brunswick, NJ: Rutgers University Press.

Benjamin, Walter. 1976. "The Work of Art in the Age of Mechanical Reproduction." In *Illuminations*, ed. Hannah Arendt, pp. 217–51. New York: Schocken Books.

Bhabha, Homi. 1994. *The Location of Culture*. London: Routledge.

Boswell, D. M. 1969. "Personal Crises and the Mobilization of the Social Network." In *Social Networks in Urban Situations: Analyses of Personal Relationships in Central African Towns*, ed. C. Mitchell, pp 245–96. Manchester: Manchester University Press.

Bourdieu, Pierre. 1984. *Distinction: A Social Critique of the Judgment of Taste*. Trans. R. Nice. Cambridge, MA: Harvard University Press.

———. 1991. *Language and Symbolic Power*, ed. J. B. Thompson. Cambridge, MA: Harvard University Press.

Bourgois, Philip. 2002. *In Search of Respect: Selling Crack in El Barrio*. Cambridge: Cambridge University Press.

Boutin, Beatrice. 2003. "La Norme Endogene du Français de Côte d'Ivoire: Mise en Évidence de Règles Différentes du Français de France Concernant la Complémentation Verbale." *Sud Langues* 2:33–46.

Butler, Judith. 1988. "Performative Acts and Gender Constitution: An Essay in Phenomenology and Feminist Theory." *Theatre Journal* 40 (4): 519–31.

———. 1990. *Gender Trouble*. New York: Routledge.

Butler, Judith, and Biddy Martin. 1994. "Cross-Identifications." *Diacritics* 24 (2/3): 3.

Callon, Michel, Cécile Méadel, and Vololona Rabeharisoa. 2002. "The Economy of Qualities." *Economy and Society* 31 (2): 194–217

Ceuppens, Bambi, and Peter Geschiere. 2005. "Autochthony: Local or Global? New Modes in the Struggle over Citizenship and Belonging in Africa and Europe." *Annual Review of Anthropology* 34:385–407.

Chappell, David. 1989. "The Nation as Frontier: Ethnicity and Clientelism in Ivoirian History." *International Journal of African Historical Studies* 22 (4): 671–96.

Chauveau, Jean-Pierre, and Samuel Bobo. 2003. "La Situation de Guerre dans l'Arène Villageoise: Un Exemple dans le Centre-Ouest Ivoirien." *Politique Africaine* 89:12–33.

Chernoff, John. 2003. *Hustling Is Not Stealing: Stories of an African Bar Girl.* Chicago: University of Chicago Press.

Chumbow, Beban Sammy, and Augustin Simo Bobda. 2000. "French in West Africa: A Sociolinguistic Perspective." *International Journal of the Sociology of Language* 141:30–60.

Clifford, James. 1994. "Diasporas." *Cultural Anthropology* 9 (3): 302–38.

Cliggett, Lisa. 2005. "Remitting the Gift: Zambian Mobility and Anthropological Insights for Migration Studies." *International Journal for Population Geography* 11 (1): 35–48.

Cole, Jennifer. 2004. "Fresh Contact in Tamatave, Madagascar: Sex, Money, and Intergenerational Transformation." *American Ethnologist* 31 (4): 573–88.

Comaroff, J., and J. Comaroff. 1993. *Modernity and Its Malcontents: Ritual and Power in Postcolonial Africa.* Chicago: University of Chicago Press.

———. 2006. *Law and Disorder in the Postcolony.* Chicago: University of Chicago Press.

_____. 2009. *Ethnicity, Inc.* Chicago: University of Chicago Press.

Conklin, Alice L. 1997. *A Mission to Civilize: The Republican Idea of Empire in France and West Africa, 1895–1930.* Stanford, CA: Stanford University Press.

Cornwall, Andrea. 2002. "Spending Power: Love, Money and the Reconfiguration of Gender Relations in Ado-Odo, Southeastern Nigeria." *American Ethnologist* 29 (4): 963–80.

"Courrier Drap." 2001. *Gbich!*, February, pp. 9–15.

Cutolo, Armando. 2010. "Modernity, Autochthony, and the Ivoirian Nation: The End of a Century in Côte d'Ivoire." *Africa* 80 (4): 527–552.

d'Aby, Amon. 1960. *Croyances Religieuses et Coutumes Juridiques des Agni de la Côte d'Ivoire.* Paris: Editions Larose.

Dadié, Bernard. 1959. *An African in Paris.* Trans. K. C. Hatch. Chicago: University of Illinois Press.

David, Philippe. 2000. *La Côte d'Ivoire.* Paris: Éditions Karthala.

De Boeck, Filip, and Marie Françoise Plissart. 2006. *Kinshasa: Tales of the Invisible City.* Ghent: Ludion Press.

Debord, Guy. (1967) 1994. *The Society of the Spectacle.* Trans. Donald Nicholson-Smith. New York: Zone Books.

Delafosse, Maurice. 1904. *Vocabulaires Comparatifs de Plus de Soixantes Langues ou Dialectes Parlés à la Côte d'Ivoire et dans les Regions Limitrophes, avec des Notes Linguistiques et Ethnologiques, une Bibliographie et une Carte.* E. Leroux: Paris.

de Latour, Eliane. 2000. *Bronx-Barbès.* Arte.

Dembélé, Ousmane. 2002. "La Construction Économique et Politique de la Categorie Étranger en Côte d'Ivoire." In *La Côte d'Ivoire: L'Année Terrible, 1999–2000,* ed. Claudine Vidal and Maurice Le Pape, pp. 123–72. Paris: Karthala.

Denot, Christine. 1990. "Petits Metiers et Jeunes Descolarisés à Abidjan." Mémoire de Thèse, Department de Sociologie, Université de Paris 1: Panthéon-Sorbonne IEDES.

Diabate, Henriette, and Léonard Kodjo. 1991. *Notre Abidjan*. Abidjan: Ivoire Media.

Dinnan, Carmel. 1983. "Sugar Daddies and Gold Diggers: The White-Collar Single Women of Accra." In *Female and Male in West Africa*, ed. C. Oppong, pp. 344–66. London: George Allen and Unwin.

Diouf, Mamadou. 2003. "Engaging Postcolonial Cultures: African Youth and Public Space." *African Studies Review* 46 (2): 1–12.

Dirlik, Arif. 2002. "Bringing History Back In: Of Diasporas, Hybridities, Places, and Histories." In *Beyond Dichotomies: Histories, Identities, Cultures, and the Challenge of Globalization*, ed. E. Mudimbe-Boyi, pp. 93–128. Albany: State University of New York Press.

Douglas, Mary, and Baron Isherwood. 1979. *The World of Goods*. New York: Basic Books.

Dozon, Jean-Pierre. 1985. *La Société Bété*. Paris: Karthala.

Ekholm Friedman, Kasja. 1991. *Catastrophe and Creation: The Transformation of an African Culture*. Chur: Harwood Academic Publishers.

Ellis, Stephen. 1989. "Tuning in to Pavement Radio." *African Affairs* 88 (352): 321–30.

Epstein, A. L. 1992. *Scenes from African Urban Life: Collected Copperbelt Papers*. Edinburgh: Edinburgh University Press.

Etienne, Mona. 1983. "Gender Relations and Conjugality among the Baule." In *Female and Male in West Africa*, ed. C. Oppong, pp. 303–19. London: George Allen and Unwin.

———. 1997. "Women and Men, Cloth and Colonialization: The Transformation of Production-Distribution Relations among the Baoulé (Ivory Coast)." In *Perspectives on Africa: A Reader in Culture, History, and Representation*, ed. R. R. Grinker and C. B. Steiner, pp. 518–35. Oxford: Blackwell Publishers.

Fanon, Franz. 1967. *Black Skins, White Masks*. New York: Grove Press.

Ferguson, James. 1999. *Expectations of Modernity: Myths and Meanings of the Copperbelt*. Berkeley: University of California Press.

———. 2006. *Global Shadows: Africa in the Neoliberal World Order*. Durham, NC: Duke University Press.

Fitini. 2000. "Parigo." From *Tout Mignon*. Jober Entertainment.

Förster, Till. 1993. "Senufo Masking and the Art of the Poro." *African Arts* 26 (1): 33–101.

Fortune, Reo. 1932. *The Sorcerers of Dobu*. New York: E. P. Dutton and Co.

Foster, Robert. 2005. "Commodity Futures: Labor, Love, and Value." *Anthropology Today* 21 (4): 8–12.

———. 2007. "The Work of the New Economy: Consumers, Brands and Value-Creation." *Cultural Anthropology* 22 (4): 707–31.

Frazer, Sir James George. 1950. *The Golden Bough: A Study of Magic and Religion*. New York: MacMillan.

Friedman, Jonathan. 1991. "Consuming Desires: Strategies of Selfhood and Appropriation." *Cultural Anthropology* 6 (2): 154–63.

———. 1994. "The Political Economy of Elegance: An African Cult of Beauty." In *Consumption and Identity*, ed. J. Friedman, pp. 120–34. Chur: Harwood Academic Publishers.

Gable, Eric. 2002. "An Anthropologist's (New) Dress Code: Some Brief Comments on a Comparative Cosmopolitanism." *Cultural Anthropology* 17 (4): 572–79.

Gandoulou, Justin-Daniel. 1984. *Entre Paris et Bacongo*. Collection Alors. Paris: Centre Georges Pompidou.

———. 1989. *Dandies à Bacongo: Le Culte de l'Élégance dans la Societé Congolaise Contemporaine*. Paris: L'Harmattan.

Gaonkar, Dilip Parameshwar. 2001. *Alternative Modernities*. Durham, NC: Duke University Press.

Gardner, Katy. 1993. "Desh-Bidesh: Sylheti Images of Home and Away." *Man* 28 (1): 1–15.

Geschiere, Peter. 1997. *The Modernity of Witchcraft: Politics and the Occult in Postcolonial Africa*. Charlottesville: University of Virginia Press.

Geschiere, Peter, and Stephen Jackson. 2006. "Autochthony and the Crisis of Citizenship: Democratization, Decentralization, and the Politics of Belonging." *African Studies Review* 49 (2): 1–7.

Gluckman, Max. 1963. "Gossip and Scandal." *Current Anthropology* 4 (3): 307–16.

Gnamba, Bertin Mel, and Jeremy Kouadio N'Guessan. 1990. "Variétés Lexicales du Français en Côte d'Ivoire." In *Visages du Français: Variétés Lexicales de l'Espace Francophone*, ed. AUPELF-UREF. Paris: John Libbey Eurotext.

Goffman, Erving. 1959. *The Presentation of Self in Everyday Life*. Garden City: Doubleday Anchor Books.

———. 1974. *Frame Analysis: An Essay on the Organization of Experience*. Cambridge, MA: Harvard University Press.

Goldring, Luin. 1999. "Power and Status in Transnational Social Spaces." In *Migration and Transnational Social Spaces*, ed. L. Pries, pp. 162–86. Aldershot: Ashgate.

Gondola, Didier. 1999. "Dream and Drama: The Search for Elegance among Congolese Youth." *African Studies Review* 42 (1): 23–48.

Gottlieb, Alma. 1992. *Under the Kapok Tree*. Chicago: University of Chicago Press.

Graeber, David. 2001. *Toward an Anthropological Theory of Value*. New York: Palgrave.

Grebalé, Gavier. 2001. *Intrigues et Politiques de 1990 à 1993: Le Dernier Coup du "Vieux."* Abidjan: SNEPCI.

Green, Kathryn. 1987. "Shared Masking Traditions in Northeastern Ivory Coast." *African Arts* 20 (4): 62–92.

Guerry, Vincent. 1975. *Life with the Baoulé*. Trans. N. Hodges. Washington, DC: Three Continents Press.

Gupta, Akhil, and James Ferguson, eds. 1997. *Culture, Power, Place: Critical Explorations in Anthropology*. Durham, NC: Duke University Press.

Guyer, David. 1970. *Ghana and the Ivory Coast: The Impact of Colonialism in an African Setting*. New York: Exposition Press.

Guyer, Jane I. 2004. *Marginal Gains: Monetary Transactions in Atlantic Africa*. Chicago: University of Chicago Press.

Hahn, Hans Peter, and George Klute, eds. 2007. *Cultures of Migration: African Perspectives*. Berlin: LIT Verlag.

Halliday, Michael A. K. 1976. "Anti-languages." *American Anthropologist* 78 (3): 570–84.

Halttunen, Karen. 1986. *Confidence Men and Painted Women: A Study of Middle-Class Culture in America, 1830–1870*. New Haven, CT: Yale University Press.

Hannerz, Ulf. 1996. *Transnational Connections: Culture, People, Places*. London: Routledge.

Harrison, Simon. 2002. "The Politics of Resemblance: Ethnicity, Trademarks, Headhunting." *Journal of the Royal Anthropological Institute* 8 (2): 211–32.

Hart, Keith. 1988. "Kinship, Contract, and Trust: The Economic Organization of Migrants in an African City Slum." In *Trust: Making and Breaking Cooperative Relations*, ed. Diego Gambetta, pp. 176–93. Oxford: Blackwell Publishers.

Hastings, Adi, and Paul Manning. 2004. "Introduction: Acts of Alterity." In "Acts of Alterity," ed. Adi Hastings and Paul Manning, special issue, *Language and Communication* 24:291–311.

Hellweg, Joseph. 2004. "Encompassing the State: Sacrifice and Security in the Hunter's Movement of Côte d'Ivoire." *Africa Today* 50 (4): 3–28.

———. 2011. *Hunting the Ethical State: The Benkadi Movement of Côte d'Ivoire.* Chicago: University of Chicago Press.

Henry, Stuart, and Gerald Mars. 1978. "Crime at Work: The Social Construction of Amateur Property Theft." *Sociology* 12:245–63.

Hobsbawm, E. J. (1969) 1981. *Bandits.* New York: Pantheon Books.

Horkheimer, Max, and Theodor W. Adorno. 1987. *The Dialectic of Enlightenment.* Trans. John Cumming. New York: Continuum.

Human Rights Watch. 2008. *The Best School: Student Violence, Impunity, and the Crisis in Côte d'Ivoire.* New York: Human Rights Watch.

Hunter, Mark. 2002. "The Materiality of Sex: Thinking beyond 'Prostitution.'" *African Studies* 61 (1): 99–120.

Inoue, Miyako. 2002. "Gender, Language and Modernity: Toward an Effective History of Japanese Women's Language." *American Ethnologist* 29 (2): 392–422.

———. 2006. *Vicarious Language: Gender and Linguistic Modernity in Japan.* Berkeley: University of California Press.

INS. 2000. *Recensement Generale de la Population et de l'Habitation 1998: Premiers Resultats Definitif.* Abidjan: Institut Nationale de la Statistique: Republique de la Côte d'Ivoire.

International Crisis Group. 2003. "Côte d'Ivoire: The War Is Not Yet Over." ICG Africa Report 71. Freetown/Brussels.

———. 2004. "Côte d'Ivoire: No Peace in Sight. ICG Africa Report 82." Freetown/Brussels.

———. 2007. "Côte d'Ivoire: Can the Ouagadougou Agreement Bring Peace?" ICG Africa Report 127. Freetown/Brussels.

Irvine, Judith, and Susan Gal. 2000. "Language Ideology and Linguistic Differentiation." In *Regimes of Language: Ideologies, Polities, and Identities,* ed. P. Kroskrity, pp. 35–84. Santa Fe, NM: School of American Research Press.

Kapferer, B. 1969. "Norms and Manipulation of Relationships in a Work Context." In *Social Networks in Urban Situations,* ed. C. Mitchell, pp. 181–244. Manchester: Manchester University Press.

Keane, Webb. 2003. "Semiotics and the Social Analysis of Material Things." *Language and Communication* 23:409–25.

Kearney, Michael. 1995. "The Local and the Global: The Anthropology of Globalization and Transnationalism." *Annual Review of Anthropology* 24:547–65.

Klein, Naomi. 2002. *No Space, No Choice, No Jobs, No Logo.* New York: Picador.

Koenig, Dolores. 2005. "Multilocality and Social Stratification in Kita, Mali." In *Migration and Economy: Global and Local Dynamics,* ed. Lillian Trager, pp. 77–102. Oxford: Altamira Press.

Kohlhagen, Dominik. 2006. "Frime, Escroquerie et Cosmopolitisme: Le Succès du 'Coupé-Décalé' en Afrique et Ailleurs." *Politique Africaine* 100:92–105.

Kokora, Pascal D. 1983. "Situation Sociolinguistique en Côte d'Ivoire et Emprise du Français: Les Variétés de Celui-ci et les Attitudes Langagières qu'Elles Suscitent chez les Locuteurs." *Cahiers Ivoiriens des Recherches Linguistiques* 13:128–47.

Konate, Yacouba. 2002. "Génération Zouglou." *Cahiers d'Études Africaines* 168 (4): 777–98.

Kopytoff, Igor. 1986. "The Cultural Biography of Things: Commoditization as Process." In *The Social Life of Things,* ed. Arjun Appadurai, pp. 64–91. Cambridge: University of Cambridge Press.

Kouadio, Jérémie N'Guessan. 2005. "Le Nouchi et les Rapports Dioula-Français: Géopolitique de la Langue Française." *Revue Hérodote* 126:69–85.

Kourouma, Ahmadou. 1968. *Les Soleils d'Independances*. Paris: Editions de Seuil.

Kramer, Fritz. 1993. *The Red Fez: Art and Spirit Possession in Africa*. London: Verso Press.

Lafage, Suzanne. 1978. "Rôle et Place du Français Populaire dans le Continuum Langues Africaines/Français de Côte d'Ivoire." *Cahiers Ivoiriens des Recherches Linguistiques* 4:54–69.

———. 1998. "Hybridisation et 'Français des Rues' à Abidjan." In *Alternances Codiques et Français Parlé en Afrique*, ed. A. Queffélec, pp. 279–91. Aix-en-Provence: Publications de l'Université de Provence.

Launay, Robert. 1978. "Transactional Spheres and Inter-societal Trade in Ivory Coast." *Cahiers d'Études Africaines* 18 (72): 561–73.

———. 1982. *Traders without Trade: Responses to Change in Two Dyula Communities*. Cambridge: Cambridge University Press.

Lawrence, Peter. 1989. *Road Belong Cargo: A Study of the Cargo Movement in the Southern Madang District, New Guinea*. Prospect Heights, IL: Waveland Press.

Leach, Edmund. 1951. "The Structural Implications of Matrilateral Cross-Cousin Marriage." *Royal Anthropological Institute Journal* 81:23–55.

Le Pape, Marc. 1997. *L'Energie Sociale à Abidjan: Economie Politique de la Ville en Afrique Noire, 1930–1995*. Paris: Karthala.

Le Pape, Marc, and Claudine Vidal. 2002. *Côte d'Ivoire: L'Année Terrible 1999–2000*. Paris: Karthala.

Lévi-Strauss, Claude. (1949) 1969. *The Elementary Structures of Kinship*. Trans. James Bell, John Von Sturmer, and Rodney Needham. Boston: Beacon Press.

———. 1963. "The Sorcerer and His Magic." In *Structural Anthropology*, trans. C. Jacobson and B. G. Schoepf, pp. 161–80. Garden City: Anchor Books.

Lipovetsky, Gilles. 1994. *The Empire of Fashion: Dressing Modern Democracy*. Princeton, NJ: Princeton University Press.

Livingston, Jennie. 1990. *Paris Is Burning*. Miramax.

MacCannell, Dean. 1989. *The Tourist: A New Theory of the Leisure Class*. New York: Schocken Books.

MacGaffey, Janet. 1991. *The Real Economy of Zaire*. Philadelphia: University of Pennsylvania Press.

MacGaffey, Janet, and Rémy Bazenguissa-Ganga. 2000. *Congo-Paris*. Indianapolis: Indiana University Press.

MacGaffey, Wyatt. 1968. "Kongo and the King of the Americans." *Journal of Modern African Studies* 6:171–81.

———. 1972. "The West in Congolese Experience." In *Africa and the West: Intellectual Responses to European Culture*, ed. Philip D. Curtin, pp. 51–56. Madison: University of Wisconsin Press.

———. 1977. "Fetishism Revisted: Kongo 'Nkisi' in Sociological Perspective." *Africa* 47 (2): 172–84.

———. 1986. *Religion and Society in Central Africa*. Chicago: University of Chicago Press.

———. 1994. "African Objects and the Idea of the Fetish." *Res* 25:123–31.

Magic System. 2000. "Premier Gaou." From *Premier Gaou*. Sonodisc.

Magubane, Bernard. 1971. "A Critical Look at the Indices Used in the Study of Social Change in Colonial Africa." *Current Anthropology* 12 (4/5): 419–45.

Malkki, Liisa. 1993. "A Global Affair: Nationalism and Internationalism as Cultural and

Moral Practices." In *Moralizing States and the Ethnography of the Present*, ed. S. F. Moore, pp. 119–37. Arlington, VA: American Anthropological Association.

———. 1995. *Purity and Exile: Violence, Memory, and National Cosmology among Hutu Refugees in Tanzania*. Chicago: University of Chicago Press.

Manning, Paul. 2010. "The Semiotics of Brands." *Annual Review of Anthropology* 39: 33–49.

Marshall-Fratani, Ruth. 2006. "The War of 'Who Is Who': Autochthony, Nationalism, and Citizenship in the Ivorian Crisis." *African Studies Review* 49 (2): 9–43.

Martin, Phyllis. 1994. "Contesting Clothes in Colonial Brazzaville." *Journal of African History* 35:401–26.

Mauss, Marcel. (1923) 1990. *The Gift*. Trans. W. D. Halls. London: Routledge.

———. 1972. *A General Theory of Magic*. Trans. R. Brain. New York: W. W. Norton and Co.

Mayer, Philip. 1962. "Migrancy and the Study of Africans in Towns." *American Anthropologist* 64:576–92.

Mazzarella, William. 2003. *Shovelling Smoke: Advertising and Globalization in Contemporary India*. Durham, NC: Duke University Press.

Mbembe, Achille. 2001. *On the Postcolony*. Berkeley: University of California Press.

McCracken, Grant. 2005. *Culture and Consumption II: Markets, Meaning, and Brand Management*. Bloomington: Indiana University Press.

McGovern, Michael. 2011. *Making War in Côte d'Ivoire*. Chicago: University of Chicago Press.

Miller, Christopher. 1990. *Theories of Africans: Francophone Literature and Anthropology in Africa*. Chicago: University of Chicago Press.

Miller, Daniel. 1987. *Material Culture and Mass Consumption*. Oxford: Blackwell.

———, ed. 1995. *Acknowledging Consumption*. London: Routledge.

Mintz, Sydney. 1986. *Sweetness and Power: The Place of Sugar in Modern History*. New York: Penguin.

Mitchell, Clyde. 1956. *The Kalela Dance*. Rhodes-Livingston Papers, no. 27. Manchester: Manchester University Press.

Mitter, Siddhartha. 2007. "The Hip Hop Generation: Ghana's Hip Life and Ivory Coast's Coupé Décalé." www.afropop.org/multi/feature/ID/709/. Last accessed April 24, 2011.

Moore, Robert E. 2003. "From Genericide to Viral Marketing: on 'Brand.'" *Language and Communication* 23:331–57.

Morrisson, John William. 1980. "Aspects socio-économiques des Maquis de Treichville." Memoire de Maitrise, Département de Sociologie, Université Nationale de Côte d'Ivoire, Abidjan.

Mukherjee, R. 2006. "The Ghetto Fabulous Aesthetic in Contemporary Black Culture." *Cultural Studies* 20 (6): 599–629.

Munn, Nancy. 1986. *The Fame of Gawa*. Durham, NC: Duke University Press.

Mustafa, Hudita Nura. 2002. "Portraits of Modernity: Fashioning Selves in Dakarois Popular Photography." In *Empires of Images: Visuality in Colonial and Postcolonial Africa*, ed. Paul S. Landau and Deborah D. Kaspin, pp. 172–92. Berkeley: University of California Press.

Nairn, Charlie. 1976. *Ongka's Big Moka: The Kawelka of Papua New Guinea*. Disappearing World Series.

Newell, Sasha. 2005. "Migratory Modernity and the Cosmology of Consumption in Côte d'Ivoire." In *Migration and Economy: Global and Local Dynamics*, ed. Lillian Trager, pp. 163–90. Walnut Creek, CA: Altamira Press.

———. 2006. "Estranged Belongings: A Moral Economy of Theft in Abidjan, Côte d'Ivoire." *Anthropological Theory* 6 (2): 179–203.

———. 2007. "Pentecostal Witchcraft: Neoliberal Possession and Demonic Discourse in Ivoirian Pentecostal Churches." *Journal of Religion in Africa* 37:461–90.

———. 2009a. "*Godrap* Girls, *Draou* Boys, and the Sexual Economy of the Bluff in Abidjan, Côte d'Ivoire." In "Transnationalizing Desire: Sexualizing Culture and Commodifying Sexuality," ed. Jakob Rigi and Cymene Howe, special issue, *Ethnos* 74 (3): 379–402.

———. 2009b. "Enregistering Modernity, Bluffing Criminality: How Nouchi Reinvented (and Fractured) the Nation." *Journal of Linguistic Anthropology* 19 (2): 157–84

Newton, Esther. 1972. *Mother Camp: Female Impersonators in America*. Chicago: University of Chicago Press.

———. 2000. "Dick(less) Tracy and the Homecoming Queen: Lesbian Power and Representation in Gay Male Cherry Grove." In *Margaret Mead Made Me Gay*, ed. Esther Newton, pp. 63–89. Durham, NC: Duke University Press.

Nooter, Mary. 1993. *Secrecy: African Art That Conceals and Reveals*. New York: Museum for African Art.

Nossiter, Adam, and Loucoumande Coulibaly. 2010. "Many in the Ivory Coast May Be Left Out of the Vote." *New York Times*, February 7, p. A8.

"'Nouchi' au Scanner des Spécialistes de la Langue, Le." 2009. *Fraternité Matin*, June 17.

Onishi, Norimitsu. 2002. "U.S. Children Evacuated from Rebel-Held Ivory Coast City." *New York Times*, September 26.

Packer, George. 2003. "Gangsta War." *New Yorker* 79, no. 33 (3 November): 68.

———. 2006. "The Megacity." *New Yorker* 82, no. 37 (13 November): 64.

Petit Yode and Enfant Siro. 2000. "Paris." From *Victoire*. Frochot Music.

Picton, John. 1990. "What's in a Mask?" *African Languages and Cultures* 3 (2): 181–202.

Pietz, William. 1987. "The Problem of the Fetish." *Res* 13:23–45.

———. 1988. "The Problem of the Fetish." *Res* 16:105–23.

Piot, Charles. 1999. *Remotely Global: Village Modernity in West Africa*. Chicago: University of Chicago Press.

Pratt, Mary Louise. 2002. "Modernity and Periphery: Toward a Global and Relational Analysis." In *Beyond Dichotomies: Histories, Identities, Cultures, and the Challenge of Globalization*, ed. E. Mudimbe-Boyi, pp. 21–47. Albany: State University of New York Press.

Ravenhill, Philip L. 1996. *Dreams and Reverie: Images of Otherworld Mates among the Baoulé, West Africa*. Washington, DC: Smithsonian Institution Press.

Reinach, Simona S. 2009. "Fashion and National Identity: Interactions between Italians and Chinese in the Global Fashion Industry." *Business and Economic History Online* 7:1–6.

Rivarol, Antoine de. 1808. "De l'Universitalité de la Langue Française." In *Œuvres Complètes de Rivarol*. Paris: Léopold Collin.

Roth-Gordon, Jennifer. 2009. "The Language That Came Down the Hill: Slang, Crime, and Citizenship in Rio de Janeiro." *American Anthropologist* 111 (1): 57–68.

Rouch, Jean. 1954. *Les Maitres Fous*. Watertown, MA: Documentary Educational Resources.

———. 1961. "Second Generation Migrants in Ghana and the Ivory Coast." In *Social Change in Modern Africa*, ed. Aidan Southall, pp. 300–304. London: Oxford University Press.

Rouse, Roger. 1991. "Mexican Migration and the Social Space of Postmodernism." *Diaspora* 1 (1): 8–23.

Saga, Douk. 2005. "Douk Saga en Fête." From *Héros National Bouche Bée*. Baierle Records.

Sahlins, Marshall. 1972. "On the Sociology of Primitive Exchange." In *Stone Age Economics*, pp. 185–230. Chicago: Aldine Transaction.

———. 1994. "Cosmologies of Capitalism: The Trans-Pacific Sector of the World System." In *Culture/Power/History*, ed. Nicholas Dirks, pp. 412–56. Princeton, NJ: Princeton University Press.

Schechner, Richard. 1985. *Between Theater and Anthropology*. Philadelphia: University of Pennsylvania Press.

Sciolino, Elaine. 2002. "Ivory Coast's Raging Conflict Draws France In." *New York Times*, December 26.

Scott, James C. 1979. *The Moral Economy of the Peasant: Rebellion and Subsistence in Southeast Asia*. New Haven, CT: Yale University Press.

Senghor, Léopold Sédar. 1977. "La Francophonie Comme Culture." In *Liberté 3: Négritude et La Civilisation de l'Universelle*. Paris: Seuil.

Sengupta, Somini. 2004. "Ivory Coast Cease-Fire Ends with Airstrikes against Two Rebel Towns." *New York Times*, November 5.

Siegel, James. 1998. *The New Criminal Type in Jakarta: Counter Revolution Today*. Durham, NC: Duke University Press.

———. 2006. *Naming the Witch*. Stanford, CA: Stanford University Press.

Silverstein, Michael. 1996. "Monoglot 'Standard' in America: Standardization and Metaphors of Linguistic Hegemony." In *The Matrix of Language: Contemporary Linguistic Anthropology*, ed. D. Brenneis and R. K. S. Macaulay, pp. 284–306. Boulder, CO: Westview Press.

Simmel, Georg. 1950. *The Sociology of Georg Simmel*. Ed. K. Wolff. New York: Free Press.

———. 1957. "Fashion." *American Journal of Sociology* 62 (6): 541–58.

Simone, Abdou Maliq. 2004. *For the City Yet to Come: Changing African Life in Four Cities*. Durham, NC: Duke University Press.

———. 2006. "Pirate Towns: Reworking Social and Symbolic Infrastructures in Johannesburg and Dovala." *Urban Studies* 43, no. 2:357–70.

Simplice, Illary G. 2001. "Ceux qui Dépense leur Salaires dans les Maquis." *Gbich!*, May 25–31.

Smith, James. 2008. *Bewitching Development: Witchcraft and the Reinvention of Development in Neoliberal Kenya*. Chicago: University of Chicago Press.

Smith-Hefner, Nancy J. 2007. "Youth Language, *Gaul* Sociability, and the New Indonesian Middle Class." *Journal of Linguistic Anthropology* 17 (2): 184–203.

Sonaiya, Remi. 2007. "Issues in French Applied Linguistics in West Africa." In *French Applied Linguistics*, ed. Dalila Ayoun, pp. 425–49. Amsterdam: John Benjamin Publishing Co.

Sontag, Susan. 1964. "Notes on 'Camp.'" *Partisan Review* 31 (4): 515–30.

Spitulnik, Debra. 1998. "Mediating Unity and Diversity: The Production of Language Ideologies in Zambian Broadcasting." In *Language Ideologies: Practice and Theory*, ed. B. Scheiffelin, K. Woolard, and P. Kroskrity, pp.163–88. Oxford: Oxford University Press.

———. 1999. "The Language of the City: Town Bemba as Urban Hybridity." *Journal of Linguistic Anthropology* 8 (1): 30–59.

Stack, Carol. 1997. *All Our Kin: Strategies for Survival in a Black Community*. New York: Basic Books.

Steiner, Christopher. 1992a. "Fake Masks and Faux Modernity: The Crisis of Misrepresentation." *African Arts* 25 (3): 18–20.

————. 1992b. "The Invisible Face: Masks, Ethnicity, and the State in Côte d'Ivoire, West Africa." *Museum Anthropology* 16 (3): 53–57.

Stereolab. 1996. "Motorolla Scalatron." From *Emperor Tomato Ketchup*. Elektra Records.

Strasser, Susan. 1989. *Satisfaction Guaranteed: The Making of the American Mass Market.* New York: Pantheon Books.

Strathern, Marilyn. 1988. *The Gender of the Gift.* Berkeley: University of California Press.

Sylvanus, Nina. 2007. "The Fabric of Africanity: Tracing the Global Threads of Authenticity." *Anthropological Theory* 7:201–16.

Tambiah, S. J. 1979. "The Form and Meaning of Magical Acts: A Point of View." In *Reader in Comparative Religion*, ed. W. A. Lessa and E. Z. Vogt, pp. 352–62. New York: Harper Collins Publishers.

Tarde, Gabriel de. 1903. *The Laws of Imitation.* New York: Henry Holt and Co.

Taussig, Michael. 1993. *Mimesis and Alterity: A Particular History of the Senses.* New York: Routledge.

————. 1999. *Defacement: Public Secrecy and the Labor of the Negative.* Stanford, CA: Stanford University Press.

Taylor, Charles. 2001. "Two Theories on Modernity." In *Alternative Modernities*, ed. D. P. Gaonkar, pp. 172–96. Durham, NC: Duke University Press.

Tera, Kalilou. 1986. "Le Dioula Véhiculaire de Côte d'Ivoire: Expansion et Développement." *Cahiers Ivoiriens des Recherches Linguistiques* 20:5–33.

Thompson, E. P. 1971. "The Moral Economy of the Crowd in the Eighteenth Century." *Past and Present* 50:76–136.

Thornton, John K. 1988. "The Kingdom of the Kongo, ca. 1390–1678: The Development of an African Social Formation." *Cahiers des Études Africaines* 22 (3–4): 325–42.

Toungara, Jeanne Maddox. 1990. "The Apotheosis of Côte d'Ivoire's Nana Houphouët-Boigny." *Journal of Modern African Studies* 28 (1): 23–54.

————. 2001. "Ethnicity and Political Crisis in Côte d'Ivoire." *Journal of Democracy* 12 (3): 63–72.

Touré, Abdou. 1981. *La Civilization Quotidienne en Côte d'Ivoire: Procès d'Occidentalisation.* Paris: Éditions Karthala.

"Tous les Étrangers Auront des Pièces d'Identité Ivoiriennes." 2001. *La Bombe*, no. 84 (March 30).

Turcotte, Denis. 1980. "La Planification Linguistique en Côte d'Ivoire: Faire du Français le Véhiculaire par Excellence." *Canadian Journal of African Studies* 13 (3): 423–39.

Turner, Terrence. 1976. "Transformation, Hierarchy and Transcendence." In *Secular Ritual*, ed. S. F. Moore and B. G. Myerhoff, pp. 53–70. Amsterdam: Van Gorcum.

————. 1991. "'We Are Parrots,' 'Twins Are Birds': Play of Tropes as Operational Structures." In *Beyond Metaphor: The Theory of Trope in Anthropology*, ed. J. Fernandez, pp. 121–58. Stanford, CA: Stanford University Press.

Turner, Victor. 1969. *The Ritual Process.* Ithaca, NY: Cornell University Press.

————. 1976. "Death and the Dead in the Pilgrimage Process." In *Religious Encounters with Death*, ed. F. E. Reynolds and E. H. Waugh, pp. 24–39. University Park: Pennsylvania State University Press.

Undie, Chi-Chi, and Kabwe Benaya. 2006. "The State of Knowledge on Sexuality in Sub-Saharan Africa: A Synthesis of Literature." *JENDAI* 8:1–33.

Van Bingsbergen, Wim. 2001. "Witchcraft in Modern Africa as Virtualized Boundary Conditions of the Kinship Order." In *Witchcraft Dialogues: Anthropological and Philosophical Exchanges*, ed. George Clement Bond and Diane M. Ciekawy, pp. 212–62. Athens, OH: Ohio University Center for International Studies.

Vann, Elizabeth. 2006. "The Limits of Authenticity in Vietnamese Consumer Markets." *American Anthropologist* 108 (2): 286–96.

Veblen, Thorstein. 1899. *The Theory of the Leisure Class.* New York: Penguin Books.

Vidal, Claudine. 1991. "Guerre des Sexes à Abidjan: Masculin, Feminin, CFA." In *Sociologies des Passions*, pp. 133–60. Paris: Karthala.

Vogel, Susan. 1997. "Baoulé: African Art/Western Eyes." *African Arts* 30 (4): 64–77.

Wallerstein, Immanuel. 1975. *World Inequality: Origins and Perspectives on the World System.* Montreal: Black Rose Books.

Warner, Lloyd. 1937. *A Black Civilization: A Study of an Australian Tribe.* New York: Harper and Row.

Warner, Michael. 2002. *Publics and Counterpublics.* New York: Zone Books.

Weber, Eugen J. 1976. *Peasants into Frenchmen: The Modernization of Rural France, 1870–1914.* Stanford, CA: Stanford University Press.

Weiner, Annette. 1976. *Women of Value, Men of Renown.* Austin: University of Texas Press.

———. 1985. "Inalienable Wealth." *American Ethnologist* 12 (2): 210–27.

Weiskel, Timothy. 1980. *French Colonial Rule and the Baulé Peoples: Resistance and Collaboration, 1889–1911.* Oxford: Clarendon Press.

Weiss, Brad. 2002. "Thug Realism: Inhabiting Fantasy in Urban Tanzania." *Cultural Anthropology* 17 (1): 93–124.

———. 2004. "Street Dreams: Inhabiting Masculine Fantasy in Neoliberal Tanzania." In *Producing African Futures: Ritual and Reproduction in a Neoliberal Age*, ed. B. Weiss, pp. 193–228. Boston: Brill.

Welles, Orson. 1973. *F for Fake.* Janus Film.

Werbner, Richard. 1996. "Introduction: Multiple Identities, Plural Arenas." In *Postcolonial Identities in Africa*, ed. R. Werbner and T. Ranger, pp. 1–25. London: Zed Books.

West, Harry. 2008. *Ethnographic Sorcery.* Chicago: University of Chicago Press.

White, Shane, and Graham White. 1998. *Stylin': African-American Expressive Culture from Its Beginnings to the Zoot Suit.* Ithaca, NY: Cornell University Press.

Wilde, Oscar. 1969. "The Truth of Masks." In *The Artist as Critic: Critical Writings*, ed. Richard Ellmann. Chicago: University of Chicago Press.

Williams, Raymond. 1980. "Advertising: The Magic System." In *Problems in Materialism and Culture.* London: Verso.

Wiredu, Kwasi. 1996. "African Philosophical Tradition: A Case Study of the Akan." In *African Philosophy: A Classical Approach*, ed. P. English and K. Kalumba, pp. 99–122. Englewood Cliffs, NJ: Prentice Hall.

Wojcicki, Janet. 2002. "Commercial Sex Work or *Ukuphanda*? Sex-for-Money Exchange in Soweto and Hammanskraal Area, South Africa." *Culture, Medicine and Psychiatry* 26:339–70.

Woolard, Kathryn A. 1998. "Language Ideology as a Field of Inquiry." In *Language Ideologies: Practice and Theory*, ed. B. B. Schieffelin, K. A. Woolard, and P. V. Kroskrity, pp. 3–47. Oxford: Oxford University Press.

Worsely, Peter. 1957. *The Trumpets Shall Sound: A Study of Cargo Cults in Melanesia.* London: MacGibbon and Kee.

Yanagisako, Sylvia. 2008. "Managing Labor Value on the New Silk Road." Paper presented at the Friday Speaker Series, University of Virginia, November 7.

INDEX

The letter *f* following a page number denotes a figure.

Bangladeshis, 184
Banque, La (*maquis*), 108
Baoulé ethnic group and language, 9–10,
   21, 27, 187, 259; and Easter, 190–92;
   and kinship networks, 75, 190–92; and
   migration, 190–92; and Nouchi speech,
   51–52, 55; and otherworld, 168–70;
   pacification of (1915), 219; and political
   crisis, 219, 222, 226–27
baptisms, 26, 80, 111f, 135f
Baraka (*maquis*), 119
Barbette (pseud.), 187
bar climatisée, 103–4
Bashkow, Ira, 167
basilica, 159–60
Baudrillard, Jean, 32, 251, 254–55
Bayart, Jean-François, 159
Bazenguissa-Ganga, Rémy, 19, 66, 88, 96,
   102, 202
BBC, 237
Bédié, Henri, 6, 9, 47, 218, 227–28, 230,
   232–33, 269n6
beer, 2, 68; and *faire le show*, 104, 106–9,
   107f, 115–17, 120–22, 124, 126–27,
   138; and life cycle ceremonies, 126; and
   migration, 187
Belleville market, 83
belonging, 60, 89–90, 193, 217, 223, 253
Beng, 11, 30–31; and clothing, 144, 150,
   162, 168–69, 177–78, 181, 223; migration to, 183–84, 186, 193–95, 197,
   199–201, 204, 207, 209, 212–13
Beng ethnic group, 169
bengistes, 2, 30–31, 183–87, 191, 195, 197–
   204; and clothing, 151–52, 156, 176–77;
   and *le descent*, 186, 197–203; and *faire le
   show*, 97, 105, 109, 121, 124, 135; myths
   of, 204–8; networks of, 201–4; and otherworld, 209; and political crisis, 239; and
   urban economy, 158
Benin/Beninois, 171, 190, 219, 235, 266n3
Benjamin, Walter, 250–51
Bete ethnic group and language, 52, 63,
   219, 226–27, 268n1
Bhabha, Homi, 14–15, 239, 250, 253
Biggie (street name), 11, 51, 96, 193
Bilé, Didier, 223
Billy (pseud.), 107, 119, 196
birthday parties, 26, 109, 125, 133, 136

bizness, 51, 80–90, 108, 121, 148; and
   migration, 193, 196–97. *See also* criminal
   networks
blackmail. See *chantage*
black market, 86, 202, 266n3; Le Black,
   51, 176
Black Skins, White Masks (Fanon), 263n5
blo, 149, 169
blofwe, 169–70. *See also* whites and whiteness
blolo, 168–70, 179–80, 254, 258, 261,
   268n5
blood brothers. See *frésangs*
bluff and bluffing, 1, 4–5, 7, 11–14,
   17, 20–22, 32, 97, 247, 251, 254–56,
   260–61; and clothing, 143–45, 147–48,
   150–55, 151f, 158–62, 164–65, 175,
   177, 180–81, 243; as cultural superiority, 155–56; and gender, 138–42; and
   hip-hop, 167; and masking, 179; and migration, 186, 192, 204, 209; and Nouchi
   speech, 37–39, 50, 61; and political crisis,
   225, 237–38, 238f, 240, 243; and state,
   Ivoirian, 7, 159–60; in urban economy,
   66–67, 79, 81, 96–98, 157–59; women
   as part of, 28, 30, 38, 79, 102–3, 130–42,
   138f. *See also faire le show*
bluffeurs, 1–3, 11, 19, 25, 28; and clothing,
   143–47, 153, 164, 181, 209; elites as,
   157–59; and *faire le show*, 100, 113, 130,
   138f, 140–41; and masking, 180; and
   Nouchi speech, 39; and political crisis,
   31, 225–26, 240; women as, 134. *See also*
   bluff and bluffing
"Bluff Inutile" (*Gbich!*), 147
bosses, 40, 125, 147, 154, 165–66, 208,
   267n1. *See also* elites, Ivoirian
Boswell, D. M., 76
Bouaké, 187, 233, 235
boubous, 163, 226, 231–32, 236–37, 238f,
   241, 267n2
Bourdieu, Pierre, 50, 157, 220
Bourgois, Philip, 84–85
bramogo, 74, 99
brand names and branding, 30, 66, 96,
   148, 170–75, 181, 248, 260–61, 264n12,
   268n7; Adidas, 2, 11, 231; Awa, 240;
   and *bengistes*, 198; Bil'iol, 240; Boos
   Sport, 189; Calvin Klein, 166; Converse,

Nouchi speech (*continued*)
  and elites, 34, 46, 49, 51–55, 59–60, 165;
  emergence of, 50–52, 106; enregisterment of modernity through, 29, 33–34,
  37, 45–46, 51, 54, 58–61; and *faire le
  show,* 101–2, 110, 125; "father of Nouchi,"
  51–52, 112; as first language, 34, 41, 58,
  60; and FPI (*Français Populaire Ivoirien*),
  48–52, 55, 59, 265n6, 265n10; and
  French language/culture, 34, 36, 40,
  42–43, 50–52, 54–60, 57f, 213; hierarchical relations in, 33–35, 41–43, 50, 54,
  60–61, 106, 125; and hip-hop, 40, 52–53;
  impenetrability of, 43, 50, 56, 59–60; as
  international export, 52, 58–59; Ivoirian
  studies of, 51; and *loubards,* 38–40; and
  national identity, 29, 33–36, 43, 49,
  52–54, 58–61, 223–24; neologisms of,
  51–54, 56; Nouchi.com Web site, 54; and
  nouchi youth, 37–42, 46, 50–54, 56, 57f,
  59–61; "original" Nouchi speakers, 41;
  "Petit Dico Ivoirien" of, 53; and political
  crisis, 35–36, 42, 60, 223–26; vernacularization of, 51; and women, 136. *See also
  specific Nouchi words*
nyama-nyama, 112

Obama, Barack, 269n4
Obi (Nigerian king), 257
Occident, 30, 71, 156–57, 175, 177–78,
  186. *See also* West, the; *and names of
  Western countries*
occult, 21, 30, 117, 162, 167–70, 178, 254,
  268n9
Olivier (pseud.), 28, 58, 121, 124, 152–53;
  and migration, 191–92, 206, 210
oridji, 176–77
Orokaiva, 167
otherness, 3, 14–15, 31, 256–57; and clothing, 168, 175, 177, 180–81; and gender,
  139, 141; and migration, 212–13; and national identity, 44, 212–13; and Nouchi
  speech, 36, 61; and political crisis, 240
otherworld, 12–13, 20–21, 124, 260; and
  clothing, 160, 167–70, 177–78; and
  migration, 186–87, 207, 208–10
Ouattara, Alassane, 6–7, 9, 157, 227–30,
  232, 234, 242, 269n9

Ouroboros, 87
Ousmane (pseud.), 97, 198, 204

Packer, George, 236–37
pagnes, 77, 105, 134, 135f, 150, 161, 164,
  170–73, 171f, 268n3, 268n6; "Fancy,"
  172; for funerals, 189; and migration,
  187, 189; and political crisis, 223, 226,
  231, 237–38; "Wax Aurlandais," 172
palm wine. *See bangi*
palsu, 260–61
panomans, 43
Papis (pseud.), 37, 148, 226
Papua New Guinea, 257
paquet of cash, *un,* 99, 121–22
"Parigo" (song), 199–200, 209
Paris, 183, 192, 221, 225; in advertisements, 157; and *coupé-décalé,* 53–54, 58;
  and *faire le show,* 97; migration to, 53–54,
  72, 94, 97, 185, 193, 195–96, 198–206,
  210, 241; and Nouchi speech, 50–51;
  Parisian Congolese, 17–18, 80, 96, 102,
  266n3; Parisian Metro maps, 177; Tour
  d'Argent in, 156
"Paris" (song), 204–6
Paris Is Burning (1990 film), 140–41
passports, 82, 97, 107, 194, 196, 202,
  266n7
patron-client relationships, 4, 29–30, 42,
  74, 237
PDCI (Parti Democratique de la Côte
  d'Ivoire), 192, 230
"peace mirage," 220
peasants, 9, 49, 158–61, 185. *See also gaous*
performativity, 1, 138–42, 256
personal networks. *See* social networks
Petit Coin, Le (*maquis*), 109
"Petit Dico Ivoirien," 53
Petit Moussa, 49
Petit Paris (clothing store), 162, 164–65,
  175–76
petits, 86, 95, 198, 204, 233. *See also fistons*
Petit Yode, 204–6
photography, 148, 149f, 151f, 164
Picton, John, 179–80
Pierre (pseud.), 38–39, 165
pierres (money, cash), 133, 193. *See also*
  CFA francs